Colección Támesis

SERIE A: MONOGRAFÍAS, 263

A COMPANION TO
THE TWENTIETH-CENTURY SPANISH
NOVEL

A COMPANION TO THE TWENTIETH-CENTURY SPANISH NOVEL

Edited by
Marta E. Altisent

TAMESIS

First published 2008 by Tamesis, Woodbridge

ISBN 978–1–85566–174–5

Tamesis is an imprint of Boydell & Brewer Ltd
PO Box 9, Woodbridge, Suffolk IP12 3DF, UK
and of Boydell & Brewer Inc.
668 Mt Hope Avenue, Rochester, NY 14620, USA
website: www.boydellandbrewer.com

A CIP catalogue record for this book is available
from the British Library

This publication is printed on acid-free paper

Printed in Great Britain by
CPI Antony Rowe, Chippenham, Wiltshire

CONTENTS

FOREWORD

The purpose of this volume is to provide an overview of the development of Spanish fiction in the twentieth century. The *Companion* is intended as a reference tool for both the specialist and the general reader interested in understanding the intellectual and aesthetic trends that have shaped the Spanish novel during what was an extraordinarily turbulent time in Spanish history. While the volume is geared towards the student of Hispanic literary studies, we hope it will appeal also to specialists in a number of disciplines such as Comparative Literature and Cultural Studies.

The eighteen contributors survey a selection of factors influencing the Spanish novel between 1898 and the end of the millennium. They trace the aesthetic evolution of the genre from nineteenth-century realism to the anti-realist, self-conscious, and experimental trends characteristic of modernism and postmodernism. The volume is structured both chronologically and thematically. Wherever possible we have tried to examine developments in the novel in tandem with key moments in Spanish history, rather than as a direct consequence of them. Five such key moments or periods are examined in turn: (*i*) the pre-Civil War years (1898–1936); (*ii*) the early years of the Franco dictatorship (1939–65); (*iii*) the transition to democracy which began with political resistance to the Franco regime and ended in a countercultural revolution (1968–78); (*iv*) the social-democratic period (1982–92); and (*v*) the present day. The different cycles and rhythms associated with each of these five periods are reflected in the novel, that most socially conscious of literary forms.

Unlike other literary histories and critical guides, this *Companion* embraces a variety of aesthetic and theoretical approaches. It has not been conceived as a rigorous history or an exhaustive inventory of modern Spanish fiction; rather, it belongs to the more imprecise territory of 'panoramic' critical studies that take a diversity of viewpoints to suggest the more important directions the novel has taken, offering what we hope is a coherent vision of the diversity and richness of the modern Spanish novel. The necessarily selective nature of the primary texts we examine means that there are significant omissions that readers may wish to made good for themselves.

The selection of material and its division into sections and chapters is perforce subjective. The first two sections adopt an historical approach, establishing a temporal framework for what follows as well as identifying examples of the specific motifs and modes that Spanish writers favored and that recur throughout the century. The broad sociocultural context in which the novels appeared is also addressed. Chapters 3–15 are narrower in nature, focusing on a trend or a group of writers and their specific intellectual milieux.

Spanish fiction is here examined in the light of fashions in contemporary literary criticism and thought both inside and outside Spain since the works studied were published. The introduction and first two essays pay particular attention to writers who pioneered the literary upheavals that have taken place and they pay due heed to the historical, philosophical, and linguistic phenomena of the day. Central to the assessment on offer are the major works that show the influence of particular phenomena (Nietzschean thought, psychoanalysis, myth theory, neohistoricism, existentialism, nihilism, structural and post-structural linguistics, Marxist theory, feminism, and postmodern relativism).

Not all these literary movements are treated in depth. As the century wore on and Spain joined other post-industrial cultures, we have laid particular emphasis on the social importance of the novel and the increasing role of the market and of mass media in the world of fiction. The importance of commercial activities associated with the book industry has transformed the novel into a consumer product and has blurred the distinction between high culture and low, and between populist and minority art forms. Some areas here considered (the novel in film, the novel as a popular genre, and the novel as historical record) point to the possible future role of the novel in a world where images are becoming for many more important than the written word.

The topics covered in this book are, we believe, symptomatic of broader sociocultural phenomena, and our aim has been to familiarize the reader with lesser-known works which have none the less contributed to change and opened new avenues for investigation. This means that we have indulged in the occasional detour into other genres and media that illustrate the progressive hybridization of the novel: autobiography, journalism, the short story, poetry, traditional narrative, modern technology, audiovisual media, and popular culture.

Among other matters treated are the vogue for detective fiction, erotic and sentimental novels, and historical romance, all of which have found a niche market and are now of interest also to academic critics of literature. The symbiotic relationship between the Spanish novel and the cinema illustrates the importance of visual media in the dissemination of Spanish literary masterpieces and best-selling novels to a non-reading public. Film creates a fusion of 'minor' and 'great' art and, by doing so, acts as a springboard for political resistance and the subversion of 'official' culture, while also providing a useful propaganda tool for both left and right.

The cultures and languages of Catalonia, the Basque Country, and Galicia have acquired a new prominence since the death of Franco and the establishment of a democratic constitution in 1978. The last three chapters are devoted to them. They attempt to show how Catalan, Galician, and Basque narrative have acquired symbolic importance and reflect national and cultural identities in conflict. Literature in these languages has earned widespread respectability both in the regions themselves and also in the broader culture of Spain as a whole. Novelists not writing in Castilian are no longer peripheral or forced to adapt their works for a Castilian-speaking readership. They now play a major role in the rehabilitation, modernization, and dissemination of their respective literary and linguistic traditions, while enriching peninsular narrative as a whole. The inclusion here of such regional literature mirrors the bilingualism that is a phenomenon of post-Franco Spain; the interaction of Castilian with these separate linguistic cultures is a trend that Francoist censorship was ultimately unable to suppress.

We have not included here the work of Spanish-born writers who went into exile as a result of the Civil War and published abroad, save in the case of those whose novels were reissued inside Spain and proved popular there. Also excluded are works by Spaniards and non-Spanish-speaking writers who, although born overseas, chose Spain as their main residence either before or after acquiring a reputation as novelists.

The main aim of this *Companion* is, then, to provide a reliable further work of reference that can stand alongside previous surveys, such as Francisco Rico's *Historia y crítica de la literatura española contemporánea* and Ignacio Soldevila Durante's *Historia de la novela española (1936–2000)*, both of which were designed for the Spanish-speaking reader. The present *Companion* should be read alongside other essays, such as the recent *Cambridge Companion to the Spanish Novel from 1600 to the Present*, edited by Harriet Turner and Adelaida López de Martínez, which focuses on a much broader historical context.

Notes and references have been kept to a minimum. Suggestions for further reading can be found at the end of each chapter and a bibliography of all works cited at the end of the volume. All quotations are given in English. Where a novel included in the compass of this study has been translated into English, this is indicated in the text by an asterisk against the Spanish title; a list of such English translations is given on pp. 264–72. Dates of publication are given for the novels discussed in each chapter; authors' dates are provided in the Index at the back of the volume.

CONTRIBUTORS

Marta E. Altisent is Professor of Modern and Contemporary Spanish Literature at the University of California, Davis.

Katarzyna Olga Beilín is Associate Professor at the University of Wisconsin-Madison.

Ramón Buckley is Professor of Spanish Literature and Peninsular Studies at the Division of International Programs Abroad at Syracuse University in Madrid.

Stacey Dolgin Casado is Professor of Modern and Contemporary Spanish Literature at the University of Georgia.

José F. Colmeiro is Professor of Spanish at the University of Michigan, Lansing.

Sebastiaan Faber is Professor and Chair of Hispanic Studies at Oberlin College, Ohio.

David Herzberger is Professor of Spanish and Chair of the Department of Hispanic Studies at the University of California, Riverside.

Carlos Alex Longhurst is Professor Emeritus of the University of Leeds, UK and a member of the Spanish Department, King's College London.

Kathleen N. March is a Professor at the University of Maine.

Cristina Martínez Carazo is an Associate Professor at the University of California, Davis.

Alfredo Martínez-Expósito is an Associate Professor at the University of Queensland, Brisbane, Australia and a fellow of the Australian Academy of the Humanities.

Nina L. Molinaro is Associate Professor of Spanish at the University of Colorado at Boulder.

Gonzalo Navajas is Professor of Modern Spanish Literature and Film at the University of California, Irvine.

Mari Jose Olaziregi is an Associate Professor at the University of the Basque Country, Vitoria-Gasteiz, Spain.

Janet Pérez is Paul Whitfield Horn Professor of Romance Languages and Qualia Chair of Spanish at Texas Tech University.

Randolph D. Pope is Commonwealth Professor of Spanish and Director of
Comparative Literature at the University of Virginia.

Josep Miquel Sobrer is a Professor of Spanish at Indiana University,
Bloomington.

H. Rosi Song is Associate Professor of Spanish at Bryn Mawr College.

The editor gratefully thanks Laura Mancheno Macià, Paula Rodgers, Eleanor
Marsh, Andrew Matt, and Carlos Alex Longhurst for their help, and acknowledges the support provided by the University of California, Davis.

INTRODUCTION

The isolation Spain endured during a substantial part of the twentieth century, with its history of anarchism, civil war, dictatorships, democracy, and finally unprecedented economic revival, has helped to shape its culture's slow and uneven absorption of the main intellectual currents of modern Western thought. Their influence would be felt in ways that were often anachronistic and marginal during the two periods of democratic transition (1931–33 and after 1975) and also in the works of Spanish intellectual dissidents living both in Spain and beyond its borders. The essays in this volume show Spanish novelists involved in a process of give and take between tradition and experimentation.

The birth of a modern novel ambitious to outdo its nineteenth-century predecessor can be traced to the intellectual impetus provided by writers who came of age in 1898 when the Spanish-American War brought to an end more than three hundred years of Empire. Yet the period of radical and avant-garde experimentalism was brief. The pre-war literary and cultural renaissance that Mainer has labeled the Silver Age of Spanish art had less impact on the novel than it did on poetry, drama, and the visual arts. After the advent of the second Republic (1931–36) and amid the increasing socio-political tensions that led to the Civil War, novelists retreated into the more mimetic and objective modes of writing that would characterize the genre for much of the twentieth century. Old and new variants of realism (*tremendismo, neorrealismo, realismo objetivo, realismo existencial, realismo dialéctico, realismo psicológico*), dominant in the post-war period (1940–65), emerge again at the end of the millennium in historical, journalistic, and testimonial writing previously silenced by decades of censorship and by an almost universal urge to forget the horrors of war.

The young writers of the so-called Generation of 98, who witnessed the end of the Spanish Empire, were the first to engage intellectually with its implications. Their reflections did not translate into political action or despair, as happened with their Romantic predecessors, but, instead, gave rise to introspection and a search for the roots of Spanish identity. *Abulia* was the term coined by Ángel Ganivet to characterize the collective apathy and inertia that had, as he saw it, prevented the country from realizing its potential since the seventeenth century. The afflictions and pessimism heightened

by the events of 1898 led writers of the time to analyze their situation from
a philosophical and cultural perspective, often using the novel to flesh out
their ideas. Reflections on the Spanish character became a regular feature
in the works of Miguel de Unamuno, Azorín, Ramón del Valle-Inclán, and
Pío Baroja, all of whom mixed fictional sketches with essays, autobiography,
journalism, and travel narratives. While echoing the existential and epistemological concerns of the day, they incorporated into their work the formal and
philosophical innovations of European high modernism, breaking with the
local concerns and depiction of customs that had characterized the writing
of earlier generations.

As Navajas and Longhurst explain in Chapters 1 and 2, Unamuno's experimentation with self-reflection, philosophical debate, *mise en abyme*, counterpoint, and multilayered utterance, together with his penchant for paradox and
the subversion of hierarchies between author and character, paved the way for
further experimentation. This took the form of Valle-Inclán's parody of the
stylistic preciousness of *modernismo* in his *Sonatas* and his debunking pot-
pourri of Spanish colonial discourses in *Tirano Banderas* (1926); Azorín's
experiments with Proustian *tempo* and the cinematic manipulation of time in
Doña Inés (1925); and Baroja's 'visionary' style culminating in *El hotel del
cisne* (1946). The centenary celebrated in 1998 – with Spain now part of the
European Union and reinventing itself as a multinational state – showed that
the founding fathers of Spanish modernism were still relevant. Their works
are now, however, re-read in a context of postmodern experimentation.

Navajas and Longhurst show how the very variety we find in their literary
practice calls into question the simple group label Generation of 98. Among the
many European influences in play they point to the late naturalism of Baroja
and of the socially engaged novels of Vicente Blasco Ibáñez, symbolist and
avant-garde experiments in lyrical prose, and the pre-existentialist philosophy
of Nietzsche and Schopenhauer. These are influences which have affected
contemporary fiction in a number of ways. The ethnocultural concerns of
Juan Goytisolo owe a debt to Ángel Ganivet and to the theories developed
by Américo Castro concerning Arab influence on the Spanish character. The
mythological status accorded Castile as the spiritual center of the nation can
be seen in the work of Miguel Delibes and other writers from the north-west
of the Peninsula. In their stories, Castile and León appear both as frontier
territories and as self-contained worlds encompassing several different realms
(historical, biblical, Roman, Iberian, fantastic, and mythological). The impoverished mountainous or remote borderlands at the very center of Spanish
civilization still feed the elegiac imagination of Juan Benet in his cycle set in
the mythical Región, the no less mythical Artámila and Mansilla de la Sierra
of Ana María Matute, and the Celama of Luis Mateo Díez. Castile as both
place and ideal also plays a major role in the imaginary worlds conjured up
by Rafael Sánchez Ferlosio and a host of other post-war writers.

Another important legacy is that of Baroja. His powers as a mythmaker find echoes in the adventure stories of Ramón Sender, in post-Franco Basque short-story writers, in the neo-picaresque, action-oriented novels of Eduardo Mendoza, in the testimonial writing of Miguel Sánchez-Ostiz, and in the internationally acclaimed best-seller *La sombra del viento* by Antonio Ruiz Zafón. Unamuno is still seen as the greatest single influence on modern and postmodern formalists, even though many of his ideas now seem reactionary and, for most radical Basque thinkers, anti-nationalist. In *Tirano Banderas,* Valle-Inclán suggested a whole host of literary possibilities by inventing a genuinely new genre, the novel about dictatorship, a trend to which both Francisco Ayala and Ramón Sender contributed from exile in Latin America, with works such as *El fondo del vaso* (1962) and *Epitalamio del Prieto Trinidad* (1942). This is a development that has influenced Latin American writers such as Miguel Ángel Asturias (*El señor presidente*), Gabriel García Márquez (*El general en su laberinto*) and Augusto Roa Bastos (*Yo, el supremo*). Valle-Inclán also influenced the generation of writers who followed him, most particularly Ramón Pérez de Ayala and Gabriel Miró; often dubbed 'decadent', they represented a new aestheticism not necessarily at odds with post-naturalist and expressionistic tendencies imported from D'Annunzio, Flaubert, Maupassant, and the Goncourt brothers.

Overall, the writers of 1898 broadened literary language beyond the range typical of the nineteenth-century novel and introduced more flexible narrative and linguistic forms. They developed the richness of dialectal and conversational speech, as Galdós had done, and introduced new registers ranging from the serious – the poetic, philosophical, musical, pictorial, metalinguistic – to the comic. The influence of Cervantes and Quevedo was now combined with images and topics predating avant-garde and surrealist aesthetics and with a highly individualized idiolect visible in the use of paradoxes and wordplay, expressionistic outbursts, absurd plots, and stylized caricature.

This spirit of playfulness and experimentation came to a head in the mid-1920s with Lorca's generation and had repercussions in the 'idle' fictions, to use Pérez Firmat's term, of the Spanish avant-garde writers Benjamin Jarnés, Ramón Gómez de la Serna, Francisco Ayala, Antonio Espina, and Francisco Granell. In Chapter 3, Buckley uses the term 'tales' to define a category of fiction that embraces the simplicity of storytelling, the lyrical improvisation of the prose poem, the instant humor and visual imagery of a *haiku,* and the magic playfulness of the *greguería*. The early works of Jarnés, Gómez de la Serna, and Ayala attest to a fragmentation of discourse and and increasing genre hybridization in avant-garde writing, exemplifying and at the same time debunking José Ortega y Gasset's concept of 'dehumanized art'. In the case of Jarnés, that experimentation evolved into a sterile overformalism that perfectly illustrated Ortega's derogatory comment on the impersonality and abstraction of the new novel – that it shows a disconcerted subjectivity slowly adapting to the pointless hustle and rudderless bustle of the modern world.

The advent of the Spanish Civil War and the social tensions that preceded it provide a good example of the disjunction between art and life that lies at the core of modern Spanish culture. The spiritual schism of a war whose consequences are still felt today moved writers to adopt a testimonial and realistic mode, chronicling their hopes and disappointments as one attempt at political reform after another ended in failure. Civil strife was to be a favorite literary theme. An earlier generation had seen fraternal envy and aggression as an essential trait of the Spanish character – for Unamuno and Machado the sin of Cain was replayed in every generation. For writers who had experienced the war and its aftermath, they were just a natural reaction to centuries of frustrated efforts to build a just and equitable society. In Chapter 5, Faber looks back over seventy years during which novels devoted to the theme of the Civil War reflect those efforts and that frustration. The process of coming to terms with the country's recent history is still unresolved and memory only reluctantly yields up its secrets; novels about the war are both fiction and testimony.

The motif of violence and class division is one frequently encountered in the post-war novel, and it takes on extra dimensions – historical, social, existential, and psychoanalytical – in two of the best-selling works from the period: Camilo José Cela's *La familia de Pascual Duarte* and Carmen Laforet's *Nada*. Both attest to resentments simmering beneath the surface throughout centuries of autocratic rule and still unexorcised, even by civil war. As both Ilie and Asís have recognized, *tremendismo* would be an aesthetic of violence based on an unmediated description of brutality. In *Pascual Duarte*, the contradictory character traits of aggressiveness and vulnerability that we find in the antihero lead to self-examination and catharsis, and to a degree of compassion towards him. As Asís explains, 'violence is something positive at root, a desire for a better life that has not found another outlet; in some undefined way, it is a reaction against frustration and claustrophobia, exacerbated by the contrast between the miserable living conditions endured by all and the possibility of overcoming them and fulfilling one's own potential; the problem appears to be brutal and simple [...] social conflict occurs when primitive people react not by analyzing their situation but by lashing out' (1992: 30, 36).

The fascist victory of 1939 called a halt to democratic government and land reform, and, under the dictatorship, the forces of reaction and conservatism forced novelists to abandon experimentation and revert to social and existential subject matter. In Chapter 4, Pérez explores neorealism and the way it was used by writers to present the injustice of continued social divisions and to point to economic problems that were potentially embarrassing to the dictatorship. She groups together as 'neorealist novels' works by authors who championed political opposition to Franco and expressed their own longing for reform in ways that owed a great deal to naturalism. Influenced by French and Italian neorealist writers, they adopted techniques from film, photography, and journalism, and also acknowledged a debt to the lean, objectivist style favoured by Hemingway and Dos Passos. Their works documented the human sacrifices behind Spain's struggle to become an industrialized country on a par with the rest of Europe, while the squalour and misery of the settings are ample evidence of the realities of life in those first decades of the dictatorship when the lack of manpower in a country decimated by war was exacerbated by the exodus of the professional elite to Mexico and Latin America.[1]

Post-war social realism focused on industrial and urban settings but also portrayed the isolation of rural communities as young people emigrated to the big cities and to northern Europe in search of work. The effects of Franco's huge irrigation projects and the attempts of the regime to keep the rural habitat alive would become recurrent motifs in both novels and short stories. Rural fiction no longer portrayed an ancient, unchanging idyll, as it had in the works of nineteenth-century *costumbristas*; instead, it now focused on the social inequities and neglect that a state-run censored press kept from its readers. As Pérez concludes, neorealist and social realist authors went back to the politically committed novel of the pre-war years (Ramón Sender, Manuel Andújar, Segundo Serrano Poncela, Arturo Barea), exposing Spain's backwardness, and ironically employing the slogan *España es diferente* ('Spain is Different'), originally launched by Franco's tourism minister Fraga Iribarne.

Other influences came to play their part as the century moved on: from France, Italy, Britain, and Latin America. As Spaniards began to travel, for political or professional reasons, married foreigners, learned foreign

---

[1] Repression, coupled with this brain drain, led to a demographic recession far more severe than anywhere else in Europe, even though war had inflicted much more extensive physical and economic damage on most European countries than it had on Spain. The Spanish population, which had grown substantially in the 1920s, and began to decline after 1939, would not recover until the mid-1950s. This decline was in sharp contrast with the rest of Europe where growth slowed during World War II but started to recover as soon as the war ended. By 1953, US aid helped to end the rationing of essential goods and put a stop to the widespread black market. Franco's three Development Programs (Planes de Desarrollo) after 1963 produced a measure of economic liberalization which, combined with the favorable international climate, produced unprecedented growth (an annual rate of 7 per cent, surpassed only by Japan), despite the regime's protectionist measures; it was only with the energy crisis of the 1970s that the rate slowed. In spite of this economic miracle between 1963 and 1974, Spain was not in a position to join the European Community until ten years after the dictator's death. After a decade of stagnation, the country once again began to prosper in the mid-1980s, catching up and in some cases overtaking other Western European countries. Even though it has recently lost some of that dynamism, Spain is now a significant player on the international scene.

languages, and had access to foreign books in the original language or in translation, novelists searched for new forms or adapted existing ones to a changing experience, incorporating cosmopolitan references and narrative devices and modes: French objectivism, magical realism, concrete prose, fantasy literature, and science-fiction.

The 1960s saw two audacious novelistic experiments. Luis Martín-Santos's *Tiempo de silencio* (1961) and Juan Goytisolo's *Señas de identidad* (1966) were both satires of a dictatorship increasingly out of touch with the modern world. The official version of Spanish realities seemed to progressive Spaniards both illusory and absurd, and a number of writers were driven to generate 'anti-narratives' by way of counterbalance to the triumphalist state celebration of the 'Twenty-Five Years of Peace'. As Dolgin suggests in Chapter 6, these two works paved the way for Goytisolo's landmark novel, *Reivindicación del Conde don Julián* (1970), which used fiction as a way of dismantling the state-sponsored myth of the 'holy motherland'. Novelists were freed from the strictures of social realism by this quest to expose and destroy the underpinnings of the arbitrary – and calculated – construction and propagation of a Spanish national identity and character. She explains how that revolutionary literary enterprise subverted and debunked such things as traditional Spanish historiography, the literary canon, social and political institutions and customs, gender stereotypes, conventional (hetero)sexual practices, and the ubiquitous power of the dictator himself.

The novels of Martín-Santos and the Goytisolo brothers proved highly effective as criticism of the official historiographical line taught in schools and universities and reiterated at every turn in the government media. They were not alone. A number of novelists played with a new kind of expressionism and began to reach a wider public. Their works were a mix of multiple and often contradictory narrative perspectives: Cervantine irony and allegory, intertextuality and grotesque paradox; burlesque mythological structures and baroque juxtapositions, wordplay and parodies of the officialese employed by the administration; high register and low. The sophisticated use of the latest modernist techniques adapted to a Spanish cultural context conferred upon these novelists a status comparable to that enjoyed by their European, American and Latin American counterparts.[2]

The precedent set by the Goytisolos and Martín Santos raised expectations among writers and their readers. As Linda Gould Levine put it in an interview with the editor in 2006, 'they not only destabilized Spanish cultural

---

[2]   Examples are Miguel Delibes, *Parábola del náufrago* (1969) and *Cinco horas con Mario* (1966); Gonzalo Torrente Ballester, *Don Juan* (1963) and *La Saga/Fuga de J.B.* (1972); Camilo José Cela *Oficio de tinieblas 5* (1973); and Miguel Espinosa, *Escuela de Mandarines* (1974).

homogeneity and hegemony but cast their readers into an open and unfamiliar verbal terrain strewn with countless images of destruction and profanation and a utopian strain toward creation that demanded their active participation in constructing the various levels of meanings'.

In the early 1970s, a number of new factors converged to shake up cultural life in Madrid and Barcelona: the liberalization of censorship, the rehabilitation of exiled writers, the rediscovery of literature in Catalan, Galician and Basque, and an interest among younger Latin American writers in identifying a European publisher's agent to help them reach a new readership (Carmen Balcells and Carlos Seix Barral played an important part in this process).[3] The resulting mix of folklore and folk myth, fantasy, surrealism and Latin American magical realism can be seen in the the self-contained mythological worlds created by Rafael Dieste, Gonzalo Torrente Ballester, Álvaro Cunqueiro and Camilo José Cela, in Galicia; Mercè Rodoreda, Joan Perucho, Pere Calders and Ana María Matute, in Catalonia; Bernardo Atxaga, in the Basque country; and Rafael Sánchez Ferlosio, José María Merino and Luis Mateo Díez, in Castile and León. These are writers who incorporate myth and the oral tradition into the novel and bring fantasy to the forefront of Spanish literature.

The avalanche of post avant-garde experiments inspired by the French *nouveau roman* and recent literary theories such as structuralism and semiotics led in the late 1970s to a largely sterile formalism. The so-called 'structural novel' soon lost its appeal for Spanish readers, just as social realism had before it; the reading public was far more interested in the novels of the Latin American Boom and in foreign works in translation.[4] Writers seemed unsure

---

[3]   In 1969, Mario Vargas Llosa's *Conversación en la catedral*, the winner of the Biblioteca Breve Prize the following year, was the most widely sold novel published in Spain; it was soon to be followed by his two instant bestsellers, *Los cachorros* (1980) and *Los jefes* (1980). The linguistic experimentation, open structure, and general cultural iconoclasm of the Goytisolo-Martín-Santos-Benet generation brought Spanish novelists closer to their Latin American counterparts. Strong affinities developed between Juan Goytisolo and Carlos Fuentes, Lezama Lima and Severo Sarduy, which would pave the way for a positive reception of innovative Spanish novelists in Latin America; this two-way street has been particularly valuable for writers such as Julián Ríos, Enrique Vila Matas, and Nuria Amat.

[4]   The influence of the French *nouveau roman* and the structuralist aesthetics of journals such as *Tel Quel* and *Poétique* can be seen in the work of the so-called *novísimos*, a group of writers so christened by José María Castellet in his influential 1970 anthology of experimental poets and novelists with Marxist inclinations. What seemed at the time to be a transient and elitist trend, represented by the novels of Germán Sánchez Espeso, José María Guelbenzu, Manuel Vázquez Montalbán, José María de Leyva, Félix de Azúa, and Ana María Moix, led to engaging iconoclastic and self-reflexive works of far greater mythical scope, as diverse as Juan Benet's *Un viaje de invierno* (1972), Cela's *Oficio de tinieblas 5* (1973), Carmen Martín

about where to go next. José Caballero Bonald tried social commitment in *Dos días de setiembre* (1962) and then mixed it in with imported magical realism in *Ágata, ojo de gato* (1974). A similar uncertainty can be seen in the early careers of Jesús Fernández Santos, Rafael Sánchez Ferlosio, Ana María Matute, Juan García Hortelano, and Luis Goytisolo.

The complex relationship between myth and history that so absorbed Goytisolo and Martín-Santos led to a number of revisionist and deconstructive works focusing on Spain's recent and remote past. As Herzeberger explains in Chapter 7, the resurgence of the historical novel and romance is a familiar feature of recent Spanish fiction. The genre was relaunched in part by the reissue of historical fiction written by writers in exile (Aub, Sender, Ayala) who had experimented with the innovative registers typical of Latin American postcolonial fiction and with the new political realities that gave writers the freedom to explore the national past. Herzeberger points to the multiple purposes (political, moral, feminist, didactic, existential, humorous, or purely poetic) that historical fiction would come to serve without compromising its entertainment value. Contemporary historical novels also question the fictional truth and incorporate postmodern techniques of double coding that can be read at several intellectual levels. They feel free to combine playful, poetic and fantastic registers with didactic and/or political purposes. It is no coincidence that there has been a revival of interest among writers and academics in Cervantes's *Don Quijote*.

The inversion of sexual norms in novels such as **Reivindicación del Conde don Julián* is still at the center of much contemporary fiction that questions Spanish sexual mores and gender roles after the sexual revolution of the 1970s. The contradictions and the insecurity felt by many men as a result of these shifts in attitudes and behavior are central themes in the psychoanalytical novels of José María Vaz de Soto, José María Guelbenzu, and Juan José Millás, and the 'homosexual' stories of Vicente Molina Foix, Álvaro Pombo, Terenci Moix, Lluis Maria Todó and Luis Antonio de Villena. Alfredo Martínez-Expósito discusses in Chapter 12 the social and legal changes that have legitimized homosexuality and also the treatments of gay and lesbian themes in recent fiction. He explains how homosexual identity has evolved from the old unspecific 'they' of post-war fiction, through a more clearly enunciated 'he' or 'she' for the first gay heroes and anti-heroes in the novel of the 1970s, through to 'I'/'me' that we find with increasing frequency in gay fiction from the mid-1980s onwards.

The first, indirect criticisms of the patriarchal nature of Spanish society

Gaite's **El cuarto de atrás* (1978), Luis Goytisolo's *Los verdes de mayo hasta el mar* (1976), Ana María Moix's *Julia, Walter, ¿por qué te fuiste?* (1973); Juan Marsé's **Si te dicen que caí* (1973), Juan Goytisolo's **Makbara* (1980), and Juan García Hortelano's *Gramática parda* (1982).

came from women writers, such as Elena Quiroga, Carmen Laforet, Elena Soriano, and Carmen Martín Gaite; after 1975, we find that discontent with the oppressive ideology of the dictatorship comes twinned with a deeper disgruntlement about the secondary place accorded women by even radical male colleagues. Lidia Falcón in *Es largo esperar callado* (1975), Lourdes Ortiz in *Luz de la memoria* (1976), Esther Tusquets in **El mismo mar de todos los veranos* (1978), Rosa Montero in **Crónica del desamor* (1979), Montserrat Roig in *El temps de les cireres* (1978) and *La veu melodiosa* (1978), and Fanny Rubio in *La sal del chocolate* (1992) all feature women's increasingly assertive role in public life, though not necessarily yet in politics. As the writers' alter egos in these novels are forced to re-examine the traps and self-delusions of their sentimental education, they are shown having to struggle with all kinds of obstacles to self-fulfilment, both external and personal.

The political disenchantment characteristic in the rest of mainland Europe of the aftermath of the 1968 countercultural revolution would not be felt in Spain until 1976 but it would continue to dog the administration of Felipe González throughout his time in office.[5] After two decades, it was clear to Spaniards that the socialist ruling class had sought to benefit from the system rather than to change it. With the increased prosperity of a new middle class now enthusiastically playing its full part in the consumerist culture of Western capitalism and the European Union, the possibility of radical political change was gone. Callinicos (1990:168) describes Spaniards, 'with all the hope of a social revolution gone – indeed, often having ceased to believe in the desirability of such revolution'. This apathy, 'combined with the political disillusionment of Spain's most articulate members, provided the context for the proliferating talk of postmodernism' (cited by Lewis 1994: 177). By the mid 1980s, the 'master narratives' of anti-capitalist resistance, adds Lewis, had become suspect, when not impossible, and could be imagined only at the level of micropolitics and personal lifestyle.

Ferreras (1970), Suñén (1978) and Sobejano (1988) all talk of this intro-

---

5   The term used by Sanz (1992) to describe fiction published before and during the democratic transition is the 'Generation of 68'. It groups together authors as diverse as Javier Marías, Eduardo Mendoza, Julio Llamazares, and Manuel Vázquez Montalbán (once a *novísimo*). Conscious of the artificiality of such groupings, Ruz (1999) explains that, when Spanish critics try to define the 'novel of the democratic transition', all they can say is that the writers of the Generation of 68 have no truck with the ideological squabbles of their predecessors. Although they reject Francoism, these writers distinguish between civic commitment and literature. They are strongly influenced by French structuralism, a theory that they expand to include postmodern metafictional tendencies. Soldevila-Durante chooses the term 'Generation of 77', the year that the Minister of Culture, Manuel Fraga Iribarne, relaxed the censorhip laws.

version in Spanish literature over the last twenty-five years.[6] Novels tend to gravitate to three main subjects: (*i*) the rituals of intimacy, ranging from the sentimental to the erotic and the pornographic; (*ii*) the recovery of the historical imagination through stories of the everyday; and (*iii*) fictions about the individual set in a broad network of autobiographical and self-referential processes (from Luis Martín-Santos, Juan Benet, Carmen Martín Gaite, Luis and Juan Goytisolo, to Luis Landero, Lourdes Ortíz, Clara Janés, Álvaro Pombo, Esther Tusquets, Soledad Puértolas, Paloma Díaz Más, Carme Riera, Marina Mayoral, and Belén Gopegui).

The belated recognition of women writers and the presence of feminine perspectives in all three of these themes are among the more remarkable features of late twentieth-century fiction. In Chapter 11, Molinaro looks at first-person feminine narratives and traces the evolution of the female voice from silence to assertiveness, 'from the selfless assertion of self' (Buckley 1996: 131) to the openly judgmental heroines of Tusquets, Lourdes Ortiz, and Marina Mayoral. Her selection of first-person *Bildungsromanen* shows their narrators' capacity for running their own lives and their willingness to step out of line whenever they feel they need to do so if they are to fulfil themselves as individuals. Sentimental traps of one kind of another may impede their achievement of full independence, many heroines tending to define themselves in terms of the redemptive possibilities of romantic love. But these female protagonists appear increasingly capable of creating their own rules, making their own reading of their pasts, and imposing their own logic on the world around them.

Just as important as the discovery of women's own voices has been the acceptance and exploration of their bodies and desires, a search that has given depth and complexity to an unprecedented boom in erotic and sentimental fiction in the last thirty years. Erotic fiction has exposed hidden taboos and placed transgressive behavior right at the heart of respectable middle-class lifestyles. Writers now use sexual material to explore loneliness, isolation, and the violence that was hitherto swept under the carpet. The crisis in the biological family is now seen as a mirror image of the crisis in the national family that was once considered the indestructible core of national life.

Now that the demons of dictatorship seem long gone and democratic

---

6   Sobejano and Suñén, following Hutcheon's term 'narcissistic novel', identify a type of self-centered writing devoted to dissecting its own genesis and growth. This they christen 'the self-absorbed novel' or 'the writerly novel'. Ruz (1999) points out that the term 'self-absorbed novel' came after the 'total novel', a label invented by Suñén in 1974 to refer to texts such as Juan José Millás's *Visión del ahogado* and *Cerbero son las sombras* in which literature becomes an autonomous entity in itself. For Sobejano, adds Ruz, the writerly novel is the latest manifestation of the lyrical novel; one that aims above all else to be a creative and autonomous text.

'normality' has set in, new kinds of realism have begun to appear in the novel. These do not always mean a return to objective reality, but instead to a conscious construction of the human mind in its ordering of experience beyond established categories; a process that places the sense of self and of the other at the heart of narration. Beilín explains in Chapter 13 how Spain's new readership is on the lookout for novels that confirm rather than deny the disquieting aspects of everyday life. The stories of Juan José Millás, Javier García Sánchez, Soledad Puértolas, or Javier Tomeo, for example, explore from within the restlessness and instability of our contemporary condition. She also uses a term, 'disquieting realism', to describe a selection of highly subjective novels by Antonio Muñoz Molina, Cristina Fernández Cubas, and Enrique Vila Matas. These works evoke the irrational forces at work on our minds and the uncertain moods of everyday life, and use the epistemological uncertainties of language and fiction to depict ordinary truths and everyday experiences. According to Beilín, 'the possible and the apparently impossible, the visible and the invisible merge and give birth to a new vision of reality which extends beyond the limits of common sense, but not beyond this world. In works of this kind, the incredible is represented as a part of reality, and the real is often exposed as incredible'. Fictional characters reflect the vacuum left by the death of ideology and the absence of common causes and metaphysical concerns, as they experience forms of alienation quite impossible to articulate in words.

The polar opposites of that kind of writing are the terse, detached, and speech-oriented novels of 'Generation X'. In Chapter 14, Song sees the Spanish equivalent in a group of writers now in their thirties (Roger Wolfe, Ray Lóriga, Ángel Mañas, Benjamín Prado, Félix Romeo, David Trueba, Lucía Etxebarria, Gabriela Bustelo) for whom literature and lifestyles have become global and amoral. She shows how the literary aesthetic of 'dirty realism', or 'rough realism', enthusiastically embraces consumerism and pop and techno culture (music, rock, comics, films, videos, and the like) just as American dissident culture in the 1960s embraced the narratives of the Beat Generation and later the 'dirty realism' of Raymond Carver, Richard Ford, Mary Russo, and Tobias Wolff. The marginalized world and minimalist style of writers such as these highlight the superficiality of a society in which success, money, and the acquisition of material goods have replaced all other values and marks of identity, where relationships are sustained by alcohol, drugs, cheap sex, and nocturnal rituals, and where any one locale is indistinguishable from any other.

The Spanish novel also chronicles Spain's 'economic miracle': the transformation in a few decades of a predominantly agrarian society into a modern, urban, high-tech nation. Since the 1970s, the rapid evolution of Spanish customs, values, and attitudes has meant that readers are more interested in city life than they are in the old, rural ways. Madrid and Barcelona, in the process of re-inventing themselves as cultural and cosmopolitan centers, continue to emulate and rival each other. Their unique traditions and cultures are foregrounded in a series of novels in which, more than merely settings, the cities become actual protagonists. In Chapters 13 and 14 Pope and Altisent show how the images of the two cities have changed in the minds of those who live in them. Right through the twentieth century, these two cities have been phenomenological realities as well as constantly rewritten palimpsests of past images and literary referents. Each has its distinctive identity and each has become increasingly detached from its past in our global post-industrial world; their traditions and their monuments have become displaced or divorced from their original function and are now increasingly the stuff of memory.

The importance of the city in today's fiction is one factor in the recent unprecedented success of crime fiction. In Chapter 8, Colmeiro analyzes the way in which detective stories have enjoyed enormous success, articulating the tensions and contradictions between the authorities and the underworld. Since the 1950s, crime fiction has increasingly told stories that are vehicles 'for social observation and cultural criticism, to voice dissent and disagreement with the prevailing political ideology'. Writers have added further elements to the objectivist style and diction of the social novel by including irony, black humor, self-examination, and repartee. Vázquez Montalbán's Carvalho series, for example, goes well beyond postmodern practice to address pressing social and moral questions swept under the carpet during the democratic transition. As Balibrea has argued, the Carvalho series is at the heart of Vázquez Montalbán's attempt to introduce a critical awareness in the face of Spain's historical *desmemoria* (amnesia); its enigmas reveal a politics of obfuscation endemic to the entire capitalist system rather than pointing to a single individual who corrupts the perfect social order (1999: 130–31). The entertainment value of such detective fiction is heightened by its polemical nature and by the moral quandaries experienced by a detective who is a fascinatingly complex authorial alter ego.

In conclusion, throughout the twentieth century Spanish fiction strove to break with traditional middle-class values and with the poetics of realism favored by readers and writers who saw meaning only in plots and situations that were familiar and predictable. A number of factors eventually helped them to break out of the monotony of social comment muted by censorship and failed political novels dominated by a mood disillusionment, even despair: the rise of journalism, the role of memory in writing and film during the transition, and, finally, the commodification of dissent each drove writers to return to more purely literary values of fiction, making the engagement of the reader their priority. The pleasures of a well-constructed story and an urge to absorb all sorts of diverse aesthetic influences and traditions have brought new vitality to the genre. The tradition of the lyrical novel and anti-novel in the early years of the century was revived in the mid-1960s and it grew into the structural novel of the 1970s which has since become increasingly multi-faceted and more in keeping with the postmodern commitment to lightness, humor, and aesthetic relativism. By the 1990s, we can see a decline in what John Barth terms 'literature of exhaustion'. Novelists' inquisitiveness, intellectual curiosity, sensuality, and fondness are what characterizes the Spanish novel today, and the pleasure principle is firmly to the fore. Spanish fiction has breathed new life into some less frequented and non-native traditions: science fiction, the Byzantine novel, the Gothic novel, and magical realism. The world of the novel is no longer limited to the Spanish countryside and the major cities: it can embrace places and concerns all the way from New York, Paris, Oxford, and Lisbon to the so-called paradises of Santo Domingo, Chiapas, Costa Rica, or the West African Spanish ex-colonies. None of these settings now seems impossibly exotic. The global awareness fostered by the media and an unprecedented influx of third-world immigrants have led novelists to address the question of exile from a fresh angle, seeing it as the collective tragedy of the dispossessed, rather than as an individual act of intellectual and ideological defiance. Violence has migrated, too: from the frustration of those, as in *Pascual Duarte* and Ana María Matute's *Los Abel,* forced to eke out an existence in deprived rural areas, to the upper classes and the urban underworld, where alcohol, drugs, and sexual addiction have dismantled the the old family values, eroding relationships and encouraging destructive rituals and gratuitous sacrifices, such as the deadly drinking binge in José Ángel Mañas's *Historias del Kronen* or the rape and murder of a friend in Lucía Etxeberria's *Beatriz y los cuerpos celestes.*

Contemporary novels also re-examine the cynicism, hypocrisy, and pretence brought on by affluence and the ways these have spawned the new standards of 'decency' and 'political correctness' portrayed by Margarita Rivière in *La década de la decencia* and caricatured by Félix de Azúa, Javier Marías, and Manuel Vázquez Montalbán. Other writers cautiously approach the new concerns that are surfacing at the beginning of the millennium: discrimination involving migrant workers from the Maghreb, environmental and ecological degradation, irresponsible land speculation, domestic violence and child abuse, and the dangers of nationalist movements. Such issues are at present addressed more effectively in film and by documentaries, but they may come to feature in the novels of the future.

What, then, of that future? Santos Alonso (2005) sees the survival of the novel as inextricably bound up with the uncertain future now facing the publishing industry. New market conditions have made the novel even more of a consumer object than before, and the market is increasingly international. The money that multinational publishing houses make from books has brought both benefits and dangers. The social status of the writer has risen. Generous prizes, large advances and commissions, and more equitable copyright laws have given Spanish authors financial independence and helped to foster their literary careers. On the other hand, the aggressive marketing of each new title, with reviews plastered all over the newspapers, makes constant demands on the writer. It also means that the critic and reader have to rely more on their own judgement. Students of literature must avoid facile assumptions based on establishment judgements about quality. The cultural mafia may be systematically skeptical of anything new or which suggests that society itself is changing, but readers need also to be wary of the siren call of the new and the fashionable.

I

CONTINUING TRADITIONS AND CHANGING STYLES

1

The Spanish Novel in the Twentieth Century

GONZALO NAVAJAS

The turn of the century: the crisis of 1898

The evolution of the Spanish novel in the twentieth century runs parallel with the twists and turns in national attitudes to the central ideas and events that shape the world at the time. For much of the century, leading Spanish novelists viewed the social and cultural condition of their country with pessimism and contempt, seeing Spain as cut off from the rest of Europe. Their works analyze the causes of this marginalization and offer a number of diagnoses for the country's ills. The extension and depth of their criticisms varied with the author's ideological perspective and the gravity of the political questions under consideration. Criticism was particularly strong at times of acute distress, such as the loss of the last remnants of the Spanish empire (1898), and the Civil War and its aftermath (1936–75).

The century begins with the rejection of the tenets of the nineteenth-century novel and in particular those held by realist authors, the most prominent of whom was Galdós. His novels provided the group of writers of the pivotal 'Generation of 98' with a benchmark against which they could measure their own achievements and a model which they could reject in favor of new kinds of writing. Apart from Unamuno, the most important writers of that Generation of 98 are Baroja, Azorín, Antonio Machado, and Valle-Inclán, writers who can be grouped together because their works reflect the decline of the country after the defeat of Spain in Cuba and the Philippines in 1898. For writers such as these, Galdós's novels represented a closed cosmos informed by a methodology both empirical and objective. His aesthetic was founded on the principles and goals of positivism and the experimental sciences that were at their most popular in the second half of the nineteenth century. But that world had undergone a profound crisis with the emergence of post-Hegelian philosophers such as Kierkegaard and Nietzsche, and, at the turn of the century, novelists and thinkers in Spain found in these new ideas a fresh conceptual framework to express views on literature and culture.

The writings of Miguel de Unamuno signal the first major break with the representational and analytical view of reality on which that old, conventional realist novel was based. He brought to fiction an intellectual complexity, internalizing the narrative process while, at the same time, subjecting the assumptions of realist aesthetics to close scrutiny. Unamuno's training as a philosopher and academic encouraged him to conceptualize the impulses of an intellectual generation that felt the need to divorce itself from historical and cultural assumptions that still remained fashionable in the country as a whole.

Paz en la Guerra (1897), written in an autobiographical format, sounds the starting-gun for the foregrounding of the self as the narrative core of the text, without any of the masks and filters which the realist novel had employed to conceal it. But it is *Amor y pedagogía* (1902) that is the first novel to break with two principles that were essential to realism: the creation of psychologically well-rounded and credible characters and the elaboration of a spatial and temporal environment that is easily identifiable because of its clear correspondence with a recognizable locale and time. As Unamuno himself said (1981: 11), the characters in his novel are 'puppets that the author parades on the stage while he speaks'. Those same characters are paraded at a time and place that are accidental and contingent, whereas space and time had been central to the realist novel. Unamuno's fictions progressively dispense with descriptions of either character or milieu, a process which culminates in *San Manuel Bueno, mártir* (1933), in which the small town of Valverde de Lucerna, where the story is set, becomes an abstract and universal space, shorn of any recognizable physical correlative. Instead, the text concentrates on Unamuno's thinking about the perpetuation of the self once the latter has abandoned the secure anchorage of metaphysical and religious truth. The book's protagonist, the agnostic priest San Manuel, is an emblem for the author's self, as are his parishioners, split between a fervent faith and the denial of that faith by reason.

The epistemological change that Unamuno triggered in the novel is both extensive and profound. He even coined a new term to describe his fictions, *nivola*, because both their conceptual framework and their language and structure were fundamentally new. Rejecting the role of the omniscient and supposedly neutral observer, his narrators became clear alter egos for an author who used fiction to explore his own sense of shifting identity.

Niebla (1914), *La tía Tula* (1921), *Tres novelas ejemplares y un prólogo* (1920), together with *San Manuel Bueno, mártir*, are the works which, after *Amor y pedagogía*, best exemplify this subjectivized and anti-representational novelistic method, one in which the processes of narrative consciousness are not concealed or disguised, as they had been in realist works, but instead are explicitly foregrounded in the text. *Niebla,* in particular, goes even further in dispensing with the conventions of the realist novel, presenting the open rebellion of the central character, Víctor Goti, against the author's decision to kill him off in order to prevent him from usurping the author's own role. Denying the rights of the author to autonomy and self-assertion, Goti proclaims (1974: 171): 'You [the author] do not exist outside me and the other characters whom you believe yourself to have invented'. In Italy, at much this same time, Pirandello was doing something similar when he explored the fragmentation of the self and the independence from their creators of literary and artistic works.

Unamuno's literary vision is usually associated with the principles of high modernism and especially with the privileging of the author as both center of creation and representative of society as a whole. Another important contribution was his questioning of traditional genre divisions. Novel, drama, essay, and poetry are all invoked to make the work of art didactic as well as entertaining and enjoyable. As for other major European modernist writers, literature for Unamuno became a way in which we may compensate for the shortcomings of natural science when it comes to explaining and interpreting the world. Literature thus replaced science and religion as the favored means for the individual to reconnect spiritually and intellectually with his or her environment.

Unamuno was the major figure in this movement toward a repositioning of the role of literature in terms of the so-called *Geisteswissenschaften*, the new approach to the humanities and social sciences most clearly articulated at the turn of the century in the writings of Schleiermacher and Dilthey. He ushered in a period in which literature was seen as a major source not only of social and political criticism but also of philosophical enquiry. Unamuno and the other novelists of the Generation of 98 expanded the conceptual repertoire of the novel and freed it from the restrictions of empirical thought and realist aesthetics, turning narrative fiction into a device for finding fresh ways to configure the self in a social and cultural environment that they felt had inhibited personal growth.

Pío Baroja, in *Camino de perfección* (1902) and *El árbol de la ciencia* (1911), created the figure of the isolated seeker of personal fulfilment in a hostile environment. Both novels reworked the mythical quest of Ulysses for a new sense of identity. For Baroja, home was not a physical or geographical concept. Instead of some second Ithaca, his novels search for a *Heimat* or spiritual and cultural refuge in which the protagonist can feel emotionally and intellectually at home. Unlike Ulysses, Baroja's characters do not succeed in their quest but, instead, become negative heroes or antiheroes. That Fernando Ossorio in *Camino de perfección* experiences a number of spiritual and near-mystical aspirations is confirmed by allusions to the Spanish mystical writers St Teresa of Avila and St John of the Cross, as well as to the painter El Greco. Fernando's quixotic struggle against the frustrating mediocrity of Spanish life concludes paradoxically when he, too, is engulfed by the general triviality around him and ends up a victim of the very environment against which he has battled.

El árbol de la ciencia takes fatalism further. The protagonist, Andrés Hurtado, attempts to find an intellectual and cultural home through his scientific research, but his quest proves fruitless and ends in despair and suicide. With his death, the possibility that Spanish science and culture might be developed to rival those of more advanced European countries dies with him. These two are among the best of Baroja's vast and uneven output as a novelist and they attest to a continual conflict between Spanish culture on the one hand and modernity on the other.

Paradox, rey (1906) extended this same fatalistic view to other aspects of Western civilization and, in particular, to the colonial European enterprise in Africa. Baroja passes the same harsh, critical judgment on other countries that he previously passed on Spain, undermining the universalist principles and objectives of modernism by demonstrating that they derived from the hold that strong nations have over weak ones. It is not surprising that Baroja's utopia is an anarchist one. The absolute rejection of all gradualist and reforming measures appears to be the only legitimate solution for his antiheroes.

Valle-Inclán's position was more diverse and complex. The *Sonatas* (1902–05), consisting of four separate segments, revel in the power of aesthetics to soften and embellish the coarseness of a degraded national culture. These are ambiguous narratives that some see as frivolous, influenced as they were by the principles of *modernismo*, the movement that permeated Spanish and Latin American poetry and literature at the beginning of the century. They may represent only a brief phase in Valle-Inclán's fiction, but they show the lure for him at this time of beautiful language and brilliant rhetorical effects that overshadow the rest of the work. It was not the *Sonatas*, however, that established Valle-Inclán's reputation and, though important, they are unrepresentative of his output as a whole. The focus of his other narratives is his uncompromising view of the historical and cultural reality of Spain and the rupture of conventional formal and ideological barriers. We can see this most clearly in his invention of the *esperpento*.

This was not some new literary form aimed at further undermining the realist credo of the objective presentation of reality. Instead, it submitted reality to a process of violent distortion through hyperbole. Unlike Unamuno, Valle-Inclán viewed Spanish culture as the underbelly of modernity, a caricature of European reality that, in a progressive and liberal society, could serve only as a model to avoid. The *esperpento* was a process that depended on an extreme deformation of an already deformed reality. The process was grounded in the expressionistic trends of Spanish art, from the picaresque novel and Quevedo to Ribera and Goya. Valle applied the *esperpento* in particular in texts that might be seen as dramatic in form: both his drama

Divinas palabras (1920) and his major narrative works. Among these, *Tirano Banderas* (1926) ridiculed the antics of a Latin American dictatorial figure whose excesses revealed the futility of much of Latin American political history and, by extension, that of Spain as well. The three volumes of *El ruedo ibérico* – *La corte de los milagros* (1927), *Viva mi dueño* (1928), and *Baza de espadas* (1958) – deconstructed the ideological alibis used to justify the many historical errors and abuses that Valle identified, in particular the manipulation of society for their own ends by dominant groups such as the armed forces, the Catholic Church, and the political class. The apocalyptic and fantastic vision of the country that emerged from Valle-Inclán's *esperpentos* served as a dire warning concerning the destructive tendencies of the Spanish collective psyche that had shaped modern Spanish history into a process of unremitting internal confrontation that led eventually to civil war.

Valle-Inclán was the most extreme and uncompromising writer of his generation. His contemporaries did not share the same critical intensity. Azorín, for instance, saw the process of reassimilating the classical tradition (as represented by the great iconic literary figures of the past, from Cervantes to Fray Luis de León) as a way of asserting a continuity between past and present and seeing culture as an instrument of collective redemption. Contemplation and apathy, '*abulia*', replaced the violent contradictions and conceptual confrontations we find in Unamuno, Valle, and Baroja. *Abulia* shaped the autobiographical *Doppelgängers* of Azorín in *La voluntad* (1902) and *Las confesiones de un pequeño filósofo* (1904). These were works profoundly different from the intensity and dynamism characteristic of the novels of Baroja and Valle-Inclán. Azorín's prose was the most refined and elegant of his generation, and it often became the predominant, or even the sole reason for writing. Time and again Azorín demonstrated a mastery of language, particularly in his cultural travelogues through the Peninsula, of which *Castilla* (1912) is just one example among many. Gabriel Miró – in *El libro de Sigüenza* (1916), *Nuestro Padre San Daniel* (1921), and *El obispo leproso* (1926) – expanded and developed this tendency towards contemplation and refinement that turned texts into exquisite *objets d'art* in accordance with an essentialist aesthetic far removed from the immediate *circunstancia* of the day.

Nietzsche and Kierkegaard were not the only thinkers to influence the seemingly new cognitive and aesthetic paradigm that replaced the epistemological self-assurance of realism and positivism. Henri Bergson and Wilhelm Dilthey also played their part. Bergson emphasized the intuition and emotion that underpinned Kant's view of time. Dilthey's theory of *Lebensphilosophie,* or 'philosophy of life', stressed the part played by the vital and the personal in the acquisition of knowledge. The scientific theories of Einstein, too, were influential, since he brought to the forefront of intellectual debate the immaterial and the invisible, things that cannot be observed or empirically verified: at the beginning of the twentieth century, physics replaced natural sciences as the model for the social sciences and the humanities.

José Ortega y Gasset was the most influential Spanish thinker in the first four decades of the twentieth century, not only in philosophy, but also in intellectual history and the arts. His works on contemporary thought (*El tema de nuestro tiempo,* 1923), experimental aesthetics (*La deshumanización del arte,* 1925), the novel (*Ideas sobre la novela,* 1925), and history as the consequence of the intervention of individuals (*En torno a Galileo,* 1942), set an agenda with which writers of the time were then free to agree or disagree. As well as a powerful intellectual force in the cultural life of the nation, Ortega was a thinker who was constantly updating the terms of intellectual debate. In the ongoing conflict between internal and external forces that he saw as defining recent Spanish history, Ortega took on the role of modernizer, opposing what he saw as a national cultural life dominated by a fixation with the past. Dismissing the fatalistic view that Spain could not alter a destiny dictated by history, Ortega advocated a policy of embracing the future and the new.

Ortega's ideas on avant-garde and experimental art influenced, among others, the novelists Benjamín Jarnés (*El convidado de papel,* 1928, and *Teoría del zumbel,* 1930) and Antonio Espina (*Luna de copas,* 1929). Both have been largely neglected by literary critics, who see their concepts of the novel as doing the same kind of thing as non-figurative painters, from Picasso and Miró to Kandinsky, were doing in the 1920s. Innovative techniques and language notwithstanding, their notion of an abstract and 'pure' novel, removed from reference to the real world and stripped of any discernable structure, led to the appearance of works that lacked the fluidity and narrative intensity so vital to the novel.

The principles of European high modernism can be seen at their most effective in the work of Ramón Pérez de Ayala, who undertook a profound critical re-examination not only of the educational and ideological limits of contemporary Spanish society but also of its recent cultural history. From *A.M.D.G.* (1910) to *Tigre Juan* (1926), Pérez explored some of the principal bones of contention in Spanish intellectual life in his search for the causes of Spain's peripheral role in the intellectual and cultural life of recent times. Ortega's influence is plain to see in the conceptual framework of Pérez de Ayala's novels, and in particular his concentration on leading figures or generational groups as a way of explaining cultural phenomena. His characters, such as the eponymous Belarmino and Apolonio, and the situations in which he places them, reveal an idealized view of development and progress that runs quite contrary to the Marxist ideas about materialism and economic determination that we find in the novels of César de Arconada (*Los pobres contra los ricos,* 1932) and José Díaz Fernández (*El blocao,* 1928), both of

which offer a dialectical and class-oriented view of social and human relationships and a radical critique of the establishment.

The first three decades of the twentieth century were one of the brightest
periods in modern Spanish culture. Politically, the country was moving slowly
in the direction of greater liberalization and was opening up to new cultural
avenues. This was also a time when political life was increasingly influenced
by prominent intellectual figures, from Unamuno and Ortega y Gasset to
Manuel Azaña and Ramiro de Maeztu. This process of modernization and
cultural and social dynamism culminated in 1931 in the proclamation of the
Second Republic. The new regime brought enormous hope to the country as
a whole, even though that hope soon proved illusory and disintegrated into
polarization and upheaval. Increasingly violent internal conflict led to the
rebellion staged by the most conservative forces in the country which ushered
in the bloody Civil War.

The implosion of the Civil War

The Civil War and the consequences of the lengthy and repressive dictatorship that followed were the most decisive factors shaping the history of Spain
in the second half of the twentieth century. Social development was halted
in its tracks and the country reverted to its old ways of isolationism and
negativity. Politically and culturally shut off from the European mainstream
and from events in the wider world, the novels of the period are redolent of
isolation and marginalization.

Among the writers forced into exile were three of the major novelists
to reflect in print upon the traumatic events of the Civil War and the divisions that it brought to the country: Ramón Sender, Arturo Barea, and Max
Aub. Sender's *Crónica del alba* (1942–66), Barea's *La forja de un rebelde*
(1941–46, not published in Spanish until 1951), and Aub's *El laberinto
mágico* (1943–67) are all multi-volume works documenting the events that
led up to the Civil War as well as the war itself. In addition to works such as
these centering on the Civil War, Sender and Aub also produced a number
of novels dealing with a variety of subjects and contexts well beyond the
traumatic events that forced them to leave the country.

Another major novelist to produce important work in exile was Francisco
Ayala. Thanks to the censorship imposed by the regime, both *Muertes de
perro* (1958) and *El fondo del vaso* (1962) remained for many years unknown
in Spain, as did the work of many other novelists in exile, such as Rosa
Chacel, Segundo Serrano Poncela, and Manuel Andújar. Recognition came
only after the death of the dictator in 1975 and the increasing liberalization
of the country; by then, although there was real public interest in the produc-

tion of exiled Spanish authors, any impact these novels might have had was blunted by the passing of the years.

Those novelists who remained in Spain during the dictatorship were forced to adapt to the limitations imposed by the regime. Camilo José Cela is the one novelist of the immediate post-war period who, in *La familia de Pascual Duarte* (1942) and *La colmena* (1951), contrived to capture some of the despair and banality of everyday life in a society both provincial and backward. Cela's works stand out among the fiction published during the first two decades after the war, though both Carmen Laforet's *Nada* (1945) and Ana María Matute's *Los hijos muertos* (1958) are of interest.

Other writers of the time struck a more militant and defiant attitude. Antonio Ferres's La piqueta (1959) and Juan Goytisolo's La resaca (1958), to take just two examples, advocate uncompromising opposition to the political and social status quo. The principles of social realism, as defined by Lukács and by Goldmann, helped to nurture the social novel of the 1960s, conceived as a weapon in the struggle to delegitimize the ideology of a despised regime and its self-serving cultural agenda. With few exceptions, works of a transparently political nature enjoyed only limited artistic success, as any artistic goals they may have had were subordinated to this other purpose. Apart from those already mentioned, the most important novel of this period is *El Jarama,* by Rafael Sánchez Ferlosio. First published in 1956, it constitutes the first serious attempt to overcome the limitations inherent in literature of advocacy and to infuse it with symbolism and poetry as well. But, overall, the novels written in the first two decades after the Civil War were marked by a narrow, albeit well-intentioned aesthetic and ideological program. The strictly local nature and immediate objectives of such works may explain why, with the exception of Juan Goytisolo, such writers remained largely unknown outside Spain.

The first and most elaborate attempt at breaking the mould is Luis Martín-Santos's *Tiempo de silencio* (1962). Its appearance in 1962 triggered a reexamination of the goals of social realism and of the function of literature as a vehicle for social and cultural criticism. Although the novel was critical of the repressive regime, Martín-Santos's artistic goals went well beyond a simple political critique. The narrative follows the pattern of much contemporary European literature and culture, but, in place of the French and Italian sources used by most Spanish novelists of the time, the models used come from the English-speaking world. The influence of Joyce, Huxley, Orwell, Nabokov, and Dos Passos can be seen in the book. Through irony and a wide array of stylistic devices, Martín-Santos was able to create an innovative and personal language that ran counter to the trite and predictable resources of Spanish fiction of the time. The novel is a tour de force when compared with the sterile artistic output of his contemporaries, and it heralded the beginning of a profound renewal of novelistic principles, paving the way for a series of works that expanded the conceptual and technical horizons of fiction. *Tiempo de silencio* is a powerful call for a broadening of the cultural horizon and for national renovation.

After *Tiempo de silencio*, there is one further novel that is especially significant because of its audacious use of new narrative structures and techniques. Juan Goytisolo's *Señas de identidad* (1966) is unlike his earlier novels, such as *Juegos de manos* (1954) and *Fiestas* (1958), which had engaged in a rudimentary process of sublimation of the author's unresolved personal issues. Instead, it skilfully foregrounds those same concerns through the creation of an alter ego for the narrator. Using flashbacks, historical documents, and an indirect stream of consciousness, Álvaro Mendiola's story traces Goytisolo's own years of self-imposed exile in Paris to present a panorama of Spanish history, from the days of colonial Cuba to the economic tourist boom of the 1960s. Álvaro assumes the voice of an entire generation struggling to survive in a hostile environment and, at the same time, Goytisolo unleashes what will become a torrent of unremitting cultural criticism of the kind we see in later works, such as *Reivindicación del conde don Julián* (1969). Álvaro Mendiola's bitter and unforgiving indictment of the situation that he is forced to endure in Spain becomes a portrait of an entire generation that felt itself excluded from contemporary cultural trends back home and condemned to the margins of European history. The sense of doom and fatalism that we find in *Señas de identidad* will persist throughout Goytisolo's work and it serves as a painful reminder of the country's history of cultural conflict and collective frustration.

The publication of *Tiempo de silencio* and *Señas de identidad*, together with the first tentative overtures of the regime to the outside world in the mid-1960s, made it possible for the novel gradually to embrace new themes and structures. The works of Juan Benet, Luis Goytisolo, and Jesús Fernández Santos signal the beginnings of more experimental types of novel. Carmen Martín Gaite and Esther Tusquets brought the issue of gender to the fore as they focused on women against a background of power structures and social attitudes that excluded and silenced them. The characters of Martín Gaite's *Retahílas* (1974) and *El cuarto de atrás* (1978), or those in Esther Tusquets' *Varada tras el último naufragio* (1980) and *Para no volver* (1985) are conditioned by a repressive environment and yet they engage in a personal struggle defined primarily by their gender rather than by politics. Women's fiction helped to make the subjective the core of the literary text.

Another important strand in this renewed interest in fiction was the emergence of a hybrid: the detective story infused with social and political commentary. Eduardo Mendoza's *La verdad sobre el caso Savolta* (1975) ushered in this development, which was then taken up by Manuel Vázquez Montalbán's *Asesinato en el comité central* (1982) and, to a lesser extent, by Juan Madrid (see below, Chapter 8). The wide acceptance of a form traditionally associated with literature of entertainment as a vehicle for the discussion of pressing social and political issues arising from the troubled history of the country is an indication of the greater freedom now enjoyed by writers in dealing with political questions. This new kind of detective story made it possible for writers to address issues from the perspective of dissent and criticism, but to do so in a format that included a broad range of registers borrowed from popular culture. All these developments prepared the way for a new kind of novel that was able to respond to the changes that took place when Franco died and the cultural barriers erected by his regime were gradually dismantled.

Spain's global postmodernity

Postmodernism reached Spain late, and at a time when its appeal as a new way of approaching art was already on the wane. By the time it was being discussed in Spanish artistic circles in the 1980s, it had lost a good deal of its philosophical and ideological vigor and had become simply yet another aesthetic option among many as well as offering an attractive lifestyle for the young in the heady days of liberalization. Rather than a critique of the excesses and shortcomings of traditional rationalist modernism (such as we find in the works of Lyotard, Baudrillard, or Venturi), Spanish postmodernism simply advocated a break with all traditional norms and canons of social and artistic conduct. Its focus was on the here and now, the present rather than any notion of historical continuity, its guiding principles a deliberate blurring and blending of genres and registers and a casual approach to cultural classics of all kinds. The central model for all this came from film and in particular from Pedro Almodóvar's stand against what he saw as the burden of an ideological history that limited the artist's freedom to approach contemporary issues in any way he chose.

The post-Franco novel found in postmodernism an attractive medium with which to express the rapidly shifting situation of the country. In the era of what Vattimo calls 'soft thought', favoring anti-systematic and non-metaphysical categories, the postmodern legitimized a new version of literature that was not necessarily associated with great ideas and causes. It also allowed for a more flexible and less politically committed approach to cultural and social issues. Taking advantage of the powerful movement in Spain toward openness, the Spanish postmodern novel explored the cultural dynamics linked to the digital revolution that had facilitated instant and universal global communication. In this way, the novel might become more inclusive, semantically as well as stylistically. Antonio Muñoz Molina, Javier Marías, Almudena Grandes, and Arturo Pérez Reverte are some of the writers at the heart of this renewal, as are a number of those who write in other peninsular languages, including Bernardo Atxaga, Suso de Toro, and Biel Mesquida.

Muñoz Molina's early novels provide a good illustration of the nature of the new epistemological and aesthetic mode. *El invierno en Lisboa* (1987) and *Beltenebros* (1989), in particular, seized these new technical possibilities in order to offer a fresh view of history. Although they both contain a central core of critical analysis of the current Spanish social and political situation, they conduct that analysis through frequent allusions to Hollywood films, jazz, and popular music, and they do so in a poetic and highly stylized language. This mixture of intertextuality and sophisticated artistic cross-referencing produces works of art that are both intellectually challenging and aesthetically compelling. In such works, political and ethical considerations become secondary.

In Muñoz Molina's later works, there is, however, a marked evolution toward the reintegration of an ethical dimension. *El jinete polaco* (1991) and *Plenilunio* (1997) tackle the controversial and painful issues of the need to keep alive in the collective memory the forgotten heroes of the Civil War and the terrorist activities of the Basque Homeland and Freedom Movement, known as ETA. The ethical imperative resurfaces alongside the re-emergence of the structures and concerns of the classical novel, such as linear narrative and descriptive contextualization.

Ethics remain a central concern for writers of previous generations. Juan Goytisolo, for instance, continues to produce works that are politically both critical and committed, while Manuel Vázquez Montalbán and Juan Marsé have written novels in which social and political agendas predominate. Theirs, however, has become a minority position. The younger generation is concerned with global issues, the new technologies of communication, and the demands of the mass-market. This shift has both ushered in an expansion of horizons when it comes to artistic expectation, and provoked, in turn, the trivialization and simplification of many of the issues involved. The work of Arturo Pérez Reverte is an illustration of this. His books span centuries of Spanish and European history, going as far back as the Middle Ages, and yet entertainment and immediate gratification dominate all other considerations. His first major novel, *El maestro de esgrima* (1988) was openly critical of government, but such criticism has all but disappeared in his later work, such as the hugely popular series *El capitán Alatriste* (1996).

The classical and modernist novel saw intellectual writers addressing the most pressing and intractable issues of their day: Galdós, Zola, and Tolstoy in the nineteenth century; Unamuno, Valle-Inclán, Aub, and Sender in the first half of the twentieth. Increasing globalization and the fashion for postmodernism have dismantled national boundaries and discredited conventional criteria for the creation and definition of personal and collective identity. They have also accelerated the process of erosion and devaluation of the great ideologies of the past. As a result, the status of the authorial voice has been diminished and its power has to some extent been drowned out by the white noise from the many other media widely available in an increasingly diverse cultural environment. There are many more writers writing today than at any time in the past, but they do not exercise the huge social and cultural authority that the comparatively small number of major figures enjoyed in the past. Globalization has seen individuality supplanted by conformism, the lone voice by the many. The old novel, written along predictable guidelines, has evolved once again into the most popular of all kinds of writing. The phenomenon of the instant international best-seller is the product of mass marketing, while other literary genres, such as poetry, have been less affected because they appeal to a much smaller readership.

The progressive globalization of the major publishing houses and their consolidation into multinational conglomerates with enormous power to dictate fashion and style has also contributed to the homogenization of narrative. The Spanish novel of the last decade of the twentieth century and the early years of the twenty-first has seen the extensive and direct involvement of such market forces and of the mass media in the promotion and distribution of popular novels. Carlos Ruiz Zafón's *La sombra del viento* (2004) and Julia Navarro's *La hermandad de la sábana santa* (2004) are just two illustrations of this trend. At the same time, the popularity of Javier Cercas's *Soldados de Salamina* (2001) not only demonstrates that commercial success is not necessarily incompatible with ambitious aesthetic and artistic goals, but also illustrates the close interconnections that today exist between literary fiction and film.

Conclusion: the future of the novel

The history of the Spanish novel in the twentieth century is an uneven one. The century began with major figures such as Unamuno and Valle-Inclán who continued to write well into the 1930s. The Civil War brought about an abrupt rupture in cultural continuity and, for two decades or more, the best works came from writers living in exile: Max Aub, Ramón Sender, Francisco Ayala (see below, Chapter 2). Inside the country, perhaps the only major author still working was Camilo José Cela, although, after *La colmena*, even his work tended to be repetitive and thematically limited. The 1960s saw the emergence of two important works: Luis Martín-Santos's *Tiempo de silencio* and Juan Goytisolo's *Señas de identidad*. After Franco's death, the number of both novels and novelists has grown exponentially, but at the same time there has been a marked tendency towards uniformity and complacency. The future of the Spanish novel will be determined by its ability to balance the demands of the new age of instant global communication, which has dismantled cultural hierarchies and canonical values, with the exploration of new scientific discoveries and fresh artistic options. Spanish fiction has overcome the parochialism that for so long penned it in within national borders and dented its international reputation. One can but hope that the novels of the future rediscover the capacity for critical analysis and intellectual depth that served them so well in the past.

Further reading

Abellán (1977: vol. IV), Alonso & Castells (1992b), Amell (1966), Epps & Fernández (2005), Gies (2004), Gullón (2006), Johnson (2003), Labanyi (2002), La Rubia (1996), Larson & Woods (2005), Navajas (2002 and 2004), Santos (2004), Spires (1988), Torrecilla (2004 and 2006).

2

The Early Twentieth-Century Novel

CARLOS ALEX LONGHURST

Literary creativity is multi-directional. It looks backwards, sideways and forwards. A writer will follow or subvert a tradition, will be aware of what his contemporaries are doing, and will hope to surpass them. Literary historiography by contrast can only look in one direction; it is a discipline that seeks to order the past and whose understanding of that past is a function of the taxonomy employed. At its simplest, the taxonomy of the modern Spanish novel consists of a series of labels that purport to describe a succession of approaches to the writing of fictional prose. After the early nineteenth-century romances set in remote times à la Walter Scott came the more earthy yet picturesque descriptions of contemporary life of the *costumbristas* (portrayers of contemporary customs), which led in turn to the more ambitious plotting and complex vision of the contemporary world that characterizes realism, the dominant mode of novelistic writing in the second half of the nineteenth century. The concomitant rise of science and the emergence of the quasi-scientific discipline of sociology persuaded some novelists to attempt to follow the example of the Frenchman Émile Zola and emulate the natural sciences by converting the novel into a tool for the seemingly scientific study of society and its ills. Naturalism was in effect a pseudo-scientific form of realism. The late nineteenth-century disillusionment with science because of its perceived failure to solve the growing social conflicts of rapidly industrializing societies led naturalism into disrepute; in Spain, rather than producing a novelist of the rank of Zola, it had spawned a vast number of second-rate novels obsessed with the seamier sides of life: sex, alcoholism, crime, and moral and environmental decay. It was against the materialism of naturalists that older realists like Benito Pérez Galdós and Emilia Pardo Bazán reacted, in their later more spiritually driven work, as did a new generation of younger writers (Clarke 1999: 3–17). In this chapter we shall consider the work of four novelists all born within ten years of one another, between 1864 and 1873, and all of whom produced work of lasting influence: Pío Baroja, Miguel de Unamuno, Ramón del Valle-Inclán, and Azorín. These four writers can be considered the advance guard of a movement whose radical novelty would not become apparent until after World War I and which reached its climax in the avant-garde writers of the 1920s (Lough 2000: 39–41). A dominant characteristic of this new kind of fiction was, at least when compared to realist novels, a generic fuzziness, or hybridity. As the genre became more porous and writers attempted to emulate techniques associated with painting, music, theatre, and even the new art of cinema, it lost its traditional structures and its dependence on storytelling. In this, the Spanish novel was no different from the modernist novel across Europe. Instead of referring to novels plain and simple, literary commentators increasingly found themselves having to qualify the kinds of novels they were dealing with, using such labels as philosophical, intellectual, psychological, lyrical, mythological, formalist, dehumanized, self-reflective, the artist-novel, and even the anti-novel.

The appearance in 1902 of this new style of fiction in the works of Unamuno, Valle-Inclán, Baroja and Azorín has left an indelible mark on Spanish literary historiography and has slanted it in favour of the new or modernist narrative, as though overnight this had actually displaced the realist and naturalist novel. Received wisdom has favoured innovation over tradition, with the result that, in standard histories of literature, the early twentieth century is dominated by modernists and avant-gardists, women writers in particular being seriously under-represented, since they continued to be more interested in the exploration of social and family relationships than they were in philosophical debate and formal experiment (Johnson 2003: vii–viii). The broader picture is rather different. During the first twenty years of the century the market continued to be dominated by realist and naturalist works. Realism's major exponent in Spain, Galdós, returned to the *episodio nacional* form of the historical novel that he had popularized in the 1870s. Among younger writers who followed in the realist tradition, Concha Espina and Carmen de Burgos enjoyed some success, while the novels of Manuel Ciges Aparicio have a certain documentary value, and those of the hugely talented Wenceslao Fernández Flórez employ a humourous satire that wavers between the realistic and the allegorical. But it was the second-generation naturalists, such as Eduardo Zamacois and Felipe Trigo, who continued to sell their sex-orientated yarns in far greater numbers than did any innovative writer of 1902. The most successful Spanish novelist by far, and one who enjoyed an international reputation in his lifetime, fêted from Paris and Buenos Aires to the West Point Military Academy, was Vicente Blasco Ibáñez, another disciple of Zola whose early works fit comfortably into the naturalist mould as long as we are not looking to find any kind of scientific rigour in them. Although his war novel, *Los cuatro jinetes del Apocalipsis* (1916), sold by the million and made him many friends among the Allies, he is remembered today chiefly for his Valencian novels which depict life in and around that bustling metropolis. Still greatly appreciated in his native Valencia, Blasco's regionalist novels, uncomplicated in style and easy to read, are among the most robust and instructive of this sub-genre.

If Blasco Ibáñez can be counted among the survivors of a nineteenth-century way of writing fiction, the quantity and diversity of output of Pío Baroja defy all attempts at classification. His earliest novels, *La casa de Aizgorri* (1900), *Aventuras, inventos y mixtificaciones de Silvestre Paradox* (1901), and *Camino de perfección* (1902), deal with topics such as alcoholism and degeneracy, bohemian life, the psychology of the artist, unconscious motivation, and sexual desire: all of them themes common in late nineteenth-century fiction. But even when Baroja borrowed themes and topics, his treatment of them was never conventional. In *La casa de Aizgorri*, the physical effects of alcoholism, so often described in naturalist novels, are superseded by the mental agonies of an imagined fear of alcoholism. In *Camino de perfección*, another trendy novel-of-the-artist, the connection between art and illness is explored through the mystical journey of a neurotic painter (the title is borrowed from St Teresa). The trilogy *La lucha por la vida* (1903–04: *La busca, *Mala hierba,* and *Aurora roja*) follows closely in the steps of Galdós in offering a vivid account of Madrid low life, but the picture is drawn in much darker hues, as befits a Spain increasingly beset by social conflict and political confrontation. Baroja, however, is not concerned with political ideologies but with human behaviour, especially of the delinquent and criminal kind, and with capturing them effectively in a racy and unpretentious style.

Baroja had a predilection for foreign writers – Shakespeare, Poe, Dickens, and Dostoyevski were among his favourites – and that is reflected in his frequent choice, unusual for a Spanish novelist, of foreign settings for his novels: Paris (*Las tragedias grotescas,* 1907), London (*La ciudad de la niebla,* 1909), Rome (*César o nada,* 1910), Geneva (*El mundo es ansí,* 1912), Calabria (*El laberinto de las sirenas,* 1923), and several other European cities. His reading of English adventure novels and seafaring yarns left a clear imprint on many of his works, but the adventure yarn in Baroja is perhaps more of an intellectual exercise: adventure not so much experienced as seen at second hand and from a distance (Alberich 1966: 103–20). Rather than a realistic account of heroic exploits, adventure at times becomes for him a simulacrum, the ironic musings of a fiction writer at work. Thus *Las inquietudes de Shanti Andía* (1911) is presented as the recollections of an ageing and sedentary seadog who looks back over a life at sea in the same way as the author himself is reminiscing about his youthful readings of Mayne Reid, Captain Marryat, and Robert Louis Stevenson.

Nineteenth-century history was a major source for Baroja's novels, historical events sometimes providing an oblique entry into, or exit from, a wholly fictional plot (for example, the attempted assassination of King Alfonso XIII on his wedding day which marks the beginning of *La dama errante* (1908), or the 1871 rising of the Paris Commune which brings *Las tragedias grotescas* to an end). But in the 22-volume *Memorias de un hombre de acción* (1913–34), which represents fully one-third of Baroja's total novelistic output, history plays a more prominent role as the writer reconstructs the life and exploits of a notorious spy employed by the Liberal government to penetrate Carlist lines and help bring about the defeat of the insurgents during the civil war of 1833–39. In the late 1920s and early 1930s, Baroja, who held pessimistic views about Spain's ability to solve increasingly violent confrontations between the ideologies of left and right, turned to contemporary events in an attempt to leave a novelistic record of those momentous years. In this, he shared the change of mood of the rather younger writers of the Spanish avant-garde, who also moved from playful esoteric creations to socially committed literature in or around 1930. In the trilogy *La selva oscura* (1931–32), which deals with the coming of the Second Republic, Baroja employs a new documentary realism based largely on newspaper reports, from which he borrows generously; but, just as his historical novels had often sought to give a new slant to the events described in the history books, so his contemporary novels recycle press material in order to raise doubts about the accuracy or impartiality of the reports. Indeed, Baroja's deep-seated agnosticism extended to all branches of human knowledge, historical, scientific, philosophical, religious, or artistic, and he summed up his personal credo with the phrase *ignoramus, ignorabimus* (we know nothing and we shall always know nothing). This did not, however, prevent him from exploring many different aspects of modern existence, often with the psychological and ethical dimensions of human conduct very much in mind.

Baroja's range of interests is unparalleled in modern Spanish literature, but that very diversity has proved a disincentive for any scholar contemplating a study of his work. Many of his novels remain unstudied, but one that has repeatedly attracted attention is his most deeply philosophical one, *El árbol de la ciencia* (1911), the story of a medical doctor (as was Baroja himself) who loses his faith in medicine and tries to construct a more solid scientific explanation of life and mankind's role in it. The hero eschews the pragmatism of his uncle and interlocutor (also a medical doctor) in favour of Kant's defence of science in the *Critique of Pure Reason* and Schopenhauer's gloomy modification of Kant in *The World as Will and Representation*. The poignant story of Dr Andrés Hurtado, whose lofty ideals are overwhelmed by personal tragedy, becomes in effect an exploration of the philosophies of Kant and Schopenhauer and their relevance to the human situation. Baroja, as was his wont, does not commit himself, so the reader is left in a quandary, but the fictional exploration of the consequences of accepting the views of these two philosophers is carried through with passion and considerable fidelity. Abstract yet intensely human, this is one of Baroja's key works and it sums up supremely well the disorientation of a new generation which had

to search for new guiding principles at a time when the old positivistic paradigm that had governed nineteenth-century thought had irretrievably broken
down. It is when we place *El árbol de la ciencia alongside Blasco Ibáñez's
La voluntad de vivir (1907) that we appreciate the gulf that separates two
writers who on the face of it had much in common, most notably a belief
in the importance of the subconscious in artistic creativity and the idea that
sedimentary impressions that have lain dormant for many years play a crucial
role in the creative process. Whereas Blasco is content to stress that man is
simply driven by sexual urges, Baroja probes much deeper and presents man
not just as biological entity but as a being driven by a passion to establish
truths about his species, his world, his conduct, and his future.

Miguel de Unamuno also sought to explore the transrational human
world, but his contribution to the novel was altogether different. He started
conventionally with a historical novel about the siege of Bilbao during the
third Carlist War of 1873–74, *Paz en la Guerra (1897),[1] but five years later
produced the first of several utterly unconventional works, *Amor y pedagogía (1902), a satire of nineteenth-century cientifismo, or pseudo-science,
conveyed through the flawed educational theories of the central character and
of the 'scientific' treatise on origami that Unamuno appends to the narrative
proper.[2] Equally mischievous but far more suggestive and influential was
his next novel, *Niebla (1914; composed 1907). Although its metafictional
interest has some precursors, not least Part II of Don Quijote which it clearly
echoes, *Niebla raises issues about an author's relationship to his work which
have radical implications, perhaps the most startling of which is the paradoxical idea, which must ultimately be true, that an author is dependent on
his characters for his continued existence rather than the other way round.
The basic storyline of *Niebla could not be more banal, involving as it does
the betrayal and public humiliation of the main character, Augusto Pérez, by
his bride-to-be, who elopes with a rival, and his subsequent suicide. Yet the
treatment that Unamuno accords this unpromising material is so unexpected
that the novel has exerted an enduring influence on Spanish narrative, both
on the vanguard novel of the 1920s and on much later experimental fiction.
The reasons for this are not hard to find. In a mock-serious manner Unamuno
raises fascinating issues about the art of writing, especially in relation to the
question of autonomy: of the text, of the author, and of the reader. Underlying
Unamuno's playful discourse is his idea of language as self-sustaining, that
is to say as a form of utterance that acquires its own separate existence independently of the speaker (Olson 1984: 91–92). The plot of *Niebla parallels

---

[1]   An earlier novel, Nuevo mundo, remained hidden away and unpublished during his lifetime.
[2]   A year earlier Baroja had satirized pseudo-scientific systems of thought in his comic
novel Aventuras, inventos y mixtificaciones de Silvestre Paradox.

the work's own genesis. As the artist struggles to draw forth the raw material from his subconscious and give it artistic shape through the organizing power of language, so his character has to learn to make sense of the world around him, and to fathom his relationship to others. This he does not just through the accretion of experiences, but through the linguistic manipulation of those experiences. Via monologues and dialogues the character turns life into words, just as the author is turning his subconscious intuitions into language. For, if the character's verbal musings displace his experiences, the novelist's linguistic execution seals his inspiration and makes it transmissible. The story of Augusto Pérez the man in effect becomes the story of *Niebla* the book, and indeed Unamuno contrives his story in such a way that the questions raised by Augusto Pérez about life are just as applicable to the writing of novels. One of these revolves around the debate between contingency and determinism, accident and design. Are our lives a succession of pure chance events or are we part of a predetermined plan? Can we control what happens to us or are we mere cogs in a giant machine with no power over our destiny? Does a novelist exert full authority over his material or is he driven by the demands of plot and character? Is he the creator of his work or does his work create him? And finally – fully anticipating the so-called reception theory of half-a-century later – how does the individual human being's attitude towards existence or a reader's attitude towards a text alter the world or the text? All these questions and more form the network of philosophical and literary associations of this ingenious and seminal text, the climax to which – a dramatic confrontation between author and character – has become a landmark of modern Spanish fiction.

Among Unamuno's dozen novels and novelettes three others in particular deserve mention. *Abel Sánchez* (1917), based on the ancient story of two close friends who fall in love with the same woman, is in effect a psychological study of envy, not in an abstract or purely discursive sense, but rather from the anguished point of view of an otherwise good and upright character who wants to know why he is driven by a consuming jealousy that poisons his life. While at the level of plot the story has its own internal logic, it is also clear that the two friends are to be seen as different facets of a single personality and that Unamuno is exploring the formidable question of whether we can ever get to know our internal self (Round 1974: 33–47), whether indeed such a self exists, and whether our self is anything more than our perception of others' views of us, an idea already raised in *Niebla*. *Abel Sánchez* is Unamuno's most profound and disturbing work of fiction and one which demonstrates that the novel was for him not a medium for passing away the hours of idleness but a instrument of self-knowledge and a way of shaking the reader from the complacency of conventional thinking.

Some of this is still evident in *La tía Tula* (1920), inspired by the Christian paradox of the Virgin Mother. Tula, who has something of the modern feminist in her and has proved to be Unamuno's most controversial character, eliciting the most diverse reactions even among scholarly critics, rejects the male of the human species as too brutal and materialistic. Driven by blind biological instinct, sex for man is mere pleasure, whereas for Tula reproduction is a sacred duty. Unwilling to marry any of her suitors, including her widowed brother-in-law, she deems it her moral obligation to appropriate the latter's children by his two marriages, act as their mother, and create a united family based on the spiritual values of a religious order. Although Unamuno does not appear to approve entirely of his character's demotion of men to the level of beasts, the novel can be read as a response to the neo-Darwinism of the late nineteenth century in which the human species was seen in terms of adaptation to its environment, and spiritual ideas were interpreted as a mirage of a purely biological self-interest. Tula's motherly interest is obviously very much more than the manifestation of the selfish gene, since she is not the biological mother of her five children. Her self-perpetuation is thus wholly spiritual, and her egotism of a quite different order. The mother figure was for Unamuno the repository of enduring values of caring and compassion handed down from one generation to the next, and in Tula he has created a character who refuses to yield to society's pressure to conform and opts instead to pursue her own secular ideal of female values. Indeed, Unamuno goes so far as to suggest that Tula's female vision of Christianity is superior to the official version based on male values and ministry. It is in this respect as radical a work as Unamuno ever wrote.

San Manuel Bueno, mártir (1931), like *Niebla*, has attracted a good deal of critical attention, but for all the wrong reasons. Disregarding Unamuno's injunction that he should not be confused with his characters, many have seen the story of the sceptical priest as a *roman à clef* in which Father Manuel Bueno is the key to Unamuno's own tortured soul. This approach does a disservice to Unamuno on two counts. First, it imputes hypocrisy to Unamuno, as far as his own religious beliefs are concerned; and second, it disregards the poetics of composition, that is to say the artistic resources of a consummate creator of fictions. On the first count, Unamuno was always very clear that religious belief did not come through logical necessity but through an affective need, and that, to be true to himself, he had perforce to be both a believer and an unbeliever. This may be a paradox, but it is certainly not a mystery. On the second count, what is crucial to an appreciation of *San Manuel Bueno, mártir* is not the veiled incredulousness of the saintly country priest but the way in which Unamuno has refracted the story through a variety of minds in order to distance the eponymous character from the reader through a deliberate technique of regression. As readers we are thus placed in the position of having to choose what to believe. Do we share the Bishop's vision of Don Manuel as a model Christian worthy of canonization? Do we accept Lázaro's account of Don Manuel as a complete religious sceptic led only by his altruistic concern for the underprivileged? Do we, on the contrary, identify with the uncomplicated adherence of the villagers for whom the parish priest is protector, consoler, and unfailing support in life and death? Or do we let ourselves be persuaded (and confused) by the contradictory account of the perplexed author of the memoir, a modern Mary Magdalene enraptured by the towering presence of a latter-day Jesus Christ? The whole story is enveloped in a poetic and symbolic language that invites decoding (Butt 1981: 67–74), but the novel remains suggestive rather than conclusive, emphasizing Unamuno's contention that language can never adequately express our innermost being.

Ramón del Valle-Inclán deserves to be remembered as Spain's most revolutionary playwright of the twentieth century, but his contribution to the novel was almost as powerful and original. The decadent Romanticism and preciousness of the four *Sonatas* (1902–05), which relate the erotic adventures of the sensual Marqués de Bradomín, just manage to avoid falling into a totally inconsequential aestheticism by the self-mockery, irony, even sarcasm that Valle confers upon his narrator. The Marqués is a poseur and his memoirs a fraud: we laugh at, rather than identify with, the narrating character, but he seems aware of his own pretence. The three *Comedias bárbaras* – *Águila de blasón* (1907), *Romance de lobos* (1908), and *Cara de plata* (1922) – which revolve around a family of Galician aristocrats, are an interesting hybrid of novel and theatre, or a dramatized novel (a format already employed by Galdós and Baroja). More generically novelistic is the Carlist War trilogy, *Los cruzados de la causa* (1908), *El resplandor de la hoguera* (1909), and *Gerifaltes de antaño* (1909). Consisting mostly of dialogue, these seeming historical novels do not share the historicizing outlook of Galdós's *Episodios* nor the radical reappraisal of Baroja's *Memorias de un hombre de acción*. History is for the most part curiously absent, save as background, entirely as if Valle had little regard for what actually happened. On the other hand, we find brilliantly original descriptive touches, such as the scene in which the violent death of a fleeing deserter is captured by a dog licking the pool of blood left on the street. The opening volume, *Los cruzados de la causa*, focuses on the Galician nobility, which was of no historical significance in the Carlist War of 1873–76, and is rather anachronistic in its evocation of a world long left behind. *El resplandor de la hoguera* moves the action to Navarre, one of the main theatres of the war, and we get a description of a military ambush in the mountains, typical of the tactics employed by the Carlist guerrilla bands. Through the conversations of characters we learn something of the rivalries among Carlist guerrilla leaders and of the ignoble political machinations of the Liberals, but the focus now is rather more on the peasantry and rather less on the aristocracy or the military. *Gerifaltes de antaño*, which centres on the ruthless savagery of the notorious Carlist priest Manuel Santa Cruz, is rather better documented and more genuinely historical than the earlier two novels, but the sentimental ending, in which the murderous Santa Cruz, deliberately allowed to escape by a Machiavellian Spanish government, is depicted as shedding tears of relief and remorse, is an illusory platitude that not only comes disconcertingly close to an apology for a brutal killer but also demonstrates Valle's mythical approach to Carlist history. These novels, then, appear to celebrate, rather than explain, a rural world that is made to seem more remote and stylized than was historically the case.

Nothing that Valle had written earlier, except his highly innovative plays of the absurd or *esperpentos*, presaged the astonishing brilliance of his return to novel writing in 1926 with *Tirano Banderas,* undoubtedly one of the most remarkable examples of narrative prose to come out of twentieth-century Spain. Had Valle been writing in any other Western European tongue this masterpiece would have enjoyed the cult status of a *Ulysses* or an *À la recherche du temps perdu*. The first thing that strikes any reader of *Tirano Banderas* is its language. Both lexically and syntactically the novel is unlike anything else published in the Spanish-speaking world at the time, even allowing for the fact that the 1920s were the years of avant-garde experiment in which the search for new forms of expression was a key element. Valle-Inclán has succeeded in devising for this novel, set in the imaginary Central American country of Santa Fe de Tierra Firme, an original idiolect which, while drawing broadly on Spanish-American usage, is sufficiently distinct to remain unique and to evoke its own ambience, an ambience that serves in turn to heighten the almost surreal events recounted, as the brutal dictatorship of Santos Banderas comes to its bloody end. *Tirano Banderas* not only set the trend for Latin American dictatorship novels (Asturias, García Márquez, Roa Bastos, Vargas Llosa) but did so in a way that established new standards for the novel as an artistic genre. The debate between the novel as representation and the novel as artificial or self-reflective construct is superseded by a concept which is much closer to the plastic arts: the novel as a style, a form of expression, a way of perceiving. The distinction between what is written and what it is written about becomes less important than the overall picture in which image and execution are one. The influence of painting is detectable not just in Valle's reference to El Greco's technique of filling out every square centimetre of canvas, but also in the explicit and implicit references within the text itself to Cubism (Dougherty 1999: 185–93). The novel has a very deliberate symmetrical structure built around prime numbers, with 29 episodes arranged in clusters of 3, each around a central nexus of 7 scenes, the whole preceded by a prologue and followed by an epilogue. The undoubted interest in the occult science of numerology, as well as theosophy and astrology, does not detract from the predominantly spatial approach to the material. The time factor is reduced to less than 48 hours, while the spatial dimension is emphasized by the theatrical techniques employed. The characters appear as puppets on a stage, manipulated not just by an invisible puppeteer but also, at the level of the fiction, by the cruel and all-seeing Santos Banderas whose words strike fear in those around him.[3]

The canvas of Santa Fe de Tierra Firme is filled with a vast array of figures, their words, and their actions. Valle depicts the sadism, manipulative methods, and intellectual preoccupations of the despot General; the mystical ideals and candour of the social reformer Don Roque Cepeda; the self-serving desertion of the brash and drunken Colonel Domiciano de la Gándara; the opportunistic self-appointment as leader of the insurgents by the rancher Filomeno Cuevas; the bombastic hypocrisy of the international diplomatic community; the hollow rhetoric of the politicians; the stinginess and dishonesty of the Spanish businessmen intent on making their fortunes at the expense of the local population; the debased adulation of the hangers-on who surround the dictator; and the misery, fatalism, and irrational violence of the Amerindians, trampled upon by anyone and everyone. As a portrait of a demented humanity bent on collective self-destruction it resembles a picture by Hieronymous Bosch rather than one by El Greco. The painterly approach is supplemented not only by repeated references to acting, as though the characters' sole function were to play out their assigned roles – the word 'mask' appears repeatedly – but also by references to a stage set, as if Santa Fe de Tierra Firme were a theatre for the delectation of some perverse spectator.[4] The characters are further dehumanized by Valle's technique of referring to them as animals: dog, frog, toad, snake, rat, owl, buzzard, and various other appellations are used in what amounts to a merciless debasement of their status as human beings. While we cannot doubt that Valle wanted to show the widespread degradation occasioned by political tyranny, the microcosm that is Santa Fe and Banderas's own fascination with the night sky and with the possibility of other distant worlds looking down uncomprehendingly at our own suggest that Valle had more than Latin American revolutions in mind. Savage in its ironic devaluation of human life right up to its closing lines, and with no hint of redemption to come after the downfall of the tyrant, *Tirano Banderas is a book about man's inhumanity to man that seems to call for the arraignment of an entire crazed humanity.

Valle-Inclán's final contribution to the novel is a highly original version of a short but critical span of nineteenth-century Spanish history (the final days of the regime of Isabel II and the coming of the Revolution of 1868): the trilogy El ruedo ibérico, consisting of La corte de los milagros (1927), Viva

---

[3]   The time factor, again based on the 'magic' number 3, extends from the evening of day one to the morning of day three. Given that Banderas is explicitly associated with Satan and that we move from life to death, a conscious inversion of Christ's death and resurrection seems a distinct possibility.

[4]   The influence of the cinema cannot be ruled out. Other novelists of the 1920s (Benjamín Jarnés, for instance) adapted cinematic techniques in their compositions.

mi dueño (1928), and the unfinished and posthumously published *Baza de espadas* (1958). The influence of the *esperpentos* is evident here in the way historical figures (and fictitious ones too) are ridiculed and reduced almost to the level of marionettes, yet the historical concern is much more palpably present than in the early Carlist War trilogy. If the earlier trilogy celebrated Carlism from an historically outdated perspective, this later one denigrates its political rival, Liberalism, by reducing it to ignominious farce. These novels are nevertheless 'exceptionally well documented' (Sinclair 1977: 120), and, despite the tendency to caricature and the adoption of a very reduced time-scale, there is a good deal of authentic history here, gleaned from contemporary accounts and historiographical sources but given added spice by Valle's mischievous pen. Indeed, what Valle does very effectively is to question the bombastic and portentous approach of much nineteenth-century historiography and to suggest that the overwhelming problem of modern Spain was not that it was torn apart by ideological confrontation but that it was led by charlatans and nincompoops whose sense of self-importance far outweighed their sense of purpose. Hypocrisy, corruption, and venality within the political establishment are the real targets of his merciless mockery and sardonic belittlement. Few figures escape unscathed from his disparagement, but the novels themselves are a testament to his extraordinary skill in subjecting the familiar to wholly unfamiliar handling and processing. This alternative history of modern Spain is both unique and a perfect example of Valle's lateral thinking as an artist. Not known for the originality of his plots, and often accused of borrowing stories and episodes, his contribution to the novel is nonetheless one of the most original of the first half of the twentieth century, matched only by the ingenious but much more elusive fictional creations of the outlandishly brilliant avant-garde writer Ramón Gómez de la Serna.

José Martínez Ruiz, better known as Azorín, was the author of some sixteen novels among a varied literary output, but several of these are barely recognizable as such, since they have neither action nor plot, being rather a series of reflections on a chosen theme. Indeed, the author has been more often admired for the quality of his limpid and elegant prose than for his novelesque invention. His novels are full of descriptive passages inspired by painting. One critic felt able to speak of the 'painterly nature of his prose', adding that 'Azorín considered much of what he thought and wrote in terms of the visual arts' (Jurkevich 1999: 18). Azorín became in real life the personage he had created in fiction. In *El libro de Levante* (1929) he wrote that the function of a creative writer was 'to create a character and make desperate efforts to be like him'. Art starts by imitating reality, and reality ends up by imitating art. Azorín's art is based on the distillation of sensations provoked by everyday objects. In attempting to capture the sensations of reality impacting upon our human sensibilities through the medium of art, Azorín is implicitly, sometimes even explicitly, claiming the superiority of art, of fiction, over history: 'legend triumphs over history', he wrote in *Doña Inés* (1925), and 'encompassing reality is the creation of the artist', in *Memorias inmemoriales* (1946). To capture the sense of reality and the effect it has on us one needs to be more than a historian, one needs to have the intuition of the artist. Azorín rejects history because the historian compartmentalizes time, ringfencing a chunk of it, a period. But time for Azorín is not divisible into periods. Time, like space, is everywhere: it is past, present, and future all at the same time. The present influences the past as much as the past influences the present. Thus, the historian's claim to separate out the past is naïve, for his judgement of the past is governed by his own experience in the present. And this applies to literature as well, which is constantly reinterpreted in the light of the reader's present. One of the constant themes of Azorín's work is the rewriting of the classics. Like the slightly younger Ramón Pérez de Ayala, Azorín rewrote the Don Juan legend begun by the seventeenth-century dramatist Tirso de Molina, while his *Doña Inés* (1925) is loosely derived from Zorrilla's play *Don Juan Tenorio* (1844), and his *Tomás Rueda* (1915) inspired by Cervantes's story 'El licenciado Vidriera', published in his *Novelas ejemplares* (1613).

Azorín's early novels, the Antonio Azorín trilogy, like those of Unamuno and Baroja, are a mixture of philosophy and psychology. The best known of these, *La voluntad* (1902), is a clear case of discussion-fiction, since the main interest is in the philosophical discussions between Antonio Azorín and his mentor, Yuste. The title refers to what Antonio lacks, willpower, and it is this which leads him to lose the woman he loves, who chooses to enter a convent, and to a lacklustre marriage to another woman who has willpower in abundance and eclipses the irresolute hero. *La voluntad* is an essay in fictional form on volition and its absence, *abulia*. *Antonio Azorín* (1903) is a lighter work, more descriptive and static. Written in the present tense throughout, it is in effect a long series of short vignettes – some in the form of letters – that focus predominantly on the external, physical world and occasionally reproduce fragmented dialogues in which a small number of characters express views on a variety of topics ranging from modern philosophers to feeding ducks. But the underlying theme is change, decay, and repetition; there is no plot, no causal connection, merely an observing mind whose senses and sensibilities constitute the text and whose perambulations give it what little movement it has. *Las confesiones de un pequeño filósofo* (1904) continues in the same vein, this time in the form of a would-be writer who sets out to fulfil his artistic calling by considering his own childhood and reactions, at once aesthetic and anguished, to the world around him. The significance of this early trilogy lies above all in the departure from the subject matter and plot lines typical of realist and naturalist works.

Azorín's novels of the avant-garde decade, *Don Juan* (1922), *Doña Inés* (1925), *Félix Vargas* (1928, later retitled *El caballero inactual*), and *Super-*

realismo (1929, later retitled *El libro de Levante*) will be of interest to those attracted by novelistic theory, for in these experimental works Azorín seems determined to strip the novel of its conventional trappings of plot, storyline, and character development. But ordinary readers looking for an element of dramatic engagement are likely to be disappointed. These novels are, in a very real sense, reflections on the phenomenon of writing, which often go hand in hand with an exploration of the nature of time, a subject that obsessed Azorín throughout his career.

The most satisfactory (and most conventional) of them is *Doña Inés*, arguably Azorín's best, in which the Gidian device of *mise en abyme* (literary recursion or self-reproduction) is used with simplicity but to great effect. Set in 1840, the novel is much more than its anecdote: the story of a daring kiss and its repercussions. Doña Inés hears the fifteenth-century story of Doña Beatriz from her writer-uncle Don Pablo and creates a parallel between Doña Beatriz's tragic love for the young troubadour Guillén de Treceño and her own infatuation with a young poet, Diego Lodares. The question is not so much whether history repeats itself as whether we ourselves through our own perceptions and sensations bring about that repetition. The real parallel, if there is one, is that Doña Beatriz's story is the creation of a writer called Don Pablo and Doña Inés is the creation of another writer called Azorín. And these two writers have at least one important thing in common: their unusual sensitivity to the problem of time. Don Pablo's memory is so attuned to sensations that a sound can make him relive an experience of many years before. He is deeply and painfully conscious of the passing of time, but what is more, he also has the capacity to project the present into the future and to see its consequences. Hoffmann's malady, an acute perception that happiness cannot last, destroys his capacity to enjoy the present. Conscious of the limits of human understanding, he is trapped by an awareness of a phenomenon that defies comprehension. The theme of time is revealed, too, through the technique of reiteration in the writing itself. Images, phrases, even entire sentences reappear in different contexts. This technique is not necessarily Azorín's attempt to reproduce novelistically Nietzsche's concept of the eternal return, as has often been alleged. Rather is it a product of the aesthetic consideration that time is repetition, that it has all been said before, that it will all be said again. As human beings we are trapped in time; we can experience it intuitively but we cannot comprehend it; it is for the artist in us to try to overcome our limited ability to convey our intuitive and non-definable experience. That seems to be Azorín's position. Past and present are a unity rather than a chronology, so that the literature of today is but a reinterpretation, or reperception of the literature of yesterday. Azorín's Doña Inés is José Zorrilla's in another circumstance, a circumstance which can be seen as future if we place ourselves in Zorrilla's perspective, but is present if we think of the work which the novelist Azorín is writing and is also past because in his work Azorín makes use of legend in order to trap his characters in a circle of time. The difficulty is not simply the concept of time, but how to convey it artistically. The authentic vocation of the novelist is to crystallize the paradox of a highly temporal creature in a universe that may be timeless. The existence of time lies purely in our perception, simply because we change and do not last. But time itself is timeless, and just occasionally perhaps we catch a glimpse of that timelessness when we sense that we have been here before. Art for Azorín, as for Unamuno, became an obsession with transcending the human boundaries of time.

The closing years of the nineteenth century and early years of the twentieth were characterized by uncertainty brought about by the waning influence of nineteenth-century forms of thought, whether scientific, artistic, social, or moral. The new or modernist fiction that emerged throughout Europe was part of a broad movement of reaction and renewal that elicited highly individual responses as writers sought to redefine the boundaries of their work. In Spain, Baroja greatly broadened the horizons of traditional narrative by exploring the role of the subjective mind in interpretations of the world and depicting a humanity caught in the snare of self-deception. Unamuno, obsessed with the mystery of personality, of what it is and how we might know it, conceived the novel as a tool of self-cognition and thereby raised intriguing questions about the role of the writer, the role of the reader, and the function of language in creating worlds that reflect the human mind. Valle-Inclán developed an approach to fiction based on ironic distortion which highlights the radical irrationality of the human condition. And Azorín condensed the novel to a stylized world of sense impressions and meditations on the transience of the human presence in a modern recasting of the aphorism *ars longa, vita brevis*. In their different ways, these four novelists produced original work of distinction which was to exert an influence for many years to come and can be seen in the work of such later novelists as Camilo José Cela, Luis Martín-Santos and Eduardo Mendoza.

Further reading

General: Butt (1978), Cerezo (1992), Eoff (1961), Fernández Cifuentes (1982), Ferreras (1988), García de Nora (1963–70), Gullón (1969), Harrison & Hoyle (2000), Johnson (1993 and 2003), López-Morillas (1972), Lough (2000), Ramsden (1974), Santiáñez-Tío (2002), Shaw (1975). **Baroja:** Alberich (1966), Bretz (1979), Ciplijauskaité (1972), Collins (1986). Flint & Flint (1983), Lecuona (1993), Longhurst (1974 and 1977), Murphy (2004), Ramsden (1982), Rivas (1998), Rivera (1972). **Unamuno:** Basdekis (1974), Batchelor (1972), Butt (1981), Criado (1986), Díez Hochleitner (1976), Gullón (1964), Jurkevich (1991), La Rubia (1999), Nicholas (1987), Olson

(1984 and 2002), Øveraas (1993), Ribbans (1971), Round (1974), Sinclair (2001), Turner (1974), Vauthier (2004), Wyers (1976). **Valle-Inclán:** Belic (1968), De Juan (2000), Díaz Migoyo (1985), Dougherty (1999), Salgués (1973), Schiavo (1980), Sinclair (1977), Smith (1971), Speratti (1957 and 1974), Tucker (1980). **Azorín:** Fox (1992), Glenn (1973 and 1981), Jurkevich (1999), Krause (1955), Livingstone (1970), Lott (1981), Martínez Cachero (1960), Pérez López (1974), Risco (1980), Villanueva (1983).

3

Tales from the Avant-garde

RAMÓN BUCKLEY

The Silver Age

Spain has traditionally boasted a Golden Age of the Arts, a *Siglo de Oro,* following hard upon the high point of Spanish empire in the sixteenth and seventeenth centuries. Recent critics have suggested that it would be equally appropriate to talk about an *Edad de Plata*, a Silver Age, extending from the final collapse of that Empire in 1898 to the outbreak of the Spanish Civil War in 1936.[1] During these three decades, both artists and men of letters sought to portray the dramatic image of a Spain torn between the conservative and traditional values it had once fostered and the advent of modernity in its myriad forms. There is a general consensus that this Silver Age reached its climax with the so-called 'Generation of 1927': Salvador Dalí, Luis Buñuel, and Federico García Lorca would then simply be the visible tip of an iceberg that includes the Nobel Prize winner Vicente Aleixandre, the great advocate of 'pure poetry' Jorge Guillén, the lyric poet Pedro Salinas, the surrealist Rafael Alberti, and neo-Romantic poets such as Luis Cernuda.

There has been a tendency amongst literary scholars to regard this Generation of 1927 primarily as an outstanding group of artists, poets, and playwrights, and to relegate their novels and short stories to relative obscurity. One of the reasons for this lack of attention to narrative may well have been the way in which the writers experimented with literary genres and the consequent difficulties encountered by critics when they attempt to comprehend (and classify) the actual nature of some of the literary artifacts produced at this time. The 'tales of the avant-garde' analyzed in this chapter clearly overflow the generic boundaries of poetry and prose, novel and short story, drama and cinematic image, and create what are in effect new modes of expression. And yet, in spite of the puzzling nature of these 'tales' (or, perhaps, precisely

---

[1]   José-Carlos Mainer was the first to suggest the concept of an 'Edad de Plata' directly linking the first two so-called 'generations' in modern Spanish literature: those of 1898 and 1927.

because of it) there is no doubt in my mind that a careful search amongst them would discover a trove of literary gems, comparable to the best works of the renowned poets and artists of the period. My search began in 1973 when I published, together with John Crispin, the anthology *Los vanguardistas españoles*, with the intention of informing the general reader that there was life beyond Lorca and the other great poets of the Generation of 1927. Much, of course, has been written on the subject since then, and this is, I believe, a good opportunity to reappraise the views we expressed in print thirty-five years ago.

The merit of these fictions is that they reflect – more than any other kind of writing – the full impact of the European avant-garde movements of the early years of the century upon the Spanish literary scene of the 1920s and early '30s: Cubism and Surrealism, Dada and Ultraism, Futurism and Pure Poetry, Vitalism and Perspectivism, Dehumanization and Social Revisionism, all find expression in the tales which we are about to discuss.

It is an easy task to select the best authors and their most successful stories, since most poets and playrights tried their hand, at one point or another in their career, at writing a 'tale from the vanguard'. The best known of them, Ramón Gómez de la Serna, can, to a certain extent, be considered the father of this literary genre and, coming as he did from an older generation, he it was who initiated a whole group of young Spanish writers into the art of experimental writing. Benjamín Jarnés is often considered the only 'true novelist' of the Generation of 1927 and he was responsible for producing the fullest and most complex examples of this new genre of the avant-garde tale. Early in his career, Francisco Ayala wrote a handful of such narratives: *Cazador en el alba* (1929) is clearly one of the masterpieces of its kind. In tandem with the writers already mentioned, he captured a rare moment of optimism when the world seemed to be spinning away from the disasters of the Great War and into an era where modernity and modern living would transform humanity forever. These hopes, of course, would soon be dashed – by the global repercussions of the Wall Street crash of 1929, by the Civil War in Spain, and by World War II – but the futuristic visions of modern living we find in these tales remain surprisingly vivid and attractive.

The most surprising thing about these tales from the avant-garde is that they emerged in one of the most underdeveloped countries in Western Europe. Having lost the last remnants of its colonial Empire, the Spain of the early twentieth century was mired in a deep economic crisis (only a few cities in the North had joined the industrial revolution) and in social chaos (anarchist organizations held sway both in the industrial North and in the rural South and frequently paralyzed the whole country through strikes). King Alfonso XIII, however, managed to steer the country away from involvement in World War I and this granted it a brief respite from its woes: those years boosted Spanish industry (which, overtly or covertly, supplied both sides in the European conflict) and jump-started the nation in its first attempt towards modernization: modern highways were built; the telephone was introduced alongside the telegraph and radio transmitters; dams were constructed: and the first skyscrapers were built in Madrid. Oddly enough, the man whom the king commissioned to modernize Spain, General Miguel Primo de Rivera, took over as dictator after Alfonso ceded power in 1923.

It is within this concept of 'modernity' that one must understand the publication in Spain of one of the most influential European reviews of the time, whose very name, *Revista de Occidente*, underlines its ambition of becoming the cutting-edge of modernity in the Western World, the mouthpiece of the most enlightened European intellectuals of the time. Primo de Rivera was well aware that, in order to build a 'modern' Spain, he needed new ideas as much as bricks or electric power and so he came to an understanding with the leading intellectual of the day, José Ortega y Gasset, that would allow the latter's *Revista de Occidente* to continue, provided that no direct criticism of his government was published in its pages. Like any dictator, Primo de Rivera used censorship to control all published material but he nevertheless allowed 'speculative' or 'intellectual' discussion to take place in such places as Ortega's *Revista*, on the understanding that the regime itself would not be called into question. This uneasy balance of power between the dictator and his intellectual opponents lasted until his fall from power in 1929. In that very brief period of time – the 1920s – Spain became a center of artistic and literary discussion, with its two capitals, Madrid and Barcelona, focal points of European intellectual debate. The desolate and backward country had suddenly sprung to life with the first stirrings in its soil of 'modernity'. It is against the background of these apparent contradictions and conundrums that we should approach these surprising 'tales' from the avant-garde. They would be unthinkable without the influence of Ortega and his *Revista de Occidente*, not only because many of them first appeared in that review but because the review itself set the agenda for everything that was about to happen: the first surrealist paintings of Dalí, the movies of Buñuel, or the dazzling poetry of Lorca.

In 1925 Ortega y Gasset published his essay *La deshumanización del arte*. This was in effect the first description of artistic modernity to reach a wide readership in Spain. He emphasized the 'intrascendence' of modern art and its 'playful' nature: 'It has often been said that art has saved mankind because of its power to express lofty ideas [...] I am closer to thinking that art has saved mankind from boredom, and that the more it returns to its playful origins the more it will engage our wit and sense of humour and the closer it will come to fulfilling its role as the greatest game man ever invented' (1925: 87). 'Homo ludens' or 'man as player' and 'man at play' (rather than 'at work', 'at thought', or 'at prayer') seemed to be the magic metaphor that Ortega would use to describe this playful sense of existence, this 'return of mankind to innocence', which had so recently been overshadowed by the cataclysm of the Great War.

Postmodern readings of these 'tales of the avant-garde' tend to emphasize their playful nature as well as to explore their aesthetic origins. Gustavo Pérez Firmat calls them 'idle fictions', so 'idle', indeed, that they can hardly stand on their own two feet. The stories they tell are practically 'untellable', since they are based on non-events, performed by non-characters, and have no beginning and/or no conclusive ending. 'What we witness in these tales is,' he asserts, 'the gradual but complete volatalization of the architecture of the novel or the short story, the vaporization of characters and plot which, before our very eyes, dissolve into thin air' (1982: 65). This process he dubs 'the pneumatic effect' of stories 'inflated with or operated by air' (66), an effect which dissolves the very structure of the narrative and any direction or 'meaning' the tale might possess. He is quick to point out that this apparent 'dissolution of form and meaning' is a challenge to the reader. Readers have to use their imaginations to fill in what is missing from the tale itself; they have to complete a story which the author has deliberately left incomplete, or in a 'nebulous state'. 'The nebula is nothing other than a monolith, pulverized, atomized, to the point that it levitates' (46–54). Such 'levitation' is both beautiful and arbitrary, and it requires an effort on the part of the reader which brings us back to the point Ortega originally made about the playfulness of modern art: the author, that is, is openly asking the reader to participate in a game.

Just as the story, in Pérez's words, 'atomizes, vaporizes, and levitates before our very eyes' (58), elements of the modern world appear in all their seductive brilliance: there may be a gag from the latest Buster Keaton movie, a jazz player puffing away on his sax, a black boxer in the ring before an excited crowd, a beautiful blonde taking the elevator to the heights of a New York skyscraper, a Michelin Man suddenly appearing on a tyre advertisement by the roadside, or an advertisement displaying the wonders of commercial aviation (by plane or zeppelin) that is busy shrinking the planet. Herein lies the *aporia* (or admission of self-doubt) that readers are invited to resolve. Are these tales of dissolution or of resolution? Do they spell the death of the novel or the birth of modernity? Does the birth of modernity signify the death of the novel? Or are they simply tales of utopia, visions of paradise soon to be dashed by the tragic turn of history? Ramón Gómez de la Serna conjured up both utopias and dystopias in his stories: utopias when he points to the brave new world ushered in by the great artistic movements of the avant-garde; dystopias when he describes the dehumanization of modern man.

Ramón Gómez de la Serna

When Ramón (as he is commonly known in Spain) was eighteen years old, his father, a high-ranking official in the Spanish Government, introduced him to Prime Minister José Canalejas. Since Ramón had, by that time, already published his first book, Canalejas asked him to become his private secretary, a post which would involve such tasks as letter and speech writing. To his father's amazement, Ramón turned down the Prime Minister's offer, saying that he most certainly wanted to become a writer, but he needed the freedom to write whatever he wished. He paid a very high price for this decision after his influential father's death, since he would run into economic difficulties that would plague him for the rest of his life. One of the most hard-working and prolific writers of modern times, he was simply unable to make a decent living, and his hand-to-mouth existence, both in Spain and Argentina (where he sought refuge during the Spanish Civil War), was the fruit of his determination to be nothing but a writer. Ramón is a unique figure in modern Spanish literature: an author who made writing a way of living and living a way of writing to the point that he became, as he himself declared, a 'one-generation' man. Ramón cannot be classified as part of a particular group, generation, style, or artistic movement. He belonged to no one but himself.

Ironically, however, the impact he had on other writers was greater than that of any other modern literary figure. He organized his famous *tertulias* (literary gatherings) at Madrid's Café Pombo, wrote for some of the most influential newspapers of the time (*El Sol* and others), broadcast live from his famous den in Madrid, known as *El Torreón*, and befriended anyone and everyone who could be described as an 'artist', whether they were poets, novelists, playwrights, intellectuals, painters, sculptors, architects, actors, or film-makers. The way in which he embraced such a catholic definition of art and artists marks him out as one of the key figures in the advent of modernity in Spain.

By 1910, Ramón had already made Paris his second home. He described his first glimpse of the Paris 'Exhibition of Independent Artists' as 'entering a new-found land, discovering a new America-of-the-Arts [...] gazing at another world' (1948: 66). From that moment on, he became a missionary for New Art, travelling the opposite route of the old religious Spanish missionaries from the great artistic centers of Europe – Paris, London, Berlin and Rome – to provincial Madrid to preach 'the good news'. Not even the Great War would stop him. In 1916, he returned to Paris and visited Pablo Picasso in his studio in the Rue Victor Hugo:

> Stout and square-shouldered, he looked like a garage handyman to me, surrounded by the strangest collection of the 'spare parts' that he was in the habit of picking up in the streets of Paris. There is no doubt this great

mechanic had given modern art a new speed, as if he were gazing at the
world from a fast car, discovering new perspectives.   (1948: 75)

Not only did Ramón write several books on Picasso and Cubism but some
of his own stories seem to be attempts at 'literary cubism'. For example,
the couple who live in *La casa triangular* (1925) are so obsessed by this
house, with its triangular rooms and triangular furniture, that they end up in
a triangular relationship, which ultimately spells the end of their own love
affair.

Before meeting Picasso, Ramón had already befriended the French
vanguard poet Apollinaire, who volunteered to fight in the Great War. It is
impossible not to see the origins of Ramón's *greguería* (which he defined as
'poetic metaphor plus humour') in Apollinaire's haiku-like snippets composed
at the battlefront for the French press. Ramón's *greguerías* were to become
his trademark style: 'A rainbow is Nature putting a colourful ribbon in her
hair after washing her face'; 'A string of pearls around a woman's neck is
sin's own rosary'; 'Old ladies always seem to be holding long conversations
with their fans'; or 'Crabs are forever young because they walk backwards'
(1945: 138).

As playful 'snap-shots' of reality, 'haiku-like prose poems', 'Nature's
utterances' or 'the fast mail of the modern world', the *greguerías* were both
the making and breaking of Ramón as a writer. As Salvador Dalí was to say
of him, Ramón 'knew when to start writing but he never knew when to stop'
(2003: 155). *Greguerías* reflects Ramón's wit as much as it does the superficial quality of his writing: his ability to capture images of the world as well
as his inability to reflect upon them in any meaningful way.

The Italian Futurist poet Marinetti was perhaps the artist Ramón admired
most. This was not only because of the latter's 'impassioned and warm character' (as he often described it) but because he was the 'most modern' of the
'modernists', a self-defined 'futurist':

> Speed is the new beauty which adds to the splendor of this world [...] a
> speeding automobile is far more beautiful than the Greek statue of the
> 'Victory of Samothrace' [...] From now on we will sing to the tune of
> roaring engines, the thump of pistons in a steam engine, the buzzing of the
> crowd, the whistling of train locomotives, the buzz of airplanes.
>
> (1975: 113)

Ramón paid several visits to Marinetti in Italy and their friendship continued
unabated even after Marinetti became an 'official artist' to Mussolini. Ramón
was one of the few avant-garde artists who refused to play politics; when civil
war broke out in Spain, he simply left the country.

It would, however, be a mistake to think that Ramón drew his inspiration only from the avant-garde styles he so enthusiastically sponsored. Cubism, Futurism and Surrealism barely scratch the surface of some of his best fiction. In novels such as *La viuda blanca y negra* the reader is confronted with a disquieting element that is both intensely personal and deeply conflictive, and that adds depth to a prose so often described as 'brilliant but superficial'.

To approach what Ramón called 'my dark side' we must turn to Sigmund Freud. Although his works were not published in Spanish until 1923, there is good reason to believe Ramón was acquainted with some of Freud's theories as early as 1917, when he published *La viuda blanca y negra*. It is a novel that could well be subtitled *The perversion of repression*. Social and religious repression and inhibited public conduct in a conservative country such as Spain were modes of behavior that obeyed Freud's principle that the greater the repression in public, the greater was the perversion that reigned in the private domain. The black attire the eponymous widow wears in public to display her widowhood only helps to attract suitors who see her as 'unattached'. More suggestively, the blackness of her clothes only emphasizes her lily-white skin once an eager lover has removed them. The Church itself becomes an aphrodisiac meeting-place for the lovers, who hear each other's 'confessions' and anoint each other's hands with holy water before raising them to their lips for a lingering kiss (1917: 15).

Leopoldo Alas, in his famous novel *La Regenta* (1884), had already explored the overt spirituality and covert eroticism of a repressed priest. Ramón, in *La viuda blanca y negra*, takes us beyond determinism into an exploration of sexual practices as conceived by a decadent imagination prepared to cross the dividing line into 'perversion'. Widowhood itself becomes fetishistic as Rodrigo discovers he is enamoured not of a woman but rather of a black dress. His obsession with the 'black widow' extends beyond her dress to thighs and breasts that become so desirable that they are edible: 'Her thighs were as soft and rich as on a well-plucked and skinned hen from Bayonne of the kind one sees displayed in the market: one cannot help admire the rich texture of the soft but firm meat on the bird's thighs', and her breasts become 'so desirable that they tremble like jelly or the flesh of a quince' (1917: 87). Such cannibalistic tendencies point to a gradual dehumanization of the female body: from 'desirable woman' to a 'tasty bit of flesh'. But Rodrigo fails to pass the ultimate test of perversion, refusing to inflict the corporal punishment the widow demands of him: 'My husband kindled my blood by whipping me [...] cruelty is the ultimate expression of love, you can only hate with so much passion someone you absolutely adore' (1917: 186).

As Spanish tradition would have it, so long as a widow is 'in mourning, she belongs to no one but herself' (1917: 58). The black dress of widowhood protects her from her husband (who, as it turns out at the end, is still alive) as well as from lovers and suitors. Ramón provided an ultimate feminist twist to his story of erotic perversion. The widow finally emerges victorious from the multiple power-games she plays with the men who desire her.

Written in the early years of the century, many such avant-garde narratives today read as postmodern texts. Freud's theories seem to have struck a deep chord in Gómez de la Serna's own troubled personality, or what he called his 'dark side'. Alongside the exuberant, friendly, charming personality of the literary figure everyone knew lived another Ramón who displayed an 'emotional numbness' that brought him close to being a psychopath. Discussing *La viuda blanca y negra*, Fidel López-Criado concludes: 'It seems safe to say that not only Rodrigo but the narrator himself could be described as a fetishist with misogynist tendencies' (1998: 59). It is only when the author introduces himself into the story he is telling that he produces his most original and profound writing.

Gómez de la Serna based his next novel, *El chalet de las rosas* (1923a), on the life of the French serial lady-killer Henri Landru, whose crimes, revealed at his trial (1921–23), scandalized European public opinion. Ramón chose a new name for his hero, Roberto Gascón, set the story in Madrid, and, more significantly, focused on the relationship between Gascón and his lovers, rather than on the moment he killed them. It could be argued, therefore, that when he conceived the protagonist the author had the myth of Don Juan in mind every bit as much as he did Henri Landru. Gascón is certainly interested in his lovers' money, but the seduction and passionate love affairs in which he engages are just as appealing as the money itself: he kills his lovers only when they are about to discover his secret ploys. Just like Don Juan, Gascón is a liar (both promise marriage to their victims) and his affairs are short-lived, but there is little doubt about their passionate intensity. Love, as Gascón muses to himself during one such seduction, can only reach such peaks of intensity when one is thinking about death: 'How intensely happy anyone would be to be with such a sweet and poetic woman as the one I have in my arms if they had the added knowledge of their imminent death!' (1923: 72), and he goes on to add a little later that 'murder brings happiness since it puts us on the same level as kings and as nature, the traditional dispensers of death' (85).

Ramón's mythmaking finds echoes in the postmodern interest in (or rather obsession with) the psychopathic personality. Indeed, the very word 'psychopath', although first used at the beginning of last century, did not become common in scientific circles until Hervey Cleckley published *The Mask of Sanity* in 1941. Serial killers, such as Jack the Ripper and Henri Landru, were popular with the public in Ramón's day, but little attention has been paid to the reflection of that interest in Spanish writing. The obsession with the psychopathic personality that we find in later novels and in American film (*American Psycho* is simply the tip of an iceberg; there are literally thousands of films of the kind routinely shown on television) transformed the psychopath into a favorite (anti)hero of the postmodern world. Roberto Gascón's behavior anticipates that of many present-day psychopaths; as Robert Hare puts it, in *Without Conscience*:

> The actions of a psychopath are not the result of an unsettled mind but rather the result of a carefully calculated plan, a cold and highly intelligent decision, combined with a total lack of empathy towards other human beings [...] What stuns us is not the crime itself but the fact that it is committed by an apparently rational and, by all descriptions, normal human being. (1988: 59)

Roberto's 'lack of empathy' and his skill at controlling, manipulating and deceiving his victims; his ability to seduce and to simulate feelings he does not have ('they know the words but they do not know the music of emotions'); and his quest for new thrills combined with a total lack of social responsibility conform to the definition of a split personality given by Hare.

Ramón was able to express both the 'shiny' and the 'dark' side of modernity. He was partly responsible for introducing into Spain the great artistic movements of the European vanguard, in the hope that they would bring about change in the conservative, traditional, and backward country that was the Spain of the time. Yet he also discovered the 'dark side' of modernity: one which led inexorably to a dehumanized and divided personality. He wrote many stories on the 'art of killing' (see Serrano 1992), not simply as thrillers or detective stories, but rather as an expression of what he himself called the 'dark side' of his own personality.

Benjamín Jarnés

Benjamín Jarnés was born into a poor family in Zaragoza (his father, a tailor by profession, had to feed as many as 20 children from different marriages). He was fortunate enough to enter the seminary of the local Pontifical University, where boys were trained for the priesthood. It was not uncommon in those days for poor families to send their brightest son to the seminary in the hope that he would become a priest or, at the very least, receive a good education. A 'good education' was unwittingly provided by the Church itself in the form of an Index or blacklist of books that seminarians were forbidden to read. Students were quick to make the volumes blacklisted their required reading, circulating among themselves clandestine copies of authors such as Châteaubriand, Dumas, Stendhal, Galdós, and Dostoyevsky. Thus it was that seminarians became more familiar than many with the most exciting literature of the turn of the century, at the same time as they were getting formal training in biblical, classical, and medieval studies. It would be no exaggeration to say that the Church unwittingly provided its trainee priests with the best training in humanities that anyone could hope to receive in Spain in the early years of twentieth century. Add to this the fact that such students, since they had not yet taken holy orders, were allowed to roam the streets of Zaragoza fairly freely on weekends and it will come as no surprise to learn that many of these would-be priests had girlfriends and sweethearts galore, as Jarnés himself acknowledges.[2] The education of mind and spirit offered in the classroom proved to be no obstacle to any student determined to develop at the same time the physical and emotional sides of his personality.

Jarnés left the seminary before being ordained and joined the army Administration Corps. He was sent to Barcelona and then to Morocco but his first permanent posting was Madrid. The timing of his arrival in the capital dovetailed perfectly with his emerging literary career. In 1923, when Ortega y Gasset founded his *Revista de Occidente*, Jarnés was invited to join a young but enthusiastic team of writers, intellectuals, and artists set on bringing modernity to Spain. He had an advantage over the rest of the staff of the *Revista*, being by far the most learned and well read of all its members, and he would soon establish himself as the top literary critic in Ortega's team. He had, however, also set himself the more ambitious task of becoming a novelist, and was well aware that, in order to write well, he had to unlearn what had been dinned into him in his years at the seminary. Before he could create his own 'idle fictions' he had to deconstruct a narrative form (the nineteenth-century novel) that was anything but 'idle'. Jarnés was joined in this task by other young Spanish writers who were by 1925 publishing their revolutionary prose in the *Revista de Occidente*. In *Paula y Paulita* he recognizes that '[conventional] art has gone down to the River Jordan to receive a new baptism for all its past sins. After getting rid of the fetters which have imprisoned it for centuries, it stands naked, trying to decide what clothes to wear. Art has taken a long and well-deserved vacation from itself and we should enjoy its new – and festive – mood' (1929a: 14).

Jarnés's best known novel, *El profesor inútil* (1926), begins with a teacher taking a vacation. 'On the seventh day,' he muses to himself: 'the gods were supposed to rest [...] Let me rest and gaze at nature and try to imagine it in its pristine state'. The professor wants to make of 'idleness' his life goal: 'I am not interested in cursing or in praying,' he declares, 'I am simply interested in being happy, or rather, I am interested in spending the whole morning considering how happy I am' (1926: 21). Happiness and idleness become identical. Since he has no students, he can become a 'professor of myself, or perhaps be my own student or, even more interesting, my own guinea pig'

---

2   *El convidado de papel* (1928), although labelled a 'novel', is thought to be a fairly accurate description of his own experiences in the Zaragoza seminary.

(27). The plot of *El professor inútil* develops into a series of non-events, as all the women the protagonist meets and tries to seduce (some of whom are his former students) appear and disappear like shadows who have none of the consistency we expect from characters in a novel. In Pérez Firmat's terms 'they vaporize into thin air' (1982: 65). The only character who does not disappear from the story is the narrator himself, who is as much a 'professor' as he is Jarnés's own persona. The novel should be read as Jarnés's attempt at establishing a new identity as the teller of avant-garde tales, fascinated as he was by the new style and perplexed and puzzled about how to put it into practice.

By the time he published *Locura y muerte de nadie* (1919) Jarnés was ready to tackle the modern world head-on. This is a novel about the modern city and Jarnés delights in taking us through cosmopolitan urban scenarios: a city bank, a cabaret, a movie house, the stock exchange, the central plaza, a luxury hotel, a brothel in the outskirts, and so on. It is also a confrontation and mediation between the Nietzschean vision of modern man and Ortega y Gasset's own ideas on the matter. Although Ortega's seminal *La rebelión de las masas* (1929) did not come out until a few months after the publication of Jarnés's novel, the latter seems to have been well acquainted with the ideas of the Master. Jarnés's protagonist Juan Sánchez is the alienated Man of the Masses whom Ortega described in his famous essay. Juan knows he has become a Man of the Masses when he realizes that he has lost all visible signs of his own personal identity. He is frequently mistaken for others and unsure about the identity of his own parents. Even his wife seems to dismiss him by having frequent affairs with other men, suggesting that she can easily exchange him for another. So acute is Sánchez's pain at his apparent loss of personal identity that he tattoos his own signature on his chest to remind himself of who he really is. When he participates in a mass rally, steals the limelight, and becomes the focus of the cameras filming the event, Sánchez becomes the epitome of the Man of the Masses, though, from his point of view, that is the same as being a nobody. To become a Man of the Masses is not as tragic as Juan Sánchez seems to think. On the contrary, it can be a source of pleasure and enjoyment, as Arturo, another character in the story, suggests:

> Arturo felt he was skidding down a rampart that would immerse him into a collective entity, into a mass where he would simply be a number, a mass that would cut him off and release him from personal responsibilities to family and friends […] Rather than being simply himself, Arturo dreamt of being a collection of other beings, of living the existence of others as well as his own […] it was a kind of multiplication of his spirit. (1929: 62)

Arturo's character seems to echo the Nietzschean idea of a man freed from his own constricting identity, a man who is about to become a Man of the Masses as well as himself. Arturo, who describes himself as a 'miner of the spirit', reminds us also of Jarnés the novelist, who vicariously tries to live the lives of others by creating new characters in his novels. Ortega's very negative vision of the Man of the Masses is therefore pitted against Nietzsche's own vision of Superman, as Jarnés tries to mediate between the two. Modernity, Jarnés seems to imply, can both shrink and enlarge the human spirit: it can imprison the mind and erase individuality (as Ortega's Man of the Masses suggests) but it can also allow him to soar, to expand his own identity, to encompass many 'selves' in his own 'self', which was the Nietzschean ideal.

The crisis of capitalism that came with the Wall Street crash of 1929 put a stop to any illusions of indefinite progress, that cornerstone of modernism. Jarnés's last novel, *Teoría del zumbel* (1930), shares this sense of insecurity and catastrophe. It hero, Saulo, meets his death in the car crash which also bring his career in banking to a sudden halt. In a memorable ending, the author has Saulo meet God who displays his collection of spinning-tops to him and points to the fact that the length of the cord of each spinning-top is different:

> I love to cast my spinning-tops down to Earth and watch them spin. They will keep turning as long as their spirits last, as long as their cords keep them in motion. Your cord, I am afraid, was a particularly short one.
>
> (1930: 198)

The playful nature of 'modern man' – Ortega's and Huizinga's *homo ludens* – extends to his fate and mirrors the game of God with us (as his 'spinning-tops'), a game that is subject to the whim of the player. In *Teoría del zumbel,* Jarnés suggested that the game of modernity was over, that fiction could no longer be 'idle'. He could no longer sit on the fence but had to take sides and move from contemplation to action.

Francisco Ayala

Francisco Ayala, who celebrated his hundredth birthday in 2006, is the oldest and one of the most remarkable storytellers Spain has ever known. His life as a writer spans most of the twentieth century, and we should begin by looking at the avant-garde prose of his youth. He himself has reflected somewhat critically on the tales he wrote at that time and on his fellow writers of the 1920s and '30s: 'How can I forget those years when we decided to tear down the past in order to build – with our fists, rather than with our hands – a brilliant new world, which turned out to be a sham? In those days, youth was a merit in itself, our cocky insolence was often applauded, and our jokes were taken seriously. In fact, we were openly invited to express whatever first came into our heads, whatever nonsense first crossed our minds, and our *boutades*, distorted images, and free association of ideas invariably won high praise' (1988a: 14). Ayala's caricature of himself and his friends is an accurate assessment of the treasure-trove of literary gems they left behind for us to enjoy.

Perhaps it was the very flippancy and cockiness of youth that inspired the young Ayala to write one of the avant-garde masterpieces, *Cazador en el alba* (1929). This short novel tells the story of a young peasant, Antonio Arenas, who comes to Barcelona to do his military service. Built into the plot is the dazzling vision of modernity itself, perceived in all its brilliance by a young peasant who had lived close to nature and away from the big cities. He is the 'hunter' looking at the 'dawn' of a brave new world. For this adventurous soldier modernity is the 'second nature' with which God has endowed humanity. As he is travelling into the city on a train, Arenas is amazed at the sudden multiplication of signposts, advertisement hoardings, and notices that seemed to spread over every spare surface of the urban landscape: 'I had never imagined nature could be labeled [...] and packaged, just like any other piece of merchandise'. Arenas quickly notices that this 'second nature' is ruled by a new generation of gods whose pictures are clearly displayed in the streets of the city: 'There was the patron saint of photography smiling down on us as she always does and, a bit further on, the god of highways looking plump and well-fed and made of tyres, the image most venerated in all the garages in town' (1988a: 68); the references are to the logos employed by Kodak and Michelin. At night these gods actually wandered through the skies 'drawing lines on the heavens with a celestial ball pen or appearing and disappearing in the form of a fish, a snake or some mythical beast' (69). Thanks to electric power, these 'new gods' could write their messages to humanity on the walls of the urban landscape for all to read. But the most admirable product of this 'second nature' were women themselves:

> For a soldier coming from the countryside, city women are indeed the most refined product of industrial civilization, certainly as articulate as a typewriter, as precise as a sewing-machine, and as exact as a computer. Modern technology reaches its perfection in the creation of the female. (69)

Not only does this 'second nature' provide a companion for our soldier-hero but even assigns him a profession that embraces both his own 'nature' and the 'second nature' of the city. Antonio discovers that professional boxing is not only about hitting a close-range target in the ring but 'hitting the whole world with your boxing-gloves once your image is reproduced millions of times around the globe, once the stories of your feats have been telegraphed to remote corners of the universe and the radio has carried your very voice across the oceans' (80).

The ultimate reward of modernity is globalization, the notion that man has ultimately jumped into another dimension where he is no longer constrained by space or indeed by time. The very essence of that modern world is captured in the brief pages of *Cazador en el alba*. The education of the hero of the story begins the very day he is taken to a military hospital to be treated for concussion after falling from a horse:

> Fever displayed before his very eyes jumbled segments of the film of his life [...] It was then that Antonio Arenas understood that reality can only be comprehended at a temperature of 40° C and that, when God wants to make himself understood, he knocks a rider from his horse, though not necessarily on the road to Damascus. (62)

Modernity is perceived as a divine 'revelation', displayed in terms of 'film' and in the 'fever' which reveals the subconscious thoughts of the injured soldier. Modernity is as much inside us as it is outside, as real as it is 'surreal'.

Avant-garde writing is a mixture of the real and the 'surreal', of film and fiction, of poetry and prose. Ayala, for instance, describes a dance-hall in *Cazador en el alba* as a beautiful meadow where a gentle cow (the pianola) ruminates harmoniously: 'The dance-hall was a beautiful, lyrical meadow, where a pianola – a cow overflowing with harmonies – grazed patiently on a pianola roll of suggestive and juicy notes'. The pianola comes under constant attack from a band of shrill horseflies – 'that poor, idyllic cow surrounded by buzzing trombones' – while 'a huge nickel insect of the sax family whimpers like some poor black musician with convulsions as it sucks the cow's blood' (72).

The young writers of 1927 had celebrated the 300th anniversary of the death of the Spanish poet Luis de Góngora, who had indulged in a style so rich in poetic tropes that his poetry could hardly be understood by the non-initiated. So, too, were these tales from the vanguard rich in a poetic fantasy that often obscured the very plot of the story the writers were trying to tell. Their 'poetic excess' was very much a part of their celebration of modernity, a celebration which, as we have seen, proved short-lived.

To sum up, the term 'modernism' in Spanish literature has traditionally been used to refer to the poetic movement initiated by the Nicaraguan poet Rubén Darío at the end of the nineteenth century. He invented what was in effect a new poetic language, and one which inspired most of the great Spanish poets of the twentieth century, including Juan Ramón Jiménez and the young Antonio Machado. Darío, however, set some of his poems in eight-eenth-century France – in an imagined world of palaces, lakes, and swans – rather than in twentieth-century Europe, and he himself chose to live, as a poet, in an 'ivory tower' rather than in that 'modern' world.

We have used the term 'modernity' here to refer to the advent of the modern world—the steam engine, the telegraph, the telephone, the radio, the combustion engine, and the airplane—and thus also to modern living. Avant-garde artists and writers were at the cutting-edge of modernity, since they saw modern living not simply as an evolution of the past but as a revolution into a future that would forever change mankind. Their hopes were soon to be dashed by the Wall Street crash and the Great Depression but the visions of the brave new world which they saw and foresaw are as dazzling today as they were when they created them. The 'idle fictions' which they wrote were snapshots of a world soon to vanish, and these 'tales from the vanguard' were in effect a new literary genre they invented to capture the very essence of 'modernity' as they saw it in their everyday lives.

Further reading

Albaladejo *et al.* (1992), Brihuega (1982), Cardona (1957), Cerezo (1992), Díez de Revenga (2005), Fernández Cifuentes (1982 and 1993), Havard (2004), Hiriart (1972), Ilie (1968), Irizarry (1971), Kirkpatrick (2003), Martínez Latre (1979), Mechthild (2005), Mermall (1989), Morris (1972), Pérez Bazo (1998), Pérez Firmat (1982), Pino (1995), Risco (1980), Ródenas (1998), Soldevila-Durante (1977), Soria (1930), Umbral (1978), Vázquez Medel (1998), Wentzlaff-Eggebert (1991 and 1999).

4

The Social Realist Novel

JANET PÉREZ

Thematic origins and political content

In the Spanish post-war novel, the term neorealism is used for the re-emergence of realist writing, never completely absent even though it had become unfashionable with the Generation of 1898 during the heyday of *modernismo* and during the so-called *vanguardismo* characteristic of the Generation of 1927. Neorealism emerges in the work of writers such as José Díaz, dubbed in 1930 the 'New Romantics'. Reacting against the vanguardist 'dehumanization' of art and the advocacy of 'pure' art, or 'art for art's sake', they felt compelled by the dramatic events of the Civil War to focus once again on social and political realities. Avant-garde writers, consciously elitist and intellectual, had looked down on 'bourgeois' taste and produced few novels (a genre still dominated in the eyes of the public by the great authors of the Generation of 1898: Baroja, Azorín, Unamuno, and Valle-Inclán; see above Chapter 1). Not long after this, a number of politically combative pre-war 'New Romantic' works appeared, among them *La turbina* (1930), *Los pobres contra los ricos* (1933), and *Reparto de tierras* (1934), all three by César Arconada; *Campesinos* (1931) and *Crimen* (1934) from the pen of Joaquín Arderíus, and works by the prolific Ramón Sender, including **Siete domingos rojos* (1932), *Viaje a la aldea del crimen* (1934), and **Mr. Witt en el Cantón* (1936). Most of these novels consist of autobiographical, eyewitness accounts or documentaries, politically motivated and socially focused. The Marxist critic Pablo Gil Casado (1973) saw Sender's **Siete domingos rojos* as coinciding with the emergence of a 'real' social novel in Spain. Many novelists of the Civil War and writers in exile also played a part in the renaissance of critical neorealism.[1]

---

[1] They include María Teresa León, Arturo Barea, and the erstwhile vanguardist Max Aub, whose epic cycle of novels *El laberinto mágico* (1943–57) depicted the war from prelude to aftermath, including the concentration camps, guerrilla warfare, and prison camps for refugees obliged to carry out forced labor. Another survivor of the Generation of 1927, Francisco Ayala,

Although that renaissance under the Franco dictatorship is often credited to the influence of post-war Italian neorealist cinema and *verismo* (generally deemed itself to be a reaction against an Italian idealized vision of traditional family and gender roles promoted by Fascism, and the result of readers' rejection of the anti-aesthetic excesses of Fascist *triunfalismo*), there had been a move in the direction of reportage and sociopolitical writing under the Spanish Republic. Neorealist tendencies can be seen in pre-war narrative (and in poetry and the arts during the war), although post-war social novelists consciously adopted 'safer' Italian neorealist cinematic techniques. Among the Italian neorealists who had an appreciable impact in Spain were the novelists Alberto Moravia and Cesare Pavese, and the film-makers Roberto Rossellini and Vittorio De Sica, many of whose films feature rootless, aimless protagonists, derelicts, criminals, and other representatives of an urban underworld not unlike that familiar to Spaniards of the time. Both cinema and the novel afforded scope for using collages, flashbacks, panoramic shots, and close-ups on print media. But Spanish neorealism differs from the determinism and fatalism of Italian *verismo* because it concentrates on tragedies that arise from sociopolitical injustice and that are not, as a consequence, inevitable.

Neorealist trends pick up the threads of this New Romantic rejection of modernist aesthetics. Traditional realism of the kind practiced by Galdós never disappeared completely in Spain: books in that vein were being produced even after the 1950s. Younger realists, some of them self-professed disciples of Galdós, such as Juan Antonio de Zunzunegui, Sebastián Juan Arbó, Ignacio Agustí, and José María Gironella, enjoyed considerable success from the 1940s through to the mid-1960s with saga-length novels, often organized into trilogies or longer cycles and usually chronicling the fortunes of a single family, either rural or urban. Despite sharing the same novelistic stage, none of these writers (or other authors of a similarly traditional bent, including the *costumbristas*) can properly be considered neorealists, since they simply followed in the realist tradition without any technical innovation or politico-social engagement. It is these last two features that divide traditional realists from neorealism or social realism, as they dictate the interrelationship

---

developed a personal, essentially realist style after the war, combining humor, satire, irony, allegory, and history in *Los usurpadores* (1949) and *La cabeza del cordero* (1949). Calm, dispassionate, and philosophical, these stories tell of Franco's usurpation of power. Ayala's subtle post-war critiques of the dictatorship coincide with neorealist opposition to the regime, although his refined style and multifarious subject matter, all of it drawn from Spanish history, range far more widely than the usual narrow neorealist insistence on socioeconomic realities. Other works by Sender are of interest in this regard: *Mosén Millán* (1953), *Réquiem por un campesino español* (1960), his multi-volume autobiographical series *Crónica del alba* (1965–71) and a further series, *Los cinco libros de Ariadna* (1957). Spanish critics of the period used the terms neorealism and critical realism almost interchangeably, although there was a stronger political thrust to the latter.

of text and context. The euphemistically named *novela social* was simply neorealism in the service of political protest. In a literary context, 'social' meant political (and being political meant being subject to censure). Social literature under Franco consisted, then, of works of political protest, necessarily covert but nevertheless subversive and critical in intent, and almost always presenting cases of socioeconomic injustice: problems which, such works suggest, would not have existed had it not been for the army revolt that triggered the Civil War. Another prohibited term at the time was 'Civil War', the regime insisting on describing the years 1936–39 as 'Our Glorious National Uprising' or 'Our Glorious National Crusade'. Because only Falangists were willing to use such terminology, social novelists usually avoided the war entirely, or treated it only obliquely. By the same token, to use the names of political parties or movements was dangerous and best avoided, and so social novelists concentrated primarily on the trials and tribulations of the poor, not limiting their portrayal to their misery and hunger, but also pointing to their unequal treatment before the law, their exploitation by employers and the upper classes, and – conversely – the *dolce vita* of the wealthy. Typically, the poor were good, while the wealthy were selfish, inconsiderate, and bereft of any redeeming feature, such dichotomies being described as 'dualistic' by commentators at the time, given the black-and-white picture such novels afforded of society and its ills.

The 'social novel', the broadest and most inclusive label of all, was used not only to indicate the limited themes and subject matter treated in such works, but also as a euphemism for political protest. The extent and nature of the realist component in such works might go well beyond neorealism, often embracing a variant of Galdosian realism with its traditional focus on socioeconomic problems, or perhaps a degree of 'poetic realism', the term applied to a number of works by Ana María Matute and Miguel Delibes, given their lyrical treatment of children and adolescents and the world of Nature, or to the novels of writers such as Dolores Medio, who concentrated more on the emotional life of her characters.

The Politics of neorealism

Shortly after the end of the Civil War, Spain's borders were effectively sealed and libraries were purged; book-burnings in the streets were a common sight (although, as often with such attempts at wholesale censorship, the private libraries of the wealthy were immune). Most foreign books were prohibited, save for works by Portuguese and Italian Fascists, and many Spanish classics were banned as well, including the works of most nineteenth-century realists and naturalists, the Generation of 1898 (because 'they criticized Spain'), and the Generation of 1927, who were guilty of association with the

Republic.[2] An entire generation grew up in complete ignorance of Spain's literary past, with the result that some practitioners of social fiction honestly believed that realism was an invention of their own. Their novels owed as much to Naturalism as they did to realism, notwithstanding the influence of Italian neorealism and French objectivism, and as a result they often read like nineteenth-century works. Though we may apply different labels to them – social literature, social realism, critical realism, objectivism, dialectical realism – these are novels which had a common denominator: they were all covertly opposed to the Franco regime. Two labels commonly used by scholars looking at this period are *literatura de evasión* (escapist literature), and its opposite, *literatura comprometida* (politically and socially committed literature). Most social novelists sought to oppose the dictatorship and to engage themselves politically, even though all political activity outside the Falange was prohibited and any open expression of political opinions was censored and the writer or speaker could easily be imprisoned.[3] Spanish neorealism held sway as the dominant artistic 'movement' from the early 1950s through the mid-1960s and it was generally well regarded by critics and writers, most of whom shared similar ideologies, including a tacit, covert opposition to the regime.

Another important influence was French objectivism, a fashion that was a feature of the French 'new novel', or anti-novel, associated with writers like Michel Butor, Nathalie Sarraute, and Alain Robbe-Grillet. Rejecting traditional plot and characterization, they produced what came to be known as 'laboratory' novels, experiments in removing the authorial voice and concentrating instead on detailed, photographic descriptions of objects and on the systematic dismantling of literary conventions. The influence in Spain of this so-called *École du regard* or *écriture objective* can best be seen in Robbe-Grillet's *La jalousie* (1957). But such objectivism was diluted by the time it reached Spain and had lost its experimental edge, becoming instead a technique for circumnavigating censorship and an instrument of political protest (and hence scarcely objective). Objectivism required that authors abstain from intervening personally in the text, speaking directly to readers, suggesting interpretations, inserting their own opinions or values, or displaying their own culture and beliefs. They had to avoid language that implied judgment, and instead portray things and people with 'scientific'

---

[2] Banned works and exiled writers were neither taught in schools nor available legally in bookstores (although many bookstores sold contraband at greatly inflated prices), nor was it safe to write about them..

[3] Early legislation by the Franco regime had established the Falange (Spanish Fascist party) as the country's only legal political organization; its only organized opposition, the clandestine Communist party, operated underground and from across the border in France (also, of course, the source of leftist literary theory).

objectivity, giving measurements and detailed descriptions, providing data that would lead the reader to sympathize with the poor, but without any overt sign that this was what the writer had in mind. The result was slow-paced narratives studded with extended passages of description, denuded of verbs of action and adverbs modifying that action. An author could not write that the protagonist 'stormed in angrily'; rather, he should describe him slamming the door, throwing his package to the floor, and breaking a plate, leaving the reader to conclude that the protagonist might be angry. Such an approach derived partially from an existential belief in the impossibility of one person's knowing what went on in the head of another.

Objectivism also owed a debt to Marxism. A leading writer on Neorealism, José María Castellet, argues in his *La hora del lector* (1957) that, just as writers achieved autonomy in the eighteenth and nineteenth centuries, and fictional characters subsequently revolted and gained their freedom, so now the reader's turn for liberation has come: readers should no longer be told what a work 'means' or forced to accept a single, fixed conclusion to it.[4] Neorealists (especially those influenced by Existentialism and Marxism) considered that the only admissible 'psychology' was behaviorism, best represented by cinematographic techniques, with the author portraying nothing that could not be captured by movie camera and sound track, an idea that can be seen to good effect in Jesús Fernández Santos's *Los bravos* (1954), Rafael Sánchez-Ferlosio's *El Jarama* (1956), and two works by Ignacio Aldecoa: *Gran Sol* (1957) and *Parte de una historia* (1965).

While social realism demanded fewer circumlocutions and permitted a measure of subjectivity (usually in direct speech), it eschewed stylistic refinement, *recherché* vocabulary, and authorial intervention. As a consequence, characters were typically flat and generic, and were often stock representatives of particular trades and occupations: bootblacks, fishermen, cooks, maids, truck-drivers, newsboys, peasants, construction workers, and so on. Authors were genuinely altruistic, striving to improve the lot of the workers and the indigent poor about whom they wrote, but always adhering to the rules of this game.[5] Their efforts to improve the lot of unfortunate groups

---

[4]   Castellet later (1970) reversed this Marxist-inspired approach, rejecting neorealism and shunning political engagement in favor of the emerging Spanish 'new novel'. Juan Goytisolo, novelist and erstwhile theorist of the social novel (1959), had also originally adopted a Marxist stance and excoriated the psychological novel, affirming that any self-respecting novelist should be embarrassed to write such things in the second half of the twentieth century.

[5]   Marxist theorists had decreed that art which did not contribute directly to changing society was immoral and unjustifiable, and thus for a novelist to cultivate a personal style was indefensible, as was teaching for artistic effects or using any lexicon except that accessible to the lowest common denominator (the audience was assumed to be the 'common man', even though he had no money to spend on books, and was more interested in forgetting his troubles than in reading about them).

had no perceptible impact, the sole exception being the novel *Funcionario público* (1956) by Dolores Medio, which exposed the plight of Spanish postal and communications workers, minor bureaucrats who were forced to dress well but were paid too little for them to afford even the bare necessities, a situation which renders the protagonist impotent and causes his wife to leave him and return to her village. Medio, who wrote at least nine novels and eight collections of short fiction in the Neorealist vein, consistently espoused feminist and workers' causes and was justifiably proud that *Funcionario público* produced a small raise for postal employees, a pragmatic impact no other 'social' writer achieved. By the 1960s, many novelists were weary of the poor financial return, negligible social impact, and limited personal satisfaction offered by the neorealist crusade.

The break came in 1962 with the publication of Luis Martín-Santos's *Tiempo de silencio*. The author, a Marxist psychiatrist repeatedly jailed by the regime, showed just how a complex, experimental, psychological novel might break nearly all the rules of the social novel (save for its political content) and at the same time achieve more impact and artistic satisfaction. Over the following five years, most social writers followed this lead, switching to neo-vanguardist, neo-surrealist, and neo-Baroque variants of the 'new novel' which became the dominant mode in 1967 with the appearance of Juan Benet's *Volverás a Región*.

Major writers, works, themes, and techniques

A critical commonplace of the 1950s and 1960s was that *La colmena* (1951) by Camilo José Cela was Spain's first neorealist novel, a somewhat arbitrary judgement which has largely gone unchallenged. It was neither the first, nor was it genuinely neorealist; still less was it a social novel, as it lacks any clear-cut political commitment. Cela presents a Manichaean division of society into 'victims and executioners', but nowhere does he suggest any connection between this division and the military uprising of 1936 or the subsequent dictatorship (nor does he ever adopt an unambiguous political stance such as would have been characteristic of the social novel).

The neorealist or social post-war novel falls into two major groupings: those with an urban settings and characters whose problems reflect the problems of life in the city, and those set in a rural environment and peopled with characters who face distinctly rural problems.[6] *La colmena* is emphatically urban, but, as we have suggested, lacks political or social commitment. Its

6   Critics who divide the novel along these lines include Gil Casado (1973), Sobejano (1975), and Sanz Villanueva (1972). In practice, few major novelists belong fully in one grouping or the other, although Delibes sets more of his novels in the countryside, while Juan

neorealist features include the characters' generic, collective nature and the presence of cinematographic techniques, probably adopted from Italian neorealist cinema (Cela is never objectivist). Direct authorial interventions in *La colmena* echo or parody those of the nineteenth-century realist authors much reviled by Spanish theorists of neorealism, such as Goytisolo and Castellet, and rejected by French proponents of objectivism. Cela's typically expressionist techniques of caricature, degradation, exaggeration, dehumanization, and deformation distance him from the mimetic approach of neorealism and the social novel. The systematic dehumanization of his characters suggests their animal nature. In the prologue to the third edition of *La colmena*, the author states that man is not good, neither is life, and that 'culture and tradition are never ideological, but instinctive' (1987: 109); similar deterministic and apolitical attitudes are repeatedly found in his work. Furthermore, Cela never ceased to privilege novelistic experimentation and style; one aspect of his work on which most critics agree is the primacy of style – an emphasis incompatible with the tenets of both neorealism and the social novel.

La familia de Pascual Duarte (1942), Cela's only other novel in the neorealistic vein, and one in which setting, characters and plot seemingly subscribe to the aesthetic of the social novel, has been seen as the source of what came to be known as *tremendismo*: a blend of aspects of Valle-Inclán's expressionistic *esperpento* and of a naturalism stripped of most of its scientific basis. Cela himself identified another influence: the seventeenth-century poet, courtier, novelist, and social critic Francisco de Quevedo. It is undeniable that here and in Cela's third novel, *Nuevas andanzas y desventuras del Lazarillo de Tormes* (1944) the picaresque plays an important role, and one that should long ago have alerted critics to the dubious nature of any suggestion that Cela was a neorealist. In his autobiographical *Memorias, entendimientos y voluntades* (1993), he classed himself as 'socially conservative'. The absence of any political commitment in his writing and the ambiguous nature of his own personal political behavior suggest he was never a leftist or a man with a political agenda.

Miguel Delibes employs traditional realism in his early novels, which date from the ten years from 1948 to 1958, and there are few traces in them of cinematographic techniques, objectivism, or any kind of political engagement. His first neorealist novel, *La hoja roja* (1959), innovative in its focus on old age, employs a modified objectivism, cloaking the authorial presence by narrating the story in the form of a dialogue between the protagonists: a widowed, retired city employee named Don Eloy and his live-in cook and maid, Desi, an illiterate, orphaned adolescent country girl. The dysfunctional

---

Goytisolo's exposés of upper-class self-indulgence tend to be set in towns (sometime in tourist resorts but more normally in the main cities).

Spanish economy that relied in the 1950s on massive forced internal migration from countryside to town led many young girls from rural backgrounds
to find themselves working on subsistence wages in towns and cities, always
in the hope that they might somehow eventually secure a dowry for themselves. It was an arrangement not unlike that of the indentured servant of
the eighteenth and nineteenth centuries. Don Eloy's plight is typical of the
elderly: unwanted by the son he struggled to educate, forgotten by his few
surviving friends, he is a social reject relegated to a hand-to-mouth existence:
poor, unloved, neglected, and left to eke out an existence on an inadequate
pension. The problem is only partly a political one, but the Spain of the
time offered precious little, if anything at all, by way of social services and
pensions. Delibes's message about those unable to cope for themselves, the
retired elderly and orphaned adolescents, is a powerful one.

But it was with *Las ratas (1962) that Delibes produced his first full-
blooded social novel, one in which the treatment of the issue of rural poverty
is unmistakably political. The point of departure is a village in which a
number of people living in caves are forcibly relocated so that foreign visitors will not broadcast the fact that Spain is so primitive that some of the
people have to live as troglodytes. It is a theme relevant to Franco's policy of
promoting tourism as a means to obtaining foreign exchange with which to
purchase plant and machinery from abroad and finance post-war reconstruction (the Spanish currency, the peseta, had plummeted as a result of its gold
reserves being shipped to Russia by the Republic's retreating Soviet 'military
advisors'). Unable to refurbish thousands of miserable villages, the regime
opted instead to build fences around those that were near roads liable to be
used by tourists so that they would not offend Northern European sensibilities. Delibes, involved in an unsuccessful campaign to convince the Ministry
of Agriculture to help the impoverished farmers of Castile, was eventually
ordered to desist, and it was this that spurred him on to write *Las ratas.
Objectivism reappears as he gets his characters to tell their stories, much of
them in dialogue, while cinematographic techniques also feature (many of
Delibes's novels have since been adapted for television and cinema, or as
plays). The 'little people' in *Las ratas end up being crushed by the jugger-
naut of progress and written off as 'collateral damage' in the government's
campaign to encourage tourism. Some critics have seen this novel as naturalist, but it is not deterministic: what precipitates the tragedy is not heredity,
environment, or social determinism, but rather the government's indifference
to the human consequences of its policies. The novel provoked public and
critical outrage, including accusations of fabrication in respect of its descriptions of the subhuman living conditions endured by the cave-dwellers. Delibes
has always insisted that he used real-life models, and has given chapter and
verse to support his claim.

Other novels by Delibes to qualify for the label of Neorealist include

Cinco horas con Mario (1966), a long monologue, in which the words
that the recently widowed Carmen addresses to her husband's corpse illustrate, via the remembered conflict between the spouses, the degree to which
the Spanish Civil War was being re-enacted daily in innumerable families;
El príncipe destronado (1973), which tells its story from the viewpoint
of a toddler (another objectivist perspective) who witnesses daily quarrels
between his parents; and *Las guerras de nuestros antepasados* (1975), a work
in dialogue whose protagonist, Pacífico Pérez, is diagnosed insane because
he rejects war. Present-day readers might do well to remember that, for over
thirty years, the Spanish government kept alive memories of the Civil War,
as well as the negative emotions triggered by such memories, by means of
a daily, even hourly roll-call of those 'heroes' (though only those that had
fought for the victorious rebel insurgency) who had fallen on that date in
history, and well as by repeatedly asserting that the Generalísimo was the
only bulwark against Communism. Delibes shows the consequences of such
a policy for succeeding generations, even for those who had not yet been
born at the end of the war. *Parábola del náufrago* (1969) is also clearly
political and contains numerous passages that many readers interpreted as
allegories or satires of Franco, but it was more experimental and expressionistic in its techniques, employing interior monologues and streams of
consciousness of the kind associated with earlier, modernist narrative and
the emerging Spanish New Novel (of which it is arguably a satire). Delibes
never abandoned his support for those living in rural areas – for villages, their
inhabitants, and their environment – but in the 1970s he began to toy with
more universal themes and conducted his own, moderate experiments with
form, perspective, and narrative.

   More self-consciously neorealist is Ignacio Aldecoa, whose first novel, *El
fulgor y la sangre* (1954) portrays the tension in the barracks of a rural detachment of the Civil Guard when their wives are notified of the death of one of
their own, whose identity has not yet been released. Each of the six chapters traces the events of one hour, depicting the difficulties and dangers that
beset the guards in their daily lives. The sequel, *Con el viento solano* (1954),
changes perspective and focuses on the fugitive gypsy who murdered the
guard, depicting the hopeless situation of the marginalized individual pitted
against society and now also against nature. In *Gran Sol* (1957), Aldecoa
employs objectivist techniques to portray the daily routines of cod fishermen
who routinely risk their lives (as well as enduring great boredom and discomfort), making voyages of several weeks from Spain to fishing grounds off
the coast of Ireland, and spending endless hour upon hour in excessively
cramped quarters with little to do but wait. Aldecoa 'lived' his story (as had
Galdós and other naturalists), by making the trip described and documenting
the routines, conversations, and the few unusual (and dangerous) interruptions to those routines. Also objectivist is *Parte de una historia* (1967), set on

an unidentified island where the presence of wealthy American tourists leads to the discovery of a body and a crime that is never solved. None of these four novels – all of them with rural settings – can rival the extraordinary mastery of the urban neorealist fiction which Aldecoa displays in the brief narratives collected in *Espera de tercera clase* and *Vísperas del silencio*, both of them dating from 1955, both written primarily in the Madrid dialect, and both featuring the poorest of the poor, from a street orphan living in a culvert to gypsies and the lowest ranks of the employed.

Rafael Sánchez Ferlosio is Aldecoa's only rival as a skilled practitioner of objectivism, his *El Jarama* (1955) showing him fully cognizant with the peculiarities of the same lower-class Madrid dialect that lends so much flavor to Aldecoa's stories. This is the only work by Ferlosio that has elements of neorealism about it, as his earlier *Alfanhuí* (1952) is in a picaresque format and offers a lyrical-cum-fantastic portrait of a central character who resembles the Sorcerer's Apprentice or Till Eulenspiegel more than he does Lazarillo de Tormes. *El Jarama*, a novel that takes place on a single Sunday one summer, beginning at dawn and ending at midnight, opens with a picture of early-morning calm and tranquility in a popular bathing spot in the Jarama, one of very few rivers in the generally arid central Castilian plateau. That peace and calm gradually vanishes as the day-trippers arrive. These comprise two generations of working-class city-dwellers: the older generation are survivors of the Civil War of nearly two decades earlier and spend the day in the bar at the top of the hill, while the young adults and adolescents go down to the river to swim and sunbathe. The cultural differences between the generations reflect more than just the generation gap: the younger group is unaware that this peaceful Jarama was the site of one of the bloodiest battles in the struggle for Madrid and that the waters literally ran red in the very place where they are swimming (the information is presented to the reader piecemeal, through hints and allusions, in answer to a question from one of the younger visitors, as any direct address of the issues would have attracted the attention of the authorities). The association that is established in this way between this place and death sets the scene for the midnight drowning which ends the party. Meanwhile, for the approximately eighteen hours covered by the narrative, there is only the most banal conversation and periodic preoccupation with what time it is. Sánchez Ferlosio experimented with equating 'real' time and 'narrated' time – that is, he attempted to make the time required for a reader to read the novel equate to the time that passes in the narrative itself, from the moment the innkeeper opens his doors until the last visitors leave at the end, the assumption being that it would take the average reader some eighteen hours to finish the book. So it is that we are given pointers to the passing of time: characters mention it when shadows shift round as the sun climbs up into the sky and later sinks; the author also inserts several references to passing trains, and several of the students, few of whom own watches, ask their more fortunate friends what the time is.

The conversations between the characters ring so true that reviewers suggested that the author must have taped them and then simply transcribed the recording. Aside from the paucity of significant content, one of the most noticeable aspects of what is said is the apathy of the younger generation, while some of the older ones are fearful of possible police eavesdroppers and reluctant to talk. The regime's regulation of public behavior, including dress, appears when one couple go for a walk in their bathing suits and a policeman detains them, warning them that they cannot go more than a few meters from the water improperly dressed. However, no narrative voice comments on such things; readers learn only from what is said by the characters. With objectivism taken to its logical extreme in this novel and in Aldecoa's *Gran Sol*, many readers were puzzled by what such works might mean, if they meant anything at all, while others complained that nothing happened in them, except that time went on passing. One reader even suggested that the only reason Sánchez Ferlosio included the accidental drowning in *El Jarama* was that he had got bored with his own story. After experimenting in this way, Sánchez Ferlosio abandoned the novel for over four decades, devoting himself to writing about linguistics.

Jesús López Pacheco is the author of one of the most highly acclaimed social novels of the period, *Central eléctrica* (1956). This narrated the construction of a dam for flood control and hydroelectric power production in the early 1950s near an isolated, backward village destined to be flooded when the plant comes into production. The story tells of impoverished, ignorant, and largely uncivilized villagers, and technical experts from the 'civilized world' who are callous, indifferent to the safety of the local workers hired to do the hard labor involved with no safety measures or insurance (several fall into the wet cement and are entombed alive in the foundations of the dam). *Central eléctrica* was greeted as the best-ever novel about the world of work when it was first published in Spain.[7] While part of the struggle pits man against Nature, the dam construction transcends its immediate regional setting to become an allegory of the exploitation of the poor by capitalism and government. López Pacheco's politics were such that he had problems with the authorities and was unable to find a job. He eventually emigrated to Canada, but not before producing several volumes of social poetry, including *Canciones del amor prohibido* (1961) which depicts the suffocating, Victorian-style regulation by the Franco regime of any public display of affection, even between spouses, and *Mi corazón se llama Cudillero* (1961), which

---

[7]   Praise came from Sanz Villanueva (1972), Gil Casado (1973), Sobejano (1975), and Soldevila-Durante (1980).

describes the harsh lives of fishermen in the Asturian village of Cudillero where the author spent a summer studying their world.

Jesús Fernández Santos began what would become a comparatively prolific career as a novelist in 1954 with *Los bravos*, in which he pictured the hard lives of peasants in the mountains of northern León, condemned to poverty, ignorance, and isolation, in the absence of any viable alternative way of life. Critics differ on whether this is an experimental novel or a collection of inter-related stories and novelettes. With a preponderance of dialogue in the manner of objectivist writing, *Los bravos* exhibits the cinematic style typical of much of this author's work (both he and his brother were cinematographers). The novel denounces the effects of *caciquismo* (the power of village bosses) in a village of some sixty to seventy residents, who suffer from the extreme summer heat which gives an edge to their resentment and aggravates their fears, hopes, and frustrations. Noteworthy are the several traditional *costumbrista* scenes describing eighteenth- and nineteenth-century folk customs, local dress, food, speech, and festivals. *En la hoguera* (1957) is also set in a village, this time on the Castilian plateau south of Madrid. Several of the characters are linked by their relationships to a man who is suffering from tuberculosis and, during the course of the story, a number of further illnesses and tragedies occur (girls are seduced or raped, robberies and murder are committed), along with incidents involving adultery or the age-old prejudices and superstitions of the community. The novel uses the same cinematographic techniques we find in *Los bravos*. The best of Fernández Santos's early social works is *Cabeza rapada* (1958), a halfway-house between novel and short story (as in *Los bravos*), consisting of anecdotes united by common characters, setting, and theme. The novelist's emphasis on social problems and objectivist narrative continues with *Laberintos* (1964), which portrays Holy Week in Segovia where the lavish celebrations contrast with the moral impoverishment of the wealthy, especially those who represent the establishment. In 1970, with *El hombre de los santos*, Fernández Santos entered another phase, incorporating aspects of the Spanish New Novel, especially a greater preoccupation with style, technique, language, and structure.

Ana María Matute combines a political commitment typical of the social, political, and moral views of her generation with themes, characters, and predominantly rural settings typical of neorealism or social literature as well as a powerfully lyrical, highly personal literary style. Her techniques are eclectic, employing devices such as interior monologue and stream of consciousness of the kind we more usually expect to find in modernist and experimental fiction. As a result, Matute is not easy to pigeon-hole, but, precisely because she never turned her back on the emotional side of her characters' lives and her language is powerful, her narratives are extraordinarily robust. Her short novel, *Fiesta al noroeste* (1952), illustrates this combination perfectly, beginning with a pen-portrait of the local *cacique* (or landowner with political power), Juan Medinao, who is a perfect example of the problems that arise from hereditary feudalism and from the system of *mayorazgo* (or entailed estates, handed down to the firstborn son and bequeathing him unlimited power). Medinao's abuse of that power allows him, as it had his even more tyrannical father before him, to ignore and trample on the rights of his social inferiors, and in particular those of women. In doing so, his figure acquires an allegorical dimension, as do several corrupt, weak, or hypocritical landlords in Matute's fiction. Her many novels, novelettes, stories, and memoirs of the 1950s and 1960s turn obsessively upon a few particular themes: social injustice, conflict within the family (the age-old tale of Cain and Abel), the Civil War, existential alienation and solitude, and man's inhumanity to man, women, children, and animals. It is social injustice that provides the central concern of her trilogy, *Los mercaderes*, comprising *Primera memoria* (1959). *Los soldados lloran de noche* (1964) and *La trampa* (1969). There are also thematic links with the fratricidal love-hate relationships we find in *La torre vigía* (1970), where Matute enters the territory of the New Novel with an unexpected hybrid, a neo-chivalric social novel which revives the Cain and Abel conflict.

Carmen Martín Gaite, who belongs to the same 'mid-century' group as Aldecoa, Matute, Sánchez Ferlosio, and Goytisolo, has been little studied in the context of neorealism, probably because of widespread ignorance at the time about the rights of women and the serious social injustices perpetrated against them. Martín Gaite's primary interests as a novelist center upon gender issues, but after two important early works – the novel *Entre visillos* (1957) and a collection of stories and novelettes entitled *Ataduras* (1960) – she concentrated on completing a doctorate in history. Viewed from today's perspective, those two works alone would suffice to establish her importance as a social novelist, as both are fully neorealist works, make ample use of cinematographic techniques, depicting a large gallery of women of different ages, social backgrounds, attitudes, and circumstances. Furthermore, they serve to illustrate the life-style options available to Spanish women in the 1950s and show the difficulties women faced in Franco's Spain if they wanted to get a decent education to prepare themselves for a career. These issues resurface throughout Martín Gaite's fiction, and can now be seen as political, even if they were never openly discussed as such during the dictatorship. Martín Gaite's remarkable understanding of gender issues, well before these became a standard subject for study, is evident in her fiction of the 1950s and leaves the reader in no doubt whatever that she viewed the regime's legislation against women as primarily responsible for their repression. That conviction in only strengthened by *El cuarto de atrás* (1978) and by her essay *Usos amorosos de la postguerra española* (1987), both of which reconstruct the ways in which the educational system, cultural mores, religious values, moral traditions, and the politics of the dictatorship conspired to keep women ignorant and chained to the stove, with no access to the law nor any possibility of achieving the slightest degree of autonomy. Surveying Martín Gaite's remarkably consistent career, it is clear with hindsight that her contribution to mid-century social literature was based on a firm political commitment.

Other works

The eight writers discussed here are the best known social novelists who had most impact on the movement's development and public perceptions of it. But there were many more writers of social novels than those eight in the 1950s and 1960s. A dozen or so other writers produced work of substance: almost all of the novels by Dolores Medio are socially concerned or feminist. Antonio Ferres not only produced *La piqueta* (1959) but also collaborated with Armando López Salinas on another form of protest literature, the pseudo-travel book. *Caminando por las Hurdes* (1960) concentrated on the depiction of poverty and backwardness. López Salinas was highly praised for *La mina* (1959), but his *Año tras año* (1960) was banned in Spain and had to be published in Paris. Ramón Nieto wrote novels such as *La patria y el pan* (1962), *La fiebre* (1960), *El sol amargo* (1961), *La cala* (1963) and *Vía muerta* (1964) as well as two collections of short stories, *La tierra* (1957) and *Los desterrados* (1958). Novels by Alfonso Grosso include *La zanja* (1961), *Un cielo difícilmente azul* (1961), *Testa de copo* (1963), and *El capirote* (1966). The most socially oriented novel by José Manuel Caballero is *Dos días de setiembre* (1962), while Daniel Sueiro produced *La criba* (1961) and Enrique Azcoaga *El empleado* (1949). Two other prolific novelists, not usually classed as social novelists, also contributed to the movement: Angel María de Lera, a longtime political prisoner, wrote *Tierra para morir* (1964), *Hemos perdido el sol* (1963), *Los olvidados* (1957) and *Bochorno* (1960), while the expatriate Juan Goytisolo (b. 1931) was responsible for **Juegos de manos* (1954) and **Duelo en el Paraíso* (1955), both of which were highly inflammatory, several of his later works also being exposés of the extreme luxury enjoyed by wealthy Spaniards and foreign tourists.

Conclusion

Spanish neorealism, with its narrow focus on the injustices of the class structure and on the economic problems that beset the country was potentially embarrassing to the dictatorship. Its advocacy of political opposition to the regime brought it closer to naturalism than to the much broader focus we find in the heyday of realism. In addition to the ample division into rural and urban novels, it is possible to discern another: that between writers who predominantly treat either the exploitation and mistreatment of the poor, the homeless, the proletariat, and the peasantry (the good) and those that concentrate on the indulgent and parasitical lifestyles of the wealthy, the aristocracy, and those in power (the egotistical, the hypocritical, the cruel, and even the criminal). Recurrent themes include emigration and the forced internal migration caused by a stagnant economy and widespread unemployment, and the resultingly high numbers of homeless and an increase in crime and illness; close scrutiny of the different kinds of jobs done by lower-class workers (in agriculture, mining, fishing, construction) and by middle-class office workers and bureaucrats, in which the emphasis is on difficult and often dangerous working conditions, inadequate pay, and the concomitant family problems and tragedies resulting from dangers in the workplace and an inability to make ends meet. In the end, the narrow range of themes treated, the limited aesthetic choices made, and the programmatic ideology espoused by the apostles of neorealism led to a uniformity and a grayness, which both bored and exasperated readers and, more significantly, writers. The latter would soon throw off these self-imposed restrictions and turn to the New Novel.

Further reading

Abellán (1980), Alborg (1993), Blanco Aguinaga et al. (1978–79), Corrales (1971), Curutchet (1973), Domingo (1973). Fernández (1992), Ferreras (1970), Gil Casado (1973), Goytisolo (1959), Herzberger (1995), Martín Gaite (1994), Martínez Cachero (1985), Pedraza & Rodríguez (2002), Sanz (1972 and 1980), Sobejano (1970), Soldevila-Durante (1980).

II

REWRITING HISTORY AND MYTH

5

The Novel of the Spanish Civil War

SEBASTIAAN FABER

For over seventy years now Spanish novelists have struggled to turn their country's most recent civil war into literature. This task has not been easy. They have had to work under changing but always problematic circumstances that posed significant obstacles and burdened them with unusually heavy responsibilities. First, there was the war itself, which broke out in July 1936 after a group of right-wing army officers tried and failed to overthrow the left-wing government of the Popular Front. From the very beginning of the conflict, writers found that they themselves and their work were being used as propaganda in support of the war effort by one side or the other: the government (also known as the Republican or Loyalist camp) or the rebellious military (who called themselves Nationalists). The latter declared victory on 1 April 1939.

Next came the long dictatorship of Francisco Franco (1939–75). Characterized by censorship, repression, and enforced exile, as well as by the centralized imposition of a self-serving version of Spanish history, the Franco regime had a direct, and mostly negative, impact on literary production and distribution. At the same time, the severe restrictions placed by the state on Civil War historiography saddled novelists both inside Spain and abroad with an additional burden: many felt obliged to turn their art into the kind of faithful representation of the past that would normally be the task of an historian.

Finally, the dictator's death in 1975 and the transition to democracy three years later did not make things much easier. While the transition did liberate novelists from the restrictions of Francoist censorship, Spain's political class collectively decided to ignore the conflicts of the past, combining a blanket amnesty with a self-imposed form of political amnesia. Many Francoist officials kept their positions; none was held accountable for actions and complicities either during the war or after it; difficult questions about the country's past were not asked, let alone answered. This meant that, once again, the novel, together with the cinema, emerged as a crucial venue for representing and explaining the war to the larger public – and, where possible, for settling accounts, coming to terms with the past, and opening the way towards true reconciliation.

Daunting numbers on a daunting topic

In spite of these difficulties, hundreds of novelists have given it a try, and dozens more have made writing about 1936–39 their life's work. The product of their efforts, the elusive subgenre that has become known as 'the novel of the Spanish Civil War', has in turn posed a distinct set of challenges for Spanish literary history. For one, the sheer numbers are daunting. While the human and political consequences of the war were nothing short of disastrous – half a million dead, half a million exiled, a quarter of a million imprisoned, and almost forty years of dictatorial rule (Ealham & Richards 2005b: 3) – the war also proved singularly inspiring to writers and artists in Spain and beyond. In the mid-1980s one critic estimated that the Spanish Civil War had given rise to twenty thousand books worldwide.[1] A more precise and specific count is that of Louise Bertrand de Muñoz (1982–87), who for the period between 1936 and 1975 identified more than five hundred novels on the war written by Spaniards in Spanish – a number that has probably doubled over the past thirty years.[2] Even then, it can be argued that the relatively narrow, purely thematic criteria employed by Bertrand de Muñoz are too limited.[3] For the first three decades after Franco's victory there were few pieces of Spanish intellectual writing that did not, in some way, deal with the Civil War and its aftermath (Ponce de León 1971: 10; Sobejano 1970: 53). The war was such an omnipresent part of post-war life that even *not* mentioning it could be read as a statement. Censorship, moreover, often forced authors living in Spain to write about the war in the most oblique of ways. Some resorted to parody, allegory, and myth. 'Because the Franco regime prohibited all writing about the war other than glorification of the victors,' Janet Pérez notes, 'any portrayal of a different version had to be covert, even – or especially – if authors had ties to the regime'. Pérez (1990: 175) mentions the case of Gonzalo Torrente Ballester, some of whose works 'portray military revolts against the legitimate government that are followed by invasion, civil

---

[1]   Haubrich (1986: 21), quoted in Monteath (1994: vii). Preston (1986: 3) estimates that the war 'generated over fifteen thousand books'.

[2]   Mainer (2005: 103) has called the theme of the Civil War an 'ever-flowing spring'.

[3]   As she explains in her introduction (1982–87: 14), she only counts novels that explicitly deal with the war and do so in Spanish and in a fictional framework; she therefore excludes novels written in Catalan, Galician, and Basque, as well as short stories, 'autobiographies, memoirs, recollections, travel and historical stories, vignettes, reportage, as well as all the books that do not at least present an "appearance" of fiction'.

war, and a totalitarian dictatorship', although they are 'often camouflaged [...] as myth, fairy tale, or "history somewhere else"' – posing, that is, as 'harmless fiction unrelated to reality'. (Needless to day, most of these covert treatments of the Civil War do not make it into Bertrand de Muñoz's bibliography.) In some of the best-known works of post-war realist fiction, the war is the proverbial elephant in the room, conspicuous for its absence and yet inexorably present. Camilo José Cela's *La familia de Pascual Duarte* (1942) is presented as a peasant's memoir, written from prison, recounting an abject life set in the first third of the twentieth century and leading up, in 1937, to an act of political murder. Although the war itself is only vaguely alluded to, it is prefigured in the violence that permeates the text from beginning to end. In Carmen Laforet's *Nada* (1945), which narrates the coming of age of a female student in post-war Barcelona, the war is a similarly oppressive but barely mentioned backdrop.

Beyond the simple questions of numbers and definitions, the Spanish Civil War novel more generally defies the conventions of twentieth-century literary history. Scholars have tended to categorize that history along national and linguistic boundaries, to confine it to literature proper, and to construct a canon based on a notion of literary quality ultimately grounded in aesthetic considerations. Yet the literary impact of the Civil War has been much too international in character to limit its analysis to novels written in Spanish. How can we talk about Max Aub's six-volume Civil War cycle *El laberinto mágico* (1943–68) without considering André Malraux's *L'espoir* (1937) or Ernest Hemingway's *For Whom the Bell Tolls* (1940)? And how can any consideration of the Civil War novel afford to bypass works written in Catalan, Galician, and Basque, including key texts by Mercè Rodoreda (*La plaça del diamant,* 1962), Bernardo Atxaga (*Behi baten memoriak*, 1991), and Manuel Rivas (*O lapis do carpinteiro*, 1998)? In addition, a significant number of Civil War novels by Spanish authors are works of exile written, published, and read outside Spain – and not always in Spanish, either. Arturo Barea's trilogy *The Forging of a Rebel* (1941–46), for instance, a novelized autobiography culminating in the outbreak of the war, had been out in English for almost ten years before its first Spanish edition was published in Argentina in 1951; it was not published in Spain until after Franco's death.

Finally, most Civil War novels also transcend the narrow category of literature in its belletrist sense. Many derive their meaning and significance not only from their political charge, but also from their intertextual relationships with non-literary or non-fictional genres such as the essay, the pamphlet, the memoir, poetry, drama, reportage, political rhetoric, and historiography: relationships that range from symbiotic overlap to parodic defiance. This is true not only of the first novels to appear on the war – hastily written and published while the fighting was still in full swing – but also of much more recent works. Texts published before the end of the war, written by witnesses and active participants, tended to have a barely disguised autobiographical basis as well as a straightforward political slant, intended as they were to bolster national and international support for one camp or the other. Ramón Sender's *Contraataque* (1938), for instance, is a passionately pro-Republican memoir covering the first six months of the war. Significantly, its English translation, *Counterattack in Spain* (1937), was published before the Spanish original. The first novels to appear towards or after the end the war, both in exile and in Franco's Spain, generally continued to be conceived as part of the political struggle for national and international legitimacy. Agustín de Foxá's *Madrid de Corte a checa* (1938), for example, recounts the author's adventures as a Franco supporter in the Republican capital, while providing a novelistic confirmation of the new regime's image of the 'reds' as cruel, godless, and anti-Spanish.

A hybrid genre

Many later Civil War novels were also autobiographical in nature, and although they were not necessarily less political than earlier works, they did tend to be less Manichean and more balanced in tone. Sender's exile novel *Los cinco libros de Ariadna* (1951) covers the same period as *Contraataque,* but where the first book praised the Communists' role in the defence of the Republic, the latter account aims to prove that Stalin and his allies actually precipitated the Loyalists' defeat (McDermott, in Sender 2004: xi). Apart from the change in the author's political views, *Cinco libros* also presents a more nuanced and disenchanted view of the war itself. Barea's *Forging of a Rebel,* also written in exile, is a barely fictionalized autobiography in which the narrator presents his own life as a window into the tensions and dilemmas of recent Spanish history. Although he is pro-Republican, Barea's narrator is as skeptical as Sender's about any absolute adherence to particular political creeds. In practice, he has a hard time maintaining his ideological mettle in the face of the country's wholesale suffering and destruction.

If Barea and Sender occupy the middle ground between fiction and autobiography, another set of challenges is posed by Max Aub's six-volume *El laberinto mágico*, whose generic ambivalence exemplifies in a different way the problematic status of the Civil War novel. While not primarily based on any memoir, Aub's novels do have a distinctly historiographical dimension. A number of his characters are historical figures who appear under their real names, and most of his narrative follows history quite closely. Begun shortly after the Republic's defeat, *Laberinto*'s main objective is to make some kind of sense of the war while representing it in all its sweep, tragedy, chaos, and injustice. The miscellaneous nature of the cycle – five novels, a film script, and some forty short stories – is mirrored on a smaller scale in each individual volume. Rather than simple narratives, Aub's texts are collages of historical and fictional material, featuring literally hundreds of characters, and written with constantly changing voices and perspectives. A sprawling epic tapestry, in scope and ambition the *Laberinto* can be compared to Tolstoy's *War and Peace*. At the same time, it often comes across as fragmentary and unfinished. In cinematic terms, the reader has the impression of viewing the rushes rather than the final edit.

This jumbled form communicates a sense of urgency but it also adds to the realism of the text. The war is represented as chaotically as it was experienced. More important are the literary and philosophical dimensions arising from the cycle's peculiar form. Literarily, *Laberinto* expresses the impossibility of capturing the war in a simple, straightforward historical narrative. Philosophically, Aub refuses to distinguish between the central and the peripheral. This refusal is driven by an awareness that his writing will be used as a weapon against the oblivion and distortion imposed on Spain by the Franco regime. Indeed, parts of Aub's novels read as textual versions of a war monument, including long lists of the names and potted biographies of victims. Since Franco was bent on destroying every trace of Republican memory, and since there was no reliable historiography available, Aub felt he could not afford to leave out any event or character who might, under normal circumstances, have been excised for artistic reasons or the sake of concision.

A large part of the exiles' fictional production on the war was written with this same awareness that it carried the burden of representing the moral, political, and historical truth about the conflict in the face of Francoist lies or silence. Something similar is true for the Civil War novel actually published in Spain in the Franco period; as David Herzberger notes, 'there frequently exists a compelling desire to confront Francoist Spain and to scrutinize the Spanish past' (1995: x). In fact, narrative fiction became one of the few forms of expression to question or subvert the regime's narrow interpretation of Spanish history.

With Aub the sense of moral responsibility leads to an all-inclusive, chaotic war chronicle. Other writers, taking the opposite route, produced simple and stylized novels that, though set in the war, suggest more allegorical readings. This is true of Francisco Ayala's *La cabeza del cordero* (1949), a collection of five short, ironic texts that, rather than dealing with the war directly, attempt to place Spain's conflict-ridden and violent history into a more universal context. In Sender's short *Réquiem por un campesino español* (1953) the allegorical impulse is even stronger: individual characters come to represent collectivities and institutions, while the war's final meaning is produced through intertextual links with the Bible and with myth. The novel narrates the life of Paco el del Molino, an Aragonese peasant's son whose growing political awareness distances him from the town priest who has taken him under his wing. After the Civil War breaks out, Paco, by now a peasant leader, has to hide from the fascists; the priest, in a moment of weakness, betrays his former pupil. The description of Paco's execution evokes the crucifixion; and the novel ends up condemning the Church's complicity with Francoism as a betrayal of the ethical principles of the Christian faith. Allegory, to be sure, had been an important modality of war propaganda, allowing both camps to portray the conflict as a universal struggle between Good and Evil. These allegories by Ayala and Sender, by contrast, point to a much more depoliticized and nuanced reading of the war as a tragic and particularly violent manifestation of universal human flaws.

Categorizing the Civil War novel

Given the generic hybridity, historiographical ambition, and political charge of the Civil War novel, it seems inadequate to approach it through the traditional literary-historical paradigm – limiting, that is, the analysis to novels written in Spanish, published in Spain, and of proven literary quality. How, then, should it be approached? What kind of path can one track through the proliferating, multilingual, and geographically dispersed jungle of Civil War fiction? The most common forms of categorization employed by critics have been political, thematic, or chronological. For a certain subset of novels it makes perfect sense to classify them according to the political sympathies of their authors; thus we can speak of Francoist and Republican novels, and even of Communist, Anarchist, or Falangist texts. Then there are the novels set in the rearguard of the forces or at the front itself; stories focusing on the outbreak of the war, on victory and defeat, and so on. Ponce de León and Sobejano both establish categories based on authors' level of participation and role in the war. Thus Sobejano speaks of 'observers' in the rearguard, 'militants' at the front, and 'interpreters' who search for the conflict's larger meaning (1970: 54). A more general thematic parameter is a particular text's level of proximity to or distance from the war, in political, emotional, or intellectual terms. In this context it is easy to distinguish a chronological development. During the first years following the conflict, novels tended to be autobiographical, anecdotal, strongly grounded in historical events, and clearly identifiable with a particular political position. The passage of time and the appearance of new generations of writers has allowed for increasing levels of symbolization, projection, political plurality, and even humor.

In the Civil War production of the final decade of the century and the early years of the present one, the increased historical distance, combined with a renewed interest in Franco's victims, has given rise to a fresh kind of politicized sentimentality. A good example of this tendency is Dulce Chacón's *La voz dormida, which narrates the dismal fate of Republican women in Francoist prisons. Other recent novels have explicitly focused on the present

generation's relationship to the increasingly distant war years. Javier Cercas's
Soldados de Salamina (2001) and Andrés Trapiello's *Días y noches* (2000)
both feature writer-protagonists fascinated by a set of mysterious documents
that set them searching for an elusive historical figure from the war. Both
novels are driven by a desire to find out the historical truth – and in both cases
this leads to a decidedly revisionist version of the war – while at the same
time they question the feasibility of that enterprise. To make matters worse,
the texts themselves continually confuse the reader with smart admixtures of
history and fiction (Mainer 2005: 102–3).

Novels like those by Cercas and by Trapiello also point to ways out of the
dilemmas facing the literary critic who tries to get a conceptual hold on the
Civil War novel. Rather than continue to attempt to catalogue or classify the
confusing multitude of Civil War texts, it might be more productive to reflect
on the Civil War novel as a *problem*, for authors as much as for the reader and
the critic. In the remainder of this chapter we will review some of the ways
in which both groups have dealt with this problem, and propose an approach
that sees the Civil War novel as part of a much larger discursive struggle over
the representation of the war.

The challenge for the critic

Given the size of the corpus at hand, three of the main problems facing the
historian of the Spanish Civil War novel are delimitation, categorization, and
evaluation. With regard to the first, we have already seen how hard it is to
define what counts as a Civil War novel and what does not. The main problem
in relation to the second issue is that the thematic category of the Civil War is
itself more historical and political than literary, and that the selection criteria
traditionally applied in literary history, such as genre or style, only take us
part of the way. For the first three decades after Franco's victory it was much
more important whether a particular text reflected a pro-Loyalist or pro-
Nationalist stance – or, more specifically, whether it was pro-Republic but
anti-Communist, or pro-Nationalist and also pro-Falange – than whether or
not it was, say, structured as a *Bildungsroman* or narrated in the first person.[4]
Even more problematic is the issue of evaluation. How should a Civil War
novel's merits be judged? What determines its relative significance? As is

---

[4]   This is true for literary history as well. As Monteath puts it, 'scholarship dealing with
[Civil War] literature has itself been heavily politicized. Even the very first step in literary
scholarship, namely the choice of a subject of study, strongly bears the mark of political
ideology. The profusion of literature stemming from the war inevitably has required the formation of literary canons, but these canons vary quite noticeably depending largely on the political
persuasions of the author or scholar concerned' (1994: xi).

well known, since the nineteenth century literary historians have generally
been occupied with constructing a canon of works that they believe stand out
from the rest because of their literary quality, their popular success, or their
pedagogical utility – that is, their potential for producing a disciplined, nation-
ally identified citizenry (Nichols 2005: 253–69). Underlying this process is a
vague notion of natural selection: it is assumed that the 'test of time' assures
the gradual emergence of those texts that deserve to survive.

Assumptions like these have always been problematic (Ríos-Font 2005).
But they are even more so in the case of Civil War literature, whose production, distribution, and critical and popular reception have been anything but
'natural', driven and determined as they have been by political, linguistic, and
geographical factors. To mention only one of the most salient points: before
the removal of precensorship in 1966 not a single novel by any Republican
exile writer could be published in Spain (Thomas 1990: ix, 3). As a result,
even established literary critics in Franco's Spain long held wildly distorted
notions of the literary landscape, mistakenly stating, for instance, that it
took several years before authors dared to take up the war as a topic (Ponce
de León 1971: 14–19). Even apart from other distorting factors, issues of
accessibility (and Francoist censorship, in particular) have had a long-term
impact on what is and what is not generally accepted as the canon of Civil
War fiction: the texts, that is, that are most often studied and taught both
in Spain and abroad. Given the inertia of scholarly and pedagogical structures, as well as the particular dynamics of Spain's transition to democracy
(which discouraged clean breaks with the Francoist past in academia as well
as politics), that impact is still noticeable today. Together, these factors have
long privileged writers living in Spain, such as the best-selling José María
Gironella, over those living abroad, like Max Aub. Among the latter, those
who managed to outlive Franco, such as Ramón Sender and Francisco Ayala,
have had a definite edge over others like Paulino Masip, who died in 1963,
and whose outstanding Civil War novel *El diario de Hamlet García* (1944)
remains largely unread.

In addition to accessibility, a second major handicap in the literary-historical treatment of the Spanish Civil War novel has been the perceived need for
the critic to be, above all else, a judge of literary quality. Among other things,
this has led scholars to dismiss a sizeable contingent of Civil War fiction
as 'mere propaganda' and to qualify another, much smaller, group as 'true
literature' worthy of comment and analysis. The unquestioned assumption
underlying this binary distinction is that concerns other than those related
to aesthetic or narrative (politics, say, or history) almost necessarily detract
from the literary merit of a text. In general terms, the rejection of politics
or propaganda as antithetical to aesthetic or literary quality has led critics to
ignore the specifically political dimensions of Civil War texts, and to bypass
novels clearly identifiable with a specific partisan position in favor of texts

that portray the war from a more 'universally human' and presumably more 'objective' standpoint (Monteath 1994: xi–xii).[5] It could be argued, however, that the criterion of literary quality – linked or not to notions of objectivity – is inadequate, if not largely irrelevant, when it comes to determining the significance of particular works of Civil War fiction. Gironella's four-volume Civil War saga, for instance, is quite uninteresting from a literary point of view, apart from its monumental size and ambition. Largely set in the Catalan town of Girona, it presents a panoramic historical narrative from 1931 to the post-war period, covering both sides of the conflict, mainly through the lives of a single middle-class family. Gironella is so concerned with the completeness and political 'objectivity' of his account – a particularly daunting task at the time – that, in formal terms, he falls back on the conventions of nineteenth-century literary realism. The novel is told by a prolix, omniscient narrator whose fatherly but ironic and moralistic view of his characters is, like those of Galdós and Clarín, largely achieved through his use of free indirect style. This does not mean that Gironella's novels – *Los cipreses creen en Dios* (1953), *Un millón de muertos* (1961), *Ha estallado la Paz* (1966) and *Los hombres lloran solos* (1986) – were not hugely important. They were in fact the first novels published in Franco's Spain to attempt to provide three-dimensional representations of the vanquished instead of merely depicting them as members of a dehumanized 'anti-Spain'. The political significance of Gironella's approach is illustrated by its decidedly hostile reception by Francoist literary critics (Southworth 1963: 27).

Max Aub's counterpart to Gironella's magnum opus, *El laberinto mágico,* is more innovative in literary terms. But it is still easy to interpret many of the formal features discussed above as aesthetic flaws. Beyond aesthetic concerns, though, it can be argued that the supposed defects of Aub's work – its lack of structure, selection, or even resolution – are significant inasmuch as they lay bare a much larger political problem: as long as national divisions are left unresolved, it is impossible adequately to represent the Spanish Civil War. Aub's case also illustrates the conscious decision of so many Spanish writers to subordinate the literary to the historical and political. As he famously declared in 1946: 'I believe I do not yet have the right to be silent about what I have seen in order to write about what I imagine' (1988: 123).

---

5 Bertrand de Muñoz argues, for instance, that a writer's having lived through the war 'leaves a peculiar imprint on the novels: the intimate knowledge [...] facilitates no doubt the creation of atmosphere and truthfulness, but the fact that the author has been implicated [...] in the conflict ... reduces his objectivity, pushes him toward a sometimes exaggerated subjectivism, since it is difficult to judge such catastrophic events without passion' (1982–87: 26).

Political narrative

Spanish Civil War fiction, then, has been too much tied up with non-literary factors, especially politics, for us to see it as a merely literary phenomenon. It makes more sense to study the Civil War novel as part of a much larger discursive struggle over the interpretation of the bloody three-year conflict. That struggle, whose beginning practically coincided with that of the war, was fought tooth and nail in Spain, Europe, and the Americas, and was much less uneven than its military counterpart. At stake was the *meaning* of the war, its interpretative framework. And while the military conflict ended on 1 April 1939 with a declaration of Nationalist victory, even now, almost seventy years and thousands of books later, the discursive struggle over the interpretation of the war shows no signs of abating, either in Spain or abroad, either in the mainstream media or among professional historians.

The competing narratives are almost too many to list. Some have presented the war as primarily an international affair, either as a battle of democracy against fascism or of western civilization against communism. Others have seen the war primarily as a Spanish conflict, with some of them emphasizing the deep-seated socio-economic problems of Spain as a root cause, and others the particular make-up of Spanish culture and the Spanish 'national character'. On the Republican side, the most salient long-term dispute, still unresolved, concerns the role of the Communists: did their insistence on central control, their subservience to Stalin and Soviet interests, and their repression of spontaneous revolutionary initiatives strengthen or weaken the Republican chances of winning the war? What exactly were Stalin's plans and objectives in Spain? Within the pro-Nationalist camp, the Monarchists, Catholic traditionalists, and Falangists all have competing stories to tell. As Paloma Aguilar has shown (2002), over time the Franco regime skilfully adapted its narrative of the war to its changing needs and circumstances, shifting from the representation of the war as a crusade – at first religious and anti-liberal, later anti-Communist – to a notion of the Civil War as a national 'tragedy' or the result of a kind of 'collective insanity' that led brother to kill brother. It was this latter representation that helped configure the dynamics of Spain's transition to democracy, largely based on an agreement not to mention the past, let alone demand accountability for it.

Since so much of this interpretative struggle is about narrative, about how to tell the story of the war, it should come as no surprise that Spanish Civil War fiction has been playing a key role in it. Politicians, press officers, authors, and readers were aware from the beginning of fiction's potential for propaganda. In 1962, the Francoist writer Rafael Calvo Serer complained that, soon after the war, foreign writers helped tilt global public opinion in favor of the Republic. As we have seen, one of the main reasons fiction played such an important part in this evolving representation of the war was the relative weakness of Spanish historiography. While exiled Republicans lacked resources, had no access to archives, and were drawn into bitter internal disputes, historians in Franco's Spain were eager, or forced, to adhere to those versions of the war that satisfied the regime's ideological needs. In effect, Paul Preston has argued, Franco all but destroyed the historical profession (1993a). The paradoxical result was that, while novelists pursued historical truth, Francoist historiography was largely based on myth: that is, on fiction. A second result was that any text about the war, fictional or not, became inexorably politicized. Even if the author's intentions were not political, the reading inevitably was.

Statements of intent

To what extent this inevitable political charge and the novel's uneasy relationship with historiography pose a problem for authors is clear from the unusual frequency in Civil War fiction of prefaces, postscripts, and meta-fictional asides. Among the issues most often addressed in these paratexts are the story's relationship to actual history (authors often point to their own war experience, or their extensive use of historical sources and interviews); the role of fictional elements (for whose presence the authors tend to apologize); the general problem of truthful representation in literary form; and the larger moral issue of guilt and responsibility: which of the two parties is to blame for the war? Writers also feel the need to explain their intentions, and to frame these in intellectual, moral, and didactic terms: the authors' stated goal is usually that readers will reach an understanding of the war that in turn will make sure it never happens again (Ponce de León 1971: 43).

Thus, Gironella opens his first novel with an 'Essential declaration', in which he defends his choice to place his action in Girona, admits to taking certain liberties with history, and at the same time expresses the hope that his text is true to life in terms of characters and atmosphere. He also emphasizes that he trusts he has adequately represented, through his limited set of characters, the opposing 'psychological forces' that drove the country to civil war. In addition, he writes, he decided for didactic purposes to unite those opposing forces into one single character (2003: 9–11). By the second volume of the series, explicitly dedicated to 'All the dead of the Spanish war', the author has become more combative. In a second preface, he now presents his enterprise as an 'orderly and methodical response' to what he sees as the one-sided and otherwise flawed novelistic attempts by foreigners and Spanish exile writers: 'These works do not stand up to deep analysis. They are often unfair and arbitrary, and make the informed reader quite uncomfortable' (1962: 12). Gironella explains that, unlike his exiled counterparts, he has been able to reach a unique level of objectivity. What has allowed him to do so, he writes, is his temporal and spatial perspective, as well as his extensive study of the facts, including eye-witness accounts in books, newspapers, and archives. But especially important has been his caring attitude towards his fellow countrymen: 'I have tried to love without distinction every one of my characters, whether they were assassins or angels' (10–11). His ultimate goal is, he says, didactic: he hopes that his novel will help Spaniards become better informed about the circumstances in both camps, and that it will allow them to evaluate the war – a tragic 'struggle among brothers' – with less passion and more comprehension.

Max Aub had opened the first novel of his cycle, *Campo cerrado* (1943: 9), with the modest announcement that this was one of four projected novels to 'depict, in my own way, some events from our war'. In the last volume, published twenty-five years later, he inserts a set of metafictional 'blue pages' in which he confesses to the impossibility of this monstruous enterprise (2002: 396): 'Here you have thousands of pages and people. What good are they?' Aub is all too aware of the fact that even these thousands of pages give only a limited picture of the past: 'To give an idea of reality, the author would have to open up thousands of skulls, expose thousands of complicated thoughts. He cannot do that' (397). He also explains the formal features of his work: 'The novelist has tried to write a pure novel […], he has tried to reduce his chronicle and turn it into a true novel, but he has failed' (398).

In the long preface to *Cinco libros de Ariadna*, Sender not only stresses the novel's anti-Communist credentials, but advances a specific interpretation of the war with clear moral and political implications: 'We are all guilty for what happened in Spain. Some through stupidity and others through malice. But the fact that we (the better ones) were the stupid ones does not save us, either in the face of history or in the face of ourselves' (1957: 20).

Francisco Ayala uses his preface to *La cabeza del cordero* to advance a similarly non-partisan interpretation of the war. Skirting the issue of guilt or responsibility altogether, Ayala emphasizes that the war in Spain was simply a local manifestation of universal conflicts, 'the tremendous event in which it fell to us Spaniards to initiate the huge and violent change that has been inflicted upon the world' (1983: 18). Moreover, the war was an outward manifestation of internal conflicts, of 'the Civil War in people's hearts' (16). In the end, all participants, 'the innocent-guilty or guilty-innocent, have the weight of sin on their conscience' (17). Going one step further, Ayala suggests that Spaniards, having had an opportunity to 'plumb the depths of the human and contemplate the abyss of the inhuman', can now contemplate the world with 'serenity of mind' (19).

Stories for reconciliation

The extent to which the Civil War novel continues to be judged by different standards than regular works of fiction, even historical fiction, is clear from the debates surrounding Javier Cercas's immensely successful novel *Soldados de Salamina*. Published in 2001, when new generations of Spaniards were beginning to feel an urge to talk about a past that their parents and grandparents had preferred to ignore, the novel narrates a writer's search for a Republican soldier named Miralles who, at the end of the war, unexpectedly spares the life of a fascist intellectual. In the process of his search, the writer-protagonist comes to understand that telling stories is the best, and perhaps the only, way to pay homage to the heroism and suffering of individuals whose legacy would otherwise be forgotten: 'as long as I told his story, Miralles would in some way stay alive' (208).

Interestingly, the book itself pays tribute in this way not just to the noble Republican soldier but also to Rafael Sánchez-Mazas, the Falangist ideologue whose life he saved. As we read the story of Sánchez-Mazas's development and his involvement in the Falange, his political choices are, if not forgiven, then at least explained with a certain measure of understanding. The novel's relative empathy for Spanish fascism did not sit well with certain critics, who, as Mainer explains (2005: 103), were particularly concerned with the way in which the novel seemed to suggest a sense of moral equivalence between the character of the Republican soldier (who in the novel goes on to become a World War II resistance hero) and that of the Falangist. It seemed to them that the novel turned an act of 'legitimate pardon' on the Republican side into 'a mutual, almost sportsman-like amnesty'. Such a level of compassion and forgiveness, some readers felt, was not appropriate, even in a novel, until there had been some more official condemnation or admission of guilt.

The discussion around *Soldados de Salamina* suggests that Spain is still not quite ready to treat Spanish Civil War fiction as just that, as fiction. Some thirty years after the transition to democracy, the nation still has not overcome the divisions of the war and its aftermath. The question that needs to be addressed is what role fiction can play in the still ongoing process of national reconciliation. Cercas's narrator, as noted above, points to the crucial role that storytelling can play in this process. It is true that there is probably no better mechanism than narrative fiction to help people see the world from others' points of view and to understand their actions, and that to do so is a first step towards forgiveness and reconciliation. The fact, however, that seventy years' worth of novels about the war have not yet managed to bring about that stage of reconciliation suggests that more might yet be needed. Perhaps the Civil War novel cannot become 'just fiction' until Spanish society, following the examples of South Africa, Chile, and Argentina, has gone through a much wider political and judicial process of coming to terms with its own recent history.

Further reading

Abellán (1977), Aguilar (2002), Calvo (1962), Cunningham (1986), Epps & Fernández (2005), Hart (1988), Herzberger, (1995), Iturralde (2000), Monteath (1994), Nichols (2005), Orwell (1967), Ponce (1971), Preston (1986 and 1993b), Rosa (2007), Thomas (1990), Ugarte (1989), Valis (2007).

6

The Novels of Luis Martín-Santos and Juan Goytisolo

STACEY DOLGIN CASADO

From the early 1960s through the decade following Franco's death in 1975, a group of left-wing Spanish writers published novels which integrate three interdisciplinary theories related to the ongoing plight of the alienation of contemporary man: (*i*) Karl Marx's socioeconomic theory of alienation (1984a); (*ii*) Roland Barthes's theory of the linguistic method by which the ruling class naturalizes social myths for the purpose of mass consumption, followed by his proposed 'demythifying' process by which the self-serving intentions of social myths may be unmasked (1957); and (*iii*) the eclectic, new realism of the German playwright, poet and literary theorist, Bertolt Brecht.[1]

The result is an amalgam: a novel that is both a story and one that debunks myths. Between 1961 and 1973 several such works attempted to counteract the rhetoric associated with the Franco regime: national supremacy, the notion that liberalism and individualism were unpatriotic, the myth of Spain's *Siglo de Oro* (or Golden Age), the code of honor, the bullfight as national spectacle, the concept of sexual decency, the Spanish State and Catholic Church as a single indissoluble entity, and so on.

The best known novelists involved in this assault on received wisdom are Luis Martín-Santos, whose only completed work, *Tiempo de silencio* (1961), initiated the sub-genre of the socio-critical realist novel, and Juan Goytisolo, whose adherence to the principles of literary demythification spans nearly two decades and who wrote five such works: *Señas de identidad* (1966), *Reivindicación del conde don Julián* (1970), *Juan sin Tierra* (1975), *Makbara* (1980) and *Paisajes después de la batalla* (1982). Jesús López-Pacheco,

---

[1] For a fuller discussion of these three theories and how their interrelationship operated in Spanish novels see Dolgin (1991). There are some excellent studies dealing with the theme of alienation in Martín-Santos' *Tiempo de silencio* (especially Rey, 1977), and in Juan Goytisolo: most notably Ortega (1972), Cox (1973), Levine (1976), and Ugarte (1982).

Pablo Gil Casado, and Luis Goytisolo each produced one such novel: *La hoja de parra* (1973), *El paralelepípedo* (1977) and *Fábulas* (1980), respectively.[2] We shall concentrate here on the novels of Luis Martín-Santos and Juan Goytisolo.

Thanks to the economic, cultural and political instability of the 1960s, the focused and objective social realism we find in works of the previous decade is supplanted – initially by Luis Martín-Santos – by a subjective approach concentrating on the psyche of the characters involved and replacing plain, accessible language with periphrasis and a more convoluted literary style which we might call neo-Baroque.[3] Among the demythifying novelists' most effective tools is ironic contrast, a technique familiar to readers of seventeenth-century Spanish poetry and satire. Visually, the reader is caught off-guard by the striking contrast between long, periphrastic sentences and short, pithy dialogue. Punctuation is often reduced to the use of colons for stringing together phrases otherwise syntactically unlinked, or else there is an overabundance of commas that serve the same purpose. Within this looser syntax, writers juxtapose and superimpose contrasting images or situations (for example, a conservative, traditional one with its contemporary opposite) and employ rhetorical devices such as polysyndeton and asyndeton, anaphora, hyperbole, and meiosis.

In novels such as these, alienated protagonists are presented *in medias res*, as they seek to reconcile a perceived incompatibility between their individual and social identities. The protagonist's fragmented self reflects a society that is fragmented and heterogeneous. By the same token, the paradoxes, inconsistencies, and anachronisms of the wider society provide a reason for that sense of a fragmented identity. The character's arduous search for coherence, both as individual and as social being, lends these novels a universal dimension that goes well beyond their immediate setting and allows the author to deconstruct social myths (historical, cultural, political, economic, religious, sexual, and so on) that are centuries-old and that have caused him to become estranged from his background, his family and class values, and denied him any sense of individuality and personal freedom. The ideology nurtured by

---

[2]   This list is not exhaustive. With the exception of Luis Goytisolo's *Fábulas*, the works that appeared after the death of Franco attack multinational myths associated with powerful groups: *Opus Dei* in the case of Gil Casado's *El paralelepípedo*, and automation and consumerism in that of Juan Goytisolo. *Fábulas* demythifies from a postmodern critical perspective the notion of progress and wellbeing as the social goal of modern society and government since the Enlightenment. Goytisolo suggests that this quest for progress and wellbeing has finally proved counterproductive, causing alienation, loneliness, depression, and the others ills associated with excessive economic and professional stress, as technology has replaced human interaction, the negative effects of environmental pollution have affected the food chain, and so on.

[3]   Gil Casado (1973) details the complex economic and cultural factors behind Martín-Santos's reorientation of the Spanish social novel of the Generation of 1954.

the social and economic structures of society serves the interests only of the powerful oligarchy that runs that society, while the masses are relegated to the status of consumers and commodities to be exploited for the benefit of the ruling classes. The authors we shall discuss attempt to develop new versions of prevailing myths in order to debunk those that serve the purposes of the ruling class. These surprise and may initially repel the reader because of their unfamiliarity, but, by doing so, they serve to distance that reader from the text and thereby prevent him from empathizing with the characters or identifying with them. By preventing the text from becoming an emotional or cathartic experience, the author induces the reader to approach the novel both intellectually and critically. For example, in his scathing demythification of the prevailing Spanish ethos in *Reivindicación*, Juan Goytisolo seizes upon the myth of the fifteenth-century Queen of Castile, Isabella 'the Catholic', as the prototype of Spanish Catholicism, nationalism, and austerity, and places her in a contemporary setting. Dressed in a revealing black negligee, the Catholic Queen prays to the rhythm of the Rolling Stones, engages in self-flagellation, and invites a group of tourists to tour her body as a symbol of the foreign (phallic) penetration of Spain by the Moors in 711. In this manner, Goytisolo compels the astute reader to recognize the arbitrary relationship between the mythical signifier and signified and, thus, to reassess what once would have been accepted as a causal, factual, and inductive correlation between the two.

Mythical concepts (the signifieds, in linguistic parlance) are ahistorical. Hence, a concept will appear to different generations in the guise of different images (signifiers), and this allows the demythifying authors to effect a metonymic association between characters taken out of their historical context, such as the Catholic Monarchs Ferdinand and Isabella, and figures from a totally different context, such as General Francisco Franco. They can be shown to share certain objectives, such as the suppression of heterodox racial, religious, and ideological groups, and to have justified that oppression in the same way, invoking the need for national and religious unity. In *Juan sin Tierra*, for example, Juan Goytisolo illustrates the paralysis induced by social myths in a most extreme way. His novel is a collage of transformed images and concepts (signifiers and signifieds) whose shared sign (signification) is contradiction. The author-narrator repeatedly asserts a principle and then denies it by stating the complete opposite of what he just asserted. The purpose is to demythify Western Civilization's obsession with the notion of production-for-consumption. He contradicts every assertion before it is even absorbed. The best example of this technique appears in the final pages of the work, where the narrative dissolves into Arabic script, an assertion of noncommunication which has the effect of casting aspersions on the point of the previous three hundred pages.

The third cornerstone of novels of this kind is the eclectic new realism of

Bertolt Brecht. The German playwright's concept of socialist-realist literature is Marxist (and hence anti-bourgeois), emphasizing as it does the inherent contradictions of life and the role of social literature in presenting man as capable of bringing about social change. To this end, Brecht opposed the Aristotelian concept of dramatic unity leading to a cathartic experience: 'Such an audience,' he argued, 'may indeed leave the theatre purged by its vicarious emotions, but it will have remained uninstructed and unimproved' (Esslin 1961: 124). In his view, the audience should not be made to feel emotion but, rather, to think both dispassionately and critically. In place of a classic, well-made play, he proposed an epic theater whose primary goal was to maintain the audience in a uncomfortable, estranged mood *vis-à-vis* the spectacle before it. Directors were to utilize any means at their disposal to minimize the chance of audience identification: 'The audience must be discouraged from losing their critical detachment by identification with one or more of the characters. The opposite of identification is the maintenance of a separate existence by being kept apart, alien, estranged' (125). If this distancing of the audience from the spectacle was successful, it would prevent the spectators 'from seeing the conflict from the point of view of the characters involved in it and from accepting their passions and motives as being conditioned by eternal human nature. Such a theatre will make the audience see the contradictions in the existing state of society; it might even make them ask themselves how such a society might be changed' (143).

The novelists we are discussing stand in relation to the novel much as did Brecht to the theater of his day. Just like the Baroque moralists referred to earlier, each and every one of them is concerned primarily with the invisible reality that lurks beneath surface; for all of them, that surface, that apparent reality is just a smokescreen concealing the true reality within. In the novels of Martín-Santos and Juan Goytisolo, the reader has to struggle with a multitude of technical and linguistic devices that serve to expose the desolate reality that lies within. This neo-Baroque style of presentation imitates the way in which social myths operate and the dialectical quality of reality. Images appear and reappear in continuous transformation; each new transformation carries something of its previous appearance while simultaneously adding some new dimension or form. For example, in *Reivindicación*, the narrator assumes in turn the transformed identities of Álvaro Mendiola from *Señas*, a modern-day version of the historical figure Count Julián,[4] the grandmother-wolf in the 'Little Red Riding Hood' story, and the snake charmer who commands his serpent to strangle Alvarito, the child-self whom

---

4   Spanish ballads and legends depict Count Julián as the traitor who facilitated the Moorish invasion of Spain in 711. Goytisolo inverts the traitor myth by re-inventing himself as a new Count Julián whose mission it is to revitalize modern Spain by destroying the age-old anachronistic stigmas he deems responsible for Spain's stagnation and decadence.

he must destroy in order to liberate himself from Spain's cultural stigmas. Each successive transformation presents the narrator in a different guise, but on every occasion he debunks the story in question.

In the specific case of *Tiempo de silencio*, the author opts for a fairly simplistic plot centering on the spiritual and professional death of a young and ambitious medical student, Pedro, on whom society has turned its back. His odyssey within and around Madrid in pursuit of a personal goal – to obtain the mice he needs to continue his cancer research as a necessary step towards his qualifying as a practising doctor – serves as a pretext for Martín-Santos to plunge into the psyche of his central character and thereby into the collective consciousness of Madrid and, by implication, that of the entire Spanish nation:

> This is how we are able to understand that a man is an image of a city and a city the viscera of a man turned inside-out, for in his city a man defines himself not only as a person and understands why he is as he is, but also discovers the many impediments and the unsurmountable obstacles that prevent him from realizing himself. (1981: 16)

Pedro's fragmented self is revealed as he is ostracized from each and every sector of Madrid society for the simple reason that he made a well-intentioned, but fatal, mistake: unlicensed to practice medicine, he performed an abortion on a young, pregnant girl who was hemorrhaging. When his attempts to save her life were unsuccessful, he was held responsible for the tragedy and imprisoned. Exonerated by the girl's mother and freed from prison, he resigns himself to the fact that the scandal has destroyed his professional future in Madrid. The novel concludes as he sits on a train taking him to his new rural post, a symbol of his professional and personal demise.

The novel is diffuse mainly because the plot unfolds piecemeal and is presented as the outward manifestation of an internal reality, a symptom of a pervasive mental illness. Psychoanalysis (and Luis Martín-Santos was a psychiatrist in a mental hospital in San Sebastián) examines the symptoms of mental illness as a way of establishing its cause, in the belief that the elimination of the cause will cure the condition. The structure of the novel resembles that psychoanalytic process as it seeks to redress the mutually dependent causes of the alienated state of a man (Pedro), a city (Madrid), and a country (Spain). One feature of life in the Spanish capital is that a majority of residents come from elsewhere: 'It would have been better if you had never come from your small town, because here you are like an out-of-towner' (17). John Lyon summarizes these two distinct, and yet mutually related forms of alienation experienced by the protagonist: 'The alienation that Martín-Santos explores in his protagonist, Pedro, involves not just a failure to relate to things outside himself, such as certain social values and assumptions, but an internal division, a failure to reconcile his actual conduct with what he believes he should be doing' (1979: 77). In essence, then, Luis Martín-Santos is here exploring the devastating consequences of an individual's dependency upon a social order that is impervious to the needs of the individual. His novel demonstrates how social structures predetermine individual and collective beliefs and behaviors and ensure the perpetuation of the status quo: 'Thus the general atmosphere generates the individual response and the individual response perpetuates the general atmosphere. The individual both forms and is formed by the society he lives in' (71).

Juan Goytisolo, whose career as a novelist spans five decades, was born in Catalonia; his work has been the subject of more critical attention than perhaps that of any other contemporary Spanish novelist. Beginning with *Señas de identidad*, he explores the theme of the alienated author-narrator-character in search of a coherent identity. His characters' alienation is presented from multiple vantage points; by using first-, second-, and third-person narrative, he establishes the psychological fragmentation of his characters, while he uses other voices – those of the established order resounding within – to illustrate their estrangement from the world around them. Frequent narrative shifts produce dichotomies of the subjective and the objective, or the individual and the collective, and these turn the author-narrator-character's individual dilemma into a representative portrait of a wider alienation in society itself; as the protagonist discovers the social forces that have denied him his individuality and effected a chasm between what society demands and what the protagonist wants for himself, his individual case of alienation comes to be seen as a microcosm of the wider alienation in society at large. Both he and society become at one and the same time the victim and the perpetrator of the economic, social, political, religious, and sexual myths within a given culture (Spain, or Western civilization, more generally) whose collective effect is to prevent man from realizing both his unique individuality and his essential humanity.

Both the thematic consistency we find in the five Goytisolo novels listed and their increasing emphasis on the universal implications of alienation for modern man, explain why they are technically so similar, and also why he gradually came to abandon characterization in the traditional sense. Taken together, the five novels constitute a wide-ranging *Bildungsroman* covering the development of an individual (Goytisolo's fictionalized, autobiographical self), a nation (Spain in *Señas*, *Reivindicación* and, to some extent, *Juan sin Tierra*, where the protagonist's landlessness is an allusion to the homeland), and global society (*Juan sin Tierra*, *Makbara* and *Paisajes*). This extensive *Bildungsroman* describes the dialectical nature of alienation; the solution to any one form of estrangement inevitably leads to another. For example, at the end of *Señas*, the narrator-protagonist opts for self-exile. On the first page of the next novel, *Reivindicación*, the reader discovers that he has carried out his plan and is now away from his homeland, struggling to acclimatize himself to his new, African home. His method of coping with his plight is a sporadic intake of hashish; the stimulant has the effect of inducing hallucinations, and these lend verisimilitude to his numerous metamorphoses throughout the novel. From this novel onwards, the narrator-protagonist, as well as the secondary characters are the product of his drug-induced state (Alvarito's mother and Queen Isabel, in *Reivindicación*; Vosk in *Juan sin Tierra*; and the woman who appears in *Makbara*).

Goytisolo debunks myths through ironic contrast and hyperbole. Throughout his works we find a number of dichotomies woven one with another: the social myths of national achievement created and perpetuated by the established order and contrasted with the depressing realities that they are meant to conceal; sexual repression contrasted with promiscuity, homosexuality, sodomy, and onanism; Catholicism alongside atheism; Apollonian rigidity linked with Dionysian frivolity; and human mechanization in the overdeveloped world (Pittsburgh in *Makbara,* Paris in *Paisajes*) contrasted with the simple, instinctive existence of the despised third world. There are others. He reveals the absurdity and dehumanization of man's automated, depersonalized existence in a society governed by bourgeois, capitalist values, and he does so by exaggerating the free-spirited, hypersexual, 'natural' existence of the people of the underdeveloped world.

Señas focuses on the life of a photographer, Álvaro Mendiola, who returns to Spain with his wife after ten years of self-imposed exile in Paris. At the time of his return to his home near Barcelona, the protagonist is suffering from a heart condition. The narrative present develops over three August days in 1963, beginning late on a Friday afternoon and ending that Monday morning. The fact that Álvaro is close to death stimulates him to try to recall the key events in his life that have led to his current sense of failure, emptiness, and solitude. By speaking to himself and about himself, most of the time in the second person, the narrator progressively effects a synthesis of Álvaro's personal identity and Goytisolo's own objective social criticism. That synthesis provides a wide-ranging personal account of post-Civil War Spain.

The narrator-protagonist of *Señas* seeks this integrated sense of himself because his worsening heart condition finds him on the point of death, and it is this which triggers his existential crisis. As he strives to assemble the jigsaw-puzzle pieces of his life, he achieves an awareness of its meaninglessness and of the mediocre, complacent values of his social class – the Catalonian bourgeoisie – which have shaped every fibre of his being through the medium of language: 'It is better to live among foreigners who express themselves in a language that is strange to you than to live amidst fellow countrymen who daily prostitute your own native language' (420). His search for a meaningful identity leaves him in a vacuum, in the ultimate alienated state of being as evidenced by the opening words of Goytisolo's following novel, *Reivindicación, spoken as Álvaro contemplates Spain from his terrace in Tangier where he resides as a self-exile: 'Ungrateful homeland, the most spurious and wretched of them all, I will never return to you' (11). The protagonist's hallucinations preclude externally induced sensorial experiences; his mind generates its own realities whose internal coherence is provided by his attack on his sacred homeland. Throughout the novel, his mind is engaged in chimerical acts of 'inventing, composing, lying, storytelling' (13) for the purpose of committing acts of treason against 'the enemy shore' (68). For example, Spanish historiography has perpetuated the myth of Count Julián as a notorious traitor. In response, Álvaro sets out to invert the myth; he fantasizes himself as a newly reborn Count Julián who seeks to revitalize Spain's stultifying and anachronistic cultural stigmas, 'sweeping away the false order, revealing the truth behind the mask, gathering your strength and your donjulianesque invasion plan: grand treason: the ruination of centuries: the cruel invasion by Tariq, the destruction of sacred Spain' (1970: 52). The fictitious identity of this second, contemporary Count Julián is marked by repeated acts of subversion aimed at undermining Spain's caste system and dismantling the rigid, intolerant, and inhumane values to which it gives rise. In this way, Goytisolo aligns himself with Américo Castro's attack (1968) on the attitude of Spanish Catholic national superiority which denied the profound part played by Arab and Jewish influences in the development of national cultural identity. Following Castro, he also points to the forced exile of the Jews decreed by the Catholic Monarchs in 1492, and the later partial exile of the Moors in the early seventeenth century as marking the beginning of Spain's rapid decline. Like Castro, Goytisolo is deeply concerned with Spain's *morada vital*: the sense of identity the nation has conferred upon itself.

In many respects, *Juan sin Tierra* is a synthesis of the two-stage dialectical process of cultural restitution we have seen at work in the two previous novels. On the one hand, the self-exiled narrator-protagonist of this, the third novel in the series, continues to be haunted by 'the hoarse voices coming from the country that you despise' (1975: 63), while, on the other, his principal target this time is global. This is a work of transition, in which the novelist attacks contemporary man's enslavement – and his concomitant alienation – by and to the consumer myth. He looks at the problem from the mutually dependent perspectives of both oppressor and victim: 'Yours is a unique civilization, condemned to live for the purpose of procreation!: producer and consumers identifiable by a single indelible stigma, like different creators of the same game' (129). The anonymous narrator of *Juan sin Tierra* utilizes both his human and literary self to debunk the consumer myth; in the process, he establishes an intimate connection between the concepts of production-for-consumption, sex-for-procreation, and terrestrial-life-for-eternal-life. As unrelated as these concepts may at first appear to be, their sustained inter-connection throughout the novel points to a broader, underlying similarity between them, and this is, ultimately, the theme of the work: the alienation that results when the value of a human being is measured by what he or she produces for something or someone else. In order to lay bare the alienation of contemporary man in a consumer society (any consumer society), the narrator presents himself as a detached observer without any particular background or culture – a mere narrative voice – searching for a universal sense of what human life is actually about and how to express it. His self-conscious literary and sexual rebellion produces a narrative whose only point of reference is its own genesis and development. Paradoxically, the reader is consuming a text that wantonly exposes its own nakedness and its unsuitability as a consumer object. It boasts (*i*) a nihilistic narrator who is neither a by-product nor a consumer of any particular culture; (*ii*) a novel that plots the strategies of its own destruction in that it appeals to none of the human categories by means of which a reader is able to perceive a coherent, fictional world dictated by cause and effect; (*iii*) a text which impedes the reader's acquisition of vital linguistic and mythical signs by keeping him or her embroiled in the process by which those signs are produced by an arbitrary collision of signifier and signified; (*iv*) a work that muddles the social problem under attack – aliena-tion – with the methods employed to expose it; and (*v*) a open-ended narrative that dissolves into Arabic, rendering the text incomprehensible even to the most educated reader of Spanish.

In the fourth and fifth novels in the series, *Makbara and *Paisajes, the author continues to wage his campaign against the alienation of contempo-rary man by means of self-referential discourse. In *Makbara, the deformed, dark-skinned narrator-protagonist is a storyteller in a Moroccan marketplace. For his livelihood he depends entirely on the money he gets from those who listen to his stories, and his only other pleasures come from the fulfilment, however imaginative that may be, of his sexual urges. Conversely, the dark-complexioned narrator-protagonist in *Paisajes is a middle-class, educated columnist living in Paris, who has withdrawn from all social contact except fantasized sex with young girls and clandestine meetings with third-world underground figures. Both novels take issue with the alienating social struc-tures that have resulted in man's marginalization, irrespective of the economic class or nationality to which he or she belongs. Both narrator-protagonists seek to add a human dimension to their solitary lives by fabricating sexual encounters and social activism in ways that underscore the impossibility of any meaningful human relationship, and then by telling (*Makbara) or writing (*Paisajes) about them as a means of self-confirmation. Despite their socio-economic differences, both characters' autobiographical accounts become an wide-ranging social testimony whose narrative structures and techniques debunk the myths surrorunding the affluent and mechanized economically advanced world, while all the time contrasting it with the meager hand-to-mouth subsistence economies of third-world countries which the richer nations exploit. In a word, they denounce the inequity of global wealth distribution, with its inevitable dehumanization and alienation of both rich and poor.

In conclusion, the narrators-protagonists of novels of this kind are alter-egos of socially committed authors who seek to dismantle the mythical structures that underpin bourgeois society. Their fictional search for identity is presented as the product of specific factors in their lives. Particular events bring about a shift in a character's self-perception, and, in consequence, that character suffers from a sense of estrangement both from himself and from society. By way of response, the authors concerned (most notably Luis Martín-Santos and Juan Goytisolo), resort to any and every literary strategy – traditional or innovative, real or fantastic, objective or subjective, narrative or lyrical – which can help them to captures man's internalization of a *milieu* of which he is the alienated by-product. These authors-narrators-protagonists see their own sense of estrangement as the direct result of social myths to which a self-serving minority has enslaved them in the name of national unity and social order. These are non-conformist writers who see their artistic mission as that of inspiring a heightened state of social consciousness in their readers as a necessary precursor to effecting a change in the existing hierarchical structures of bourgeois society.

Further reading

Anderson (1978), Bieder (1981), Blanco-Aguinaga (1975b), Cox (1973), Dolgin (1991), Epps (1966), Gil Casado (1981), Goytisolo (1978), Humphrey (1968), Labanyi (1985 amd 1989), Maravall (1986), Martínez Cachero (1979), Navajas (1979), Ortega (1969 and 1972), Pérez (1987), Pérez Firmat (1981), Pope (1995), Rey (1977), Saludes (1981), Sánchez Vázquez (1980), Schaefer-Rodríguez (1984), Ugarte (1981 and 1982), Zulueta (1977).

7

Post-War Historical Fiction

DAVID HERZBERGER

Nearly all the historical fiction published in Spain during the Franco years (1939–75) can be fully understood only in the larger context of the writing of history during that period. While it is clear that Franco used raw military power to win the Spanish Civil War and to establish his regime by force, the need to sustain his authority and legitimacy over time required other and more elaborate mechanisms. One of the most compelling was the regime's attempt to assert control over the history of the nation, to make history an instrument of the government's own progamme – in other words, to exploit history as a source of power. This entailed a number of coercive practices – regulating academic appointments in history, controlling funds for research, creating publishing venues for books and journals, censorship, and so on. Above all, it meant that the regime sanctioned a historiography that defined Spain as a unified nation whose essence grew from the Christian reconquest of the Iberian Peninsula beginning in the late eighth century and culminating in 1492. The origin of the nation was thus located in the heroic deeds of Christian warriors who defined and defended Spain against all that might threaten it. In this way of thinking, the Francoist regime was part of a continuum, along with the imperial Catholic Spain of the past, and fully embodied Spain's historic destiny. For Francoist historians it was as if history in 1939 had come to its inevitable and perfect climax, with the new Spain of Franco representing a return to the nation's glorious past too long forsaken by those in power.

Since historians of the regime asserted their authority over narration of the past, and since they made the truth and meaning of history largely the private property of the State, any narrative that set out to represent the past of Spain necessarily stood in some relation to the historiography of the regime. Much historical fiction of the period is necessarily polemical, because it is written explicitly or implicitly against the grain of the predominant discourse of Francoist historians. As a result, the historical novel during the Franco period to a large extent addresses not only historical events *per se*, but is also intimately concerned with just how the past can be known, with the nature of storytelling, and with the contingencies of historical meaning. These novels are therefore less focused on contesting Francoist historiography on the terrain of fact, disputing what may or may not have occurred at one historical moment or another, than they are on emphasizing the ways in which narrative constructs meanings about the past and is shaped by the needs and wishes of the storyteller.

One of the most compelling forms of historical fiction during the Franco years emerges from the desire for demythification of both the historical events portrayed and the way in which those events are represented (see Chapter 5). Francoist historians generally set out to write history as a form of myth whose primary goal, as Roland Barthes has observed about myth in general, is 'to immobilize the world' (1972: 155). In other words, myth establishes a set of beliefs about the past as asserted by the regime, and these in turn are set forth as unassailable truths. Such a view is embodied by what Pérez Embid (1949: 149) termed: 'the permanent meaning of the history' of Spain, and by Calvo Serer's insistence (1949: 161) that 'it is unthinkable to have more than one Spain'. Within this scheme of permanence and unity, Spanish history is created and sustained by a powerful metadiscourse whose purpose it is to preclude any reinvention or representation of the past from alternative, unsanctioned perspectives. Not surprisingly, however, many Spanish novelists do offer a counterview of history that aims precisely at demythifying the Francoist representation of the past and its foundational core of beliefs. Such novelists perceive both the Francoist version of events and the strategies of mythic narrative not only with skepticism but with disdain.

Demythification and history

One of the most widely read post-war novels in which a contempt for Francoist historiography emerges forcefully is Juan Goytisolo's *Señas de identidad* (1966), the first in a trilogy of novels tracing the life of Álvaro Mendiola. Goytisolo's concern with history in the novel is two-fold: first, he sets out to show how narration of the Spanish past cannot be contained within a story told from a single perspective and with a single purpose; and, second, he refuses to endorse the myths of either faction of the Civil War (the victorious Nationalists or the defeated and exiled Republicans), since both groups sought to assert themselves as the single, authentic voice of Spain. In his criticism of each, Goytisolo shows how strategies of narration determine meaning. For example, to a large extent *Señas* is overrun with texts from both the past and the present. Álvaro draws upon photos, postcards, maps, letters, government reports, and other documents to stitch together his family's biography (from the nineteenth century to the present) within the larger context of Spanish history. The various texts collated are suffused with meanings based upon the contexts in which they are placed, and in this way they confirm that the meaning of history is always contingent and changeable.

Goytisolo's strategy is patent on a number of occasions in the novel, but none more poignantly than in the series of juxtapositions in the final chapter, where the author specifically undermines the language through which the Franco regime has laid claim to the past. As Álvaro listens to fragments of tourist conversations in foreign languages while viewing Barcelona through a telescope, he reads a pamphlet outlining the official history of the city. Fragments of each text are absorbed into the others to produce a tainted view of both the present and past of Spain that belies the official version put out by the regime. The point in this case, as elsewhere in the novel, is to show how mythic history has been constructed on the basis of a particular desire or need of the government to control the past, but that it is easily reconstructed when other desires and needs are asserted. Goytisolo does not lay claim to the truth (or falseness) of the myths, as Álvaro examines the history of Spain, but instead emphasizes that meaning is always impermanent.

Juan Benet (1927–93) is one of the more important and complex novelists to engage Spanish history in novels and essays on the nature of historiography. What shapes all of his writings (both fictional and non-fictional) is his insistence that narration itself structures and gives meaning to history, whether the so-called facts of the past are being represented or an imagined past is being set against the real. Benet's documented history of the Spanish Civil War, *¿Qué fue la guerra civil?* (1976), challenges the Francoist version of specific events during the Spanish Republic and the military strategies of the war, but it is in his novels that he most unsparingly seeks to demythify and undermine the official past.

Benet's subversion of history occurs in matters both large and small. For example, in his 1967 novel *Volverás a Región* he explicitly proposes that chance and indifference, rather than any intense commitment to ideology, often determined the make-up of opposing forces in the Civil War. His imagined town of Región, which sees heavy fighting between Republican and Nationalist armies, further suggests how personal vengeance and incompetence were more important than were ideological factors in determining the outcome of the fighting. While readers would be hard-pressed to distinguish between the prose of Benet's fact-based *¿Qué fue la Guerra civil?* and his fictional depictions of the Civil War in *Volverás a Región* (both draw on the referential capacity of language and the details of military strategy to represent the past), the idea of history in Benet's novel is quite different from that dictated by regime. Above all, and in strong contrast to Francoist historians' insistence on the heroic and mythic past of Spain, Benet sees history here as a wholly destructive force. Indeed, as he writes in the novel, the people of Región 'have opted to forget their own history' (1985: 11), but, more importantly, they view the past as consisting of 'everything that we are not, everything that has been wasted and failed' (301). These are key passages in Benet's fiction because they encapsulate the way his characters embody and envision the past. First, Benet makes it clear that the residents of Región are conscious of being actors in the very history that they reject. Above all, however, he shows in *Volverás a Región* and throughout his fiction that to live historically means to bear a grim burden: the burden of a past that inevitably led to present ruin. This explains the desire to forget that is shared by the characters and it also provides the conceptual impetus for his use of the metaphor of the diseased body to define Spain and its history. While Francoist historians see the body of historical Spain as healthy and productive, and predict progress growing out of the myths of empire, unity, and destiny, Benet paints Spain and its history as suffering from a tragic and terminal illness.

Benet explores the nature of Spanish history most fully in his fiction in the three-volume *Herrumbrosas lanzas* (1983–86), which presents Región as it was in both the nineteenth and twentieth centuries. More importantly, he is here reflecting on the nature of writing history as well as on what readers might actually be led to believe about its capacity to recapture the past. He includes documents, footnotes, letters, and maps in his narrative, all of which reveal a desire for facts upon which to build a historical narrative as well as enhancing the illusion of authenticity and truth. Benet's approach makes it appear that he adheres to a concept of writing history in *Herrumbrosas lanzas* that is not all that different from that used by historians of the regime.

But of course it is only a grand illusion. For while the 'objective' presentation of data seems to lend an air of reliability to the narrative, all the other aspects of the work subvert it. Rather than offering a single perspective from a unified perceiving subject whose goal is to restrict ambiguity, Benet's narrative is continually so imprecise that it undermines any faith in the existence of a preeminent and logical truth about the past. He achieves this indeterminacy by inserting enigmas at the core of the novels and by employing a number of technical strategies, such as contradictory and multiple explanations for an event, an emphasis on the plot requirements of storytelling, and recurrent oxymoronic constructions that collapse the paradigms of myth established by the dominant historiography of the regime. Benet thus avoids the complacency that comes from a full and coherent view and also denies his readers any certainty or unitary meaning for the events related, leaving them with an uncertain and hence polysemantic view of the past. As the narrator of *Herrumbrosas lanzas III* remarks, in what is perhaps the most succinct rendering of Benet's thinking on the writing of history: 'Most assuredly, the final verdict concerning such a frequently disputed fact is not found, nor will it be found, in any one place, because for each moment history has many explanations' (1986: 123). In this way, he prevents any mythic underpinning of history in his novels and challenges at every turn the Francoist version of history. What he offers in its place is a past fully open to rearrangement, re-presentation and, ultimately, reenactment.

Metafiction and history

At first glance, it may seem that metafiction and history ought not to be talked about in the same context. After all, metafictional works generally set out to reveal the inner workings of their composition in order to insist upon their nature as fiction. Further, they seem to distance themselves from the realist illusion that a novel is (or is able to be) a faithful reflection of a real world beyond the text. Yet, far from eschewing metafictional constructs, many Spanish novelists embraced them in the 1970s and 1980s as a way of asserting their claim that historical writing entails more than telling a story that is embedded naturally and obviously in the facts of history and then simply brought to life by the writer. Indeed, the use of metafiction in the historical novel grows from a desire to show the constructed and contingent nature of what we know about the past.

Recuento (1973), the first instalment of Luis Goytisolo's tetralogy entitled *Antagonía*, illustrates this point. The main character, Raúl Ferrer Gaminde, proposes to write a novel about himself and his friends during the 1950s and '60s. For the most part, *Recuento* then becomes a discussion of how to do that. Raúl rejects the assumption of realistic novelists that they can imitate the real world, and instead proposes to involve extratextual elements through narrative construction. This decision is especially pertinent to the writing of history. Through Raúl, Goytisolo shows in *Recuento* that the received history of Spain (the history, that is, written by historians of the regime) is based on facile historiographical assumptions about the nature of narration and how it enables us to understand the past. For example, in a long and complex sequence at the end of Chapter VII, the narrative recounts the history of Catalonia and Spain. Here, as elsewhere in the novel, the self-referential focus of the narrative undermines the foundations on which the mythic history of the regime has been built. The narrator in this instance proposes 'an intricate history' (1973: 278) of Spain that recognizes the diversity and dissent inherent in the very nature of writing. More importantly, through the protagonist, the novel proposes that subjectivity and narration constitute the foundation of all historical writing. In *Recuento*, Goytisolo proposes multiple historiographical meanings rather than a single truth. Further, these meanings are linked to a narrator who is bound up with the past through the double projection of his self and his view of history. As Goytisolo shows, nothing can be preserved and then evoked about the past without its passing through the filter of the subjective and narrative demands that are the very essence of writing.

Goytisolo clearly asserts here that, for Raúl (and for the writing of history more generally) the meaning of history is not 'given' by a perceived chain of events; rather it is wholly constructed. This construction takes place within the crucible of the self (the perceiving subject) and is projected onto the world by means of narration. Thus, when Raúl contemplates his novel in relation to history, he rejects 'the heroic prose of his militant period' (626) when his defence of the Communist Party echoed in many ways the historical writing and mythic perspective of the regime. Fully conscious now of his task as a writer, he proposes that the voices and mechanisms of narration can open up history to the inevitable subjectivity that lies beyond the reach of the particular goals and myths espoused by official historiography.

Metafiction also shapes the representation of history in one of the most widely read novels of the post-war period, Carmen Martín Gaite's *El cuarto de atrás* (1978). The narrator of the novel, a fictional Carmen, has vowed to write two novels: one in which she will explore the history of post-war Spain and the other based on Todorov's theory of the fantastic. When a mysterious (and perhaps imagined) man dressed in black visits her one night, she seems to have written, during the course of her conversation with him, a novel entitled *El cuarto de atrás* that fulfils both these promises. The novel clearly lays out for the reader its strategies of composition, from the intention to place uncertainty and ambiguity at the core of the narrator's experience of the real to the understanding that history as taught in Spanish schools and universities is deformed by deceit. Her reflections on her own past are often tied to the past of Spain, and she grows to understand how she has been deprived of that past by being force-fed the history written by supporters of the regime.

From Carmen's perspective, the way in which the reign of Isabel la Católica and her influence on Spanish identity are taught to students best exemplifies this mythic version of the past. Francoist historians linked Isabella to Spain's glorious past, portraying her as the visionary mother of the nation who made Christianity the cynosure of all that would become quintessentially Spanish. As Carmen puts it, 'They told us how she held the ambition and the despotism of the nobles in check, how she had created the Holy Office, expelled the traitorous Jews, and gave away her jewels to finance the most glorious undertaking in our history' (1978: 95). The narrator of *El cuarto de atrás* recounts these myths not because she believes them, but to expose them as tools of official historiography aimed at exerting strict control over the past and its relationship to the present. In contrast, the metafictional thread of the novel compels us as readers (and as interpreters of history) to become aware of the indeterminate and fragmented nature of the past and of the meanings constructed by various narrative strategies. Memory, narration, ambiguity, desire, and need are among the forces that shape the writing of history, and Martín Gaite's novel suggests the open-endedness of the past within a narrative that itself is malleable and open-ended.

Memory and history

Novels of memory (fictions that evoke the past through subjective memory, most often with a first-person narrator) come to the fore in Spain in the late 1960s as a way of exploring a past largely eschewed by Francoist historiography: the lived past of the Civil War and the dissent that both led to the conflict and persisted in its aftermath. Juan Goytisolo's *Señas de identidad*, Luis Goytisolo's *Recuento* and Carmen Martín Gaite's *El cuarto de atrás* can be seen in this context. Each seeks to draw elements of the past into the present as narrators define their own identity in relation to Spanish history, and each explicitly engages with Francoist historiography as a negative point of reference for the proper understanding of history as many-voiced and indeterminate.

One of the most complex novels to link memory and history is Antonio Muñoz Molina's *El jinete polaco* (1991). Published sixteen years after the death of Franco, by which time Spain had emerged as a modern Western democracy and member of the European Union, it stresses the persistence of history as a critical component of the Spanish novel. Muñoz Molina's work evokes the Civil War and the desire to forget the past that characterized much of Spain during the early years of democracy. As many critics and historians have pointed out, 'disremembering' the past grew into a central tenet of political and cultural life in Spain following Franco's death. It became convenient (many argued necessary) to forget the Civil War and forty years of oppression when what was needed was a new and forward-looking programme to promote progress and modernization. Indeed, many Spaniards claimed that the past was no place to find the future; hence the desire in many intellectual and political circles to control personal and collective memories for the good of a new democratic Spain that would emerge unfettered by any complications arising from recent history.

This is precisely the premiss that informs the actions of the individual at the center of *El jinete polaco*, and it is a premiss that is quickly shown to be both impractical and harmful. The protagonist, an international interpreter named Manuel, has attempted for nearly two decades to isolate himself within the present by wilfully forgetting everything that happened in the past. In other words, he has sought to live outside history. However, when he returns to his hometown of Mágina, he is forced to recall his own past and to evoke the lived history of the Civil War, the Franco regime, and what he has always thought of as the vacuous period of transition to democracy.

In a town and in a family overrun with memories, ancestors, images, and stories of the past, Manuel cannot for long maintain his isolation in the present. Thus, while the novel begins with a compulsion to annul the past, it shows just how impossible this is to achieve. Remembering quickly becomes important for Manuel, and through it he compensates for the absence of history.

The war, his youth in post-war Spain, and later the transition to democracy are each pregnant with meaning as they move in and out of his consciousness, often as he browses through photographs of the past. He comes to understand how historical forces have shaped his life, but he learns at the same time that these forces are often beyond his control.

What is most important about history for Manuel, however, and indeed what takes pride of place in the novel of memory in general, is the recognition that our knowledge of the past not only grows as we learn more but it grows also as we narrate and remember it. While for many members of Manuel's family the past represents a deadweight that stultifies and stifles, Manuel eventually understands that the past provides a sense of continuity and permanence in their lives as they both remember and tell stories about it. These may not bear reliable witness to what actually happened in the past, but they allow individuals to define themselves with reference to the past and so incorporate many versions of the past into the living present. Manuel's conscious recollection of all that he had once renounced is muddled, uncertain, and contingent. But these turn out to be only small vexations, as history rescues him from oblivion. Remembering and narrating the past ultimately merge into a single process and neither of them can exist independent of the other. It may be that a process like this threatens the authenticity of history by suggesting why and how we can never know everything about the past. But for Manuel, and for the novel of memory as a whole, such reclamation of the past is a risk worth taking.

Women narrators and the distant past

With the exception of Isabel la Católica, women most often exist on the margins of written Spanish history, especially during the early years of the unification of the Iberian Peninsula and the birth of Spain as a nation. Women as objects of historical representation, as well as women whose voices shape our understanding of the Spanish past, have indeed traditionally appeared only fleetingly in either fiction or historiography. However, as the Franco regime drew to a close with the death of the dictator in 1975, and as Spain moved quickly to redefine itself as a progressive and modern country fully integrated into Europe, many perspectives on culture in general, and on the Spanish past in particular, begin to emerge. Women narrators and women writers gained a new prominence with the emphasis on the recent past; examples of this are Josefina Aldecoa's trilogy: *Historia de una maestra* (1990), *Mujeres de negro* (1994), and *La fuerza del destino* (1997). Two novels that focus on the more distant past, however, have attracted attention for their compelling representations of women as both object and voice of their narrations: Jesús Fernández Santos's *Extramuros* (1978) and Lourdes Ortiz's *Urraca* (1982).

Fernández Santos's novel revolves around the lesbian relationship between two seventeenth-century nuns living in a convent experiencing severe financial hardship. Narrated by one of the nuns, the novel focuses on the amorous relationship between the two women and the other nun's intentional cutting of her hands to represent the wounded hands of Christ. However, her stigmata become part of a deliberate deceit, as she tells the community that the wounds were made by divine intervention. The miraculous sign of Christ's blessing draws attention to her and the convent, while the drought and plague that have afflicted the area begin to attenuate. The nun is soon hailed as a saint, but the narrator declines to reveal the truth about the wounds, fearing that she and her lover will be separated. Eventually the fraud unravels and both nuns are punished.

Within the somewhat sensational focus of the plot of *Extramuros* lies an intense interest in history. The first-person narrator gives voice to religious mysticism in the context of earthly love between two women, but equally importantly she places herself in the context of the Inquisition and the other sociopolitical structures of seventeenth-century Spain. The conditions of the time include some of the most devastating in the country's history: economic depression, heavy taxation, starvation, and disease all serve as historical forces which establish the conditions for a religious 'miracle' associated with her fellow nun's rise to eminence. The historian J. H. Elliott has shown how Spain was in the 1600s divided into two classes, the rich and the poor, and that the big difference between them was the amount of food that they had to eat (1963: 307). The nun who narrates the story is clearly swept up by her confusion between mystical and carnal love, but she is also fully aware of the social disparities of the time and of rampant poverty. By means of the narrator's historical contextualization of her dilemma we are led to picture a nation in full decline. When the poor are punished for defying the laws decreed by the king simply in order to survive, and when the Inquisition in all its ruthlessness is evoked as enjoying absolute authority over moral and religious transgressions, the official Spain of the seventeenth century can easily be linked to the Spain of Franco, as the pervasive climate is one of terror. What makes this view new and persuasive is, of course, the fact the narrator of this society in decline is herself a woman: a marginal figure further marginalized by prohibited love. The narrator exhibits no postmodern angst as she seeks to justify her behavior, but her narrative capitalizes on a modern way of looking at things that allows a woman to speak about Spain and her own place within it.

This writing into the historical record of a woman's experiences, and the way in which those experiences shape history, is even more startling in Lourdes Ortiz's *Urraca*. Narrated by Urraca, who lived from 1080 to 1126 and was the first Queen of the Christian kingdoms of Leon and Castile, the novel recounts her life and times from a perspective that gives her authority and identity as both subject and object of the story. More importantly, she engages history through the creation of a story of her own, offered in the guise of a chronicle that quickly turns into autobiography and challenges both the form and the content of traditional historiography. As she puts it at the beginning of her narrative: 'A queen needs a chronicler, a scribe capable of transmitting her deeds, her loves and her misadventures, and I, here, enclosed in this monastery, in this year of 1123, am going to become that chronicler' (1991: 10). She thus affords herself the opportunity not only to write herself into a story, but to write herself into a history whose truth and meaning she will seek to control.

Urraca's historical perspective depends primarily on defining both herself and medieval Spain against the grain of received orthodoxy. This means above all that hers becomes a gendered writing of history, one that shuttles back and forth between chronicle and apology for her actions in a society dominated by men and by their stories of power. Urraca is by no means loath to assert her power as actor and chronicler: she recounts her struggles to win and sustain control of her kingdom through both erotic desire and brutality as she alternately sees the need to use first the one then the other. From her father Alfonso VI she learned, as she explains, the value of both. Much of the novel then consists of her story as told to her interlocutor, the monk Roberto, in a manner that reveals her intelligence, her ruthlessness, and above all her willingness to secure power at nearly any price. She assigns herself a variety of roles (queen, mother, wife, and political warrior) and in each of these pits herself against the historical forces of her times. From a contemporary perspective, of course, we are able to measure Urraca against the figure of Isabel la Católica, the queen who ruled Spain nearly four centuries later. While Isabella was elevated to heroic, even saintly grandeur by Francoist historiography for uniting Spain under Christian rule and imposing strong central authority, Urraca's reign, as she tells it in her own voice, entails treachery and an instability marked by short-lived alliances and sexual dalliance. Urraca thus clearly locates herself in the midst of turbulent political and historical conflicts that she at one and the same time sought both to instigate and to restrain.

Above all, the world that Urraca constructs in her writing is deeply rooted in something that was hotly rejected by mainstream Spanish historiography for many centuries: the essential hybridity of Spain as a nation born of many cultures. Rather than represent medieval Spain as a space divided between Christians and Moors, each defined and bound by difference and conflict, Urraca's narrative shows us a world in which Christians, Jews, and Moors not only lived together but enriched each others' cultures in ways that are at variance with the traditional historical narrative of difference, implacable enmity and conquest. The many characters that appear from these cultures in Urraca's narrative (including the beautiful Moor Zaida, mother of Urraca's step-brother Sancho) pointedly tell of a Moslem society in many ways superior to that of her father's own court. Yet what the Spanish historian Américo Castro termed *convivencia*, or 'living together', most directly describes Urraca's view of her times: the essence of Spanish history, as well as its identity, grows not from the unifying imposition of Christianity on diversity but rather from a commingling of cultures that allowed diversity to engender a richness unique to Spain and central to its national identity.[1]

Spain and its multicultural past

While *Urraca* gives prominence to the diverse foundations of Spanish history (gender, race, culture), it is hardly alone over the past two decades in challenging the monolithic view of Spanish national history that had long held sway. The compulsion to absolute unity in all things that characterizes the Franco years now gives way to a desire to explore those other cultures from the past that have for so long been excluded. It is a process which ensures that history continues to play a prominent role in Spanish fiction. In a survey conducted in 1990 by the literary periodical *Ínsula*, several writers were asked to identify dominant trends in current Spanish fiction; nearly all of them pointed to the centrality of history, especially the tendency to open the past to new perspectives. Antonio Muñoz Molina's *Sefarad* (2001) is one such novel that peers into history to present a picture of Spanish Jewry from fifteenth-century Iberia to the twentieth-century Holocaust in Nazi Germany. The novel turns on two closely related conceptions of history and of how it may be written. First, Muñoz Molina roots his narrative in the imagined community of voices in Sefarad (the name Jews gave to Spain in the Middle Ages), at the same time linking those fictional voices to the real personal histories of Spanish Jews (the horrors of Sephardic Jews sent to concentration campus during World War II, for example. or the suffering of the Jews in Russia during the 1930s and '40s). Second, he draws attention within the narrative to both the fictionality of history and the historical accuracy of stories (so important in the Jewish tradition), so that his novel becomes a hybrid that conveys the story of Spain as a hybrid nation. That is to say, *Sefarad* is 'a novel of novels', as announced on the title page, but also a documented representation of the past, as indicated by the bibliography that the author includes in an Afterword.

As Muñoz Molina sees it, Spain can be understood fully only by recog-

---

[1]   Américo Castro developed his idea of *convivencia* over many years and in a number of books. The last and most complete development of the concept can be found in his masterwork (1971).

nizing the cultural differences it has accumulated and assimilated throughout
history. He sets out in *Sefarad to represent Jewish otherness (which in so many
ways has marked their community throughout history), but he does so only to
represent its continuity over time so that it cannot be ignored or excluded as a
component of Spain's past. Multiculturalism and its consequences (including
the trauma experienced by those whose lives are constantly at risk when they
are perceived as a threat to a desired or imposed homogeneity) are given
voice and substance through a narration that itself is multi-voiced. Thus, the
hybrid form and content of the novel work together to produce an exploration
of the undeniable hybridity of national history.

This same sense of the diversity that lies at the heart of Spanish history
shapes the narrative of *Moras y cristianas* (1998), a novel written by two
women authors, Ángeles de Irisarri and Magdalena Lasala. Here a series of
loosely related stories of Moorish and Christian women are woven into a
tapestry of the social history of medieval Spain. Offered primarily as a series
of portraits of individuals and professions (slaves, intellectuals, prostitutes,
religious women), the work at once suggests both the cultural difference
between Christians and Moors and the symbiosis between them. The attention to detail in such matters as the daily life of a slave or of a noble arises
from a keen nose for historical accuracy, and is clearly designed as a textual
strategy to alert the reader to the referential base (both temporal and spatial)
of the novel and to establish its historical authenticity. Medieval objects and
their uses, customs and mores, as well as forms of entertainment in both
cultures move to the fore and serve to impress on the reader that this is a
text grounded in fact. More importantly, however, the authors offer a fusion
of Christian and Moorish cultures that points to a new set of historical meanings and works in a way not unlike that of a metaphor. That is to say, just
as metaphor turns upon a writer's ability to perceive likeness in difference
in order to place seemingly disparate words or images in the same semantic
context (and thus create a new way of looking at something), so Irisarri and
Lasala set Christian and Moorish cultures beside one another and, out of their
apparent dissimilarities create a new way of looking at Spanish culture and
history. This result is reminiscent of the *convivencia* of cultures described by
Américo Castro, but it goes further by creating a fictional story that forces
the reader to look afresh at the past. The historical agenda we find in novels
like *Urraca* and *Sefarad* with their depictions of a multicultural society, has
now come to constitute an important feature of the historical fiction written
in recent years as part of a re-presentation of the Spanish past.

It is both impractical and unfeasible, short of formulating a schematic list
of novels and novelists, to take full stock of all the issues affecting historical
fiction in Spain over the past six decades or so. It is hard enough to put the
historical novel itself, and the use it makes of history into neat, discrete
categories. One might easily add to the writers discussed here such authors

as Arturo Pérez Reverte (with his series of novels on the fictional swordsman Captain Alatriste, which depict history in seventeenth-century Spain); Eduardo Mendoza (in novels such as *La verdad sobre el caso Savolta,* 1975, and *La ciudad de los prodigios,* 1986, portraying social upheaval in late nineteenth- and early twentieth-century Barcelona); or Manuel Vázquez Montalbán (in works such as *Galíndez,* 1990, about the disappearance of a Basque nationalist in 1956, or *Autobiografía del General Franco,* 1992, which addresses important historical events in the latter half of the twentieth century). In much of their writing these authors have used history as a key component of plot as well as a critical determinant of character development and social criticism. Yet none of these writers forms part of a particular movement or has a narrowly drawn view of the past.

In broad terms, however, the historical novel written during the Franco years strains against traditional historiography and in doing so offers a dissident perspective to counter the orthodox, monolithic, and Christian view of the nation used to underpin the authority of the regime. Following Franco's death, the writing of history has afforded new opportunities to broaden our insight and understanding of the past, especially as the political context for critical enquiry no longer demands a single, unitary perspective. During this period novelists have continued to explore the history of Spain in two main ways: first, by countering the tendency of Spain's nascent democracy to disremember the recent past; and second, by opening the more distant past up to multi-voiced and multicultural enquiries of a kind largely eschewed during the Franco period. As a genre, the historical novel explores ways in which the past can be represented, which bits of the past should be reconstructed, and the meanings that might be given to them. In this sense, novels of this kind engage with time and history to scrutinize the slippery terrain between narration and truth. Above all, history in the Spanish novel written after the Civil War is portrayed as mutable and contingent. In the context of a nation where history was viewed for much of the twentieth century as an instrument of power, the novel demonstrates the power of fiction to offer an array of stories about the past, as well as lending them serious and potentially useful meanings.

Further reading

Bertrand (1996), Boves (1996), Buckley (1996), Carr (1986), Carrasquer (1970), Colmeiro (2005), García de Cortázar (2003), Herzberger (1995), Hutcheon (1988), Irisarri & Lasala (2002), Lukács (1976), Medina (2001), Middleton & Woods (2000), Pons (1996), Pulgarín (1995), Resina (1994), Romera *et al.* (1966), Soldevila-Durante (1989), Suárez Cortina (2006), White (1987), Williams (1992).

8

Spanish Detective Fiction as a Political Genre

JOSÉ F. COLMEIRO

One significant aspect of the development of detective fiction in Spain in the latter part of the twentieth-century is its emergence as a political genre. The modern Spanish detective novel, and the urban thriller or *novela negra* in particular, has been used by Spanish writers, both during the Franco regime and since, as a vehicle for social observation and cultural criticism, to voice dissent and disagreement with the prevailing political ideology.

The new Spanish *novela negra* often subverts the traditional detective story, with its firmly roots in the idea of preserving bourgeois legal and social order and punishing transgression. Detective fiction is traditionally teleological, ending in the triumph of reason and stability and the reinstatement of narrative and social order. On the other hand, the *novela negra* tends to offer a destabilizing view of crime in society, exposing and criticizing repression, punishment, and social control, and focusing instead on the underlying social and political causes of crime. Rather than celebrating the reimposition of the status quo, as the traditional detective novel does, the *novela negra* questions the rationality of the prevailing social order, of the justice meted out by courts, and of the ethics of the police force, offering instead a moral critique of the shortcomings of ordered, capitalist society.

From timid beginnings in the 1950s and '60s, detective fiction grew in confidence during the last years of the Franco regime, and began to explore social issues and shifting moral values, as well as memories of the Civil War, questioning the status quo, investigating political and economic power, and offering a more or less camouflaged political allegory or indictment of the Franco dictatorship. Contrary to the traditional Marxist view of the alienating effect of detective novels and other forms of popular fiction which reinforce conservative cultural values, the new detective story resorted in Gramscian fashion to taking a popular cultural genre and infusing it with a with a heterodox message. The detective novel offered an opportunity for the writer to present a veiled critique of the dictatorship, affording oblique glimpses of economic injustice, social inequality, the lack of freedom and human rights, economic corruption, and the repressive police and legal system of the dictatorship.

The earliest sign of this trend can be seen in *El inocente* (1953), a highly literary story by Mario Lacruz often considered the first Spanish *novela negra*. *El inocente* offers an implicit denunciation of police and state repression, and of the psychological alienation that is the product of living in a police state. While the action of the novel was transposed to a fictional place and characters were given vaguely exotic names in order to avoid censorship, it is not hard to relate the climate of obsessive fear and anguish represented in the novel to the reality of post-war Spain. By presenting an indirect criticism of police corruption, torture and brutality, state oppression, and the lack of human rights, this work is the first clear instance of the Spanish detective novel being used as a political genre. It was to provide a model for subsequent Spanish authors of detective fiction.[1]

During the dictatorship a small group of dissident writers from Catalonia, including Manuel de Pedrolo, Aurèlia Capmany, and Jaume Fuster, resorted to writing detective novels in Catalan as a form of protest at Francoist repression of Catalan language and culture. Capmany published *Vés-te'n ianqui! o, si voleu, traduït de l'americà* (1959, revised 1980), a clever and ironic metafictional work with veiled political overtones. It uncovers the hidden links between police corruption, organized crime, and political dictatorship in a fictional Albania, exploring the dangerous territory between 'Tirana' and 'Valona', easily understood as Madrid and Barcelona. Capmany's second foray into the genre, *El jaqué de la democràcia* (1972) is an innovative and experimental novel stretching the conventions of the *novela negra* to their limit. It is a metaphor for the social and political turmoil of 1920s Barcelona (this time 'Salona' in the novel), and is a clear precursor in both theme and literary technique to Eduardo Mendoza's widely acclaimed *La verdad sobre el caso Savolta* (1975). The detective investigates the mysterious deaths of a wealthy industrialist and a labor leader, and in the process he uncovers an underworld of political intrigue, anarchist movements, and counter-revolutionary mercenaries. The real protagonist of the story is the city, its landscape, and the human conflict in its streets. As in Dashiell Hammett's Poisonville, the violent, corrupt, and treacherous atmosphere of the urban underworld predominates. In similar fashion, Pedrolo published a series of crime thrillers during the post-war period, *L'inspector fa tard* (1954), *Joc Brut* (1965), and *Mossegar-se la cua* (1967), which, although less overtly political, nevertheless implicitly criticized living conditions in Franco's police state, its corrup-

---

[1] For more detailed analysis of Mario Lacruz's novel, see Bértolo (1984); Hart (1987: 26–36), and Colmeiro (1994a: 140–51).

tion and injustice, and its victimization of the innocent.[2] Towards the end of the Franco era, Jaume Fuster published his first detective novel *De mica en mica s'omple la pica* (1972), a realistic depiction of contemporary Barcelona that afforded glimpses of corruption among the political and economic elite. In a more explicit and realistic way than the other two writers, Fuster offered his readers a depiction of the absence of any basic rights among the Spanish working class, who were forbidden to join a union or go on strike, issues that clearly resonated in the political and social context of 1970s Spain.

At the same time as these modern experimentations with the urban thriller in Catalonia, a much more traditionally Spanish approach emerged in central Castile. The case of Francisco García Pavón is an anomaly in the development of Spanish detective novels with a socio-political subtext written during the dictatorship. Instead of experimenting with urban and/or foreign locations, hidden political symbolism, or veiled social critique, García Pavón opted for a brand of rural detective fiction that was all his own, emphasizing the quaint and the picturesque. Written mostly in the late 1960s and early 1970s, his detective series features Plinio, a police inspector from the small town of Tomelloso in La Mancha, a self-confessed *paleto*, or country bumpkin, proud of his origins and at odds with everything about the modern world. Pavón's novels, frequently nostalgic for an idealized past identified with the Second Republic, reflect (and oppose) the policy of rapid industrial growth, or *desarrollismo,* favored in the 1960s and characterized by rural industrialization, urban migration, and consumerism. They depict the rapid cultural transformation of Spain from an agrarian to an urban society in the last decades of Francoism. The most obviously political of his novels, and for many critics his best, is *Las hermanas coloradas* (1969), a mixture of detective fiction and what is known as *costumbrismo* (sketches of typical local customs) with the addition of a new historical and political twist: after the general pardon for all Civil War political 'crimes' offered in 1969, thirty years after the end of the conflict, stories from the past started to emerge, among them several about republicans who had lived in hiding for many years for fear of reprisals by the regime. *Las hermanas coloradas* was the first novel to deal openly with the issue of men and women who had made themselves prisoners in their own homes, and they were seen as a metaphor for all those living an inner exile in their own homeland under the dictatorship. While the Plinio novels were a highly successful series with critics and the public, especially after receiving the prestigious Premio Nadal in 1969 and their subsequent adaptation into a popular TV series, interest in Plinio declined after the restoration of democracy, and the stories of rural *paletos* became

---

[2]   For further reading on Catalan detective fiction written during the dictatorship, see Hart (1987) and Colmeiro (1989 and 2002).

more anachronistic and came to be regarded as out of touch with a rapidly modernizing Spanish society.[3] Contrary to Briones García's contention that the Spanish detective novel only started to restore historical memories of the past in the 1980s (1999), and Godsland and King's argument that only in the 1990s did it actually start to investigate that past (2006), *Las hermanas coloradas* is an explicit attempt to investigate and restore fragments of the past erased from the collective memory.[4] This is a novel which demonstrates that the key to solving the mysteries of the present lies in uncovering hidden stories from the Francoist past, something which we will see again and again in novels of the transition by Manuel Vázquez Montalbán, Andreu Martín, Eduardo Mendoza, Juan Madrid and Jorge Martínez Reverte in the 1970s and 1980s.

With the transition from dictatorship to democracy, the detective novel metamorphosed in Spain from a popular genre, widely considered a subcultural product of little serious importance, and one largely neglected by critics and demonized by intellectuals, into a new hybrid form, a mix of urban thriller, investigative journalism, and political exposé, which was embraced by many respected authors and in turn gained a wide readership and the recognition of the literary community and the cultural industry. In the mid-1970s, at the time the Franco regime was beginning to collapse, two Spanish authors in particular, Manuel Vázquez Montalbán and Eduardo Mendoza, pioneered the political use of detective fiction to explore openly current as well as historical social issues that had been off-limits during the dictatorship. Detective fiction became an ideal medium for criticizing the legacy of Francoism, as the political transition began to expose the shortcomings of the regime. So it was that the forgery of a counterfeit historical past, the corruption of the financial elite, and its connections with the corruption of the legal system and the police force, all surfaced as frequent themes in the new *novela negra*.

Mendoza's *La verdad sobre el caso Savolta* (1975) is widely credited with inaugurating the postmodern novel in post-Franco Spain. This is a work characterized by narrative fragmentation, the interplay of high and low cultures, parody, and pastiche, and the ironic questioning of orthodox narratives, including that of history. *El caso Savolta* offered a refreshing mix of some of the innovative narrative strategies of the experimental 'new novel' of 1960 and 1970s, and a new-found interest in traditional and popular genres (the suspense and violence of crime fiction, the episodic structure and ironic view of the picaresque, among others), as well as historical narrative. The

---

[3]   For a closer analysis of the Plinio novels, see Marqués López (2000) and the introduction of my edition of García Pavón (1999: v–xciii).

[4]   The many efforts by Spanish writers to recover historical memories of the war and the post-war period are discussed in detail in Colmeiro (2005).

novel follows the investigation of the collapse of an industrial family, the Savoltas, and it turns into a complex historical panorama of the social and political climate of the Barcelona of the late 1910s and early 1920s, exposing social turmoil, the establishment of anarchist worker movements, and the ensuing police repression. The novel furnished a fresh and vivid portrait of the social and political movements of an epoch that had been silenced during the years of Francoism. In the process, *El caso Savolta* breathed renewed life into the moribund Spanish novel, even winning the prestigious Premio de la Crítica.

Mendoza later returned to the detective genre with three other novels, the highly original *El misterio de la cripta embrujada* (1979) and *El laberinto de las aceitunas* (1982) and almost 20 years later the largely derivative *La aventura del tocador de señoras* (2001). All are set in contemporary post-Franco Barcelona and feature an unnamed maverick detective, a deranged modern-day *pícaro* constantly in and out of mental institutions and police stations. Highly parodic in tone and playful in nature, these novels, particularly the first two, offer an insightful and hilarious dissection of Spain's transformation during the political transition, as seen from the abnormal, almost surreal perspective of this investigator. As such, they offer a radical critique of the legacy of Francoism through an exploration of the internal workings of Spanish institutions, particularly the legal system (still largely in the hands of Francoist police and judges) and intellectual and scientific institutions (Catholic schools and mental hospitals from the *ancien régime*). In *El misterio*, the investigator goes back and forth between three places – the prison, the school and the mental hospital – all of which are targets of the most intense social criticism. The fact that the final key to solving the mystery in the novel is the revelation of the hidden paths between many of these distant locations, suggests metaphorically the mutual implication of such institutions in the control of power and knowledge, as well as the connections between the Francoist past and the transitional present. These locations function as metaphors of the repressive and ideological Spanish state apparatus, still very much in the hands of Franco supporters: the fascist Comisario Flores, the ultraconservative Mother Superior, and the retrograde Doctor Sugrañes, each a caricature of similar representative figures of Francoist National Catholicism. In these three novels, Mendoza give us a comic and surreal portrait of *la España cutre* (the ugly side of Spain) still struggling to come out from under the heavy weight of Francoism: a Spain which would like to see itself as modern, free, and European, but which is still to a large extent premodern, imprisoned in its own past, traditional and backward.

Vázquez Montalbán was instrumental in the development of detective fiction as a political genre in Spain, and his example also has been enormously influential overseas. The original contribution of his detective novels lies in its generic hybridity, their mixing (or one might say their ironic and self-aware abuse) of generic convention, their incorporation of social, cultural, and political analysis of the contemporary world, and their acute insights into the legacies of the past, the imbalances between North and South, and the new pressure for globalization. Through a series of more than twenty titles he documented the Spanish cultural climate of the years from the end of the Franco regime to the beginning of the new millennium. His novels provide a critical examination of many facets of Spain's political, economic, social, and moral transformation in the last thirty years, including the collapse of both Francoism and Eurocommunism, Spain's entry into the European Union, the pleasures and excesses of late capitalist consumer society, the transformation of Barcelona into a global city thanks to the Olympic Games, and the cultural and economic devastation wrought by globalization.

Although written in the last years of the dictatorship, *Tatuaje* (1974) is the novel that set the stage for the remainder of the detective series featuring the Catalan-cum-Galician Pepe Carvalho, a former anti-Franco Communist militant and ex-CIA operative now a a skeptical and cynical private detective working in Barcelona. Carvalho is a profoundly disillusioned dissident, distrustful of ideologies and government explanations, whose déclassé social position allows him to dissect contemporary Spanish society from the margins and to offer almost voyeuristic satirical insights into its shortcomings. In spite of censorship, the novel offers an implicit denunciation of the other side of the Francoist *desarrollista* 'miracle', revealing the poor living conditions of the lower classes under the dictator, and the great rural exodus that forced millions of Spaniards to find employment in proletarian urban centers like Barcelona or as migrant workers in northern Europe.

Only a few months after the first post-Franco elections in Spain, Vázquez Montalbán published *La soledad del manager* (1977). Government censorship had gone, prohibitions had been lifted, and certain subjects that had been taboo under the dictatorship, particularly politics and sex, were now openly explored, discussed, and celebrated. This general celebration of newly gained freedoms is reflected in the explicit sexual scenes in this novel, the realistic depictions of corruption, and the critical portrayal of Spanish institutions linked to the Francoist past, in particular the financial community, right-wing political parties, and the police. The first democratic elections after Franco's death provide the backdrop for the story and the novel accurately conveys the sense of excitement as well as confusion that surrounded these historical events. Unpalatable social realities of the kind that fully emerged from the shadows after Franco's death – unemployment, drugs, street violence, and crime – are also present.

Vázquez Montalbán's highly praised novel *Los mares del Sur* (1979), which won the Premio Planeta, was one of the triggers for the emergence of the Spanish *novela negra* during the years of the transition. It captures the general sense of disillusionment that followed the initial euphoria that greeted the restoration of democracy. The old dreams and utopias of the past had gone, as a revolutionary break with the past was exchanged for a consensual moderate transition and a political pact to forget, a consensus which implied immunity for all crimes committed by the Franco regime. The story investigates the murder of an entrepreneur with a guilty conscience who became a millionaire during the economic boom of the 1960s fuelled by Franco's technocrats, and who built substandard housing complexes for the huge number of rural migrants who moved to the new working-class suburbs of the big cities. With its flexible prose style and its perceptive observations on social customs and the political climate, the novel achieves a masterful balance between the fast-paced action of the thriller and the ironic social commentary of the new *novela negra*.

Perhaps the most overtly political of the Pepe Carvalho detective novels is *Asesinato en el Comité Central* (1981), a sort of hybrid locked-room mystery-novel and political *roman à clef*, best described by the term coined by the author himself: 'political fiction'. It investigates the internal dissensions within the Spanish Communist Party and other movements opposed to the dogmatism of the past. Pepe Carvalho travels to Madrid to unravel the mysterious assassination of Garrido, the Party president, and in the process explores the decline of Eurocommunism, the general sense of confusion and disillusionment of those years, and the political turmoil that would cause the downfall of Spanish President Adolfo Suárez and the failure of the military coup on 23 February 1981, one of the last public manifestations of the Francoist political legacy. In *Asesinato* Vázquez Montalbán not only investigates the social and historical crimes of the dictatorship, as in other Carvalho detective novels, but also exposes the fissures in the anti-Franco resistance and its own political skeletons.

Los pájaros de Bangkok (1983) is set during the collapse of the Communist Party, the euphoric victory of the Socialists in the general elections of 1982, and the political, economic, and cultural opening up of Spain to the outside world. As the world moves inexorably towards globalization, this is a theme which will reappear frequently in later novels. Likewise, *El balneario* (1986), set in the context of Spain's recent entry into the European Union, offers a biting satire of the hermetically sealed comforts of the first world, figuratively presented as an exclusive health club of rich nations, thus metaphorically criticizing the unequal power relationship between North and South, a concern that will also reappear in later novels dealing with the problems of globalization. *El delantero centro fue asesinado al atardecer* (1988), set against the backdrop of extensive renovations in Barcelona for the 1992 Olympic Games, explores the connections between the national obsession with soccer, the excesses of urban planning, and the loss of collective memory, key issues in Spain at the time and ones with a clear connection to Francoist history. *El laberinto griego* (1991) and *Sabotaje olímpico* (1993) both of which use the Barcelona Olympics as the setting for the action, are more like social caricatures, sometimes bordering on the surreal, particularly the latter. They reflect the other, darker side of the Olympic years in Spain, when political tensions and government corruption seemed to be at an all-time high. That is true also of *Roldán, ni vivo ni muerto* (1994), a political cartoon published with accompanying comic-strip illustrations, which fictionalized the search for and capture of the notorious Director of the Spanish Civil Guard, Luis Roldán, who had fled the country after embezzling public funds. In *Quinteto de Buenos Aires* (1997) Pepe Carvalho travels to Buenos Aires in the aftermath of the military Junta to investigate the case of a distant uncle who has been 'disappeared' and in the process offers the reader a detailed account of political violence in contemporary Argentine society. Here again, the ghosts of the fascist past make their comeback in the form of the return of the repressed.

Galíndez (1990), published after a gestation period of exhaustive research lasting several decades, is the first Vázquez Montalbán novel to react from a directly postmodern perspective against the emerging tide of globalization, and it is also one of the best examples of interplay between detective fiction and the recovery of historical memory on a global scale. *Galíndez* is a novelistic tour de force. It is a novel of investigation and denunciation written at the end of the cold war and the beginning of the new world order. In the process of unraveling the 'disappearance' of the exiled Basque Jesús de Galíndez, many allegations surface which implicate the military apparatus of General Trujillo, the laissez-faire attitude of Franco's government officials, as well as the secret services of the United States and the collaboration of the Partido Nacionalista Vasco, united in a common front against the Communist menace, and the historical amnesia of the socialist Spain of the 1980s. *Galíndez* is a hybrid, mixing heterogeneous elements of the detective genre with characters from the historical novel, the subjective exploration of the novel of memory, the questioning of the master narratives of postmodern historiographical metafiction, the suspense of the political thriller, and the moral imperative of testimonial literature. It is not a coincidence that this novel was published in 1990 when the neoliberal face of the new world order was beginning to be dubbed globalization. After the fall of the Berlin wall, the end of utopian ideologies, the acceleration of history, and the loss of memory, the intensification of communication technology, the huge global population movements, everything and everybody is subject to a neo-imperial supranational order that imposes political, economic, and cultural homogeneity. Faced with this devastating post-cold war panorama, Vázquez Montalbán seems to be asking several questions. What are the possibilities of ethical resistance to the neoliberal market ideology? Can historical memory survive under these conditions? Could it serve as an antidote to the erosion of cultural identity and of an ethical code of conduct opposed to impunity?

Vázquez Montalbán redefines the boundaries of detective fiction, as well as its geopolitical and generic borders. The action takes places in a number of widely dispersed locales across the globe which are nevertheless surreptitiously linked to one another through complex political and economic connections. The narrative is a collage of sketches cleverly stitched together to reflect the tensions in post-Franco Spain between the Basque Country and the socialist government in Madrid, the third-world provinces of the global neoliberal empire such as Santo Domingo and their dependence upon the neo-imperial centers to the North, Miami, New York, and Washington, where resistance movements are monitored and controlled, and intelligence plans drawn up. *Galíndez* could well provide a new model for Hispanic detective fiction, a political detective fiction on a global scale, given its heterogeneous structure, international and multilingual, and its concern with the political, ideological, economic, and cultural connections of global neo-imperialism. The novel won several prestigious awards, including the Premio de las Letras in Spain and the Europa Prize awarded by the European Union.[5]

The last novel of the Carvalho series, *Milenio Carvalho*, published posthumously in 2004, consists of a journey around the contemporary world examining the dismal legacy of European colonialism on four continents, and offers a critical view of the devastating effects of globalization from a postcolonial perspective. Instead of the pleasing and exotic vision provided by colonial and neocolonial travel literature, *Milenio* examines in depth the present climate of violence in the Middle East, the assaults of terrorism and counter-terrorism, the devastation in Afghanistan, the lost paradises of the Far East, the eternally postponed promise of the Southern Cone and Brazil, ending with the terrible and miserable reality of black Africa, before returning full circle to the starting point. As the author suggested in *El Pais*, 3 August 2003, '*Milenio* is not just a geopolitical journey, but an anguished, secular pilgrimage through a world ever more hypocritically religious, where gods are invoked every day to justify holy wars and economic-military hegemonies'. It presents a human gallery of the victims and victimizers of globalization, as the new colonial phase of international neoliberalism produces an inequitable division of power between globalizers and globalized.

One consequence of the pioneering work of authors like Mendoza and Vázquez Montalbán is that detective fiction, in its Spanish *novela negra* version, has achieved a new status of legitimacy and popularity and come to be associated with the new Spanish novel of the transition. Following suit, many other Spanish authors have found that the detective novel seems the medium best suited to the exploration of the contradictions and the fissures

---

[5]   The most insightful essay on *Galíndez* is Gabilondo (2007), which sees it as an alternative to nationalist nostalgia and the global loss of historical memory.

in the new democracy. Their novels offer a critical view of the new urban consumer-driven Spanish society, plagued with the social realities of unemployment, crime, terrorism, drug trafficking, corruption, and the continuing legacy of the Francoist past.

Andreu Martín is an established writer of Spanish *novela negra*, both in Spanish and Catalan, having published more than 25 novels since the late 1970s. His works of hard-boiled detective fiction which the author has characterized as 'novels of urban terror', often depict acts of extreme irrational violence and cruelty as they attempt to explore the roots of evil in contemporary Spanish urban society. They reveal the dark side of Spain's 'model' political transition, built on a conspiracy of mutual amnesia about violence, past and present. The return of repression re-emerges with avengeance, producing profoundly disturbing effects and destabilizing any sense of normality.

His detective novels, such as *Prótesis* (1980) or *Barcelona Connection* (1987), show how corruption among the powerful (the economic upper classes, the law-enforcement authorities, and the political class) lies at the root of crime, through the systematic use of violence, oppression, and extortion. The workings of organized crime constitute a mirror and a metaphor for institutional social violence in late capitalist Spanish society, characterized by an obsessive lust for power and wealth, irrational violence, rampant corruption, and dehumanized aggression. The struggle for power among both groups follows the same principle of the survival of the fittest at any price. They often use similar methods and have similar objectives, and they often seem interchangeable and indistinguishable. The novels reveal the schizophrenic character of bourgeois morality, and the barbaric and undemocratic nature of violence, oppression, machismo, and racism. Martín's novels constitute a harsh indictment of the rapacious and irrational structure of late capitalist society in post-Franco Spain.[6]

Juan Madrid, like Martín, is a long established author of the *novela negra*, with more than 30 novels published in the last 25 years. His six-novel saga constructed around the investigator Toni Romano is a mini-chronicle of the Spanish transition, originally intended to span the period from the restoration of democracy to the installation of the Socialist party in government, but later extended up to the present. In the author's own words, this series is 'an anti-epic of political discourses and the praises they sing' (Colmeiro 1994a: 247); it offers a critical view of the socio-political transition as seen from the lower strata of society and the marginal world of crime. In his novels, Madrid frequently makes his central policeman figure a privileged observer and mediator of power relations between the bourgeois order and the criminal world. The first instalment features ex–cop Toni Romano, once

---

6   There is further analysis in Hart (1987: 109–27) and Colmeiro (1994a: 230–45).

active during the dictatorship and now recycled as a private security agent, occasional investigator, and debt collector during the transition. Madrid openly denounces the moral duplicity of Spanish society and the persistent legacy of Francoism, as he depicts the recycling of Francoist politicians and public figures as democratic citizens after the end of the dictatorship. His novels offer an unambiguously critical view of the past and a cynical and bitter vision of a present still haunted by corruption, injustice, extreme right-wing terror, and violent repression, and they betray a certain longing for the lost collective dreams typical of leftist *desencanto*. His political critique of post-Franco Spanish society continues in his later saga, *Brigada central* (1989), centered around the figure of the gypsy police inspector Flores, and other novels such as *Días contados* (1993), which focus on ETA terrorism and delinquency against the backdrop of the decline of Madrid's counter-cultural *movida* (a movement that arose in the 1980s and extended to other Spanish cities such as Valencia, Vigo and Bilbao).

Another author who has created a mini-saga documenting the years of political transition is Jorge Martínez Reverte. This features an investigative reporter, Julio Gálvez, who is involved in unraveling unsolved social economic and political crimes. His first novel, *Demasiado para Gálvez* (1979), follows Gálvez' investigation into the fraud scandal committed in the last years of the dictatorship by the Serfico real-estate company, a fictional conglomerate representative of the most corrupt aspects of Francoist *desarrollismo*, with Francoist generals and admirals as well as politicians and members of the aristocracy serving on its board of directors. The novel is a humorous exposé of the fraudulent practices of companies protected by the power elite, such as the real Sofico fiasco a few years earlier, and anticipates the Rumasa scandal that broke a couple of years later. *Gálvez en Euskadi* (1983) was one of the first Spanish novels to tackle the issue of ETA terrorism and state counter-terrorism, and focuses on the disappearance of a Basque executive who was about to pay a ransom to the terrorist organization. The novel explores the continuing legacy of Francoism as the main cause for chronic violence in the Basque Country (see King 2005). *Gálvez y el cambio del cambio* (1995) offers a view of the crisis of the Socialist party, haunted by the corruption and scandals that would eventually see it swept from power. The title of the novel is an ironic allusion to the socialist political campaign slogan 'El cambio del cambio', which echoes the original political message, 'Por el cambio', that had brought the Socialists to power a decade earlier. The novel explores the competition between different groups for control of new media technology: monopoly interests, lobby groups, privatized companies, banks, multina-tionals, and even the autonomous governments (Gálvez goes to Catalonia in the course of his enquiries). Gálvez uncovers a case of corruption in illegal backhanders and witnesses the regrouping of conservative forces under the banner of neoliberalism, in another return with avengeance of the repressed Francoist past.

The latest novels in the series examine the recurring violence associated with the rebranding of Spain's cultural identity in the twenty-first century. *Gálvez en la frontera* (2001) explores the redefinition of borders, real and metaphorical, brought on by the process of globalization, ethnic clashes, the struggle for survival among migrant workers, the drama of human trafficking, and the 'new economy'. *Gudari Gálvez* (2005) looks at the multicultural remapping of contemporary Spain, and offers a new take on political violence in the Basque Country, seeing it in the context of peace negotiations with the Spanish government.

One of the most important events that resulted from the transition has been the redefinition of the political structures of the Spanish state and the return of political power to the regions. This, in turn, has strengthened regional claims to separate cultural identity, always closely associated with use of the local language. As a result, a crop of detective novels from the periphery has sprung up, written in Catalan (Andreu Martín, Maria Antònia Oliver, Ferran Torrent), Galician (Carlos Reigosa, Roque Morteiro, Manuel Forcadela, Ramiro Fonte, Daniel Álvarez Gándara, Suso de Toro) and Basque (Xabier Guereño, Jon Arretxe). Detective novels like these are also political, but in a different way, as both the subject matter and the medium employed are a conscious response to specific political and cultural conditions, and they have proved themselves effective in bolstering the use and status of peninsular languages other than Castilian.[7]

A further recent trend in the politicization of detective novels in Spain has been the emergence of women writers (Lourdes Ortiz, Alicia Giménez-Bartlett, Maria Antònia Oliver, Margarida Aritzeta) and the introduction into the stories of domestic violence and abuse, gender inequalities, land exploitation, and ecofeminism.[8] Gay and lesbian issues are also highly political, and sometimes appear as important subtexts in the novels of Andreu Martín (*Prótesis* and *Si es no es,* 1983) and Vázquez Montalbán (**El laberinto griego* and *La rosa de Alejandría,* 1984). They play a more central role in Blanca Álvarez's, *La soledad del monstruo* (1992), Javier Otaola's *Brocheta de carne* (2003) and a trilogy of novels by Lola Van Guardia: *Con pedigree* (1997), *Plumas de doble filo* (1999) and *La mansión de las Tríbadas* (2002). To my knowledge, no detailed study of these has yet been published.[9]

In all the cases we have examined, Spanish detective fiction has become

---

[7] For a case study of two detective writers writing in Catalan (Maria Antònia Oliver) and Galician (Carlos Reigosa), see Colmeiro (2001: 176–92), and for detective fiction in Basque, Cillero (2000).

[8] See the articles by Colmeiro (2002) and Thompson-Casado (2004).

[9] Mandrell (2007) studies gay characterization in several novels by Vázquez Montalbán.

an effective medium and one selected by many Spanish writers for an exploration of current social and political issues reflecting the cultural anxieties of contemporary Spanish society.[10] In this sense, detective fiction is a good indicator of the tensions and conflicts in the political landscape in Spain today, both the continuing legacies of the repressed political past and the new challenges that the future may bring.

Further reading

Amell, Samuel (1986), Balibrea (1999), Bértolo (1984), Briones (1999), Buschman (2002), Bussière-Perrin (1998), Christian (2001), Cillero (2000), Colmeiro (1989, 1994a, 1994b, 1996, 1999, 2001, 2002, 2005, and 2007), Gabilondo (2007), Garino (1998), Godsland (2002), Godsland & Moody (2004), Godsland & King (2006), Hart (1987), King (2005), Mandrell (2007), Marqués (2000), Pérez (2002a), Pérez & Pérez (1987), Resina (1993 and 1997), Rix (1992), Schaefer-Rodríguez (1990), Valles (1991).

---

[10] The trend is not restricted to Spain. The example of the Spanish *novela negra* has been influential in the development of a new detective genre in Latin America dubbed 'neo-detective fiction': examples are the novels of Paco Ignacio Taibo II, Justo Vasco, Leonardo Padura, and others. Writers of detective fiction in other languages, such as Andrea Camilleri and Donna Leon in Italy, Petros Márkaris in Greece, or Filipa Melo in Portugal, have also acknowledged a debt to Vázquez Montalbán who showed them the possibilities that were open to a writer of political detective fiction.

III

THE CITY AS LITERARY SPACE

9

Madrid in the Novel

RANDOLPH D. POPE

The word Madrid covers a huge, diverse, and ever-changing city that became larger and more complex during the course of the twentieth century. It went from half-a-million inhabitants in 1900 to close on six million today (Parsons 2003). The new city grew around the capriciously laid out center of what was known as the 'Villa', with its Plaza Mayor, Royal Palace, Puerta del Sol, and Retiro Gardens, to name but a few of the landmarks made famous by the novels of Galdós, especially *Fortunata y Jacinta* (1886–87). As it did so, it incorporated the old, reinterpreted it, and completely altered its dynamic. There was plenty of evidence of the modern: the grid layout of new middle-class neighborhoods, the spread of electricity, the changing fashions adopted by the inhabitants. But incontrovertible evidence of the continuing plight of the poor and the exploited amidst this growing prosperity made it harder to integrate the whole city into a single narrative. Pio Baroja described this new situation perfectly in *La busca*:

> The inhabitant of Madrid who finds himself accidentally wandering into the poor neighborhoods close to the River Manzanares is surprised by the spectacle of destitution and squalor, misery and ignorance afforded by the outskirts of Madrid with their wretched streets, full of dust in summer and mud in winter. The Court [as Madrid was usually called, as the residence of the royal family] is a city of contrasts. It offers intense light alongside dark shadow; refined styles of living, almost European, in its center; African, small-town life in its suburbs. (1904: 282)

Baroja's narrator clearly suggests that those native *madrileños* who may be taken aback by the poverty on the outskirts of their city do not live in those areas but rather in areas with electric light and fine living, and are perturbed lest their almost European lifestyle (the 'almost' is deliberate) is swamped by the African suburbs (no 'almost' here).

La busca is the first novel in a trilogy entitled *La lucha por la vida* (1904–05), which follows the adventures of Manuel, an adolescent who arrives in

Madrid from a small town in Soria where his mother had sent him while she
tried to make a living in the capital, and where her status has plummeted: she
now works as a maid in a boarding house. Meanwhile, Manuel will encounter
people of all walks of life who have been thrown together in that lodging
house where there is no real privacy, the food is inadequate, and everyone is
prey to despair and fading ambition. The boarding house appears in several
of the novels we will examine in this chapter: it is a symbol of those random
communities created by a growing city which acts as a magnet for provincials
seeking a better life and who, though their hopes may be dashed, remain
dazzled by the thought that the city offers golden opportunities.

Baroja's portrait of the harsh conditions of life in Madrid is a startlingly
audacious one. Surrounded by petty criminals, prostitutes, and drunks, the
hero is unapologetic, does not seek to justify his behavior, and entertains no
romantic illusions about the future. While there are echoes of Baudelaire in
the novel, there is no sense that evil is attractive, and no fascination with
commerce or progress. Women are routinely battered, children sleep out in
the rain, stealing is just one more job, and murders happen. People are making
do, with the desperate creativity that comes from finding oneself on the edge
of ruin. One printing press produces several small-circulation newspapers, all
of which are ignored by the better-off who do not need to struggle every day
to find food and shelter, and whose lives are entirely cut off from the world
inhabited by the characters of this novel. One rich English woman does come
slumming on a kind of literary tour and readers may have the uncomfortable
feeling that she represents them. Arriving in Madrid, poor and unschooled,
as Manuel does, the experience is not a pleasant one:

> When one of his traveling companions announced they were already in
> Madrid, Manuel experienced real apprehension. The sunset illuminated
> the sky, blood-red, like the eye of some monster. The train was slowing
> down, going through poor neighborhoods and past grim houses. The elec-
> tric lamps cast a dim glow onto the signs along the track. (1946: 269)

This sunset on Manuel's arrival is the counterpoint to the dawn presented in
the last volume of the trilogy, *Aurora roja* (1905), a tribute to Nietzsche and
an assertion, albeit a profoundly skeptical one, that anarchy might prove one
road to salvation. The monster is too unwieldy, insensitive and bloodthirsty.
Regardless, Baroja frequently finds a redeeming quality in the almost theatrical illumination of the landscape through which his characters wander:

> There was still no trace of the green tinge of grass on the hills and in the
> hollows around Madrid. The trees of the Campo del Moro [the gardens of
> the Royal Palace] were reddish, skeletal, among the perennial foliage. Dark
> wisps of smoke emerged, hugging the ground and soon to be swept away by

the wind. As the clouds flew over the plain it changed color: in turn purple, gray, yellow, copper. The road to Extremadura looked like a broken line, with its parallel rows of gray, filthy houses. That austere, grim landscape on the outskirts of Madrid, rough, cold, and brutal, moved Manuel to the depth of his soul. (*Red Dawn* 1905: 328)

This is more than impressionistic aesthetic evasiveness with just a touch of the modernist verbal palette. The anticipation of spring, the transitory nature of the wafting smoke, the delicate tracery of some of the deciduous trees in the Royal Palace garden, enduring through winter alongside their evergreen companions, the shifting colors, and the road that stretches into the distance all point to the grim existence of Manuel and his friends, but they also harbor the faint hope that it may all change. The succession of colors, from funerary purple to a range of sunny yellows and the deep orange of copper, may indicate the implacable march of the seasons, indifferent to individual suffering, but it also lends an energy to the whole city.

There are several other novels that provide glimpses of Madrid in the following decades, but to find a similarly powerful evocation of the city one must wait until *La colmena* (1951) of Camilo José Cela. This novel, consisting of just six chapters – not ordered chronologically – plus an ending, rambles along, presenting snippets from the lives of hundreds of characters as they kill time in a café, gossip in a boarding house, walk the streets of a poverty-stricken city still haunted by war, share an apartment building where a murder is committed, and hang out together in a brothel. The character around whom the delicate narrative thread is woven is appropriately named Martín Marco, *marco* meaning 'frame' in Spanish (though he frequently disappears from view amid the profusion of truncated stories in which the only continuity is provided by the city itself). While in *La busca* the struggle for survival has a sense of life and energy, in *La colmena* the characters hunger after petty things, action is minimal, and dialogue, rather than convey information, simply serves to identify faces in the crowd. Cela's genius is to convey character in a few words. In *La busca* everything is movement, anger, denunciation: Madrid is enervating, insatiable, harsh. In *La colmena* people mostly sit around, bored and cowed; the tables in the café are made from old tombstones, and on the reverse of one of them is the name of the deceased: Esperanza (or Hope).

But not everything is bleak. The first sentence of the novel is spoken by the owner of the café, Doña Rosa, a Fascist who mistreats her staff and embodies the feeling of oppression that characterized the 1940s: 'Let's not lose a sense of proportion; I tire of repeating it, but it's the only thing that matters' (1987: 119). A growing city will give rise to many different points of view, especially one like Madrid, which does not even have an iconic landmark, such as the Eiffel Tower or the Empire State Building, from which to seek a common bird's-eye view of the emerging metropolis. The repeated admonition that Doña Rosa feels obliged to inflict on her regulars is necessary precisely because of the enormous variety of customers she has. Their refusal to agree on a common take on the city is the result of the waves of incomers who patronize the café, isolated each from the next, or else clustering around one of the tables; the clientele changes with the time of day; it is a constant flow out of control.

But as the novel draws to a close something new occurs. A group of very different characters, all of them related in one way or another to Martín, read an announcement in the newspaper which seems to indicate that he is being sought by the police in connection with murder. Readers have up to this point seen the city as governed by money, earned and spent, lost and found, anonymously transferring its power from one person to the next. This concluding section of the novel, simply titled 'Final', opens with a sombre thought:

> The air is tinged with the colors of Christmas. Across Madrid, which is like an old plant putting out tender green shoots, one hears, from time to time, amid the hurly-burly of the street, the sweet tolling, the loving tolling of a chapel bell. People walk past each other, each of them in a rush. Nobody thinks about the person next to them, about that man who is perhaps looking down at the ground; his stomach shot to pieces, or who has a tumor on one of his lungs, or a screw loose. (398)

But in fact Marco does observe the squalor around him, and he is moved by it:

> From the road that goes East, one can see some wretched shanties, built out of old iron and broken boards. A few children play, throwing stones at the ponds left by the rain. Some women are scrabbling amongst the piles of garbage. (401)

Now the newspaper generates solidarity among family, friends, and even simple acquaintances. Our last glimpse of Marco is of his returning in late December from a visit to the cemetery, where he has gone, probably on the anniversary of his mother's death. He is happily planning his future, not knowing that the trap is closing around him. The reader, though, can still harbor the hope that the city has a heart and that Marco will be rescued by his friends. The beehive, then, is coming together and finding its strength, as indeed Madrid would begin to wake up in the 1950s and take on a fresh vitality that would have been unthinkable for Doña Rosa and her customers in Cela's unforgettable café.[1]

---

[1] For an assessment of the arguments for the emergence of an active opposition in the early 1950s in Spain, see the excellent overview by Jordan (1995).

It is surprising that a novel that concludes the vogue for objective, social narrative of the kind prevalent in the 1950s should, because of its free-wheeling narrator and ironic approach, present a view of late-1940s Madrid that is not nearly as interesting as those we find in Baroja and Cela. The main character of *Tiempo de silencio* (1962) by Luis Martín-Santos, is Pedro, a doctor working on cancer and living in a boarding house. He visits the shantytowns, and interacts with different social classes, while the narrator indulges in long sentences bemoaning the random and accidental nature of the city: the fact that it has no cathedral, for example. With hindsight, it seems far too predictable that this researcher should fall for the daughter of the owner of the boarding house – a fall from grace, according to his upper-class friend – and that he should fall foul of the machinations of his incestuous assistant, Amador. It is also sadly predictable that the assassin of Pedro's bride turns out to come from the poorest of the poor. Regardless of the novel's other merits, its portrait of Madrid is outdated and simplistic. To refer to Madrid as a city 'lacking historical substance' (1976: 13) seems more like a complaint, a yearning for a different past, than any kind of insightful comment.[2] The very rich are criticized for having bird-like brains and being irredeemably frivolous, but at least they get to listen to the musings of a philosopher very much like Ortega y Gasset, and are compared to a painting by Goya. As one goes down the socio-economic ladder, characters become more unpredictable and animalistic. Amador's wife, supposedly a representative of the innocence of the educated, is described as a walking lump of clay as though she were just emerging from some prelapsarian paradise. At the end of the novel, Pedro abandons Madrid, apparently going into what will be a miserable exile, as there is no salvation outside the capital. In practice, the 1960s witnessed the beginning of a drastic transformation in Spanish society which would make social class less rigidly predictable, shatter the sense of superiority enjoyed by the capital (one might, after all, it now seemed, live a full life in Barcelona, or Santiago, and more or less anywhere of Andalusia, not to mention Bilbao), and displace the center of Madrid to a largely upper middle-class *barrio* centered around the commercial outlets of Calle Serrano and the newer neighborhoods that sprang up in the inner suburbs. Ultimately Madrid would get a cathedral, Nuestra Señora de Almudena, consecrated on

---

2   Madrid does not even merit a mention in two of the most influential books about cities by Mumford and Hall respectively, even though Mumford's description of citizens gathering around a Court might well apply to the Spanish capital: 'Pleasure was a duty, idleness a service, and honest work the lowest of all degradation. To become acceptable to the baroque court, it was necessary that an object or a function should bear the marks of exquisite uselessness' (1961: 375). The main question addressed by Hall could also be asked of late twentieth-century Madrid: 'What makes a particular city, at a particular time, suddenly become immensely creative, exceptionally innovative?' (1998: 3).

15 June 1993. Martín-Santos's representation of the city, then, is both archeological and backward-looking.

Historical events during the transition from dictatorship to democracy brought about a profound transformation of Madrid, and this, in turn, has given rise to two quite different visions of the city. One is nostalgic, based on a sense that new buildings, changing moral codes, technology, and a culture that is global rather than local is rapidly erasing traditional *castizo* Madrid. This is the city we encounter, for example, in *Días del Arenal* (1992) by Soledad Puértolas. The other is experimental, marked by repressed desires and by excess. This is the Madrid of *Historias del Kronen* (1994) by José Ángel Mañas. In appearance these two novels are quite different. *Días del Arenal* has a leisured narrator who tells the story of the lives of a number of people who have come into contact with Antonio Cardús, now a seventy–year old recluse living in a neighborhood untouched by the modernization of the city:

> Manises is one of those streets, in Madrid as elsewhere, which, without anyone knowing why, have begun to look abandoned, with little traffic, and inhabitants who live, perhaps, outside time itself. (1992: 7)

Cardús had his moment of glory long ago, during an affair with a married woman, Gracia, whom he met at a country wedding. For her, Cardús and Madrid, and the hotel in which they met in Arenal Street provided the occasional spice to a provincial life she found comfortable and never wished to give up. Cardús's own life enters a phase of paralysis and inertia when Gracia rejects him and later dies. Yet the city keeps changing and when a young woman, Susana, arrives to live in the same building as Cardús, they strike up a friendship that eventually leads the old man to re-engage with life and temporarily leave the cocoon of the neighborhood. This is a novel than harks back to Galdós, steeped as it is in a muted romanticism bordering the trivial. But that is precisely its power, for it represents a whole way of life that is caught napping and finds itself out of date, not because of anything it has done, but simply because the world has gone on changing while it has stayed the same. The neighborhood is neglected and run down, the small shops have been boarded up, friends and family have left, and the future holds no allure. Susana, though, and the troubles of one of her friends finally convince Cardús to take action and to enter a present he has hitherto kept at bay: 'He crossed streets, looking up to the terraced roofs that crowned the buildings, astounded that the city could be so large, that it could contain so many lives. Immersed in his own ignorance he felt a completely unfamiliar feeling: curiosity' (212). After Cardús realizes that his is not the only story in town and that he has lingered on in a kind of coma induced by emotional trauma, he is capable of looking up and experiencing new feelings. The novel ends with an epiphany in which Cardús and his two younger friends drink tea, eat pastries, smoke, and enjoy a drink together: 'it was a moment of fulfilment' (238). The city, then, brings together different generations; it is not just a network of streets with a constantly changing skyline, but a living organism. A similar situation occurs in the highly successful *La hija del caníbal* (1997) by Rosa Montero, in which a middle-aged woman befriends two of her neighbors, a younger man and an older one, when her husband is apparently kidnapped at Barajas airport and she finds herself liberated from a dull marriage and a boring job.

The new Madrid, where sex, drugs, and rock music take over at night, is pictured in *Historias del Kronen*. As if completing the cycle initiated by *La busca*, readers are now treated to a view of the flipside of a city characterized by frantic hustle and bustle. The young protagonists in *Historias* have few if any economic needs, yet they are constantly on the move, crisscrossing town at high speed in their cars, courting danger, hungry for excitement and peer-group approval. Their search is prompted by affluence and boredom, fuelled by cocaine and pornography, modelled on violent literature, and they have no sense whatever of social responsibility. They get away, literally, with murder. The city has become a playground, in which they are granted immunity by the fact that they have money and are in a crowd, and by the excuse that they have acted under the influence of alcohol. The city has lost its previously local character and is now just another global metropolis. Appropriately, there is little to distinguish this novel from others by non-Spaniards: the American Bret Easton Ellis, for example, and his *Less than Zero* (1985) or the Chilean Alberto Fuguet's *Mala onda* (1991), translated as *Bad vibes*. That is precisely the point: Madrid has become a world capital.[3] Baroja's monster has been domesticated, though one may well feel some nostalgia for the old beast.

Once Madrid begins to be perceived as a place where all things are possible, then appetites grow according, aided and abetted, among other things, by film, advertising, urban myth, and tourism. The old frustration of living in an urban misery leavened by tantalizing glimpses of opportunity, real or imagined, has now been supplanted by a new frustration: that of living in a modern city where one is encouraged to have it all and yet not being able to afford to do so. Real life puts real obstacles in the way of enjoyment: there is work to do, a salary to earn, a family to look after, a daily grind. Most people are not like the pampered youths of *Historias del Kronen* on a summer vacation. But just knowing that everything is out there and could be had if one had the money and the contacts, the power, can be a painful experience, as it is for the two protagonists of *Dos mujeres en Praga* (2002), a novel by

---

3 Lehan (1998: 3) declares that the modern city has evolved 'through three stages of development – a commercial, industrial, and "world stage" city'. Madrid never quite achieved the first two, but it has managed at least flashes of the third.

Juan José Millás. Here, two frustrated writers and two women whose lives lack the glamour they yearn for become entangled in a web of fantasy in which stories and identities are stolen, and literary games are played with point of view. The anonymity of the city allows the characters to invent and reinvent themselves, even if they are shackled to each other by contracts, money, the telephone, radio, and e-mail. The two women can imagine that they are in the more exotic Prague, a place of liberation, even when they are actually stuck in Madrid. Simulation is everywhere, so there is no reason not to adopt it as a way of life.

We have gone over the century from a desperate quest for survival in the poverty-stricken Madrid of *La busca*, to an equally desperate quest, this time for meaning in lives stripped of any meaningful sense of self in a much more affluent but still challenging city. All along, the novel has attempted to catch the prevailing wind by describing a city that shifts and changes every day with greater speed.

Further reading

Baker (1991 and 1999), Barella Vigal et al. (1995), Barella & Gutiérrez (1997), Conde & Longares (1993), Graham & Labanyi (1995), Jordan (1995), Lacarta (1986), Ugarte (1996).

10

Images of Barcelona

MARTA E. ALTISENT

Barcelona, the second largest city in Spain and the capital of Catalonia, is often defined by comparison with Madrid. Throughout the twentieth century, the widening gulf between the two cities has determined much of Catalonia's national ethos, itself defined by reference to Castilian-speaking Spain (Arkinstall 2004: 22). For Spaniards, Barcelona is both the place where European novelties first arrive in the Peninsula and also a narcissistically self-regarding city. Barcelona's physical peculiarities have both nourished and curtailed its political aspirations, but it has always been the driving force behind a Catalan nation with no state but a desire to define its identity in terms of literature, art, and culture.

As a port, Barcelona shares with other Mediterranean capitals more than a millennium of colonization and expansion. The physical constraints on the city, sandwiched between the mountains and the sea, have also made Barcelona extremely conscious of the importance of urban planning. There has been endless discussion of the city's charms, the labyrinthine medieval city has been shaped and reshaped by wave after wave of planners, and elaborate gardens of iron and cement have been created which have helped to make its architecture sharply distinct in character (Hughes 1992: x).

In the early twentieth century, Barcelona's literary heart was the humble district of La Ribera, a *barrio* wedged between the Ciudadela fortress and Las Ramblas Boulevard. This is the urban backdrop to Santiago Rusiñol's autobiographical novel *L'auca del senyor Esteve* (1907), a saga depicting three generations of a petit-bourgeois family of shopkeepers full of an 'apolitical charm' that would soon emulate the behavior of Castilian-speaking gentry. As a modernist painter and playwright, Rusiñol tried to redeem his own class by giving it a sense of beauty, art, and poetry. This tender evocation of the author's humble origins does nothing to hide his scorn for the hideous *senyors Esteve* who are unable to rescue their city from its sordid and petty limitations. Sr Esteve's economic rise from *botigaire* to landowner and his purchase of a villa in Gràcia foreshadows the modern Barcelona of luxurious mansions, apartment buildings, shops, and mausoleums side by side with the dilapidated old buildings, dirty alleys, slums, and barren lots of the Gothic quarter. As Josep Pla put it, *L'auca* contains two turn-of-the-century Barcelonas: the popular and the Parisian.

Josep Pla made the subject of his own fictional autobiography, *Un senyor de Barcelona* (1942–44), another quintessential *barcelonés*. Rafael Puget is the aristocratic son of a family of liberal landowners. He is a *bon vivant* and a gentleman of means, who is generous with his virtues of elegance, affability, tolerance, friendship, and discreet charity. As the last in a line of impoverished oligarchs, his influence now stretches only to the cultural and the spiritual. His activities are those of the idle city *flâneur*; he divides his time between 'ocio atento', or intellectual pursuits, and 'el cultivo de la amistad', keeping his friendships in good repair. His daily rounds of the Círculo Ecuestre club, the Athenaeum, the elegant cafés of Las Ramblas – La Fontana de Oro, El Café de la Ópera – the theatre, the grand hotels and the music halls of the *Paral.lel* recall the landmarks of 1920s Barcelona. This rich web of human relationships and social spaces, which have become a daily ritual, totally ignores the rest of a city in which artistic fervor is a habitual way of transcending social crisis. Pla's novel also captures the feel and the shape of Barcelona with its sterile ritual of the *tertulia de café* and the empty rhetoric of what it is discussed there, the café being a masculine sanctuary away from domestic life and without female intrusions. The cluster of idle characters at the *tertulia* and their trivial conversation and gossip, much of it already incorporated into the structure of the Madrid-based novels of Galdós, would became an important motif in depictions of urban life by Pío Baroja, Max Aub, and Camilo José Cela. In postmodern fiction and the more recent urban chronicles of Barcelona by writers such as Quim Monzó and Sergi Pàmies, the *café* will be replaced by the *bar*, that ubiquitous oasis of calm amidst the turmoil of everyday urban tension and drudgery.

The bloody anarchist revolts that led to in 1909 to Barcelona's so-called *Semana trágica*, or Tragic Week, and the brutal repression by the city authorities provided the *modernistes* with the backdrop to their urban narratives, one that contrasted sharply with the orderly and abstract *polis* dreamt of by their successors, the *noucentistes*, who were determined to turn the city into a lively, modern capital, a unified cultural entity that would replace the legacy of fragmentation bequeathed by the socio-nationalists. That they were so optimistic about the future was due to the joint political-cultural venture of the recently established *Mancomunitat*, or autonomous Catalan government, which fuelled an unprecedented revival of interest in both Catalan language and Catalan culture.

The contrast between the utopian Barcelona of the *noucentistes* and the reality of social unrest in the interwar period was to become a central paradox in historical post-war representations of the city by Max Aub, Ignacio Agustí, Mercè Rodoreda, and Eduardo Mendoza. In their novels, urban experience becomes more and more contradictory as the customary images of the city are replaced by images with strong social and political connotations. Mendoza's retrospective *La verdad sobre el caso Savolta* (1975) weaves the tensions of anarchist Barcelona into an ambitious social tapestry, with a panoramic perspective and a degree of documentation that results in a nineteenth-century saga or 'totalidad decimonónica'.[1] Mendoza intersperses true and apocryphal data on the assassination of a Catalan businessman (the fictional Savolta), allegedly by anarchist union members and/or German spies as an act of revenge for his role in manufacturing arms for the Allies during World War I. The murder is finally attributed to the machinations of an American power company, 'Barcelona Traction Light and Power', that journalists of the time implicated in Savolta's death. Mendoza uses lawyer Javier Miranda's careful reconstruction of this homicide, as he prepares a deposition for the US court a decade later, to paint a vivid socio-economic tableau that stretches from the reign of Alfonso XIII and the first year of the Primo de Rivera dictatorship in 1923 to the proclamation of the Second Spanish Republic in 1931. He depicts the economic advantages and privileges the Catalan entre-preneurial class drew from Spain's neutrality in World War I and places it against a backdrop of ongoing tension between management and workers. The main events the time, such as the General Strike of 1902, the organiza-tion of anarchist factions into the two political alliances, Solidaritat Obrera (Labor Solidarity) and CNT (National Confederation of Workers), and the popular uprising against conscription for the Moroccan Wars – which in turn led to the bloody repressions of 1909 and 1921 – are all going on while the protagonist's story unfolds. The Great War had awakened new social animosities as it enriched the entrepreneurial class of the Savoltas-to-be, a class that did not hesitate to seek the support of the local military when they were looking for protection against the threat of terrorism. Businessmen like Savolta surrounded themselves with *pistoleros a sueldo* (salaried gunmen) while the street violence and the climate of repression promoted by the civil authorities reached unsustainable levels.

The advent of the Spanish Second Republic in 1931 reunited the Catalan avant-garde with the liberal and increasingly left-wing nationalism of the *Ezquerra Republicana de Catalunya* (Catalan Republican Leftist Party). As in Madrid, the Civil War would label Barcelona a 'proletarian capital' super-seding its previous identity as 'the city of bombs'. Max Aub's choral novel, *Campo cerrado* (1939), published as he went into exile in Mexico in 1943, captures the socio-political turmoil that the city experienced between the end of the end of the dictatorships of Primo de Rivera and Berenguer and

---

[1]   Santos Alonso (in Mendoza 1988: 19–20) establishes the strong influence of Galdós and Baroja on the novel.

the beginning of the military insurrection of 1936. The escalating political tension is here seen through the eyes of Rafael Serrador, a sixteen-year-old boy who arrives in Barcelona from Castellón at the opening of the 1929 International Exhibition. As Rafael tries to forge a cohesive image of a city full of contradictions by striking up an acquaintance with a series of anarchist, nationalist, and Falange mentors who leave him wary of party commitment, the reader enters into a labyrinth of political factions and party allegiances via a cacophony of opinion and conversation garnered from a broad sociopolitical spectrum. In picaresque fashion, Rafael moves from job to job, from apprentice to clerk and back to industrial worker in a nickel foundry in Hostafranchs. His political education gives him a dense topographical map of the city, consisting of factories, workshops, warehouses, cafés, shops, working-class libraries, and working-men's clubs of a kind that will vanish with the onset of the war. In July 1936, Barcelona's *barris* and slums become stages for festivals (like the Proletarian Olympics), protests, strikes, fires, and barricades, leading up to the heroic hand-to-hand fighting of the civil militia defending the city as Franco's troops are overwhelmed in a counterattack.[2] Only then does Rafael Serrador feel ready to defend the Republic's legitimacy and join the Durruti militia which drives Franco's insurgents out of the city. As in other moments of Barcelona's tumultuous history, the burning of churches and buildings becomes a symbol of purification from which a new social order is to be born:

> Rafael Serrador wandered the streets bumping into people and sensing the ties that bind him to the other men. He felt trapped in a web as though he was one of its threads; one of the threads of the night. The world had gone mad; everything was out of kilter. Leaning on a downpipe, Rafael Serrador thought of the falling water: a savage torrent, swift, implacable, uncontain-

---

[2]   George Orwell's *Homage to Catalonia* reports the same jubilant revolutionary atmosphere at the outbreak of the Civil War that first attracted him to the cause: 'The presence of the oppressed and invisible masses is felt in Las Ramblas as they organize to collectivize industry and appropriate the city's technical structures: Down the Ramblas, the wide central artery of the town where crowds of people streamed constantly to and fro, the loudspeakers were bellowing revolutionary songs all day and far into the night. And it was the aspect of the crowds that was the queerest thing of all. In outward appearance it was a town in which the wealthy classes had practically ceased to exist. Except for a small number of women and foreigners there were no 'well dressed people' at all. Practically everyone wore rough working class clothes or blue overalls or some variant of militia uniform. All this was queer and moving. There was much in it that I did not understand in some ways, I did not even like it, but I recognized it as a state of affairs worth fighting for' (1967: 5). *Homage* immortalized for the democratic world the abortive efforts of Catalan anarchists, after the removal of president Lluís Companys and the death of Andreu Nin. Orwell's political disenchantment with the left moved him to make changes to his account of the fighting among the antifascist factions that took place in Las Ramblas during the first two weeks of May 1937.

able, falling with an untamed force like that of a fiery bull, a rainbow of fire, above the victorious city. (Aub 1943: 271)

The city's contagious revolutionary euphoria is also captured in *La plaça del diamant (1966), in which Mercè Rodoreda chronicles the change of collective mood from joy to disenchantment, from that 'sunny day' (14 April 1931) when the Second Republic was proclaimed – a day 'bathed in spring air and smelling of tender leaves and roses that would be never enjoyed again' (1962: 80) – to the day in February 1939 when Franco's troops recaptured the city. The readiness of the young to fight for the democratic regime in 1936 is in sharp contrast with the feelings of anger and frustration aroused in the second part of the novel by the nationalist victory.

Post-war Barcelona

Franco's dictatorship restored powers to a conservative loyal-cum-collabora-tionist ruling class. He decreed that the entire life of Catalonia and its capital – official, cultural, and educational – had to be conducted in Castilian, and this decree had profound implications for literary life in the city. Following the initiative taken by a group of intellectuals, writers, and editors with links to Falange ideology to establish a journal, Destino,[3] the local publishing industry, which boasted editors such as Dalmau, Milá, Aymá, Freixinet, Barna, and Delfos, was keen on publishing apolitical books about the city. Thus Barcelonismo became a substitute for the banned Catalanismo.[4] A good example of one such project approved by the regime in Madrid was Ignacio Agustí's best-seller, Mariona Rebull (1944), the first instalment of what was to become the five-volume saga La ceniza fue árbol, the last part of which was not completed until 1972. The cycle spans more than seventy years in the life of Barcelona and is packed with entrepreneurial and amorous adventures

[3] Destino started as a weekly Falange magazine launched in Burgos during the Civil War on the initiative of Barcelona editor Eugenio Nadal. It was reconstituted as a private enter-prise after 1939. The journal eventually came to adopt a more liberal stance and became one of the main channels for the diffusion and promotion of Catalan culture in Spanish. Among contributors were a number of renowned Catalan authors and critics who wrote in Spanish as a way of reconnecting with their readers. They included such figures as Josep Plá, Josep Fuster, Josep Maria Sagarra, Joan Ramon Masoliver, Joan Teixidor, Jaume Vicens Vives, Josep Maria Espinás, Joan Oliver, Joaquín Marco, Antonio Vilanova, Pere Gimferrer, Baltasar Porcel, and Montserrat Roig.

[4] One undertaking worthy of mention was the ten-volume collection entitled Barcelona y su historia, published by Librería Dalmau in 1942–43, which had a number of eminent contrib-utors, among them Joaquín Nadal, Carles Soldevila, Aurelio Capmany, José María Ràfols and Ramón Alberich. Alberich also wrote the highly successful Un siglo de Barcelona, published by Freixenet in 1945.

that fill the empty and depressed post-war years with nostalgia and romanticism. It portrays a traditional, conservative, hard-working city, with a stable
hierarchy of guilds and professions, social classes which neither mix nor
envy each other, and the promise of a new, more ambitious and productive
future. Agustí's Barcelona was to be a city attuned to the official concilia-
tory rhetoric of the Francoist regime (Alberich 1970: 298).[5] Mariona's high
spirits, extravagance, and frivolity are easily identified with the Catalan old
families with economic ties to Madrid, as well as with social climbers and
those newly rich from the black market who were anxious to legitimize their
status by becoming anti-Catalanist.[6] Significantly, the author chose the anarchist bombing of the Liceo Opera House on 7 December 1893 as the stage
on which to sacrifice the superfluous heroine and her lover at the end of the
novel. Mariona's adultery would not change the values that her widower,
senyor Ríus, would pass on to their son Desiderio, the man destined to transform the 'face of Catalonia' in subsequent instalments of the novel (Alberich
1970: 298).

Brought to the silver screen by director José Luis Sáenz de Heredia in
1945, Mariona Rebull breathed new life into bourgeois myths popularized
by the turn-of-the-century novels of Narcís Oller and Dolors Monserdà, and
the plays of Serafí Pitarra, Ignasi Iglesias, and Santiago Rusiñol. The fiction
of José María Segarra, Xavier Berenguel, Jaume Cabré, Eduardo Mendoza,
Nuria Amat, and Montserrat Roig would take up many of its symbols of
identity.[7]

---

[5] Agustí recognized that the furore provoked by his novel has nothing to do with literary
merit and everyting to do with the current situation in the city. This is what gave the work its
'civic aura': 'Mariona was the symbol of an outlawed, beaten and humiliated Barcelona... Its
people accepted Agustí's book, thinking that, at last, someone without patriotic or ideological
alliances had understood the way they were, and was trying to make it clear to the rest of the
world' (1974: 156–57). Film critic Román Gubern has suggested that, 'as the cycle of apologies
for Franco's crusade was interrupted by the struggle for Stalingrad, films and fiction looked to
the previous century for their subject matter' (1997: 62).

[6] Mariona Rebull was followed by El viudo Ríus (1945), Desiderio (1957), 19 de julio
(1965) and Guerra Civil (1972), chronicling Barcelona's history from 1879 to 1936 from a
personal perspective (in all but the first novel). Soldevila-Durante points to Agustí's claim
of political impartiality – 'my novel neither puts out candles nor sets off bombs' – and to the
detached, impersonal style in which the author reports the political turbulence from the side-
lines, and suggests that the work does indeed furnish an authentic portrait of a certain sector
of Catalan society (1980: 134–37).

[7] The same myths inspired Catalan fictions and dramas popularized by films and TV, such
as Eduardo Mendoza's play Restauració, the movie La ciutat cremada (Antoni Ribas, 1976)
and the film based on Narcís Oller's La febre d'or. Mercè Rodoreda's *Mirall trencat and *La
plaça del diamant, Montserrat Roig's trilogy Ramona, adeu (1972), and Eduardo Mendoza's
*La verdad sobre el caso Savolta are among the most successful TV-3 series.

The Barcelona *flâneuse*

The return to realist modes and existentialist concerns in the post-war novel meant that there was interest once again in the psychology of character, an introspection attuned to the restoration of urban middle-class values and the new interest in female self-awareness. The freedoms women had tasted during the war, though halted by the neo-conservative and religious offensive that was *nacionalcatolicismo*, prompted young women to question the way their mothers lived, submissive to their husbands and bound to the house. Spanish authors, influenced by the European best-sellers of Stefan Zweig, Lajos Zilahi, and Daphne du Maurier, attempted to reflect the new ways women contemplated, dreamed of, lived in, and appropriated urban places from which they were previously excluded. Their heroines and alter egos searched for promise and possibility in the big city, overcoming the ubiquitous vigilance of the authorities and their own apprehensions, and feminizing the city in the process. In the *Bildungsromanen* of Carmen Laforet, Carmen Kurz, Mercedes Salisachs, and later, in those by Lidia Falcón, Esther Tusquets, Carme Riera, Montserrat Roig, and Maruja Torres, the heroine's passage into adulthood equates to leaving, returning to, and coming to terms with her own city. Rebellious adolescents, idle students, housewives in distress, unmarried office-workers, maids, and hesitant prostitutes roam the streets of Barcelona in search of lost memories or new possibilities, often stumbling into brief encounters or being awakened by personal epiphanies. In a quintessential post-war novel, Carmen Laforet's *Nada* (1945), Andrea, the protagonist, finds in her walks through the city an escape from the stifling tutelage of her adoptive family and a cherished privacy in which to indulge her adolescent self-absorption. Arriving at Barcelona's railway station, she plunges into the evening air and 'the urban tide' becomes an exhilarating experience, intensifying her sense of risk-taking and her openness to new sensations, her will to take possession of this unknown city:

> A sea breeze, strong and fresh, entered my lungs along with my first sensations of the city: a mass of sleepy apartment buildings, shuttered businesses, and street lights standing like sentinels drunk with loneliness. A deep breath, hard won, came from the first whisper of dawn. Behind me, just across from the mysterious alleys that led to the Borne market, was the overwhelming presence of the sea. (1945: 4)

The invigorating presence of the Mediterranean in a city of cement, a glimpse connected to flashbacks to the protagonist's idyllic past or lost childhood, is a recurrent motif in Carme Riera's *Te deix, amor, el mar com a penyora* (1975), Esther Tusquets's *El mismo mar de todos los veranos* (1978) and Clara Janés's short story 'Un punto de humedad en el aire' (Regás 1989: 155–63). *Nada* introduces yet another urban ritual: the incursion of the adolescent into areas of Barcelona's dangerous and off-limits red-light district, or Barrio Chino, somewhere that soon loses its appeal once penetrated, and once the misery and sordidness of the city at night is plain too see.[8]

In Mercè Rodoreda's novels, past and present converge in a typically cramped space in an old area of Barcelona – a *barri,* a square, a street, a house – where the heroine was born and has always lived. Natàlia's entire life has been spent in and around the Plaça del Diamant both before and after the war, and she has journeyed just a few steps from the dilapidated apartment she inhabited as a young wife to the more conventional flat where she now lives out her old age. During the war, as hunger and despair set in, Natàlia's walks round the *barri* become a symbolic race against death. She rushed through her house-cleaning jobs because she feared for the children she had left on their own at home, and she attempted to commit suicide in the square where once she danced and fell in love. Her small urban world has a powerful component of legend, myth, female and Catalan folk wisdom that allows for the presence of nature in the midst of the impersonal march of progress and the twists and turns of history. The close-knit social texture of the neighborhood in which Natàlia's tale unfolds is severely affected by the war, but not entirely ruined. Houses, shops, park benches, squares, and churches become personal emotional landmarks, or, at best, hideaways where she can grab a moment's respite; refuges where she can see her life's sufferings and accomplishments in perspective.

El Carrer de les Camèlies (1966) and *Mirall trencat* (1983) are structured around the concentric circles of *la torra* and *el barri*. The childhood home (*torra*) functions as a substitute for lost parents. It and, by extension, its garden, street, or square, remain inviolate in the protagonist's memory while time and events desecrate it, leaving only ruins, echoes, cracks, wild vegetation, rats, and cockroaches. The melodramatic nature of *Mirall trencat*

---

[8] 'The "Devil's glitter" about which Angustias had warned me seemed impoverished and loud, with a great abundance of posters with pictures of dancing women and male dancers. The doors of the nightclubs with shows seemed like booths at a fair. The music left one in a daze, coming as it did from all sides and mixing together and clashing inharmoniously. Rushing along in the midst of a human wave that sometimes exasperated me, because it kept me from seeing Juan, I experienced the vivid memory of a carnival that I had seen when I was little' (1945: 121). The charged sensuality of Las Ramblas on a June afternoon also appears in a narrative by Esther Tusquets as a carnivalesque operetta performance and a reflection of the protagonist's sexual awakening: 'The whole city – such a sordid, vulgar, marvellous, miserable city – had gone mad [and Sara] had gone out into the street hiding under her thousand disguises; she made her way, pagan and wild, down towards the sea, between the leaden sun in an unchanging blue sky and the sticky, burning asphalt, because Las Ramblas boulevard was a blooming jungle: dirty, obscene, stinking, wild, indescribably beautiful' ('He besado tu boca, Yokanaán', in Tusquets 1981: 185–86).

makes a central issue out the middle-class dream of *la torreta i el jardi* (a little house with a garden) surviving the ravages of time. Teresa Godoy de Valldaura's mansion in the Sant Gervasi de Cassoles hills personifies her social success and her personal misfortunes. As a beauty born to a fishmonger in the Boquería market and married twice to Barcelona businessmen with connections in Paris and Vienna, Teresa languishes in her villa, embodying in her aging frame and dispassionate soul the city's many tribulations and transformations. Her legitimate, illegitimate, and adopted offspring are living reminders of the social changes and personal rivalries that have destroyed her family and dictated her affections.[9] Her attachment to *la torra* after her favorite grandson drowns in the fishpond is strengthened by the tutelary presence of her old servant Armanda, who runs the house and stays out of blind loyalty, even after all her masters have left.

The agoraphobia from which both Teresa and Armanda suffer contrasts with Cecilia's attachment to the streets in *El Carrer de les Camèlies*, as she progresses from streetwalker to prostitute to kept woman. The streets of Barcelona are 'a source of financial opportunity fraught with danger for the single working girl' (Arkinstall 2004: 120). Cecilia is a restless woman whose interminable wanderings through the city lead her back to the street where she was abandoned and propped up against the fence of her adoptive parents' home by the angel-like figure of the *vigilant*, or neighborhood night-watchman. At thirteen, she runs away with a seventeen-year-old street boy to the old districts of Las Ramblas and the Liceo Opera House, where she meets elegant gentlemen, figures who in her future years will become symbols of tutelage, corruption, and redemption associated with her lost father. As a young woman, immersed in a solipsism that becomes the narrative matter itself, Cecilia's endless perambulations through the streets and squares of post-war Barcelona are voyages of self-discovery. This self-absorbed, semi-unconscious *flâneuse*, short on character and assertiveness but long on resilience, is an excellent observer, an all-seeing eye.[10] As Arkinstall has noted, *Carrer* is not driven by action and plot so much as by the drifting of an endlessly reflective mind; a female mind meandering as she walks through

---

[9]   Feminine icons of the city include La dama del paraiguas (The Lady with the umbrella), a statuette of 1814 who evokes Barcelona's Romantic period, and the Frederic Maillol statues flanking Catalonia Square which recall the Classicist Mediterranean ideal of Catalan woman-hood. Close to the spirit of the *Noucentistes* were the cubist figures of Picasso and the paintings of Joaquim Sunyer. The literary idealizations of women recur in Catalan poetry and in journalism on the subject of Barcelona, such as Eugeni d'Ors's *La ben plantada* and Gabriel Miró's 1911 chronicle 'La hermosa señora' (see Altisent 1992: 169–72).

[10]   The crowds and streets, like drugs that pull the *flâneur* back time and again onto the city streets, are features derived from Baudelaire (see Benjamin 1968b).

the city; a mind ruminating and occasionally going off on tragic tangents involving abortion and suicide.

In *City women*, Liz Heron notes how difficult it is, given middle-class gender divisions between masculine and feminine, public and private, for the modern woman writer to conceive a female equivalent of the *flâneur*, whom Baudelaire defined in his famous sonnet 'La passante' as 'the passionate spectator [...] who can set up house in the heart of the multitude'.[11] Cecilia's desire for total freedom to come and go as she pleases points to the simi-larities between *flâneuse* and prostitute in those poverty-stricken post-war years. Arkinstall sees her as an example of 'how the conceptual categories of working woman and prostitute soon become fluid and exchangeable entities' (2004: 121), as for most of her adult life Cecilia is the 'kept woman' of a string of wealthy and married 'protectors' from whom she obtains the income to maintain the house she inherits from one of them. The contradictions in her status – a market player but only because she sells herself – and the ways she gradually reclaims the male-dominated space that is Barcelona, show Rodoreda challenging the masculinist premiss of the T.S. Eliot quotation used in the preface to the novel: '[She too has] walked many years in this city'.

The ambiguity of the post-war *flâneuse* and the pejorative connotation that the expression 'mujer de la calle' (street woman) still holds for females who walk the streets also casts a dark shadow on Rosita, the twelve-year-old protagonist in Juan Marsé's *Ronda del Guinardó* (1967). Like Cecilia, Rosita is an orphan, a precocious child who loves to wander the streets, has male friends and, eventually, is raped by a stranger (an incident later used by the police to pressurize her into falsely identifying as her rapist a political prisoner who has died as a result of police torture). Just like the afternoon Rosita reluctantly accompanies the police to the morgue to identify her predator, Rosita's routine rounds through the neighborhood and her pica-resque-like transactions with her friends are metaphors for the meanderings of the narrative itself. They lead in a certain direction and point to a certain end: the disclosure of her longing for affection and her obsessive need to fill the void of her lost family. These, in turn, lead to her final encounter with a counterfeit cousin, who corrupts her by becoming her lover and her pimp. Rosita's vagrancy and freedom from social convention in the hills of Mount Carmel and her knowledge of the territory is a sort of self-imposed destiny. Like young Cecilia, she is a socially marginal figure who proudly rejects middle-class charity and prejudice in favor of an independent life bordering on prostitution.[12]

---

[11] Charles Baudelaire, 'A une passante' (1980: 68–69), quoted by Heron (1993: 7–9).

[12] The sordid character of post-war Barcelona provides neo-picaresque scenarios in which 'la mujer de la calle', 'hacer la calle', or 'vivir en la calle' acquire their familiar connotations: spinsters live a double life, out-of-town students and impecunious single ladies find themselves

Displacement, re-familiarization and reconciliation with one's own city after a long sojourn abroad are key motifs in *El temps de les cireres* (1977) by Montserrat Roig. The wanderings of photographer Natàlia Miralpeix through the Barcelona streets constitute both a physical and an emotional collage of flashbacks covering the years from her political militancy as a student to the present, when the end of the Franco dictatorship is imminent. After self-imposed exile in Paris and London, Natàlia returns to Barcelona in 1974, the year that the ailing dictator strengthened his iron rule by ordering the execution by garrotte of anarchist student Salvador Puig Antich and imposing a curfew on the city. The deafening noise of the streets becomes a metaphor of Natàlia's need for oblivion: 'The first thing she noticed that was different was the noise. Barcelona had become very noisy. It was not the roaring noise of any big city, the roaring of cars and people, but different ... as though the city were screaming as a way of not feeling' (1974: 97). Alienated in a city swamped with traffic, the noise of construction, concrete towers, and flash luxury apartments, she evokes the politically-charged city of a decade earlier, when the anti-Franco student resistance promised adventure and risk and when her love for Emili, who disappeared into a Francoist jail leaving her pregnant and confused, was still full of promise. In her present estrangement from an overdeveloped and consumerist Barcelona, her thoughts turn to the political agitation of the late 1960s and to a city not yet ready for the same personal freedoms that would drive the riots of 1968 in Paris, the Mecca where she and her comrades eventually learned to release 'the fear of the police and of their own bodies' (97).[13] Natàlia's sentimental reminiscences abruptly shift to the hidden tragedy of her abortion, the decision that triggered a confrontation with her father and led her to leave home. But, now, her father's senile retreat into himself makes Natàlia see him as yet another victim of unrequited love (for Natàlia's mother) and of political defeat. Especially significant for a protagonist coming to terms with her own

---

on the fringes of prostitution, while prostitutes assume decorous and bourgeois façades. During the last years of the Franco regime and the transition, a hedonistic nightlife, fuelled by alcohol, drugs, sex and easy money, will transform the working-class Ramblas, as well as the more elegant Rambla de Cataluña, Ensanche, and Las Corts districts, into stages for a masquerade in which social decline rubs shoulders with the social aspirations of a new and ambitious political elite. In the novel of the 1980s and 1990s, idleness and social intercourse are more and more reduced to corruption and political intrigue, as we can see in Lluis Maria Todó's light comedy of the Barcelona bisexual scene, *El joc del mentider* (1994) and the more sombre drug-related downward spiral portrayed by Lidia Falcón in *El juego de la piel* (1982).

[13] Ironically, the 'Song of the Cherries' or the communist hymn sung on the Paris barricades in May 1968 and which gives the novel its title ends up being a call of the homeland: 'She became homesick when she was happiest. She missed a smell, a street, the flood of people descending into the *Ramblas* in small waves, the shadows around Santa María del Mar, the chill of the early morning, the leaves swept from the plane trees in the fall' (97).

city is the encounter with her nephew. As a younger version of herself, Pere personifies the city's ability to regenerate itself. Their common enjoyment of a nocturnal promenade through the gothic maze of Santa Maria del Mar triggers in Natàlia a new recognition of a city that has kept its charm and zest for life, even though its has taken a completely different political path from the one she had imagined.[14]

Debunking Barcelona's myths

The writers of the Escuela de Barcelona and their contemporaries use their writings to question the myths of the tribe, creating an aesthetic of destruction and hatred as a stylistic counterpart to the inaction, censorship, inertia, and procrastination that beset Spanish society after two and a half decades of dictatorship. The uncivil diatribes of Juan and Luis Goytisolo, Terenci Moix, and Juan Marsé were targeted at their own social class and the fusty nationalist emblems of Catalonia and Spain. They also denounced the cultural elite's narcissism and exhibitionism and its urgency to embrace European modernity at its most frivolous and uncritical. Álvaro de Mendiola's return to Barcelona from his Paris exile in Juan Goytisolo's *Señas de identidad* (1966) is as disappointing as that of Roig's alter ego. Álvaro enters into dialogue with his city in a tone that is both desperate and irredeemably loving: 'This love which, though you never asked for it, I have given you for years now, despite everything' (1976: 332). He, like the author, is torn between the complicity with Franco's establishment of the class to which he belongs and his own awareness of social injustice. As he visits the Montjuich military fortress and cemetery, his memories of the Civil War massacre of Republican Catalans are interrupted by a group of foreigners, whose voices become a polyglot collage underlining the tourist *verbena*, or carnival that Spain has become. In *Señas*, Barcelona is a 'labyrinth', a 'ghost town', a 'mausoleum' built

---

[14] As in Virginia Woolf's *Mrs Dalloway*, Natàlia's self-absorption provides a whole host of images and sensations that connect the city to the awakening of lost emotion. Her monologue, interspersed with flashbacks and free associations, is a dialogue between the heroine and her city, a city at once welcoming and alienating, carefree and repressed (as though Franco's ubiquitous police surveillance also reached into the mind): 'Barcelona was a gigantic corpse with its guts wide open' (97), 'I don't like this city. It is as if it were sinking gradually... I also thought this city was sinking, but while abroad I have realized that we always carry our city inside us' (216). The dictator's iron rule, in the form of Puig Antich's brutal execution, shows that Natàlia's exile has been time spent waiting for nothing. Later, in her Ensanche apartment, the family ghosts transmit to Natàlia the power to endure loss and degradation indifferently. Thus she can accept the present, hoping, as in the 'Song of the Cherries', that 'there is also a time for life and love, in spite of history' (1977: 217).

by a bourgeoisie 'whose preposterous artistic taste is equivalent in degree to the city's greediness', (73).[15] Its socio-historical referents, pregnant with meaning, are similar to those we find in Luis Goytisolo's *Recuento* (1972), Esther Tusquets's *El mismo mar de todos los veranos* (1978), Félix de Azúa's *Diario de un hombre humillado* (1987) and *Historia de un idiota contada por él mismo* (1986), and Nuria Amat's *La intimidad* (1998) and *El país del alma* (1999). In Juan Goytisolo's autobiography, *Coto vedado* (1982) and in Amat's novels, the empty spaces of post-war Barcelona are filled with rituals, memories, epitaphs, and rambles, all of which provide structures for the internal dialogue of the narrators with dead poets, writers in exile, and obscure artists who struggle to preserve Catalan culture against an uncertain future. The Sarrià-Pedralbes-Sant Gervasi enclave, where the shadows of writers, musicians, editors, and foreign and Latin American novelists (from J. V. Foix, Carles Riba, Joan Fuster, and Carlos Barral to Gabriel García Márquez) still haunt the streets, has become a ghost town, a 'city of the soul' which has vanished beneath the overdeveloped and multicultural Barcelona of the 1990s.

Barcelona also takes center stage in novels and memoirs by Terenci Moix, Manuel Vázquez Montalbán, and Lluis Maria Todó,[16] and, in doing so, it re-emerges as an overly social, nocturnal, and carnivalesque capital whose streets have become a stage for *happenings* and *boutades* and in which those in fashion are always at risk of becoming outdated. The city is nothing more

---

[15] The cemetery is a recurrent metaphor in *Señas de identidad*: Barcelona is, in 1963, 'a prosperous and flourishing city of a million and more corpses, fat and full of themselves' (24); it is also a metropolis full of the sleeping and the waking dead, the only difference between them – the poor southerners who live in the Montjuich barracks and the rich buried in the cemetery – is 'strictly a question of horizontality' (54) in a place where 'Gaudí-like and Modern Style mausoleums are a cross between funerary monument and summer villa' (70). Nuria Amat's *La intimidad* (1997) establishes an intertextual dialogue with the city we find in Juan Goytisolo's *Coto vedado* (1982), which is set amid the frigid, neoclassical architecture of Bonanova, alongside the medieval monastery of Pedralbes, the church of Sarrià, and the Sant Gervasi cemetery.

[16] As Moix puts it in *Lleonard, o El sexo de los ángeles* (1992: 293), 'You would have had to live through the post-war years to understand what that resurgence meant to all of us. ... We would say "Barcelona is dead, Madrid is more of a capital city", and things of the sort. Suddenly, the tables were turned: intellectuals from Madrid came on pilgrimage to Barcelona and dropped their pants in honour of the cosmopolitan air that we were breathing here. One felt superior whenever those cavemen exclaimed: "Barcelona is closer to Europe, in fact it *is* Europe; you people are freer, more modern, more cool". Listening to such praise constituted one of Lleonard's pleasures since he, borrowing from a controversy fashionable at the time, called intellectuals from Castile "the cabbage eaters" '. 'Every night we would practice all the hobbies we had acquired, all those habits that had helped us survive the barrenness of Spain's dark years, and had turned us into the most eminent members of an ultra-refined civilization (427).

than a network of social encounters in the places where it is fashionable to hang out: *boîtes*, bars, night-clubs, boutiques, bookstores, art galleries, bordellos, and flamenco taverns, as well as a number of particular venues, such as the Liceu Opera House, the Bocaccio and Zeleste discotheques, the Seix Barral publishing house, the bookstore Dau al Set, the 'Drugstore' on Las Ramblas, Tuset Street, and the jazz clubs in the Plaza Real (Jazz Colón and Jamboree), which are frequented by locals, American sailors, and tourists. These were the obligatory stops in the nocturnal wanderings of a liberal bourgeoisie eager for improvisation and the celebration of anything new, in search of illicit sex, or keen to cause scandal, to dress up in disguise, or just to be provocative.[17]

The experimental and anti-realist innovations of the mid-1970s led to new ways of describing the urban alienation of late capitalism. The rapid and disconcerting transformations to which Barcelona was subjected by Josep María de Porcioles, its mayor from 1957 to 1973, in his zeal to accommodate ever-increasing waves of immigrants, are depicted in Luis Goytisolo's *Recuento* (1973). A decade later, Eduardo Mendoza would recapture in *La ciudad de los prodigios* the rapid modernization of turn-of-the-century Barcelona and question the no less hasty and controversial city replanning that occurred in the late 1980s during the term of office of Mayor Pasqual Maragall, when the Olympics enterprise gave the mayor an opportunity to 'modernize' and 'revitalize' a dormant and dilapidated Barcelona.

In Luis Goytisolo's *Recuento*, the physical Barcelona, occupying a social space rebuilt over centuries, becomes inseparable from the written city. Its disparate social, ethnic, and political archetypes are paraded before us and contrasted with their opposites in an attempt to convey the contradictory nature of Catalan history, both internally and in respect of its relationship to the rest of Spain. As Ricardo Gullón puts it, '[*Recuento*'s] broad sweep and detailed exposition [...] and the description of the city as a living entity and of its daily rhythms makes it a sort of *Comédie humaine*. The elements that go to make up and undo that entity are written with a verve that stands

---

[17] The cross-dresser and the transsexual are important figures of the Barcelona nighttime scene. An early literary example was Terenci Moix's protagonist 'Lilí Barcelona' in the title story of his *La torre dels vicis capitals* (1968). Robert Hughes points out (1992: 46–47) how the *travestit* would come to represent 'the spirit of permanent mutation, voyeurism and exhibitionism that lead to Barcelona's fixation with design'; a self-conscious attitude, used as a way to escape the triviality and the mass consumerist taste that overwhelmed the city and transformed Spanish society itself. In the *travestits* of Les Corts, this critic sees a projection onto the human body of Barcelona's wrenching and sacrificial architectural projects, 'as if its authentic self were struggling to manifest and reinvent itself by a series of painful surgical interventions' (47). This narcissistic obsession would be at its most exasperating during the 1992 architectural reinvention of the city.

comparison with Balzac' (1983: 56). The novel's parallels with James Joyce's *Ulysses* lie in its articulation of the crisis of a society and a nation living under the heel of a hated imperial power while trying to cling to its own petit-bourgeois identity. But Luis Goytisolo's perspective is that of systemic parody: 'mystification and the elegiac-cum-burlesque being the decisive contrasting factors between the imaginary and the real, generating a literary space that is the recreation rather than the representation of the everyday world' (Gullón 1983: 57). *Recuento*'s narrator is a historical guide, offering an uncompromising overview of Catalan history that quickly shatters into a number of different points of view. He distances himself from the here and now in order to contemplate the city and the region *sub specie aeternitatis*. In Chapters VI and VII, the narrative voice is speaking from right in the heart of the Gothic Quarter or *Casc Antic* (specifically, from the Museum of the History of the City on Mons Tabor where Barcelona was founded) and there it attempts to explain the conflictual relationship between Catalonia and Spain since pre-historical times.

Recuento is the most ambitious chronicle of Barcelona's continual process of self-definition, self-destruction, and survival during the 1970s. The narrator gradually vanishes from view to be replaced by a series of speeches, ready-made formulae, slogans, and rhetorical clichés that prevent the reader from arriving at any impartial evaluation of the world that is shown him, a device which suggests that it is impossible to synthesize all the obsessions, megalomania, and distortions of the collective unconscious. The frantic enumeration of icons and stereotypes of *Catalanitat* (Catalanity) becomes more and more stylized, until history itself takes a back seat. These demagogical, apologetic, axiomatic, elegiac, and deprecatory echoes are fleeting points of reference in an inscrutable reality that defies any attempt at rational synthesis. Silence is also used to dramatize an increasing emotional and autonomous text:

> An historical personality with features not respected by fate, a random and inconsistent fate, cast adrift by events and the whim of destiny, the separatist Barcelona of 1934, the anarchist Barcelona of 1936, communist Barcelona in 1937, fascist Barcelona in 1939, cheering victory, given to apotheosis, under military leadership, a characteristic versatility, an ominous spectacle, ignominy exalted in memory to the point of volatility, presumably a nightmare or even a carefully staged setting along the lines of Potemkin. A history of a people, more rewritten than written, adapted to the historical needs of the people, linked to its *reinaxença*, a grand epic, an epic in the flesh, made real in the realms of fantasy. Chopping and changing, events, the hope of change in a battered cause, Catalonia, the romantic bourgeois sublimation of misconceived collective behavior, the heart kicked out of the ideal of independence, now listless and with no drive left, political ineptitude masquerading as individualism, an unfortunate narrow-mindedness confused with stubborn and Pyrrhic resistance, a clumsy greed rebranded

as virtuous endeavour, a stubborn wretchedness marketed as good sense, a miserly poverty seen as a symptom of austerity, age-old inherited character traits, images made magnificent in the mirror of time [...] traces of the past transformed into an excuse for present impotence, transmuted into dreamy visions of the future, fanciful after-dinner talk, being the best thing in the world, a gift from God, a Messianic quality, the promised land, a mythic Mediterranean homeland now made real [...] Catalan territories – more than forty of them – stretching from Alicante to Roussillon, even perhaps from Murcia to Provence, spiritual Catalanity made real [...] the fortunate isles, the true paradise with *charnegos* as laborers and financed by tourism. (1973: 279–80)

This series of mutually contradictory and disjointed snippets – amorous, didactic, propagandistic, political, religious, military – reconfigure the map of the conscious and unconscious mythologies that have been planted in the mind of every citizen of Barcelona, every Spaniard.

The anti-romantic projection of Hispanic and Catalan myths reaches its *reductio ad absurdum* in Terenci Moix's *roman-à-clef*, **Lleonard, o El sexo de los ángeles*, written between 1959 and 1972 but not published until 1992. The fictional author elevates the level of individual experience to that of national archetype, without sacrificing the immediacy of the former or the stature of the later. Behind a complex collage of real-life personalities and a cacophony of voices, the reader can follow an autobiographical thread as the author tells how he came to be shunned by society as as result of the *malditismo* that is the very essence of Moix's outspoken public persona. He was the *enfant terrible* Barcelona society loved to despise.

And once more, the city appeared to him as a daughter-cum-whore. I know that Barcelona is like that. Beloved and pampered. Beautiful like the dim-witted daughter we all of us take under our wing; clean and polished among all the pearls in the Mediterranean, but in the end a whore. A murderous city, today and always. ... If the price we pay to obtain a certain measure of success means that we have to leave Barcelona forever, we all of us have to pay a high price, too, for our preordained return (1992: 421).[18]

---

[18] *Lleonard o el sexo de los ángeles* is a vitriolic satire of the collapse and transformation of a very small group of people: the gilded youth of the 1950s, a nationalist and leftist intellectual elite that slipped the leash of Madrid and adopted neocapitalist European attitudes and fashions. Moix targeted those Catalans who, since the 1960s, had proved resistant to change and had argued for of a type of nationalism which opposed the growth of political factions, and also those conservative nationalists who were reinventing a nationalist mystique incompatible with life in a modern city. Theirs was the neo-romantic and reactionary rhetoric that Catalonia's then president-to-be Jordi Pujol successfully appropriated in the 1980 elections and continued to regurgitate for two further decades.

While Goytisolo and Moix targeted the sins of the old nationalist elite, the next generation of writers, Juan Marsé and Manuel Vázquez Montalbán, were focusing on Barcelona's proletariat and the emerging immigrant classes that had until then been marginalized. In their novels and essays, they rejected the historical Catalonia and instead chose to portray social evolution from dictatorship to democratic transition and to show that the changes that have occurred had done nothing to alter the Francoist legacy of injustice and corruption.

Barcelona's other Catalans

In his early best-seller, *Els altres catalans* (1964), Francesc Candel had called his readers' attention to the culture of immigrants from the South now living in Barcelona. He offered a striking picture of these 'Catalans without the Catalan language' who were at the bottom of the social heap. These were the slumdwellers of Can Tunis, Casas Baratas, Verdún, La Torrassa, and the other outlying areas where, during the Civil War, one could see posters that read 'Catalonia ends here. Murcia begins here'. Candel's lightness of touch and mastery of local color did not obscure the pathos of his observation of the frictions between Southern customs and local ones, and the way they came together to produce a mixed culture (*charnego/xarnego*) born out of the co-dependency and interaction of two marginalized working-class cultures: Catalan and Andalusian.[19]

Juan Marsé, in *Últimas tardes con Teresa* (1966), **Si te dicen que caí* (1973), *El amante bilingüe* (1990), *Ronda de Guinardó* (1984), and **El embrujo de Shangai* (1993) explores with ironical bitterness Barcelona's 'bicultural' world, ignored by earlier writers. An exponent of 'possible literature', written in Spanish, harshly critical of class differences, and presenting Barcelona class warfare in all its sociocultural complexity, his is a very dramatic take on the history of the city.[20] In Marsé's novels, the relationship between the Catalan lower classes and southern immigrants – both groups popularly associated with exotic local color but enjoying common ground only in their rejection of modernity – is both complicit and resentful. Stories

---

[19] The book underplays the difficulty of getting southern immigrants to become Catalanized. When reviewing the novel in 1967, Maurici Serrahima noted that 'Catalonia not only has no means of enforcement [of the Catalan language]; it even lacks the means for teaching [the language]. Thus, it becomes extremely difficult, and sometimes impossible, to attend to the incessant demand from those who want to learn Catalan as the language of the land where they live and intend to settle permanently. Even so, correctly or not, they learn it and they use it' (Serrahima: 78).

[20] See Conte (1978) and Buckley (1996: 14–17).

such as 'El fantasma del cine Roxy' and *El amante bilingüe* show Marsé resorting to architectural metaphor to portray an impossible idyll between social down-and-outs: 'a story of unrequited love of a kind frequent in Catalonia, the love of the uprooted and uneducated *charnego* for an oppressed land, woman, culture' (Marsé 1987: 67).

In *El amante bilingüe*, satire and caricature go beyond the denunciation of Catalan nationalistic fervor and examine Catalan society since the political transition. The parody of the linguistic tyranny of the *normalització* serves here to explore the deeper psychological ramifications of Catalan bilingualism and this in turn leads to the question of the 'other'. The very title of the novel suggests a bold and sarcastic examination of the zealousness of linguistic conformity as a reversal of the previous linguistic situation, when Castilian was imposed as 'the language of the oppressor'. But, as Manuel Vázquez Montalbán observes, 'the protagonist's linguistic, cultural and sentimental schizophrenia touches on a more elusive alienation: Juan Marés-Juan Faneca, in his two alternating roles of Dr Jekyll and Mr Hyde, or the Catalan lumpen versus the *charnego* lumpen, takes us down to unsuspected depths. We penetrate the muddy waters of an anguished man struggling to present a single conventional face to the world. From the nausea of idiomatic evangelism, the novel moves to the nausea of this bilingual, Janus-faced, and lovesick individual whose wife is a militant in the fight for Catalan cultural resurgence only from the waist up' (Vázquez Montalbán 1990b: 3). An indication of Faneca's false assimilation to his wife's superior social class, bolstered by the fundamentalist rhetoric of the Catalan 'Divine Left', is the building they live in: the controversial apartment complex Walden Seven designed by Ricard Bofill in Sant Just de Desvern in 1975 that became an icon of 1970s counterculture. That postmodern and prematurely dated cluster of cubicles was designed as a space for communal living and as an alternative to the depressing apartment blocks erected during Porcioles's term of office as Mayor. The setting of *El amante* in this 'hulking castle-like structure with half-cylinder balconies, all sheathed in cobalt blue terra-cotta tiles (Hughes 1992: 50–51) demonstrates that the 'pseudo-progressive' stance of the couple is a masquerade: behind it lies the *charnego* disguise that Marés adopts to win back the love of his ex-wife, Norma, and her erotic attraction to southerners. The chameleon-like building that nurtured so many dreams in the 1970s was itself a dream, a living space conceived for the nonconformist and progressive couple that Norma thought they were; a building erected by its architect to promote an alternative life-style and sets of relationships that went beyond the traditional couple, exalting the freedoms of the individual and fostering the idea of community. But 'everything had gone to hell and Marés kept wondering why, while hearing the water dripping from the façade tiles in the outside darkness' (Marsé 1991: 36).

Olympic and post-Olympic Barcelona

The Olympic Village would indeed benefit the new middle class, but the Barcelona '92 project disturbed the old parameters that isolated the middle-class city from the hybrid city, uncovering forgotten neighborhoods and making them functional, viable, and visible. As Félix de Azúa observes, 'The new Barcelona, the Barcelona of the Olympic Games, is a product of hybrid-ization and has taken for itself nothing less than an entire sea, the same sea that for centuries symbolized evil, poverty, invasion, and illness. The patri-cians always lived with their back to the sea. Once they disappeared, the sea returned to the city' (1999: 139).

In the post-Olympic years, as Barcelona has became a must-see city on the European itinerary, its sacred spaces have been transformed and revamped to fulfil new functions or have given way to more profitable secular and tourist alternatives; its human landscape has become as multicultural as that of any other European city; its fictional mirrors have become increasingly imper-sonal and fragmented. Julià Guillamón's perceptive account of this change, *La ciutat interrompuda* (2001), shows how Barcelona novelists have felt increasingly uneasy as the old certainties vanished from the homogeneous town they grew up in and they find they have no compass with which to navigate the new city. Their political disenchantment with an official culture that seeks revenue and popularity through ever more exhibitionist forms of culture (ethnic festivals, art exhibitions, musical events, sporting attractions, urban monuments) has led them to go back to portray a city that is no longer there: a nostalgic memory far removed from the present-day reality. Such, for example, is the romantic Barcelona of Carlos Ruiz Zafón's international best-seller *La sombra del viento* (2001), a visually gray Barcelona of the 1940s not yet associated with iconic modernist architecture. Other authors resort to minimalist, impersonal, and interchangeable backdrops for their Barcelona fables of urban alienation, as witness Javier Tomeo's *La ciudad de las palomas* (1989), Quim Monzó's *Self-service* (1977), Enrique Vila-Matas's *Suicidios ejemplares* (1991) and Sergi Pàmies's novella, *La gran novela de Barcelona* (1997). These dystopian views of the manipulative powers of the city are also treated in depth in Miquel de Palol's futuristic allegory *El jardí dels set sepulcres* (1989). The impossibility of writing the 'great Barcelona novel' has led to new angles of humor and parody, as in Eduardo Mendoza's melodrama *Sin noticias de Gurb* (1991), a science-fiction tale about an alien visitor from another planet who navigates the chaotic Barcelona of the pre-Olympic years and decides to impersonate some celebrity and pop culture icons in order to immerse himself in the collective celebration of confusion. Pàmies's *La gran novela de Barcelona* is another ironic tale in perpetual motion and structured around the motif of traffic, with the city apparently a labyrinth with no exit (Guillamón 2001: 242). Opening with a huge view of

Barcelona from an airplane accompanied by a summary voiceover detailing its thousand-year history, the novel then contrasts this with the feeling of claustrophobia felt by a taxi driver and his passenger, who spend most of the novel gridlocked in the new motorway system, an image suggestive of Luis Romero's 1951 novel *La noria*.

The return to realism in the 1990s has meant that the experiences of immigrants to the city are no longer treated as those of 'the other' but as experiences of citizens in their own right, protagonists living in the new and renovated neighborhoods on the north-eastern edge of the city. Once again, it is the *carrer*, the *barri*, and not the apartment building, which affords refuge, sanctuary, security, and identity to these *nous barcelonesos* who create their own lively communities around the ever changing, chaotic, hostile, and hugely expensive city center. Many immigrant stories are set in the ruined and depopulated industrial *barris* that have survived, now renovated, increasingly accessible and identical to each other, many of which have fought to preserve their Catalan identity. Such *barris* provide the settings for Josep M. Benet i Jornet's successful TV-3 series *Poble Nou* and *Històries urbanes*.

An emotional attachment to the *barri*, new or old, is a common thread in stories of immigrant girls coming of age in the city. The heroines reminisce about the bittersweet challenges of growing up poor and getting an education that will enable them to escape the cosy and yet hideous neighborhood in which they grew up. Such is the experience of the central character of Maruja Torres's semi-autobiographical *Un calor tan cercano* (1996), set in Las Ramblas/Raval district, and of Rosa Rodríguez-Fisher's literary *alter ego* in *Batir de alas* (1998), a tale chronicling the success of an adolescent for whom the Santa Coloma/Besós public high school became the route to rapid assimilation and social integration. Maria Barbal's *El carrer Bolivia* (1999) is another multivoiced novel set in a street upgraded from a slum to an ordinary city street in recognition of the solidarity and communal spirit that marked the colony of Andalusian workers moved to the El Besós area in the 1960s. Here, the central love story reunites two symmetrical experiences, that of a Catalan family seeking their fortune in Jaén, and that of an Andalusian family that goes north in search of work. The *nou barris* born out of the expansion of the city and the new megaprojects of the once neglected and segregated Barcelona North shore (the 1992 Olympics and the 2002 Forum) have become the backdrop for many short stories, as one can see from the selections published in Rosa Regás's *Cuentos de Barcelona* (1998) and *Barcelona, un día* (1998). These stories juxtapose images new and old, Barcelona's eternal dreams and plans and its present realities.

Barcelona literature continues to produce images of complacency, estrangement, and exile that contrast starkly with the utopian and/or anachronistic aspirations of its community and planners. The lessons learned from history fail to bridge that gap between the imagined city and the living city.

Writers may try to disassociate their work from the mystique that their city continues to see in its popular and sentimental emblems, symbols, and rites. They may praise or curse their city, but their fervor, their prophetic diatribes, their elegies, and their self-ironies continue to be indicative of a partial or total adherence to the customs and culture they depict. This at times unwitting adherence to the past is all the more striking when the old images and the old usages are contrasted with the prefabricated images favored by the authorities, the uniformity of mass culture, and the gradual encroachment of the lifestyles of the global village.

Further reading

Abella (1992), Agustí, Ignacio (1974), Alberich (1970), Altisent (2002), Arnau (1991), Arkinstal (2004), Azaña (1977), Azevedo (1993), Azúa (1999), Ballester (1992), Barral (1975), Bermúdez *et al.* (2002), Benjamin (1968), Berman (1988), Bohigas *et al.* (1990), Bordons & Subirana (1999), Bru & Tusell (1990, 1997, and 1998), Buckley (1996), Carbonell *et al.* (1979), Castells (1983), Certeau (1993), Epps (2002), Estruch (1994), Guillamón (2001), Gullón (1983), Labanyi (2002), Maragall & Guillamet (1986 and 1991), Marías (1994), Moix & Moix (1988), Molas (1996a and 1996b), Regás (1989 and 1991), Roig (1987), Roig & Simó (1985), Rivière (2000), Sánchez (2002), Sempronio (1980), Smith (2000a and 2009b), Sobrer (1978), Sotelo (2005), Subirats (1995), Vázquez Montalbán (1992b), Vidal-Folch *et al.* (1994), Vilarós (1998).

IV

NEW VOICES, NEW PERSPECTIVES, NEW MODES

11

Narrating Women in the Post-war Spanish Novel

NINA L. MOLINARO

Women writers have participated in all the movements, styles, genres, debates, and themes that we find in twentieth-century Spanish literature. However, peninsular literary historians, if they have considered them at all, have tended to group these women together in order to segregate them from their male counterparts, as if their work was in some way inherently inferior. This phenomenon continues to occur well into the twenty-first century. The writers themselves complain that, as a result of this kind of gender-based segregation, they feel compelled to tell different stories. As Laura Freixas reports (1996: 19–20, my translation): 'it is not surprising that many women writers aspire to write asexual literature as a way of writing literature of quality, true literature; that they aspire to being considered *writers*'. Alternatively, proponents of women's literature have argued for the affirmation of gender differences as intellectually, culturally, and creatively significant. Women write because, and not in spite of the fact that, they are women. Gender, along with other differential indices of cultural identity, matters in ways both tangible and intangible to stories of particularity and collectivity.

We shall here adopt a compromise between a critique of strategies of exclusion and a celebration of gender differences. In order to explore Spain's post-war literary history as it has, until very recently, been written, I will discuss five 'canonical' novels published by well-known peninsular women writers after the conclusion of the Spanish Civil War in 1939: Carmen Laforet's *Nada* (1945), Ana María Matute's *Primera memoria* (1960), Carmen Martín Gaite's *El cuarto de atrás* (1978), Almudena Grandes's *Las edades de Lulú* (1989) and Lucía Etxebarria's *Beatriz y los cuerpos celestes* (1998). Insofar as these are texts that share some intrinsic and extrinsic similarities they will help us to investigate continuity and contiguity.[1] It is not coincidental that in all five novels female protagonists narrate in the first person,

---

[1] The five novels selected have won prestigious and lucrative national literary prizes, they were all written in Castilian and released in Spain by major national publishing houses, and the narrator-protagonists are all middle-class Spanish women.

albeit with varying degrees of temporal and psychic dissonance, their socio-cultural, intellectual, spiritual, artistic, sexual, and/or emotional development. As a result, the novel of formation will be a particularly relevant backdrop against which to examine the innovations and revolutions introduced by women novelists in post-war Spain.

By the same token, changing sociohistorical circumstances and discrete artistic visions have shaped these novels, and the differences between them may well be more significant than the resemblances. First-person narrative by women provides ample opportunities for an exploration of the potential connections between the narrative 'I'/eye and memory, nation, sexuality, history, language, trauma, family, and friendship, to name only some of the themes.[2] These five novels converge, however, at the intersection of voice, vision, and vocation and illustrate the contribution that women have made, and continue to make, to the peninsular novel.

Perhaps because of its intimate links to autobiography, testimony, confession, and didactic prose, first-person narrative is one of the foundational strategies employed by novelists. People have always told stories, and first-person narrative holds out to the storyteller the promise of psychic immediacy, consistency, and authority. Within the mode of first-person narrative, the novel of formation, the *Bildungsroman*,[3] has been especially important in Western literature at least since the publication of Goethe's *Wilhelm Meisters Lehrjahre* (1808).[4] Works of this kind traditionally relate the youth or adolescence of a self-aware and often articulate protagonist who tries to acquire knowledge, experience, and direction, often by overcoming environmental and relational obstacles. Ideally, by the time the protagonists have reached a certain maturity, they are psychologically stable, socially integrated, and comparatively prosperous.

---

[2]   The catalogue of first-person novels of female formation written by women in post-war Spain is considerably longer (and becoming more so every day) than can possibly be accommodated in the present essay. For example, any of the following could have been substituted for the novels studied here: Rosa Chacel, *Memorias de Leticia Valle* (1945); Dolores Medio, *Nosotros los Rivero* (1953); Elena Quiroga, *Tristura* (1960) and *Escribo tu nombre* (1965); Esther Tusquets, *El mismo mar de todos los veranos* (1978) and *Para no volver* (1985); Rosa Montero, *La función Delta* (1981); Adelaida García Morales, *El Sur* (1985); Josefina Aldecoa, *Historia de una maestra* (1990); Lourdes Ortiz, *Urraca* (1991); and Almudena Grandes, *Malena es un nombre de tango* (1994). Our criteria regrettably do not permit us to consider female formation novels by women in peninsular languages other than Castilian, novels that employ narrative voices other than the first-person, and/or novels that feature male protagonists or more than one protagonist.

[3]   Other English terms include the novel of development, the novel of self-cultivation, the apprenticeship novel and, especially in the case of women's fiction, the novel of awakening.

[4]   A glance at recent English-language scholarship on novels of formation confirms its continuing relevance and adaptability. Monographs published since 2000 include Kushigian (2003), Japtok (2005), Jeffers (2005) and Castle (2006).

Novels of formation expose the inherent conflict between knowledge of self and adjustment to societal expectations: the difficult balance between 'I' and 'we'. One way of looking at the conflict, as Sammons suggests, is to see novels of this type as tracing the evolution of an individual self or subject:

> The *Bildungsroman* should have something to do with *Bildung*, that is, with the early bourgeois, humanistic concept of the shaping of the individual self from its innate potentialities through acculturation and social experience to the threshold of maturity [...]. There must be a sense of evolutionary change within the self, a teleology of individuality, even if the novel, as many do, comes to doubt or deny the possibility of achieving a gratifying result. (1991: 41)

Because these novels are usually structured around a single central character, readers are encouraged to value the consciousness, imagination, and struggles of a protagonist whom they may well see as representative of a larger group. The discord between the individual and society is resolved when the protagonist willingly conforms to a dominant ideology, and achieves 'advancement', or else rebels, withdraws, is forced to conform, or dies, in which case the socialization process has failed.

Another way of looking at this perennial conflict between the individual and society is to examine the communal and economic factors that produce all novels of formation. In Moretti's words (2000: 10): 'When we remember that the *Bildungsroman* – the symbolic form that more than any other has portrayed and promoted modern socialization – is also the *most contradictory* of modern symbolic forms, we realize that in our world socialization itself consists first of all in the *interiorization of contradiction.*' Protagonists are defined (and define themselves) in terms of those around them, and a measure of socialization is desirable, if not inevitable. Societies accommodate and reward, to a greater or lesser degree, notions of individuality that complement the prevailing social values and goals. Both these ways of looking at the novels are useful here because gender pulls at the two sides in the conflict: women want to express their individuality, especially in the face of a normative society, and they also want to belong to a community, especially if that community welcomes their specificity.

Until well into the second half of the twentieth century, novels of female formation were about men or about how human beings, whichever their gender, measured up against 'universalized' masculine behavior, perceptions, and values. With the advent of feminist literary criticism, readers began to recognize that 'the sex of the protagonist modifies every aspect of a particular *Bildungsroman*: its narrative structure, its implied psychology, its representation of social pressures' (Abel *et al.* 1983: 5). In these texts girls and women struggle against gendered social mores to articulate and assert their desires and dreams. Whereas the female protagonists are only too well aware of the innumerable pressures to conform, they are not nearly so quick to cultivate their individual selves. Social integration frequently presents far fewer viable options for women and exacts a high price for non-conformity in terms of material wellbeing, sanity, professional success, motherhood, and sexual fulfilment. The price increases if gender is then complicated by race, ethnicity, social class, sexuality, age, and/or ability. In these five novels, development occurs at the fault line between subjectivity and society, and in every case, the female narrator-protagonist conveys an awareness of her own psychological complexity and her necessary place in the larger network of her community.

Literary scholars and historians are unanimous in acknowledging Carmen Laforet's *Nada, which won the inaugural Nadal Prize in 1944, as the first indication that women writers in post-war Spain could achieve commercial and critical recognition. It is no coincidence that Laforet effectively managed to avoid the censorship imposed by the Franco regime at the conclusion of the Spanish Civil War. Set in Barcelona during the early 1940s, *Nada centers on the life and times of eighteen-year-old orphan Andrea, who recounts, from an unspecified future vantage point, the year that she lived with her maternal relatives in their ancestral house on Aribau Street. The story begins with the unexpectedly delayed arrival of the protagonist, who has journeyed from her childhood country home to the city in order to attend the University of Barcelona. The family with whom she now finds herself living is supplemented, over the course of the novel, by 'public' relationships that emerge from Andrea's encounters at the university and on the city streets. The latter group encourages her to imagine herself and her future differently, although Laforet situates that future well beyond the spatio-temporal confines of the novel.

In addition to depicting lyrically a city characterized by the widespread hunger, poverty, and deteriorating environment that characterized the Spain of the 1940s, Laforet deftly integrates memories of the recent fratricidal conflict into the irresolvable discord between Andrea's maternal uncles. During the Spanish Civil War these two uncles, Juan and Román, had aligned themselves respectively with the liberal Republican and conservative Nationalist causes; each has experienced a distinct and yet interrelated trauma. Those traumas propel the action forward and eventually contribute to Andrea's climactic shift from observer to agent when she rescues her friend Ena from the malevolent grip of Román. Her actions are implicitly rewarded in the *deus ex machina* finale when Ena's affluent father literally whisks Andrea away to Madrid with an assurance of employment, further education, an apartment and, perhaps most importantly, a symbolic place in what appears to be a perfect nuclear family.

By the end of her year in Barcelona, Andrea has progressed in a number of recognizable ways: she is fully functional in a major city; she has passed her university courses; and she now possesses an acute aesthetic sensibility. She has survived hunger, cold, illness, and violence, and has felt deep emotions ranging from despair and panic to elation and hope. She has experienced friendship, infatuation, rejection, and duplicity. Because everyone has something to hide in *Nada, she has become adept at reading and keeping secrets, and at embracing both solitude and affiliation. And she can, after her year of apprenticeship, recognize and express beauty, generosity, and delight. In sum, she has become a moderately successful member of her society.

At the same time Andrea has also been trained to internalize resignation and fatalism, something echoed in the novel's title as well as in the epigraph lifted from Juan Ramón Jiménez's poem of the same title. Her excessive propensity for sentimentality leads her to entertain an unrealizable vision of family, friendship, and romantic love. Although she discards the models of femininity represented by her maternal relatives, she also realizes, albeit painfully, that she can only fantasize about the material and emotional comforts enjoyed by women from a higher social class, such as Ena and her mother, as well as the female relatives of Pons, Andrea's temporary love interest. As an educated woman with few financial and personal resources in post-war Spain, her agency is severely constrained and her awareness of this grounds both her socialization and her narrative.

With *Nada, Laforet contributes to Spain's continued fixation with its recent and distant past. As Andrea sorts through her family genealogy she increasingly, if unconsciously, reflects the national damage wrought by a civil war and its aftermath through her permanent sense of doom, stagnation, and victimization. And in order to become a woman, she learns to conform, compromise, and endorse the status quo. When she leaves Barcelona her future is essentially out of her hands, but she realizes, in retrospect, that her experiences in Barcelona were crucial. Andrea's individuality manifests itself most openly through the force of retelling her story, a vital step towards the realization of self and art. Her 'interiorization of contradiction' also propels her story forward because she longs equally for motherhood and romantic attachment, on the one hand, and financial independence and artistic expression on the other – a difficult combination in Francoist Spain, although Laforet herself would attempt to live just this paradox.

Ana María Matute shares a number of obvious similarities with Carmen Laforet. Both women saw the Spanish Civil War through adolescent eyes, both began to publish novels while in their twenties, and both won the Nadal Prize, albeit fifteen years apart. Matute's *Primera memoria and Laforet's *Nada are also quite different, in part because during the 1950s Franco was forced to look beyond Spain's tightly monitored borders in order to secure economic aid, entry into the United Nations, and international acceptance. Moreover, the same decade witnessed the influx into Spain of foreign influences, including Sartre's existentialism, Italian neo-realism, and the North American realist novel (see Jordan 1990; 84–128). Although the country seemed on the brink of economic and social progress, Francoist ideology continued to herald the country's past as a source of national pride and moral justification.

Although Matute dabbled with some of the novelistic trends involving realism and political commitment that were popular during the 1950s, in *Primera memoria* she returns to the decidedly intimate format of the novel of formation to creatively mine the legacy of guilt, repression, and betrayal that emerged from her country's Civil War. This novel, her sixth, tracks the memories of the adult protagonist Matia as she relives her forced exile to her arch-conservative maternal grandmother's house on the island of Mallorca during the last four or five months of 1936. During that formative period, fourteen-year-old Matia lost her childhood innocence, discovered love, lust, and longing and came face to face with her own cowardice and complicity. Unlike the events in *Nada,* all of these experiences haunt the much older adult narrator and profoundly affect her narrative present.

When the Civil War breaks out in Spain in July 1936, Matia is spending the summer with her grandmother Doña Práxedes, her cousin Borja, and his mother Emilia. Although the two cousins have the run of the island, they are bored with each other and with the constrictions of childhood. Their lives change irrevocably when they discover a body and agree to let the dead man's son Manuel use their boat to take it back to his family on the island. As a result, the three teenagers become entangled in the ideological and sentimental tensions that have shaped previous generations of Mallorcans. Matia befriends the solitary Manuel and their friendship quickly deepens into a mutual need for refuge, companionship, and acceptance in an otherwise hostile world. Borja, who covets the attention of his female cousin, jealously manipulates the larger community into punishing the innocent Manuel, who figures in the novel as both martyr and sacrificial victim.

On Matia's personal history Matute superimposes three versions of the clash between idealistic liberalism and hypocritical conservatism that, in the novel, underwrites Spain's political history and culminates in the Spanish Civil War. First, while Matia's father reportedly fights on the mainland for the Republican forces, Borja's father, a colonel in Franco's army, defends Nationalist interests. Second, the adolescent boys on the island have organized themselves into two rival factions, divided along class lines, and they spend the summer months 'playing war', complete with weapons, intrigues, and periodic truces. And third, in a lopsided adult adaptation of this same war, the leading citizens, and Matia's grandmother among them, punish Manuel's family in order to expiate the repressed sins of the entire island community: illegitimate passion, sexual transgression, defiance, and independence. The human instruments of this communal punishment are distant cousins of the transgressors, and they kill Manuel's father, shave his mother's head, exhibit her in the public square, poison the family well, and, in the final scene of the novel, condemn Manuel for a theft he did not commit.

It is part of her move from youth to adulthood that Matia should witness the effects of these actions and conclude that injustice, inequality, and hypocrisy permeate the society in which she must now find a place for herself. In order to conform to the requirements of the group, she learns passivity and collusion, and her need for both is heightened by her emerging (and barely understood) sexuality, which must, according to her elders and her peers, be controlled at all costs. Competing modes of femininity and masculinity are found at every turn in the novel, and they intersect at the junction of desire. In contrast to *Nada, *Primera memoria elaborates a complicated sexual subtext by juxtaposing, in the narrator's memory, the quasi-platonic affection between Matia and Manuel with the wanton behavior of the romanticized aristocrat Jorge de Son Mayor and his peasant lover Sa Malene, the perverse desires of Lauro for his male student, the frustrated fantasies of Emilia, and Borja's incestuous attraction to Matia. Matia is forced to recognize that it is dangerous to become a woman and that in order to survive she must comply with normative gender roles and class distinctions, even if that means compromising her integrity and losing her self-respect.

Unlike Andrea in *Nada, Matia does not get rescued or rewarded at the conclusion of the novel. Instead, she learns to forego rebellion in favor of shame, fear, and cowardice: a lesson that weighs heavily on the mind and on the narrative style of the much older Matia. She has become so adept at internalizing the destructive vigilance of others that it now inflects her every response in the narrative present. She peppers her recollections with self-directed reflections on the futility of her choices. Whereas Laforet's novelistic method was chronological and there were few references to the narrative present, Matute frequently uses her narrator's paralyzing nostalgia to introduce winding parenthetical interruptions that stress her passivity and her ignorance. By searching, finding, and then losing, Matia discovers that some damage is irreversible and some experiences unrecoverable. Female friendship does not redeem her (or anyone else) in the end, and she, in turn, does not redeem Manuel. Her eventual conformism signifies a complete abdication of her values, dreams, and sensitivity; the past has trapped her innocence and she is now beset by guilt and remorse. The mature Matia has not outgrown her trauma; rather, she has broadened it and made it into a way of life.

Eighteen years after the appearance of *Primera memoria, Carmen Martín Gaite published *El cuarto de atrás. Winner of the National Prize for Literature, this novel pulls away from mimesis and psychological realism to explore the twin strategies of metafiction and self-reflexivity. Like her two predecessors, she experienced the Spanish Civil War as a teenager and published her first novel while still in her twenties. She also witnessed Spain's transition, after Franco's death in 1975, to a functional multi-party democracy. By contrast, however, where Laforet and Matute wrote little during the 1970s, Martín Gaite contributed to the linguistic, thematic, and formal innovations of post-transition narrative by bringing together in one fictional text fantastic literature, social history, the romance novel, the memoir, autobiography, the epistolary novel, fairy tales, and detective fiction. That it is also a *Bildungsroman* enables her to anchor the narrator-protagonist's far flung memories, confirms her psychological and social maturation, and welds together past and present.

Arranged around a single night of insomnia and writer's block, *El cuarto de atrás* traces the dreams, visions, and memories of an adult female narrator, who refers to herself by her first initial, 'C', as she shuttles between personal, literary and national histories (several clues suggest that 'C' may stand for 'Carmen', the writer's own first name, but this is never made explicit). At the beginning of her present-tense narrative, C falls asleep in her Madrid apartment while reading Todorov's book on fantastic literature, only to be roused at midnight by a phone call from a strange man who claims that he has an appointment to interview her. The narrator-protagonist and 'the man in black' (who may be the devil or a transmuted cockroach) subsequently spend several hours together in her cluttered apartment sorting through her recollections of life in post-war Spain, her fears and fantasies, and her writing process, before she drifts back to sleep. When she is awakened several hours later by the return of her adult daughter, she initially believes that she has dreamt the entire encounter with this unidentified stranger. But she and her daughter each find traces of his visit: a tray with two glasses, a small golden box, and a neat stack of 182 numbered pages that bear the title *El cuarto de atrás*. It appears that C has broken through her writer's block in order to produce, in dialogue with the stranger and her memories, the novel that we have just read.

Like *Nada* and *Primera memoria*, *El cuarto de atrás* examines the triptych of searching, finding and losing, but, unlike the previous two works, Martín Gaite's text celebrates the link between the recovery of personal memories and artistic creativity. In much the same manner as Andrea and Matia, C revisits her past in order to make sense of her present, but, unlike the other two, firmly and expansively places herself in the current moment of narration. As in the earlier novels, the narrator-protagonist's imagination functions as a buffer against the harsh economic and physical realities of post-war Spain, but in the case of *El cuarto de atrás* this buffer evolves into a mental habit and, eventually, a lucrative career.

If Andrea's future hinges on the goodwill of others and Matia's mirrors the emotional angst of her youth, then C's future, more independently conceived and realized, is the most promising of the three. All of the protagonists encounter and overcome obstacles, compromise their ideals, and forge contradictory social identities, but Martín Gaite's narrator views both compromise and contradiction as productive. Unlike those of her earlier fictional counterparts, C's narrative is itself an act of successful socialization, as both it and she affirm the desirability of dialogue, either by subconsciously dreaming up an interlocutor or by consciously inviting a stranger into her conversational space. Because C has someone with whom to exchange herself, someone who can validate her memories and her forgetting them, she can and does tell a coherent story, one that successfully integrates past, present, and future, as well as individuality and society. The internalization of contradiction, including the contradiction of gender roles, moves the narrator to remember, and this in turn moves her to write anew and again.

In response to the surge in market capitalism and consumer culture, and the rise in the disposable income of the average Spaniard, the 1980s saw a publishing boom, most notably in the so-called popular genres of science fiction, children's literature, detective fiction, and erotica. While written and visual male pornography had existed during the Franco regime, albeit often only on the black market, any explicit exploration or exploitation of female sexuality was banned by the censors and by the rigid moral teachings of the Church. In 1989 Almudena Grandes rocked Spain's literary establishment and appealed to scores of readers by publishing *Las edades de Lulú. The novel, which won the Sonrisa Vertical Prize, features a woman narrator who connects her psychological and social formation with the emergence and intensification of a decidedly unorthodox sexuality. Grandes's novel might, on the surface, read as a daring exposé of one woman's sexual experiences, which range from paedophilia and incest to voyeurism and sadomasochism. By choosing a female narrator-protagonist to explore non-normative sexual practices in startlingly direct language, some have argued that Grandes effectively facilitated women's sexual agency. Others counter that her central character instead absorbs and then promotes her own abjection and subjugation. Whichever view one takes, *Las edades de Lulú turns the novel of formation upside down by concentrating on sexuality as the principal site of female maturation.

The adult Lulú begins her story by remembering her immediate past when she watched and then masturbated to a pornographic video involving two men and a woman. This narrative frame marks the starting point for two parallel stories: in the first she retreats to her adolescence and to the turning point of her relationship with Pablo, and in the second she moves towards the reenactment of that first turning point. The thirty-something Lulú recalls how, as a precocious fifteen-year old, she attracted the attention of twenty-seven year old Pablo, best friend to her favorite brother Marcelo. Pablo's primary fantasy involved the seduction of young girls, and the younger the better. He immediately indoctrinated his eager protégée into his fantasy, which Lulú then adopted and tried to repeat with and without Pablo throughout her life. From her initial sexual experience she learns to link pain and pleasure, punishment and reward, aggressiveness and dependency. After a five-year separation, Lulú and Pablo renew their daughter/father seduction, pushing at the limits of their desires to make way for additional participants, more sexual variety, and stronger physical sensations. When Pablo orchestrates recreational sex between himself, the blindfolded Lulú, and her brother Marcelo, she decides finally to emancipate herself from her master. Unfortunately, her freedom, illusory in its conception, becomes more and more difficult to sustain, since, in the absence of her object of desire, she must constantly raise the stakes by recruiting more sexual partners (which requires more financial incentive) and relinquishing more control. Her desperate quest sends her further into alternative sexual scenarios that culminate in a sadomasochistic orgy in which Lulú, one of nine players, is chained to a stake and tortured into unconsciousness before Pablo, who may have arranged the whole sequence of events, comes to her aid. Afterwards, the two narrative threads come together in the final scene of the novel when the adult Lulú returns to the primordial promise of reconciliation and protection as she waits expectantly for Pablo to arrive at her bedside with food and affection.

In keeping with the conventions of the novel of formation and with the three novels previously discussed, the adult protagonist narrates retrospectively (though not chronologically) the salient moments of her childhood and adolescence in order to establish a cause and effect relationship between the past and present. Like her fictional predecessors, Lulú chafes at any social expectations that would prescribe her behavior, especially those that might prevent her from fully expressing her sexual wishes. In all four novels the protagonist's desire is expressed along decidedly heterosexual lines. And her fantasies, in every case, generate and are generated by fear, need, and lack.

*Las edades de Lulú differs from the other three novels in ways both obvious and oblique. Sexual exhibitionism, in all its imaginable versions, replaces sexual repression, and female formation appears to hinge entirely upon the reproducible associations between physical sensation and emotional wellbeing. Where the texts by Laforet, Matute, and Martín Gaite offer a critique, in various ways and to various degrees, of the conservative ideology that spawned and sustained the Franco regime, Grandes implicates liberal politics in the fictions of dominance and defeat that control the novel. Pablo and Marcelo, leftist students who are jailed in 1969 for their political activities, literally use Lulú's body to consummate their homosexual attraction to one another. As an allegory of progressive intellectual life in 1960s Spain, the novel ruthlessly denounces the so-called liberalization of gender relations, which promulgates the reflective drive of men to perversely script women's desire (and desirability) as a confirmation of heteronormativity and a projection of male homoeroticism (see Morris & Charnon-Deutsch 1993–94: 311–14).

Finally, *Las edades de Lulú* is unique among the novels discussed in that the narrator-protagonist reifies her sexual regression to childhood as her only means of obtaining unconditional love and acceptance. The problem with Lulú's inverted quest is that she cannot truly revert to childhood, just as she cannot narrate backwards, and the simulation of either in the present tense has dire consequences. She rejects sexual maturity as inadequate and false because she has been thoroughly programmed to deny her own story by Pablo's sexual and emotional needs. She cannot go back in time and she will not go forward without Pablo.

Our fifth and final novel, Lucía Etxebarria's *Beatriz y los cuerpos celestes* (winner of the 1998 Nadal Prize) reiterates familiar patterns and suggests yet another model for the novel of formation. Etxebarrria has been linked to a new group of peninsular novelists that emerged in the 1990s. Born between 1960 and 1971, these authors participate in a globalized and globalizing economy, live in a relatively stable democracy, and benefit from widespread technological literacy. It is no coincidence that they have also matured artistically at a moment in history which, in Spain as elsewhere, has seen the development of an omnipresent commodity culture that emphasizes the prevalence of marketing and puts a high value on 'youth' and 'newness'. As the most visible woman in this group, Etxebarria has used market forces and self-promotion to great advantage.

In *Beatriz y los cuerpos celestes*, the eponymous protagonist decides, at the age of twenty-two and in the midst of a profound depression, to reconsider her life and to return from Scotland to Madrid. The 'celestial bodies' of the novel's title refer to the other inhabitants of Beatriz's vital orbit, a metaphor that she has picked up from her friend Mónica and which she weaves into her narrative of development. In parallel tales, Beatriz situates her narrative present in the moment of her decision to return to Madrid and her narrative past in the months leading up to her departure from Madrid four years earlier. These two storylines revolve, in part, around her unconsummated desire for her best friend Mónica.

Beatriz recounts how, as the only child of a critical mother and an emotionally detached father, she felt constrained and abandoned, always destined to disappoint others. When tensions between the teenaged Beatriz and her mother began to escalate, she fled to Mónica's welcoming arms and apartment, and she was instantly drawn into the underworld that supports her friend's heroin addiction. During their summer together Beatriz falls hopelessly in love with Mónica even though she knows that her devotion will not be reciprocated. Her involvement in Mónica's precarious activities leads Beatriz to carry guns and drugs to prospective buyers, even knocking one of those buyers unconscious when he tries to rape her and all but strangles her.

It is after this episode that she convinces her father to send her to Edinburgh to attend college.

Some months after her arrival, she meets Cat and the two women enter into a three-year romance. During that same period Beatriz also has an affair with a fellow student, Ralph, who abruptly terminates their relationship. Unable to resolve her feelings for Mónica, Beatriz deserts Cat to go back to Madrid and search for her friend, at which point the narrative begins. She arrives 'home' only to find that her father is ill and her mother considerably aged. After a series of overdoses, Mónica ends up in a rural treatment facility where as an in-patient she now exists in a state of permanent drugged compliance. After confirming that Mónica, around whom Beatriz has faithfully revolved even during her friend's absence, no longer exerts any gravitational pull, Beatriz elects to move forward into a possible renewal of her relationship with Cat.

Like the other narrator-protagonists, Beatriz makes sense of her life by narrating her memories. Like Andrea, Matia, C, and Lulú, recollection provides necessary distance as well as a creative filter. Like the other characters, Beatriz rebels against gendered social expectations. And like them, she accommodates those expectations, to a degree at least, by returning to Madrid and to her family, rejecting the follies of her youth, and assuming responsibility for her past, present, and future actions. The five women search for, find, and lose themselves and their places in the world, and in the process they imagine themselves and those worlds differently. Even though they remember their pasts, the five narrators gravitate towards those who can forget and can help them to forget.

Beatriz y los cuerpos celestes departs from the other four texts in a number of ways. First, Etxebarria challenges heterosexism by presenting female homosexuality and bisexuality as normal, and making a link between the pleasure both can produce and authentic sentiment. Like Grandes, Etxebarria concentrates on the formative role of sexual desire in gendered identity, but, unlike Grandes, she gives Beatriz's exploration of sexuality a happy ending. The protagonist learns how she can revise past trauma and dependency by revisiting them. Self-knowledge, and the narration of that knowledge, leads to freedom, optimism, emotional self-sufficiency and, in the final instance, social integration.

Perhaps the outstanding feature of all novels of this type is that people change and are changed. By concentrating on the first-person novel of formation, we have emphasized the capacity of the five narrators to direct the course of their lives. In telling their stories, these five women claim authority and coherence. By focusing on novels of female maturation, we have emphasized the mandate of the protagonists to mature according to rules that frequently oppose their authority and coherence. If the consequence of failed integration is death, then none of the five protagonists fails completely. If the ultimate proof of successful individuality is independence, then none of the five succeeds completely, either, as they are all drawn to define themselves in relation to the redemptive possibilities of romantic love. Nevertheless, women novelists in Spain have clearly taken up the challenge of narrating their individual and collective stories, and it remains to be seen where those stories will take us next.

Further reading

Abel *et al.* (1983), Brown (1991), Castle (2006), Ciplijauskaité (1988), Davies (1993 and 1998), Freixas (1996a), Galerstein & McNerney (1986), Hart (1993), Henseler (2003), Japtok (2005), Jeffers (2005), Jordan (1990), Kushigian (2003), Levine *et al.* (1993), Manteiga *et al.* (1988), Mayock (2004), Moretti (2000), Morris & Charnon-Deutsch (1993–94), Nichols (1992), Ordóñez (1991), Pérez (1988), Rodríguez (2000), Sammons (1991), Schumm (1999), Servodidio (1987), Vollendorf (2001).

12

Changing Sexual and Gender Paradigms

ALFREDO MARTÍNEZ-EXPÓSITO

The emergence of overt sexual themes in the Spanish novel of the last quarter of the twentieth century is closely related to the profound changes (political, legal, religious, and social) taking place in Spanish society over those years. While some of these changes affected other Western nations at approximately the same time (and there was a corresponding boom in homosexual themes in mainstream literature), there are some peculiarities in the case of Spain. Strictly censored during the dictatorship, erotic literature gradually became associated with a set of forbidden topics, such as violence, nudity, drugs, and critical comments about the conservative values defended by the regime and the Church. Not surprisingly, these were the themes that dissident writers of fiction embraced to express their opposition to the authoritarian regime. The same happened with the expression of outlawed identities, such as Catalan and Basque nationalism and all forms of sexuality outside marriage. Since in one way or another all these themes and identities were closely associated with the cause of freedom and anti-Francoism, it became relatively common for Spanish writers of the second half of the twentieth century to combine them. In this chapter, we shall look at positive versions of homosexuality in relation to ideas of freedom, at both political and individual level.

Under Franco's regime, homosexuals and other sexual minorities had been severely repressed by the law, both indirectly (public scandal, moral diktat, and so on) and also directly with the promulgation of a *Ley de peligrosidad social*, an act introduced in the last years of the regime that targeted tramps, prostitutes, procurers, homosexuals, and others deemed potentially dangerous to the wellbeing of society. Homosexuals sentenced under this legislation were typically confined to a psychiatric hospital and forced to undergo corrective sexual therapy; three-year jail terms were common. The act was enforced between 1970 and 1978 but criticized on many fronts; after Franco's death in 1975 that criticism increased both in frequency and in volume. *Dignitat*, a Barcelona-based homosexual liberation group led by a Jesuit, Salvador Guasch Figueras, issued in January 1977 a statement signed by a number of psychiatrists. Known as the *Documento de los 24,* it asserted that sexual orientation was not a choice, that homophobia was culturally determined, and that homosexual acts constituted natural behaviour for homosexuals.

Socialist-led governments in the 1980s adopted a tolerant stance towards homosexuals, while visible communities of sexually diverse people began to form in the larger cities. An incipient gay pop culture emerged in alternative circles and produced not only works of art but also organizations and associations with clearly stated legal objectives. In 1995 the Socialist government passed a Criminal Code that introduced anti-discrimination legislation and abolished the laws that had been used against homosexual and sexual minorities. Soon afterwards the conservative government led by the Popular Party gave *de facto* couples some rights regardless of sex and sexual orientation, although no changes were made to existing legislation on partnership and marriage. An increasing number of local councils enacted laws granting gay and lesbian couples full partnership rights as civil unions. Some autonomous governments, Catalonia (1998) and Aragon (1999), for example, passed comprehensive partnership laws.

In 2004, the newly elected Socialist government announced its intention to remove from the statute book all legislation involving any discriminatory element against sexual minorities. A year later, all gender-specific terms were removed from the Marriage Law, thus making possible, for the first time in the nation's history, marriages between people of the same sex. On 2 July 2005 Spain became one of only three countries worldwide to give legal recognition to same-sex marriages; a few days later Canada joined Spain, the Netherlands, and Belgium.

At the same time as these changes in law were being enacted, a visible evolution in social values and attitudes was taking place. In Europe, Spain is the most extreme example of changed attitudes towards homosexuals. Attitudes in most Western countries shifted significantly in the last quarter of the twentieth century, but there was little or substantial change in the US, Australia, or Mexico, while other countries, such as Portugal, Ireland, and Japan, actually made things more difficult for homosexuals. In many countries, homosexuality still remains a crime (Inglehart 1990–97 and 2004).

For many years the history of homosexuality in modern Spain remained unexplored territory. Spanish scholars and university leaders in the humanities largely avoided the topic; surprisingly enough, it was commonly recognized that Spain was 'one of the countries with the richest homosexual history', which was 'gradually becoming better known', and that 'an appreciation of same-sex love, along with a cult of beauty and poetry' had been 'present during many periods of Spain's history' (Eisenberg 1990: 1236). Despite legal and social changes, that academic attitude has not totally disappeared. In literature and fiction, homosexual issues are not regarded by critics as of interest in themselves. Gay characters or situations are not mentioned in most critical works, book reviews, or even book covers, and those in a position to define the literary canon apparently remain impervious to gay, lesbian, bisexual, and transgender realities. It is no surprise, therefore, that no master-work of gay literature has ever been included in any account of the Spanish literary canon. For many, the theme of same-sex relationships is irrelevant, and the reasons for acclaiming openly gay authors, such as Álvaro Pombo, Juan Goytisolo, or Eduardo Mendicutti lie elsewhere: their concern with the nature and the culture of homosexuality is, for the majority of heterosexual critics, hard to understand.

The rapid change that affected gay and lesbian culture in the last quarter of the last century does not show signs of slowing. One of the palpable effects of the same-sex marriage legislation of 2005 has to do, precisely, with the normalization of sexually diverse themes in literature. For instance, gay readers no longer need mainstream literature to deal with gay themes, as a distinctive gay market now caters to their cultural needs. Gay writers now write for gay readers in ways unimaginable in the 1970s. Gay writers, of course, do write mainstream literature as well, but new players in the literary market are already bringing about changes to the way homosexual literature is produced and consumed that may not be apparent to the general public for some time yet. A proper understanding of the literature of this period of tran-sition (from a predominantly heteronormative to a non-homophobic society) has to be based on certain premisses (Martínez-Exposito 2004).

The first is that homosexuality is not a stable term, either politically or ideologically. The history and evolution of the word 'homosexual' in the last century reveals a discontinuous and fragmented succession of different meanings – from physiological malformation to cultural trend. For nationalist ideologues at the turn of the twentieth century homosexuality represented a destructive moral disease, similar in its effects on the life of the nation to a lethal virus in a living organism. For modernist and avant-garde poets, homosexuality was often a social pose, a sign of distinction, an emblem of sophistication and sensibility. In Francoist Spain, it was taboo. Popular mass culture from the 1970s onwards made comic use of homosexuality, frequently degrading and insulting both male and female homosexuals. The list goes on and on, revealing that homosexuality is an elastic concept whose precise definition has not been settled. Essentialists and constructivists have made use of the semantic instability of the concept to argue their respective posi-tions – although in the Spanish case the debate was more tenuous because homosexuality has never been understood as an identity issue (the persistence of a 'Mediterranean homosexuality' has been adduced as a probable reason for this rejection of homosexuality as identity).

The second premiss is that the Spanish literary canon has never accepted writing about homosexuality as of any real interest. Traditionally excluded from the canon on ideological and moral grounds, homosexuality has now entered the works of literary historians as a secondary attribute of writers who are considered great for reasons other than their homosexuality or their contribution to homosexual literary traditions. For example, the poets Federico García Lorca and Luis Cernuda are rarely credited as great gay writers by literary historians. The same happens with the important confessional voices of Terenci Moix, Juan Goytisolo, Luis Antonio de Villena, and Jaime Gil de Biedma. Álvaro Pombo may be frequently praised as a magnificent stylist, Luis Antonio de Villena as an eminent aesthete, and Juan Goytisolo as a sharp critic of national myths, but very rarely is Pombo given any credit for his extraordinary analyses of internalized homophobia, Villena for his contribution to pederast dandyism, Goytisolo for his exploration of Spain's sodomite past. Typically, the works of major Spanish gay and lesbian writers are meticulously de-homosexualized by the literary establishment.

The third premiss is that the so-called 'gay community' has created its own mechanisms to reward literary and cultural products in part as a consequence of the mainstream literary establishment's unwillingness to acknowledge homosexuality as of literary value in itself. Some of the authors canonized by the gay community, such as Eduardo Mendicutti or Jaime Bayly, are well known to mainstream readers; the works of others circulate mainly in gay and lesbian circles (Llamas & Vidarte 1999). The fourth premiss is that gay culture is heavily influenced by North American gay cultural models. In other words, there is a delocalization or dislocation of homosexuality *qua* cultural paradigm, which makes it less obviously Spanish or local than it may have been in the past. And, finally, there is a fifth premisses: that the gay community has created a new orthodoxy (a new canon) independent of mainstream society that regulates many aspects of gay culture. Together with this orthodoxy a new heterodoxy has been created that has produced a dissident gay culture.

With these premises in mind, it is easy to understand that, despite the positive changes in legislation and a favorable evolution of social attitudes, homosexuality largely remains a controversial topic, both in society and in its literary and artistic representations. The third-person approach of many early attempts to present homosexual characters reveals the difficulties that gay writers faced under the Franco regime. Such a distancing approach to homosexuals as 'they' or 'people like that' was favored by writers deliberately choosing to present an unsympathetic view of the subject. Sometimes a 'they' narrative focuses on one particular character and studies in some detail his or her homosexuality. First-person narratives, typically autobiographies or pseudo-autobiographies, represent a courageous step forward and one that required some sort of personal coming-out; in some instances, writers adopted the plural 'we' to denote the identification of the homosexual writer with a cause or a community. These rhetorical positionings ('they', 'he/she', 'I', 'we') are associated with different kinds of homosexual literature.

Authors critical of homosexuality have often use distancing rhetorical devices. Camilo José Cela adopted a 'they' discursive strategy in relation to all the homosexuals that appear in his densely populated novels, such as *La Colmena* (1951), *San Camilo, 1936* (1969), and *Mazurca para dos muertos* (1983); only in *Madera de boj* (1999) is a homosexual character treated kindly by the narrative voice. Cela's homosexuals are simply ridiculous and naive, mere caricatures of what a homophobic tradition has commonly led us to believe homosexuals are.[1] The same distancing, disgusted approach can be found in novels by Carmen Laforet (*La insolación*, 1963), and Ana María Matute. The latter offers negative depictions of male homosexuality in *Fiesta al noroeste* (1953) and of lesbianism in *Los soldados lloran de noche* (1964). In the former, a dysfunctional need to exert control leads a rural cacique to rape the mother of the young man he secretly desires, who happens to be his half-brother. In the latter, the narrator does not offer a direct account of the relation between the two female protagonists, and this only serves to make the whole narrative more sordid. In both novels the main homosexual characters are portrayed as repulsive and perverse. An exception is Francisco Umbral's novel *El Giocondo* (1970) describing a sleazy gay piano bar in the Madrid of the 1960s, from the point of view of a gigolo, with a depth of character that elicits the empathy of the reader.

During the last years of Franco's life homosexuality became a more fashionable literary topic, and the trend gathered momentum when censorship was abolished in 1977. As a result, those who intended to explore the 'new' field were confronted by some important questions about models and sources. What sort of homosexuality was to be portrayed? What intertextual links were to be established? What purpose would the new theme serve? In short, where and how were the new writers going to get their material?

A quick answer to the last question could have been, of course, real life. Writers would only need to go to those recently legalized bars and cafés where homosexuals gathered and take notes on what they saw. That is what the anthropologist Oscar Guasch (1991) and the journalist Leopoldo Alas Mínguez (1994) claim to have done, and not without some measure of success. And that is precisely what many well-intentioned novelists and authors did in the 1980s. Many of them had been frequenting those same bars for years, or had long-standing contacts with lesbians or gay men, and decided just to tell their personal stories in a more or less literary manner. One writer even claimed to have modeled his characters on real-life people:

> I do not intend to name the recipients of this open letter because, even where they are based on real models their names would not be relevant to my purpose. I will not hesitate to name persons, trade marks, or businesses

---

[1]   One of Cela's more cruel portraits of a homosexual is Matiítas el Profeta, a character in *San Camilo, 1936* who commits suicide by inserting a pistol in his anus and shooting.

of a dubious reputation if I need to do so. There is nothing more despicable than those warnings at the beginning of certain novels or films: 'All resemblance with real facts or persons is a mere coincidence'. I maintain that all resemblance with real facts or persons is pure observation.

(Domínguez Olano 1974: 8).

An autobiographical element, or first-hand knowledge of homosexual ghettos is evident in several 'I' narratives: Moreno García's *Confesiones de un homosexual* (1977; written under the pseudonym of 'J. M. West'), Antonio Roig Roselló's *Todos los parques no son un paraíso* (1977) and *Vidente en rebeldía: Un proceso en la Iglesia* (1979), Lluis Fernàndez's *El anarquista desnudo* (1979), Luis Antonio de Villena's *Amor pasión* (1983) and *Chicos* (1989), Carlos Sanrune's *El gladiador de Chueca* (1992), Juan Soto Puente's *Un hombre llamado Katy* (1993), and José Ángel Mañas's *Historias del Kronen* (1994). Others simply used the raw material from real life to decorate stories had had little to do with homosexuality as such. This is the case of the majority of Spanish films, particularly comic ones. Examples include Pedro Almodóvar's *¿Qué he hecho yo para merecer esto?* (1984), in which a rather repulsive pederast is somehow presented as an alternative to a low-class family; Fernando Colomo's *Alegre ma non troppo* (1994), with its humorous but shallow parody of Freud's theories on homosexuality; Manuel Gómez Pereira's *Boca a boca* (1995); and Olea's *Morirás en Chafarinas* (1994). And finally, a number of heterosexuals have used their first-hand experience to strengthen a moral judgement against homosexuality, as do Cela and also Francisco Umbral (*Tratado de perversiones*, 1977).

Homosexuality may well have been a radically new topic on the Spanish literary scene of the 1970s and '80s, but this does not mean it was unconnected to older traditions of various kinds. Let us understand both terms of the paradox: homosexuality offered a thematic literary field which was absolutely new for those who had been living under Francoist National-Catholicism (that is, the vast majority of Spaniards). But as a literary *topos* it was well established in the cultures of the ancient world, and it would be preposterous to imagine that Spanish gay authors of the 1970s were actually embarking on something totally new. There is a paradox, then: there are two ways one can look at the theme: homosexuality as novelty and homosexuality as tradition. While fiction writers and essayists (such as Juan Goytisolo, Terenci Moix, Juan Gil-Albert, Alvaro Pombo, Luis Antonio de Villena, and the others mentioned below) did indeed have a detailed knowledge of the literary homosexual tradition, an overwhelming majority of their readers (including critics and reviewers) regarded their homosexual-themed books as a radical and sometimes shocking innovation.

Juan Goytisolo makes a special use of homosexuality in many of his novels and autobiographical writings. Instead of associating homosexuality with moral perversion or criminal tendencies, he uses it as an emblem of difference and distinction. In *Señas de identidad* (1966), *Reivindicación del conde don Julián* (1970), and *Juan sin tierra* (1975), homosexuality is presented in opposition to historical notions of Spanishness. While Spain is meant to represent, in these novels, oppression, intolerance and fanaticism, homosexuality is portrayed as part of a more liberal, tolerant, and sensual culture. There are many autobiographical elements in Goytisolo's novels, which may help to explain their ideological content, and he may be foregrounding homosexuality as a way of criticism of Spanish politics and society.[2]

Ramón Moix Messeguer, known as Terenci Moix, claimed to have been the first intellectual to come out as a gay man in Spain in the 1960s, but was frequently accused by gay activists of superficiality and excessive mannerism. Moix was an important gay voice in the 1970s, in particular in Catalonia, where gay liberation was intimately linked to Catalan nationalism (Catalan, rather than Spanish, was the language used by most gay intellectuals). Some of his early short stories in *La torre dels vicis capitals* (1967) were censored and homosexual relations had to be camouflaged as heterosexual. The first edition of his novel *El dia que va morir Marilyn* (1969) was also affected. His Catalan-language novel *Lleonard, o El sexe del àngels* was denied an important prize in 1969 because its strong criticism of Catalan cultural milieux; eventually, Moix would become uneasy with the Catalan literary world of letters and it was his output in Spanish that won him national and international acclaim. Moix's fictional approach to homosexuality is twofold. It appears as an unproblematic and joyous fact of life and as a carnivalesque element in the background. But it has also a darker side, as in the recurrent sadomasochist scenes of his science fiction dystopia *Mon mascle* (1971) and the story 'El dimoni'. Most of his gay protagonists are troubled, unbalanced individuals, who rarely achieve their goal of sentimental happiness and sexual fulfilment. Their sadomasochism is an allegory of the absolute loneliness of the individual, which is at times the loneliness of the individual who has no regard whatever for others. As Forrest put it, 'Moix's characters seem to have reached that supreme state of dominion and moral indifference that allows them to fulfil their potential without inhibitions' (1977: 926). This tension between comic pose and tragic pathos is indeed one of the most obvious features of Moix's gay-related novels. In 1990, he started publishing his long autobiography, *El peso de la paja*, the first part of which was signifi-

---

2   In his autobiographical work of 1982, *Coto vedado*, Juan Goytisolo reveals the decisive moments in his psychological and sexual development. The author claims it was the French writer Jean Genet who first helped him overcome his personal taboos and come to terms with his sexual orientation. He had sexual relations with both men and women, but admits to feeling reservations in his dealings with the opposite sex.

cantly titled *El cine de los sábados*, subsequent volumes being *Extraño en el paraíso* and *El beso de Peter Pan*. The work is particularly interesting to gay readers for his accounts of different experiences as an openly gay writer both in the last years of Franco's dictatorship and during the country's transition to democracy and new ethical values.

The poet and essayist Juan Gil-Albert made an important contribution to gay narrative prose both during and after the dictatorship. Exiled in France and Latin America, he returned to Spain in 1947 and went on writing prose and verse in private. *Heraclés*, a prose treatise on the culture of homosexuality, was written in 1955 but published only twenty years later. He was rehabilitated following a 1966 article by José Domingo in *Ínsula* which paved the way for a more general recognition and which eventually led to publication of *Fuentes de la constancia* in 1972, a book of poetry that influenced gay writers such as Jaime Gil de Biedma and Luis Antonio de Villena. Gil-Albert's more explicit gay works are *Valentín* (1974), *Razonamiento inagotable* (1979), *Los arcángeles* (1981) and *Tobeyo* (1989).

The Barcelona publisher Esther Tusquets is also well known as a novelist who explores female sexuality from a lesbian perspective. A late starter, Tusquets published her first novel, **El mismo mar de todos los veranos* in 1978, when she was forty-two years old. The book pioneered the coming-out lesbian novel in Spanish fiction and is one of the best novels of the late 1970s. Its psychoanalytical prose is full of lyrical imagery and Proustian digressions, actualized epiphanies, and the traumas and desires of a middle-aged protagonist undergoing a mid-life crisis. It was courageous of Tusquets to portray an asymmetrical love affair full of semi-autobiographical references between an adolescent Colombian girl and her college professor, a married woman from a privileged Barcelona background, who doubles also as narrator and subject in this story of unfulfilled desire. Tusquets' name has become associated with feminist and lesbian causes because of the openly erotic content of her novels, but she has rarely entered any public debate on the issue. **El mismo mar* was followed by **El amor es un juego solitario* (1979) and **Varada tras el último naufragio* (1980). These three novels portray women undergoing identity crises in a convoluted and hostile world. Their powerful lesbian sexuality and imagery has no precedent in Spanish literature and has made of the trilogy a landmark of lesbian narrative—although many of the relationships are more by way of female attachments than lesbian affairs. Other Tusquets novels that have received critical attention are **Para no volver* (1985) and *Con la miel en los labios* (1997), as well as the highly autobiographical short stories collected together in *Siete miradas en un mismo paisaje* (1982). In Tusquets' fictional universe, lesbian love is not seen as deviant; on the contrary, it leads to a better understanding of the self, to rebirth and to renewal. Relationships typically arise between women of different conditions (age, nationality, class); the reproduction of (patriarchal) stereotypes is deliberately avoided.

Tusquets has influenced the way the other women writers, such as Teresa Barbero and Marta Portal, deal with the topic of lesbianism.

Ana María Moix is another to explore female love and conflicting (or emerging) sexual identities in her short stories and poems, and in three novels: *Julia* (1970), *Walter, ¿por qué te fuiste?* (1973), and *Vals negro* (1994). Common characters and similar themes make the first two something of a diptych, although *Julia*, written as an internal monologue, is stylistically the more complex of the two. Lesbianism is presented here quite ambiguously: on the one hand, it is linked to the female/maternal universe, an idea which the first-person narrative voice clearly cherishes, but there is, on the other hand, a strong element of hatred against men in the work. Only retrospectively does Julia's fear of heterosexual love appear inexorably linked to the trauma of the rape she suffered when she was twelve.

Not all women novelists who write about homosexual themes are or identify themselves as lesbians. Rosa Montero explores in *Crónica del desamor* (1979) and *La función delta* (1981) some of the most controversial topics of early post-Franco years, such as abortion and male homosexuality. In her novels, the male homosexual is clearly disempowered by his own homosexuality, which is a source of unhappiness and frustration and eventually leads gay characters to self-harm and alienation from a heteronormative society. Olga Guirao masquerades as a shy homosexual in *Mi querido Sebastián* (1992), a novel in the form of a long letter written by an older gay male to his much younger former lover. This first-person novel represents one of the most interesting cases of transvestite narrative in contemporary Spanish novel (a women writer ventriloquizing a first-person male narrator). Among the younger writers, Lucía Etxebarría's *Beatriz y los cuerpos celestes* (1998) and Gabriela Bustelo's *Planeta hembra* (2001) introduce bisexual and lesbian themes as part of a larger array of uncommitted perspectives, registers, and narrative modes, from existential coming-of-age angst to sci-fi caricature.

Luis Antonio de Villena is one of the most conspicuous gay intellectuals in Spain today. Mainly a poet, he has also published literary prose, essays, and literary criticism, and maintains an active profile as a translator of gay poetry (the Greeks, Catullus, Michelangelo, Cavafy, and others). He has published essays and critical editions of major and minor Spanish 'decadent' writers, such as Antonio de Hoyos and Álvaro Retana, contributing to a greater knowledge of Spain's hidden gay literary traditions. His first narrative piece was a collection of short stories, *Para los dioses turcos* (1980), and since then he has published some twenty novels, including the strongly autobiographical *Ante el espejo* (1982), *Amor pasión* (1983), *Chicos* (1989), *Divino* (1994), *El mal mundo* (1999), *Huesos de Sodoma* (2004) and *Patria y sexo* (2004). Villena's approach to male homosexuality combines a decadent glorification of youth with a vivid awareness of literary and cultural traditions, in particular Hellenic and Mediterranean. His own persona, often characterized as one of rebellious and epicurean dandyism, is very often found in the first-person narratives of his stories. Over the years, he has changed his own attitude towards his own homosexual persona, in ways that parallel the changing experiences in the country: while in the 1970s and '80s he preferred to use the term 'ambiguity', in more recent times he has become much more explicit in embracing an openly gay identity and has published in some of the most visible publications of the gay community.

Álvaro Pombo produced *Relatos sobre la falta de substancia* in 1977. This was a collection of short stories some of which have an explicit homosexual content; a second collection was published in 1997 under the title *Cuentos reciclados*. Novels with explicit or oblique homosexual themes and characters include **El héroe de las mansardas de Mansard* (1983), *El hijo adoptivo* (1986), *Los delitos insignificantes* (1986), *El metro de platino iridiado* (1990), *Donde las mujeres* (1996), *El cielo raso* (2001) and *Contra natura* (2005). Pombo's openly gay literature has seldom received due attention from the critics. While *Los delitos insignificantes* is one of the most historically interesting novels of its kind, most reviewers did not focus in on its homosexuality as such, and in some cases the central gay storyline was cursorily dealt with as though it were mere anecdote. Gay themes and characters, however, have been a constant feature in many of Pombo's novels, together with a considerable presence of autobiographical elements. Pombo's gay characters problematize their own sexuality in ways that make the reader think of the author himself; for instance, many of them happen to be troubled fiction writers, such as Ortega in *Los delitos insignificantes* and Pancho in *El hijo adoptivo*, suggesting the same kind of link between writing and sexuality that we find in other homosexual novels such as those of Esther Tusquets. Pombo's greatest novel, *El metro de platino iridiado*, contains an important gay sub-plot which, as in most of his gay novels, presents a depressing and guilt-driven view of homosexuality. Pombo has often replied to critics of his unhappy portraits that it is the world they inhabit, rather than the characters themselves, which is depressing. His contribution to the gay novel consists of an extraordinarily detailed study of guilt, homophobia, and homosexual panic.

Eduardo Mendicutti is one of the most original voices in Spanish gay literature and one which succeeds in normalizing homosexual themes through a combination of autobiography and humour. Mendicutti is one of only a few openly gay Spanish writers, but he does not take an aggressively militant stance on the subject. Instead, his achieves his purpose by means of purely literary techniques, such as the conscious reworking of narrative genres, a detailed study of popular speech, the careful composition of character, and an apparently simple use of street humour (as opposed to the intellectual humour of Juan Goytisolo, Terenci Moix, or Alberto Cardín). Mendicutti's gay humour is effective in revealing other realities: typically, lives that go unrecorded by mainstream society because of an unwillingness or inability to conform to accepted lifestyles. Mendicutti's gay characters are always slightly different from those around them, and the difference lies in their perception of things, their values, and their use of language. Mendicutti has also reflected upon his own approach to gay narrative, so often marked by the erratic, agonized search for happiness, and by unhappy endings to romantic storylines (usually because of the insurmountable differences between partners or the tragic and melodramatic frame narratives typical of homosexual romances). Mendicutti's gay novels include: *Cenizas* (1974), *Una mala noche la tiene cualquiera* (1982), *Última conversación* (1984), *El salto del ángel* (1985), **Siete contra Georgia* (1987), *Una caricia para Rebeca Soler* (1989), *Tiempos mejores* (1989), *El palomo cojo* (1991, the inspiration for Jaime de Armiñán's 1996 film of the same title), *Los novios búlgaros* (1993, which inspired Eloy de la Iglesia's last film in 2003), *Yo no tengo la culpa de haber nacido tan sexy* (1997), *El beso del cosaco* (2000), *El ángel descuidado* (2002), *Duelo en Marilyn City* (2003), and *La Susi en el vestuario blanco* (2003). There is a significant difference between the novels he set in the aristocratic Cadiz of the 1950s, where he spent his childhood, which are more lyrical and elegiac in tone, and his urban fiction set in a multicultural and postmodern Madrid, where absurdist and farcical plots involving homo- and heterosexual love do not hide Mendicutti's critical attitude towards Spanish cultural norms and modern practices.

With the advent of AIDS, Spanish gay literature took on new existential dimensions. The theme appears in novels such as Luis Antonio de Villena's *Chicos* that give voice to individual tragedies that are no respecters of background and social class. The ravages of the epidemic, far graver in Spain than in northern Europe, are not for Francisco Umbral the sign of any specifically Spanish crisis in health care, but rather a metaphor for a generalized defencelessness: the fear of religion and politics may have receded but AIDS has now become a 'punishment for the crime of believing ourselves free at last' (1993: 301). As Paul Julian Smith suggests, even homosexuality, once exploited and celebrated by Umbral in his column and his novels as a defining symptom of modernity, has now faded from view; it flowered for a single day in a 'grotesque fiesta of liberty', but gay men have now become 'ordinary people', their lives much like those of 'strange but acceptable' businessmen (Umbral 1993: 155–56).

Since the early 1990s, gay communities in Spain's main cities have developed a flourishing cultural market which has led to a redefinition of gay literature. The meaning of gayness has nowadays more to do with the act of consuming certain goods and services than it has with traditional notions of identity and desire. The needs of this emergent consumer market have favored the expansion of gay or gay-friendly providers in all areas, and literature is no exception. An example of this flourishing sector, publishers

Odisea and EGALES, are now publishing and promoting gay fiction specifically targeted to the gay/lesbian/bisexual/transgender communities. This is
an all-gay business, where gay writers create characters and plots for a gay
audience. However, the impact of this sort of literature outside the boundaries of the gay community is negligible: it is very hard to find gay books and
magazines in mainstream bookstores, mainstream newspapers rarely review
them, and academic literary critics tend to ignore their existence (although
there are signs that academic attitudes in Spain are slowly changing).

Further reading

Alas (1994), Aliaga *et al.* (2001), Aliaga & Cortés (1997), Alonso & Castells
(1992a), Barthes (1978), Bergmann & Smith (1995), Bristow (1997), Butler
(1990), Buxán (1997), Cardín (1991), Dollimore (1991), Domínguez (1974),
Forrest (1970), Foster (1999), Foucault (1976–84), Guasch (1991), Kelly
(2000), Krauel (2001), Llamas (1998), Llamas & Vidarte (1999), Martínez
(2004), Martínez-Expósito (1998), Mira (2004), Smith (1992 and 1998),
Weeks (1985 and 1995).

13

Disquieting Realism: Postmodern and Beyond

KATARZYNA OLGA BEILÍN

In this chapter we shall examine the common narrative strategies and world views that surface in the works of Antonio Muñoz Molina, Juan José Millás, José María Merino, Enrique Vila-Matas, Adelaida García Morales, and Cristina Fernández Cubas. Many of the narrative techniques and ideas that these authors share could be considered postmodern; others, however, might better be though of as examples of something Navajas (1996b) calls 'beyond postmodernity'. He suggests (1987) that one important characteristic of post-modern narratives is the lack of any unitary meaning of the kind we find in the typical nineteenth-century realist novel, and that this has been replaced by multiple, vaguely connected meanings that often lead to an open and incon-clusive ending. A second postmodern feature is metafictionality, the purpose of which is, in Waugh's words, 'to create a fiction and to make a statement about the creation of that fiction' (1984: 6). Logically that statement has to be made outside the fiction proper, as, were it to be included in the text of the story, it would blur the distinction between fiction and reality. Metafic-tion, then, points either to the fictional character of reality (postmodernism) or to the reality of fiction (beyond postmodernism). Reflections of this nature often come in the form of intertextual dialogues which a writer establishes with other literary works, often from previous centuries, or occasionally with literary critics. The dialogues recycle old fictions and apply them to a contemporary context, and the result is a new understanding both of those texts and of today's reality.

In postmodern narratives, writing runs counter to our everyday common-sense perception of the world, and readers are not permitted what Navajas calls (1987: 17) 'an asylum for awareness': a place where one may escape consciousness and avoid the challenge of the unknown by repressing it or clas-sifying it as 'fantastic' and unreal. Contemporary narrative often focuses on the realities we try to avoid and exposes our unwillingness to confront them. While it would be typically postmodern to think of the realities from which we hide as negative and as posing a threat not only to our society's ethical and social stability but also to its ethical and social ideals, several Spanish novels of the late twentieth century turn that source of potential negativity into a fount of new meanings and new perspectives on history and ethics. These are the novels Navajas categorizes as being 'beyond postmodernism'. In these narratives of the 1980s and '90s, history is viewed subjectively through individual stories, and postmodern nihilism is often replaced by an ideal which Levinas describes as the 'little goodness' of everyday life that appears inviolable despite any dissolution of 'big' ideals (1999: 118). It is precisely this which brings us to what Navajas calls the 'partial assertion' of literature that is beyond the postmodern (1987: 21).

For example, Cristina Fernández Cubas's *El año de Gracia* (1994) presents Western civilization as having failed. As the main character, Daniel, travels the world to discover its wonders and to discover himself at the same time, he lands on the island of Gruinard, which has been contaminated by anthrax spores, a fact that is kept from the world at large. Paraphrasing Žižek (2000: 49), the 'Holy Grail' that Daniel seeks appears on this island as 'a pile of shit': the bodies of mutant sheep, and a shepherd, Grock, covered with lesions and emitting a nauseating stench. And yet the relationship that Daniel strikes up with Grock in the middle of all this destruction turns out to be the most enlightening and precious experience of his whole life. The lesson would seem to be that it is precisely in such outlandish places that we learn most about the contemporary world and that human relationships actually flourish.

Novels apparently so different as Antonio Muñoz Molina's *Sefarad* (2001), José María Merino's *Los invisibles* (2000), *Bene* (1985) and *La lógica del vampiro* (1990) by Adelaida García Morales, *Bartleby y compañía* (2000) and *El mal de Montano* (2002) by Enrique Vila-Matas, Cristina Fernández Cubas's short stories, and *La soledad era esto* (1994) by Juan José Millás all have as a common denominator an interest in the dark recesses of reality and of the human consciousness, and the dependence of life and of social order on language. These are writers who aim to reveal the hidden ways in which the invisible loom of language, which Lyotard sees as the most powerful force of all (1983: 86–127), conditions the mind. One could label all these interests 'disquieting realism'. In this 'disquieting realism' the possible and the apparently impossible, the visible and the invisible merge and give birth to a new vision of reality which extends beyond the limits of common sense, but not beyond this world. In works of this kind, the incredible is represented as a part of reality, and the real is often exposed as incredible. Some works contain no element of the fantastic; others may evoke a fantastic mood or theme, but none are fantastic in the way Tzvetan Todorov uses the term in *The Fantastic* (1973).

Todorov's idea is that the fantastic emerges at the moment of hesitation between the rational and the marvelous interpretations of events, and that it shows that our rational understanding of the world is incompatible with what happens in a story. In traditional fantasy literature, the reader, incapable of explaining strange events, dismisses them as unreal. By contrast, recent literature treats these events, inexplicable by traditional logic, differently: reality is not negated but rather conceived of as otherness, the incomprehensible part of reality or of human consciousness. The works in which this process takes place are neither fantastic nor realistic in the classical sense, but they are realistic in this new broad and disquieting sense of realism as literature that challenges our commonsense view of the world and the conceptual frameworks we use to understand it.

Disquieting realism in contemporary Spanish fiction and film owes much to Latin American magical realism, which inherited a zeal for the marvelous from the avant-garde. In *Foreigners in the Homeland* (2000), Santana shows the enormous impact that the writings of the Latin American Boom had in Spain in the 1960s and '70s. It is, then, hardly surprising that José María Merino, Enrique Vila-Matas, Cristina Fernández Cubas, Juan José Millás, and Antonio Muñoz Molina all name one or more of the 'Boom' writers as the model they were trying to emulate (Beilín 2004). Several critics agree that magical realism serves to 'naturalize the strange', by showing that the bizarre is after all part and parcel of reality (Llarena Rosales 1996). Like 'disquieting realism', magical realism can be linked both to the avant-garde (Anderson Imbert 1976) and to realism (Senov Kanev 1976). In disquieting realism and magical realism alike, the revolutionary rhetoric of the avant-garde may have been abandoned, but language is still subversive, as it questions not only the traditional positivistic approach to learning, but also the structures of power and the sociopolitical discourses that accompany it. While we have defined disquieting realism as a new mode and one that recognizes the reality of otherness, Zuffi (1967) argues the same for Latin American literature, considering 'alterity' as more appropriate for the cultural definition of Latin America than 'magical realism'. In both magical realism and disquieting realism, narratives which traditionally would be classified as fantastic because of their prevailing mood can make the same ontological claims as apparently realistic ones. Good examples of this process are José María Merino's fantasy novel, *Los invisibles,* and Antonio Muñoz Molina's realistic narrative, **Sefarad.*

In *Los invisibles,* José María Merino tells an impossible story, insisting on its veracity as a way of challenging his readers. The first part of the story concerns Adrián, a young man who has been invisible for some three months by the time we encounter him. In the second part, the author turns the tables on his readers by explaining that the story is based on a real event. This second part is entitled 'Ni novela, ni nivola' because, the author claims, this is not a piece of fiction but rather a rewriting of Adrián's confession. Through the reference to **Niebla*, the author suggests that, in contrast to what Miguel de Unamuno tried to claim in the story of that name, reality is not fiction, it being far more likely that fiction is reality. Merino reflects on how Adrián's story cannot be explained on the basis of nineteenth-century fantasy literature because the fantastic is a thing of the past; only the incomprehensible remains, and we often refuse to see this because it challenges our sense of how the world works. In order better to explain the mechanisms of doubt which lead the reader to disbelieve Adrian's story, Merino recalls the refusal of the civilized Western world to recognize what was going on in the Nazi extermination camps: these, he argues, were 'invisible' simply because no one wanted to know what was happening there. He concludes that there are a lot of things that people treat as a fiction simply because they do not want to have to face them.

Antonio Muñoz Molina's *Sefarad narrates real events as though they were fantasy, and in doing so makes much the same point. In historical reality and individual experience otherness is ignored just as it is in fairy tales, and by ignoring it we distort our view of the world. Even though Muñoz Molina's novel appears to be realistic and Merino's novel fantasy, they share the same theme: the marginal, the hidden (beneath its everyday disguise), and those facets of existence and consciousness which we banish from our everyday lives. Both writers tell incredible stories, focusing on the invisible and claiming that it is real. In the chapter of *Sefarad entitled 'Narva', the narrator interviews José Luis Pinillos, a member of Blue Division which fought with the Germans at the Battle of Stalingrad in World War II. Pinillos believed that Germany was the vanguard of Western civilization because Ortega y Gasset had said it was. He had studied in Germany in the 1930s, and his mind was shaped by the debates that went on at the time. At the start of the war, he joined the army, certain that he would be fighting with right on his side. When his division halted for a spell in Narva, Estonia, he witnessed for the first time imprisoned Jews being marched along a road to their death in a concentration camp. That same night he danced at a German Army party with a Jewish woman, who had been spared because she was a beauty, and who whispered in his ear the terrifying story of the extermination of her race. Only then did Pinillos start to perceive 'something monstrous, very close, yet still invisible' (2001: 483). Many years later, talking to the narrator of *Sefarad, Pinillos acknowledges that this 'something monstrous' was intimately connected with his unwillingness to recognize the real face of fascism. Both *Sefarad and Los invisibles suggest that the same intellectual processes are responsible for our refusal to face up to horror, both real and imagined, and that we have no infallible way of telling one from the other.

The narrator of *Sefarad relates his own temptation to falsify reality as he writes about it. This metafictional reflection leads him to question one of the most important principles of realistic narratives: internal cohesion. While the realist writer tries to bring some cohesion to the reality he is recounting, he also tends to embellish it with what Barthes (1970: 156) calls 'paste': descriptions, names, and intermediary episodes that never happened or at least do not figure in the memory, whither the past usually emerges fragmented and disordered. While in *Sefarad* the narrator uses 'paste' to bring together episodes as they emerge from Pinillos's memory, he precedes them with metafictional comments, such as: 'now I am tempted to invent' (2001: 479). Muñoz Molina's realism is, then, self-conscious, honestly displaying the structure of its narrative, explaining the propensity to produce a unified meaning and yet undermining it at the same time. Such realism accepts that everything disappears as a result of constant change: the healthy fall sick, the young get old, the hangman becomes a victim. The chapter 'Eres' ('You are') shows everybody constantly turning into someone else. We always define ourselves by reference to those around us, and this perception of otherness is the most important factor in our sense of who we are. Otherness is the main concern in this novel of 'exile' narratives about those who are forced out or who voluntarily move away from everyday reality: not only the victims of war, but also those suffering from addictions, illness, or even of a surfeit of literature.

The novels that Adelaida García Morales wrote in the 1980s and early 1990s share some of these same concerns. Her short novel *Bene*, for example, adopts the conventions of the fairy tale to show that everything that it deals with is ultimately part of human experience. Here, the thoughts of middle-class women in post-war Spain, based as they were on superstition and fantasy, manage to bypass any of the real sociopolitical problems of the day. Those who, like the narrator's aunt, Elisa, choose to view the marginalized as the agents of the Devil, and human suffering as the result of demonic posses-sion, do so as a way of denying any personal responsibility for such matters. By doing so, however, they condemn their own children to misunderstand the world around them. The novel makes it obvious that the image of a damned gypsy approaching the house by night is a figment of the narrator's imagina-tion, fevered as a result of the conflicting erotic tension and moralistic senti-ments that run right through the novel. The novel's central concern is with language, and the truth lies somewhere between this imagined gypsy (the signifier) and the real suffering of the gypsies (the signified).

The same is true for *La lógica del vampiro*. Like *Bene* and several other narratives of the kind, this is a novel that establishes an intertextual dialogue with nineteenth-century fantasy literature. While *Bene* can be read as a contemporary version of Henry James's *The Turn of the Screw*, *La lógica del vampiro* makes frequent allusions to *Dracula* and seems to suggest that the role of vampire stories is, by keeping the images absurd, to protect us from something far more real that lurks behind such patent fictions. As one of the protagonists suggests, the fantastic image of a vampire could well serve as a shield for real vampires, for 'if they existed, their best defence would be the fact that nobody believes in their existence' (1990: 71).

La lógica del vampiro is preceded by an epigraph from Bram Stoker's *Dracula*, and both stories have main characters who deny the reality of vampires until there is no longer any room for doubt. The nature of vampirism is different in the two novels, however. While Dracula is an aristocrat who has been officially dead for hundreds of years but keeps himself alive through the blood he sucks from beautiful women, Alfonso, the protagonist of García Morales's novel, is a middle-aged man who sucks vital energy from people whom he manages to attract to himself. Elvira, who narrates the novel, explains that when you are around Alfonso something very strange occurs, something for which there are no words, and which sounds absurd every time you try to put your finger on it. Such thoughts make us ask about the way language conditions our vision of the world and make us see that reality is not built out of words or mental constructions, but rather precedes them. Elvira concludes that:

> Everything was determined by the fortuitous and random distinction between what was known, and thus might be real, and the unknown for which there were no names or measures, and which ran flat counter to common sense. (189)

The lack of words for particular concepts means that a broad range of phenomena are banished to the shadows, where we refuse to acknowledge their presence. Common sense, which suggests that anything for which there is no word cannot possibly exist, merely confirms the cognitive status quo by preventing us from engaging with the unknown. It is our lack of an adequate terminology, perhaps, which ensures that to Stoker's question, which here serves as an epigraph to *La lógica del vampiro*: 'Who was he? An animal, a man, or a vampire?', there comes no answer. As Docherty has shown, an open ending like this is one that helps a reader to accept the inconclusive character of real experience (1996: 36–68).

The short story has traditionally been a genre where the ending is of decisive importance. During the transition and the subsequent years of the fledgling democracy it enjoyed a renaissance in Spain (Valls 1989). Among the best contemporary practitioners of the short story in Spain are José María Merino and Cristina Fernández Cubas. While their stories often have surprise endings, the surprises do not explain the strangeness of the events related but instead make them even more mysterious. Fernández Cubas's short story 'El ángulo de horror', for example, tells of a young boy returning home from school, who, as he nears the family home, suddenly sees it from a strange angle. The sight plunges him into a deep depression, and after a few days he commits suicide. At the end of the story, his little sister, who is also the narrator, also sees that same terrifying angle, but the mystery is never solved. Similarly, in Merino's short story 'La imposibilidad de la memoria' (1990a), published in the collection *El viajero perdido*, a middle-aged couple suddenly find their perceptions altered. Once they were lovers and rebels, committed to changing the world, but after twenty years of the monotonous routine of daily life they have lost their enthusiasm for love, life, and politics. First one disappears, then the other, and so ends the story. Mysterious, open endings like these can only have a symbolic meaning: disappearance as a metaphor for spiritual death or resignation, the angle of horror as a metaphor for a new and terrifying perspective on life that comes with adolescence, and vampirism as a metaphor for the fight for power in interpersonal relations.

If, as De Man contends (1984), the principal characteristic of romantic storytelling is the transformation of ancient beliefs into metaphors, then postmodernism turns that process upside-down and metaphors become again part of the real and function as allegories. Foster claims that postmodern art is allegorical not only because it focuses on the fragmentary, but also, and perhaps most importantly, because it explores the space between the signifier and the signified, and in doing so illuminates reality (1996: 86). The interest in creating metaphor, so that literal meanings collide with figurative ones, is characteristic of avant-garde art, as we can see, for example, in the dissolution of time in Dalí's famous painting of clocks or the representation of female duplicity in Buñuel's alternation of two different actresses playing the same part in his film *The Obscure Object of Desire* (1977). The same procedure is in play in Enrique Vila-Matas's *Extraña forma de vida* (1997). Juan Goytisolo's narratives also show a renewed interest in the exploration of the gap between the figurative and literal meanings of metaphor. While his *Reivindicación del conde don Julián* (1970) derides the old metaphors he considers responsible for the stagnation of Spanish culture, his *Juan sin tierra* (1975) proceeds to deconstruct them. In the last sequence of dialogue with the director of the psychiatric institute, the narrator pokes fun at what the director has to say by taking literally the figurative meaning of his speech. Taken literally, metaphors become too obvious and too visible and so lose any power they may have had to change our minds about things.

Arguably the most frightening metaphor in contemporary Spanish literature is that of 'death in life'. This may have originated with the Romantics like Espronceda and Larra but it reappears in a great number of narratives and films of the Spanish post-war period and argues for a nationwide loss of energy and a generalized social inertia. During the transition to democracy and afterwards, it returns as yet one more obstacle to overcoming the old rhetoric in which illusion always leads to disappointment. In *Las virtudes del pájaro solitario* (1988), Juan Goytisolo attempts to overcome 'death in life' through a different approach to death, transforming it, like the mystics used to, into a source of life and of love. Thus, he pretends to turn 'death in life' into 'death which gives life'. This same approach to a language that shackles but which can also liberate appears in several novels by Juan José Millás, among them *La soledad era esto*. Just as in *Las virtudes del pájaro solitario,* degradation expressed through the metaphor of 'death in life' is the point of departure for Millás's novel, and the body is the space where the change of meaning occurs. The central character, Elena, feels that she is carrying a foreign object around in her intestine and she attributes the feeling to the recent death of her mother and to apprehension about what the future may hold. She comes to think that this strange tumor, as she thinks of it, is her mother's death and will eventually turn into her own. It is a mysterious condition and one that triggers a reawakening in her: she breaks up with her corrupt husband and sets out to improve her life. The 'death' which she has been carrying inside herself turns out to offer wise counsel, causing her pain when she reverts to old habits (she is a drinker and hashish addict) and then lying dormant whenever she succeeds in moving towards liberation through the new life in which she partially recaptures the idealism of her rebellious youth. As she gradually stops drinking and smoking, she begins to keep a diary to make sense out of her experience. Little by little, she regains the capacity to think for herself and to react emotionally to her discoveries, and in this way rids herself of the mysterious illness. Before she cuts herself off entirely from her old lifestyle, though, like Larra in his memorable sketch 'El Día de Difuntos de 1836', she sees the world around her as 'dead' and the people moving in it as the 'living dead'. Once free of the past, this vision of metaphorical death changes and, in the last scene of the novel, in a manner reminiscent of both the mystics and *Las virtudes del pájaro solitario,* death reappears as a harbinger of love and the promise of new life. It is not insignificant that, just before the novel ends, Elena compares herself to Kafka's Gregor Samsa, imagining herself as an insect that has regained its old, human form.

Several contemporary Spanish narratives allude in this way to Kafka (Adelaida García Morales's 1985 *El silencio de las sirenas* is one such), for they are essentially to do with the experience of otherness and attempts to overcome 'death in life'. In Muñoz Molina's *Sefarad,* real-life accounts by victims of political persecution read like Kafka stories, and Kafka himself appears as a character in various chapters. In Enrique Vila-Matas's *Historia abreviada de la literatura portátil* (1985), 'portable writers' in Prague (Juan Gris, Stephen Zenith, Witold Gombrowicz, and others) encounter *odradeks* (or virtual suicides) from Kafka's story 'The care of the family man'. Juan Gris describes them as creatures 'like shadows' (1985: 58) which hide in dark truths, and Zenith in his letter to Gombrowicz talks about 'a reel of black thread which tries to make me say things that I do not think and never will' (15). This amorphous emanation of otherness epitomizes one of the most important characteristics of disquieting realism in that otherness is perceived both in the inner consciousness and outside in the real world, appearing in a variety of subjective and objective guises.

Vila-Matas's works are perhaps the best example of how much this disquieting realism owes to the avant-garde. His exuberant imagination allows him to disregard the rules of probability and to add spice to his fantasies with surrealist humor. However, the often absurd events and ideas lead to conclusions that are not without their serious side. As Ignacio Echevarría observes, Vila-Matas devotes himself to 'the difficult task of preserving meaning amid absurdity'.[1] Not only does his humor originate in surrealism, but so, too, does his horror. The eye sliced by a razor blade in the first shot of Buñuel's film *Un chien andalou* (1929) comes to mind. That powerful metaphor for the search for meaning in the process of seeing rather than in what is seen points also to the need for a wound in the body through which the world can enter and in the depth of which truth may be found. In *Suicidios ejemplares* (1991), Vila-Matas demonstrates the human proclivity to perceive truth in horror. It is not a proclivity to which he himself is addicted as a storyteller, but it shows how our darker instincts can be manipulated to our advantage. In one of the short stories in that same collection, 'Rosa Shwarzer vuelve a la vida', he suggests how a virtual suicide might prove a valid substitute for a real one. A similar idea returns in *El mal de Montano*, where the narrator, walking in a park, imagines in morbid detail the death of passers-by and reflects that by exercising his imagination in this way he is outstripping André Breton who, after all, did no more than kill himself. By imagining horrors instead of living them, we can simultaneously indulge in perversion and be saved from the results of succumbing to our morbid tendencies. Thus, the ventriloquist from *Hijos sin hijos* (1993) believes that literature can transform readers' attitudes to reality because, as he puts it, to learn how to read is to learn how to live, 'believing in a fiction that is known to be a fiction, knowing that it is nothing more, and then realizing the exquisite truth that one can know that it is a fiction and then, knowing it, believe in it' (1993: 141). This assertion is not the same as Unamuno's position in *Niebla* where he posits life as a fiction vis-à-vis divine truth, for according to Vila-Matas there are no realms that are either more or less fictional than any others; nevertheless, we choose to believe in some of them as though they really were true. The fictions that Vila-Matas's protagonists choose to believe in tend to have a certain element of otherness to them, beginning with the reality of *odradeks*, in *Historia abreviada de la literatura portátil*, or a trip away from home to a final dissolution and silence, in *El viaje vertical* (1999).

Vila-Matas's narratives display an attraction to otherness in all its forms. The ventriloquist in *Hijos sin hijos* spends his life imitating the voices of others and fantasizing about being many different people and in many places at the same time because it is not enough to be just one person and in just one place. **El mal de Montano* evokes the madness of Hölderlin, who, while

---

[1]   Ignacio Echeverría's words, originally published in *El País*, are reprinted on the back cover of Vila-Matas's *El viaje vertical* (1999).

he was staying in the house of a friend, used to open the door for all his guests and greet them with gestures of excessive reverence. These gestures, according to Vila-Matas's narrator, are an expression of the attitude of a true poet, for whom the other, whomsoever he or she may be, is always someone who deserves veneration and respect. According to Vila-Matas, the true goal of a writer (in common with every human goal) is to cheat death through one's work, and yet to be subsumed into that work just as Kafka might have wished, disappearance being a part of universal transformation. Vila-Matas's *El viaje vertical* (1999) tells the story of just such an eventuality. The protagonist, abandoned by his wife in old age, travels to Portugal, there to vanish without trace. This ending of the story is a figurative representation of the resignation of self for the sake of otherness.

In *Bartleby y compañía*, an avant-garde fascination with otherness takes the form of silence. The novel is about writers who stopped writing in order to live, a decision that leads the narrator to reflect upon the relationship between life and literature and to ask what the purpose of literature is (the question that Lyotard insisted in 1983 was the main one posed by postmodern art). He concludes that literature only emerges when passion is in the driving seat, as those who seek literature for literature's sake never find it, and those who do find it, find what lies beyond it, which is life. If that is so, then the modernist faith in art for art's sake has to cede ground to Bakhtin's (1990: 1) distance from art which is too self-confident and accordingly unlikely to provide any answer to life's big questions. In *El mal de Montano*, the priority of life over art would seem to be affirmed, but this novel also shows that as fiction gives priority to life, it paradoxically also leaves us outside it. To put it another way, using fiction to help us to understand experience paradoxically makes that experience impossible, albeit that the understanding we are vouchsafed seems to be more important than the experience itself. Blanchot (1968) addresses this central paradox in postmodern art by evoking the story of Orpheus. Orpheus's artistic power stems from his love for Eurydice (life), but the gods so love him for his musicianship (art) that he is permitted to descend into Hades to rescue her (life again). Yet he ends up losing Eurydice and is left with just his art, for which he is famous. This story also conveys a sense of art as mission.

The literature and film we have dubbed 'disquieting realism' take as their mission the retrieval of what has been lost: the silent voices, the past, the hidden, the forgotten; the secrets stories of persecution, violence, harm, and neglect. They do so through stories about the marginalized, the exiled, the ill, the alienated, the disappeared, and also those who, like the protagonist of *El viaje vertical,* just go away and never come back, dying after having discovered something that they never tell to another. Such stories tell us about our own cognitive processes and teach us an appreciation of the multiple meanings that lurk in the dark spaces of otherness. They lead us to the unsettling conclusion that we learn something about reality precisely by being forced to deal with things that our language and our culture have taught us do not exist.

Further reading

Amell (1992), Cahoone (1996), Folkart (2002), Labanyi (1989), Moreiras (2002), Navajas (2002), Pereiro (2002), Scarlett (1994), Smith (1991), Sobejano (1987, 1989, and 1996), Spires (1984 and 1996), Vilarós (1998), Waugh (1992).

14

Anti-conformist Fiction:
The Spanish 'Generation X'

H. ROSI SONG

The works of the late 1980s and 1990s from a new generation of Spanish writers have proved popular but have been dismissed with disdain by many established critics. Some of these writers achieved recognition very young, as in the cases of Pedro Maestre, whose *Matando dinosaurios con tirachinas* won the 1996 Premio Nadal, and José Ángel Mañas and Juana Salabert, shortlisted for that same prize in 1994 and 1996 respectively for *Historias del Kronen* and *Arde lo que será* (Urioste 1997–98). Some, more open-minded critics have seen this new crop of writers not only as professionally successful but also as representative of a generation far removed historically from the Franco regime, having come to adulthood in a democratic society (Dorca 1997). As Urioste puts it (1997–98: 457), these are writers who seem to embrace the ethos of the new democracy: youth, success, and change.

Those writers were born in the late 1960s, but there are others born in the early 1970s who are of the same generation, the equivalent of Coupland's 'Generation X' (1991). Though the following list is not exhaustive, the names that crop up most frequently in discussion are: Almudena Grandes, Mercedes Abad, Benjamín Prado, Gabriela Bustelo, Roger Wolfe, Belén Gopegui, Ángela Vallvey, Lucía Etxebarria, Juan Bonilla, Ray Loriga, Daniel Mújica, Juan Manuel Prada, Care Santos, José Machado, and Espido Freire (Izquierdo 2001). The work of these young writers and their coherence as a group are often debated in terms of their aesthetic preferences and thematic choices, although Encinar and Glenn (2005: 12–14) do not use the term 'literary generation' in this connection, given the differences between them in terms of style and subject matter, preferring to see them as a series of subgroups with distinct literary styles but all affected in different ways by the experience of the Franco dictatorship. Considering the extent to which literary expression was conditioned by political reality only a few decades ago (by both censorship and ideology), it is unsurprising that these writers have attracted such attention, seen as they are as the first clear beneficiaries of democratic change. From this perspective, even the differences between them are worth examining closely. We shall in this chapter focus on the subgroup usually identified with Coupland's 'Generation X' and whose work could be considered the most representative of their peers, not only in terms of critical attention but also because of certain features they have in common. Labeled rebellious and non-conformist, their fiction is best understood as a rejection of traditional literary and cultural forms, and an enthusiasm for a new, global aesthetic shaped by consumerism and popular culture.

After the death of Franco in 1975, the years of transition to democracy were a time of change, not only in politics but in society as a whole. Spanish culture was revolutionized by access to previously taboo topics, such as sex and drugs, as well as by unprecedented contact with the outside world.[1] The transition is usually said to have ended with the general election of 1982 and the victory of the socialist party, PSOE, whose political slogan was, appropriately, 'Por el cambio' (For Change), a motto that captured the expectations of Spaniards who hoped that the break with the past would be final (Pérez-Díaz 1993). The sense of possibility and freedom, accompanied by the feeling that Spain seemed finally to have joined the ranks of the developed countries of Western Europe, also had links with the unofficial cultural scene of the 1980s, known as the *movida*, which now exploded into the open in towns and cities throughout the country, and especially in Madrid. The transition was also a time of expansion beyond national parameters, when technological change and the new, global economy brought rapid change across the developed world, of which Spain was now part.

The expectations associated with the period of transition had quickly to confront the reality that political change had brought not a clean break with the past but a compromise; the so-called 'reforma pactada', or negotiated reform. It is the view of Juan Luis Cebrián (1982), for one, that, in practice, this political reform meant leaving intact the institutional and power structures of the dictatorship. Reaction to the compromise and to the recognition that the future would now be just the past adapted to the present meant that the ebullience of the immediate post-1975 period quickly dissipated, as commentators began to use by words like *desencanto* (disenchantment) and *pasotismo* (indifference) to sum up the prevailing attitude. Subsequent government shortcomings and the corruption scandals that enmired the first democratically elected Socialist government contributed to this general feeling, as did a sense of disconnection between the younger generation and politicians. The rapid evaporation of that early optimism was fuelled by economic recession,

---

[1]   A glance at studies of the political and social transformation of Spain after 1975 that were driven by the 'economic plans' of the 1960s reflects the enormous changes experienced by Spaniards and their new place among the most advanced capitalist societies of the Western world. See, for example, Carr & Fusi (1991) and Preston (1986).

both at home and abroad, along with a rise in unemployment which left many young Spaniards with no real prospect for the future and no opportunity of entering the ranks of mainstream society through work or a stable emotional relationship (Dorca 1997: 309). This paralysis was accompanied by a boom in visual culture thanks to the huge advances in technology, the mass media, and an increasingly materialistic consumer society. Spaniards quickly realized that traditionally accepted paradigms of cultural literacy were inappropriate to this new instant, popular culture and its symbiotic relationship with consumption. The information revolution was global, but it arrived in Spain just as the country was frantically trying to modernize its outdated economic and political structures, the legacy of decades of conservative measures. The result was a tension that has often been referred to as the schizophrenic tendency of Spanish culture: a culture, that is, born out of the clash between accelerated development and the unresolved issues of recent history and contemporary national identities (Graham & Sánchez 1995).

In this context, the rapid market success of novels by Mañas, Loriga, Wolfe, Bustelo, and Etxebarria, among others, came to be seen as a reflection of the tastes of disenchanted Spanish youth, living in a fast-paced consumer-oriented culture, plagued by unemployment and fragmented family structures, awash with drugs, and bombarded by images of sex and violence. What we find in Mañas's *Historias del Kronen* and *Mensaka* (1995), in Loriga's *Héroes* (1993), *Lo peor de todo* (1992), and *Caídos del cielo* (1995) or Etxebarría's *Amor, curiosidad, Prozac y dudas* (1997), are stories of young adults who are disaffected, unable to engage with the society around them, and seeking ways to break out from an increasingly stultifying and vacuous daily routine. Non-conformist to the core, the characters may be seen as waging all-out war on their surroundings, cultural and political, in a total rejection of political structures, economic realities, and social norms. These are works comparable to the hard (neo-) realism of Anglo-American narrative which have been labeled 'blank fiction', 'fiction of insurgency', 'downtown writing', and 'punk fiction': narratives characterized by a profound awareness of their own time and place and, by dint of constant allusions to brand names and styles, speaking 'in the commodified language' of their own period (Annesley 1998: 6–7). In both Gabriela Bustelo's *Veo veo* (1996) or Lucía Extebarrias's *Amor*, for example, the female characters are constantly defined by shopping and the products they acquire or display on their bodies, as well as by the places they frequent in order to see and be seen by others. The long litany of brand names not only defines the environment the characters inhabit, but also depicts the social settings that structure these novels. In much the same way, the cultural referents included in the works (predominantly from pop art and music and the world of rock and roll, television, and film) serve to create a connection between the characters. They also underline the main preoccupations of that subculture, such as violence and sex, also essential components of 'blank fiction'. Violence, in this context, is a metaphor for the processes of commodification, where the proliferation of media simulations of violent acts has a dehumanizing effect. The explicit sexuality in fiction of this kind reflects the way sex has permeated mainstream culture through popular culture, such as cinema and television. This sexual obsession may be widely understood as symptomatic of an increasingly decadent and immoral culture and of a new period of political and imaginative freedom, but the act of visualizing sex is also linked to forces fundamental to capitalist society and its core principle of consumption (Annesley: 40–49). From that perspective, even when drugs, random violence, and rough sex appear to offer an escape route, as they do in the novels of Mañas and Loriga (as in the murder of a friend in *Historias*), they nevertheless mimic a pattern of consumption based on the throwaway principle (of consumer goods and, now, of people).

Although fiction of this type is considered realist in terms of its portrayal of everyday life, these are writers who utterly reject the Spanish literary tradition and whose break with a previous generation shaped by ideological struggle, is total. Aesthetically, works by these new writers can be thought of as postmodern, in that their narratives are fragmented and transgressive and their style eclectic. Urioste (1997–98: 466) remarks on the disorder, ambiguity, and fractured nature of these fictions, filled with images that bring to mind Jean Baudrillard's exposition of postmodern culture. The success that these writers have enjoyed is seen by some as a passing fad whipped up by an aggressive publishing industry interested in marketing best-sellers by means of consumer research. Critics have for some time now voiced misgivings about the marketing strategies employed by publishers to introduce new young writers and their work as the sensation of the year: as prepackaged products designed to be sold, consumed, and promptly discarded.

When, in 1996, German Gullón wrote his now seminal article on this young generation of Spanish writers, he deplored the mainstream critics' negative attitude towards their work, judging its harshness as an indication of an unwillingness to accept social and cultural change. These writers, he insisted, were the products of a society that allowed them total creative and personal freedom and swamped them with visual images from popular culture. Their work would profoundly and forever change our previous understanding of literary fiction. Gullón's provisional use of 'Generation X' as a label for these writers – especially for those producing Anglo-American inspired hard neorealism like Mañas, Loriga and Wolfe – soon became the standard way of referring to them, thereby suggesting a comparison with those depicted in Douglas Coupland's hit novel *Generation X: Tales for an Accelerated Culture* (1991). As with the young Anglo-American generation of the 1990s, the label reflects socio-economic realities like the global recession of the 1980s and its attendant economic retrenchment, a rise in unemployment, and the struggle with the political and cultural legacy of the 1960s. Acland suggests that

'Generation X' refers to the experience of coming of age in the late twentieth century, but doing so with 'a certain lack of distinction'. The 'X' has come to denote an inability to define a whole generation faced with diminishing economic opportunities, a looming sense of failure, and the impossibility of attaining any group identity save by way of negating the preceding generation's lifestyle and political accomplishments. In other words, it stands for 'a structure of feeling, describing the unavailability of satisfactory markers of youthfulness and maturity, announcing that prevailing models of "growing up" did not suit the historical context' (2004: 32).

The application of the term 'Generation X' to Spanish writers of the 1990s has been much debated. Some argue about whether or not the economic, political, and social progress experienced by post-Franco Spain warrants such a label. Some, like Encinar and Glenn (2005: 12–13), suggest that lumping all these writers together in this way – and focusing on disaffection, disillusionment, and the propensity for gratuitous violence, sex, and drugs – is to turn a blind eye to many of the other narrative qualities they possess, such as an interest in storytelling, and in narratives that unearth past experience and historical memory. Colmeiro (2005) argues that using the term 'generation' has always been problematic, as it presents a group as homogenous, underplaying diversity in order to create the idea of a natural and spontaneous movement directly reflecting lived reality. The term Generation of 1898, for example, constantly used (and often abused), is open to this kind of criticism, as that particular term became shorthand for supposed Castilian national characteristics and concerns, thus reaffirming and reinforcing the idea of Spanish 'difference' when compared with intellectual movements in Europe and the US. He stresses the 'happy' coincidence (209) that the term 'Generation X' reflects both in Spain and elsewhere a period of inertia and dependence on foreign culture, especially on American popular film, television, music, and literature. If there exists a common thread between these writers, he argues, it is their connection with a popular culture that serves them not only as a cultural reference, but also as a mode of expression. That dependence has seemingly entitled reviewers to dismiss these fictions as by-products of fashionable and transient trends. The poor grammar on which they comment so slightingly, the use of colloquialism, slang, neologisms, fragmented narrative, predictable subject matter, and ubiquitous references to pop culture are all cited as proof of an asbence of aesthetic appeal and originality. The whole argument that the chaotic nature and political agnosticism of such works means that they are of no lasting artistic value provides a good illustration of what has been and is a constant tenet of the modern Spanish intellectual establishment: that art must always be conditioned and judged in terms of its relationship with politics.

Interestingly, the contempt that Gullón identified towards this Generation X and its obsession with popular culture ignores political connection. If the political positions adopted by the 1968 and 1977 generations of Spanish writers were easily understood in the context of the Francoist regime and the neo-anarchist reaction that followed it, that was no longer the case for those who came of age in the 1990s and later, in a consumerist and hedonistic Spain that excluded those without purchasing power. Once political positions that did not involve some negotiation or rejection of the country's recent authoritarian past had disappeared from view, the young experienced an increased commodification of dissent. It is not surprising that the sociocultural structures of the Spanish 'Generation X' can no longer be understood in a traditional political context.

Tara Brabazon, in her study on the Generation X phenomenon (2005), traces the invention and decline of this youth culture and the sociopolitical forces that underpin it. Starting out with Grossberg's definition of youth as 'a saturation point of hegemonic techniques of normalization, disciplinization, and the institutionalization of difference' (1984: 107), she notes that youth is also 'shorthand for institutions that maintain control over young people' (10). Youth, then is a lot more than just a particular age group at a given time: it is a product, not 'an amorphous result of ill-defined social changes, but determined by an economic system that requires niche markets to continue and increase the rate and role of consumption', and can be understood as the by-product of the ways in which different social groups achieve meaning. In the case of Generation X, no such market ever emerged because of systemic unemployment caused by the global recession of the 1980s. Unable to fulfil their economic potential, the younger generation embraced radicalism and revolution, seeing these as just another trend, a style to be borrowed, adopted, and rejected as whim dictated, not as a conscious betrayal of the 'authentic' political movements of the 1960s.[2]

Brabazon argues (11–14) that we should pay more attention to style, as this operates, she suggests, as a force not of revolution but of revelation, and shows just why a fresh approach is called for if we are to understand the different models of change now in play. The younger generation has, she says, opted for consciousness over class struggle as a way to expressing themselves, because they recognize that

---

[2]   Brabazon argues (2005: 11) that 'if political change is found only in a masculinist, heterosexual, productive public domain, then style-lifting is demeaned as an ephemeral, trivial waste'. Although her study focuses on Britain, her insights are helpful when it comes to understanding the development of youth culture in Spain. All the time the political situation was precarious, Spain would echo the student movements and student radicalism of the 1960s in terms of political opposition, always in the hope that the tide of change would eventually arrive there, too.

instead of reading 'against the grain' in an attempt to recover 'authentic selves,' there is much to be gained by glancing at surfaces and revelling in the superficiality. In *not* looking for a substantial cultural statement – a revolution – the revelation of (post-) youth culture on popular memory and popular culture can be revealed through subtle shifts of consciousness.

Spanish society post-Franco, as Moreiras has shown (2002), is going through a dark age politically in which there is little or no possibility of political and social change, a state of affairs which is reflected in Generation X texts, which break with any sense of historical continuity and immerse themselves instead in the here and now. Moreiras flags up the importance, in *Historias del Kronen* and *Mensaka*, of that here and now, the only sense of time being that provided by the actions of the characters and the unfolding of the story. The prominence of violence and indifference, the absence of any sense of community or history, the use of drugs and alcohol, and sexual behavior that is random and impersonal are all commonplace in these novels. What makes them extraordinary is the way action gives way to narration, activity occupying every movement of the text: clear evidence of a 'fictional vacuum' devoid of anything that might provide an overarching meaning (Moreiras 2002: 206–7). This vacuum is arguably a long-term effect of an historically traumatic past not yet healed, and a present that has no truck with memory. In *Historias*, for example, the nightly outings of Carlos to meet his friends at Bar Kronen to score drugs and seek thrills, his predatory sexual encounters, his obsession with violent works such as Easton Ellis's *American Psycho* or Kubrick's adaptation of Burgess's *A Clockwork Orange*, his indifference to the death of his grandfather, and ultimately, his participation in the killing of a friend in a moment of brutality fuelled by alcohol and drugs, constitute a sequence of events that is meaningless. Moreiras argues that the cultural references here illustrate both a new a way of looking at life and, more importantly, a new novelistic manner which sees characters as the subjects of experience.

The relationship between those subjects and their experience is based on consumption. The characters that inhabit these novels are simple consumers; their repetitive everyday routines show them seeking not meaning but rather experience in a casual, throwaway, consumerist world. Their lives are meaningless and disenfranchized. At the same time, it is precisely through consumption that they deal with the legacy and burden of the past. The consciousness that characters achieve is a byproduct not of an intellectual or moral quest but of an instant aggression, a tacit recognition that life is no longer functional according to any traditional social yardstick. Always mediated by a sense of style and a sharp focus on the present moment, the daily routines and mental processes of such characters are unlikely to prove constructive in any political or social sense, but consist instead of a series of particular moments in which an individual is conscious of nothing more than his or her own powerlessness. David, one of the main characters of *Mensaka*, whom we see as he struggles to stay sane while working at his day job as a messenger, muses that: 'what I should do one morning is carry a video camera with me and film everything that happens to me for a month as if it were a TV report and then I could shoot myself and anyone that watched the video would understand why' (Mañas 1995: 22). David's daily experiences show that even the big break he and his band have been waiting for all these years will not rescue him from the mediocrity of his life. It is telling that the reason David will not be allowed to share in the later success of his band is simply the tragic result of chance: he falls victim to a random act of violence thanks to the stupidity of those around him and his own failure to understand what is happening to him. Even if the brief moment of enlightenment that we see David achieve in the novel does not last, we are invited to view it as it is at that precise moment, one that might be caught on camera, the spectacle more important that any need for a narrative that might give lasting meaning to his awareness or actions. As a visual product, his moment of enlightenment is not a matter for narrative but yet another consumer product.

By creating this shift in consciousness, popular culture plays an important role. Brabazon argues that theirs is not a lost generation, but one that has discovered itself through popular culture and consumerism. Film, television, and pop music have an impact on culture, and 'Generation Xers' possess a media literacy which allows a celebration of an investment in the images that is not linked to the real.' (2005: 21). Analyzing Ray Loriga's *Héroes*, Colmeiro observes how these marginalized products of a hyper-developed capitalist society always define and identify themselves by what they consume because in the end they also consume themselves. The possibility of achieving an identity comes to be the same thing as the possibility of access to consumer goods. Thus, in Loriga's novel, the culture of rock music becomes an alternative world in which the main character can achieve his only possible socially acceptable identity (236–37). Even the possibility that they may acquire a real identity is only temporary, as the narrator fully understands the fluidity of the popular identity he wants to assume. That such an identity can serve as a mask, easily donned and just as easily doffed, is vital because it can mediate a reality that has become unbearable. As the protagonist of *Héroes* confesses, 'Feeling like Jim Morrison does not make you Jim Morrison, but not feeling like Jim Morrison makes you next to nothing. I would never go out without feeling like Jim Morrison or at least like Dennis Hopper' (Loriga 2003: 73). His decision to retreat into his bedroom is strikingly similar to the actual phenomenon of the Japanese *hikikomori*, where young people simply decide to 'withdraw' from the world and shut themselves in their rooms for days, months, and years at a time. In *Héroes*, the reluctance to engage with the world, and the urge to retreat inward and shut oneself off becomes a way in which the protagonist can achieve a new identity through musical heroes, like David Bowie, Lou Reed, or Jim Morrison. This is reality mediated by popular culture, but a culture that is by nature ephemeral. When characters are summoned by the narrator they appear as symbols not of the future but of a past stuck in the present, refusing to budge. The result is an impasse, one that leaves the narrator stuck in his room, with more questions than he has answers. His question about the passing of time is pointless: 'When all this has come and gone, where will this present me be and where will he be the moment after and where will I be in the middle of it all?' (180). The 'he' of the present and the future is meaningless, given that time does not guarantee change in this novel, and even were it to do so, it would be not a personal experience but an objectified one. As the narrator's last sentence in the novel indicates, 'I feel like a store that is changing owners' (180): the change is not experienced in the self but rather as an objective fact, and as such, it is always open to the whim of the consumer. It is not personal change that dictates character; it is consumption, or the possibility of consumption.

While dependence on popular culture to mediate identity and society might be seen by some as a sign of an incapacity to engage with reality, and therefore a recognition of social failure on the part of the characters involved, some commentators see it as truly subversive. Agawu-Kakraba argues, for instance (2002: 192), that constant references to the world of rock music in Mañas's work suggest an alternative cultural identity, one that does not belong to mainstream culture, and that the use of music and other forms of popular culture give the reader the opportunity to 'discern an urban cultural tribe bound together to express what may, surprisingly, be the plurality of a cultural experience that constitutes an important segment of contemporary Spanish society'. The possibility that there is here an alternative to traditional views of the world and to a homogeneous national culture based on ideology is an interesting way of looking at Mañas's refusal to set his work in the context of what we might think of as mainstream culture. That is not to suggest, however, that popular culture provides us with an easy key to understanding this new generation. What popular culture does do is help us understand how such writers have come to such a negative view of coherent individuality, by taking us through their many references to film and fiction, and their alternative views on the world. Popular culture, in this sense, can supply us with an iconographic database which may help us to read contemporary social structures. Music, film, and television might not be instrumental in building a political opposition or developing an alternative lifestyle and they might even reinforce a sense of impotence and defeatism, but, as Brabazon argues, 'youth cultures are silent consumers who build literacies, not capital', and their politics of consumption cannot be simply dismissed as mutinous or nihilistic, because they also give pleasure and so deserve closer critical attention (2005: 23). Popular culture, then, is not revolutionary; instead, it offers a way to read and unveil social inequalities. The resulting awareness does not provide the motivation or the wherewithal for any intervention aimed at resolving those inequalities. What the 'literacy' of popular culture permits both Generation X writers and their characters, is the chance to recognize each other, to raise consciousness of the moribund state of the social and political models that regulate all their lives. More importantly, the link with popular culture expresses the ways in which the relationship between literature and politics has been changing. No longer can we understand it in terms of opposition or resistance; the response of today's fiction to the status quo is dictated by consumerism.

Consumption is not empowerment. It simply reflects the frustration of a generation whose expectations have been thwarted by an economy dominated by uncertainty in the job market and in everything that flows from that. In such a world, coming of age in the 1980s and 1990s has meant facing an unclear future, being locked into a protracted transition to adulthood and an inability to discharge any socially traditional role. The result has been a fragile sense of identity in a world of rapidly changing values. Consumerism, both cultural and material, has reshaped the landscape while the old, inadequate socio-economic structures persist. The kind of critique mounted in the novels of recent years is not easily recognizable as a critique, since it is not articulated in the traditional language of opposition. Instead, it depicts a consumerist world in which characters participate fully, not always critically, and often with pleasure. The absence of any clear thesis of opposition and rejection is what makes the reading of this fiction so problematic.

Disapproval of Generation X on the ground that they fail to take a clear political stand is understandable, given that their work displays not coherent opposition, but seemingly random aggression and pleasure-seeking. It is unsurprising that the pleasures portrayed have not been well received, and that the role and place of popular culture in fiction of this kind has proved controversial. But that same popular culture, with its colloquialism, slang, neologism, and fashion-driven cultural referents can no longer be considered merely frivolity and self-indulgence: it is there both as subject matter and as part and parcel of a narrative structure that deserves closer examination. The popular worlds we discover in the fiction of writers like Mañas, Loriga, and Etxebarria should not just be seen as evidence of a passivity and negativity among the younger generation, but as an attempt to break with traditional ways of incorporating politics and cultural resistance into fiction.

Media literacy and non-conformity with social convention figure prominently in the works of this generation and, ultimately, bear witness to a shift in the parameters of political and social change that challenges our understanding of established social institutions. In the case of Spain, the significance of this challenge is that it is taking place in a political context which, having embraced democracy, is, with all its faults, the only available option, and yet one which is loath to contemplate the possibility of real structural change. The works of these young novelists demonstrate that the need for compulsory political compliance in a fledgling democracy is no reason not to face up to cultural changes which offer a daily challenge to our view of the world.

Further reading

Acland (2004), Agawu-Kakraba (2002), Annesley (1998), Cebrián (1982), Fortes (1984 and 1996), García & Sánchez (2001), Gracia (2000), Graham & Sánchez (1995), Gullón (1996 and 2004), Henseler (2003), Henseler & Pope (2007), Izquierdo (2001), Molinaro (2005), Moncada (1995), Perriam (2000), Redondo (2003), Rus (2000), Sabas (1997), Senabre (1995).

V

VISUAL NARRATIVE

15

Film, Politics, and the Novel

CRISTINA MARTÍNEZ CARAZO

The twentieth century was the century of the cinema. Its establishment as an art form is inseparable from the rich dialogue it has maintained with litera- ture. The relationship between author, work, and society that informs all art has a particular relevance for the cinema, since it is both a stage for artistic performance and a mass medium. There are also strong links – ideological, aesthetic and economic – between cinema and the novel, as indicated by Rafael Utrera's remark that: 'by providing characters and stories for the screen, novels shape the themes and modes of expression in popular cinema' (1985: 20). In Spain, the long cultural drought of the Franco years had a real affect on the development of independent cinema, dictating the relationship between word and image. As Sally Faulkner observes: 'twentieth-century Spanish history teaches us nothing if not that creative activity is embedded in its ideological context, especially during the Francoist dictatorship and subsequent democratic emergence from that era' (2004: 7).

The input of literature into 'the field of collective [film] performances', says Francisco Ayala, popularized the written word through a mass medium, where it became more accessible to an audience more inclined to watch than to read. In addition, the alliance between film and literature had helped cinema to overcome its early status as a kind of lowbrow spectacle, or sideshow.[1]

While some writers like Machado, Azorín, Valle-Inclán, and Blasco Ibáñez enthusiastically celebrated the relationship between film, drama and the novel, others like Unamuno, convinced of the written word's superiority over the image, refused to become involved. Blasco Ibáñez was given the

[1] This is particularly true of film adaptations of text-based drama. In the first decade of the twentieth century, theater supplied the film industry with many of its plots and stories. As early as 1907, Fructuoso Gelabert filmed segments of Ángel Guimerá's drama, *Terra Baixa*, and a year later *María Rosa*, by the same author, was well received by cinema-goers. Other successful stage works, such as Jacinto Benavente's *Los intereses creados*, flopped when transferred to the silver screen. Benavente continued to believe in dialogue between screen and stage, and in 1924 went on to form a production company with the film director Benito Perojo.

Hollywood red-carpet treatment because of his huge international success as a novelist. He sold the film rights to several of his novels, among them *Entre naranjos* (1900) and *La barraca* (1917).[2] He even directed, in collaboration with Ricardo Baños, the 1922 adaptation of his *Sangre y arena* (1908) starring Rudolph Valentino, of which there was a 1941 version featuring Rita Hayworth and Tyrone Power. Both Azorín and Antonio Machado's brother, Manuel, remained open on the question of the new art form and praised its capacity for creating a sensation of reality and bringing images to life. In the 1950s, Azorín published many articles about film in the Madrid newspaper *ABC*, and these were collected together in two volumes, *El cinema y el momento* (1953) and *El efímero cine* (1955).

Similarly, Valle-Inclán defended 'the seventh art form' and its ability to tell a story without words, and, as Zamora Vicente has shown in *Las Sonatas de Valle-Inclán*, he incorporated cinematic techniques into his texts. Unamuno, on the other hand, considered the cinema a 'disturbing', 'anti-artistic', 'fateful', 'revolutionary' spectacle, not worthy of speaking of in the same breath as literature. So adamant was he on this score that, when offered a chance to have one of his books filmed, he declared: 'If it were ever to occur to some filmmaker or other to make a movie out of one of them – and I would not go to see it – I would not think that he owed me any more than would a painter who painted a picture showing a character or scene from one of them' (Utrera 2002: 57).

The most fruitful relationships between literature and the visual arts, however, came with the poets of the so-called Generation of 1927. The poetry of Lorca, Salinas, Alberti, Cernuda, Aleixandre, and Moreno Villa provide many examples of intertextuality between writing, painting, and the films of the time. Avant-garde novelists wrote the impact of film into their works, as we see with Ramón Gómez de la Serna's *Cinelandia* (1923b) and Francisco Ayala's *Cazador en el alba* (1929), both of them fictions 'composed as literary transcriptions of a film seen on the screen or imagined in the mind' (Gubern 1999: 131).

In the mid-1920s, the importance of narrative in film grew with adaptations of classic stories such as Cervantes's *La ilustre fregona* (1927) and the anonymous 16th-century classic *Lazarillo de Tormes* (1925), as well as nine-teenth- and twentieth-century masterpieces like Armando Palacio Valdés's *La hermana San Sulpicio* (1927), Juan Valera's *Pepita Jiménez* (1924) and Pío Baroja's *Zalacaín el aventurero* (1929), one of the first Spanish movies to be distributed by Metro-Goldwyn-Mayer outside Spain.

With the arrival of sound in the 1930s, several novels and plays were

---

2   The Spanish screen versions of these were entitled *La tierra de los naranjos* (1914) and *La barraca* (1917), respectively. An American version of the former was issued as *The Torrent* (1929).

readapted, their popularity as silent film guaranteeing some measure of success the second time around. The popularity of these 'remakes' was due more to the novelty of having voices added to the images than to any intrinsic qualities they may have had as films.

   With the advent of the Spanish Civil War and its aftermath, imperialist and fascist propaganda came to dominate aesthetic considerations, so that literary works were selected and reinterpreted cinematographically on the basis of how well their content aligned with Francoist political aims and the message the authorities wanted to spread. Pérez Bowie (2004: 51) calculates that, out of a total of 432 Spanish movies made between 1939 and 1950, 196 were literary adaptations. The new pro-Franco government encouraged the filming of works that it believed would reinforce the regime's religious and patriotic values; it also encouraged the diffusion of apolitical literary and cinematic works that offered the public the escape it needed in the dark years of the post-war period. As Gubern puts it (2002: 57), 'The Spanish cinema of the 1940s preferred to watch literary texts rather than the harsh social realities that surrounded its executives on a daily basis'. *Raza* (1942), a film based on a script by the Generalissimo himself and directed by José Luis Sáenz de Heredia, is a good example of the determination in official circles to defend the religious, moral, and patriotic values of the newly installed government. Other adaptations were designed to idealize the supposedly glorious past of the Spanish empire and its cultural Golden Age by exalting the honor, religion, and national unity so close to the hearts of the regime's ideologues. Historical and romantic dramas, based on Golden-Age classics such as Lope de Vega's *Fuente Ovejuna* (Antonio Román, 1947), Tamayo y Baus's *Locura de amor* (Juan de Orduña, 1946), and even *Don Quijote de la Mancha* itself (Rafael Gil, 1948) were among the box-office successes of those early years.[3]

   During this initial phase of Francoism, the cinema resorted to the most conservative novels of the nineteenth century and to historical sagas that promoted the status quo, such as Pedro Antonio de Alarcón's *El escándalo* (José Luis Sáenz de Heredia, 1944) and *La pródiga* (Rafael Gil, 1944), Fernán Caballero's *La familia de Alvareda* (adapted by Rovira Beleta in 1950 under the title *Luna de sangre*), and Padre Coloma's **Pequeñeces* (Juan de Orduña, 1950). Ignacio Agustí's 1944 saga of three generations of a Barcelona entrepreneurial family, *Mariona Rebull,* filmed by José Luis Sáenz de Heredia in 1944, was promoted by the regime because of its author's ties to the Catalan *Falangistas*. The film was enthusiastically received by the public: evidence of the symbiotic relationship between political power and success. As Pérez Bowie points out:

---

3   Gutiérrez Aragón also adaped the *Quijote* for Televisión Española in 2001. Reviews were uneven.

The Spanish cinema's favorite image of nineteenth-century Spain is the one presented in the novels of conservative authors of the Restoration: an exaltation of the Christian meaning of life, and of a philosophy of acceptance of the constituted order at a time when the Catholic Church, and a society still run along feudal lines, had to fight off the ideological attacks of liberals and revolutionaries. This was an image perfectly attuned to the situation in which Spain found itself after the Civil War, with a regime that needed ideological and moral arguments to justify its legitimacy and also the systematic elimination of its opponents, which was still ongoing.
(2004: 56)

A small number of novelists opposed to Francoist ideology managed to get their works filmed because of the prestige they enjoyed among intellectuals and film directors at the time. Works like Baroja's *Las inquietudes de Shanti Andía* (Arturo Ruíz Castillo, 1946), Unamuno's *Abel Sánchez* (Serrano de Osma, 1946), Blasco Ibáñez's *Mare Nostrum* (Rafael Gil, 1948) and Carmen Laforet's *Nada* (Edgar Neville 1947) were not blocked by censorship, because of the intellectual prestige of the authors. There was no shortage of cases of 'ideological backsliding' by writers such as Wenceslao Fernández Flórez, whose pre-war production was marked by humor and nihilism, but who managed to find a niche in Francoist cinema by aligning himself with the regime once the conflict had ended, successfully managing to get both his *El hombre que se quiso matar* (Rafael Gil, 1942) and *El destino se disculpa* (José Luis Sáenz de Heredia, 1945) screened. Directors interested in works like these enjoyed the total confidence of the regime, either because they shared its ideology, or because they so skilfully disguised their dissidence that they remained free from suspicion. In addition, the publication of the novels on which these films were based guaranteed their approval. Mata Moncho believes that the censors allowed a certain freedom when a prestigious text was involved (1986: 5), while Hopewell confirms that choosing Spanish classics was an effective way of evading censorship (1986: 77), and Faulkner points out that 'while consensual film-makers adapted potentially radical texts in such a way that they promoted Francoist ideology, there is little evidence to suggest, conversely, that ideological opposition was voiced by subversively adapting conservative texts' (2004: 10).

At the beginning of the Franco era, the promotion of apparently neutral texts and of escapist cinema helped to raise the morale of readers and spectators who could temporally forget the squalor of their lives. The romantic novels of Luisa María Linares and the folkloric cinema, directed at the general public, were part of this pure entertainment.[4]

---

[4] Two genres adapted for the cinema achieved a high degree of popularity: the traditional *sainete* (or comic sketch) and Jacinto Benavente's drawing-room comedies. Almost twenty

During the 1960s Spain experienced a relative opening up to the outside world and the tentative introduction of a measure of tolerance, but there was still no let up when it came to state interference in the arts. The importance of literature in the cinema decreased, with adaptations declining from 32 per cent to 23 per cent of total output, while the number of films made from original screenplays increased. In 1955, one of the most politically significant milestones in Spanish cinema occurred: the 'Salamanca Conversations', in which the ideological and aesthetic shortcomings of Spanish cinema were denounced along with its lack of political commitment. These paved the way for an increasingly critical posture in the so-called 'metaphorical cinema' of the 1960s, the most important work of the period being Juan Bardem's *Calle Mayor* (1956), based on Carlos Arniches's *La señorita de Trevélez* (1916). This critical tendency blazed a trail for a new, complex and sophisticated cinema, best represented by Carlos Saura, which succeeded in dissecting the current Spanish realities and making a mockery of censorship.

In the 1960s there was still room for re-adaptations of classic novels of a conservative kind, including more by Alarcón, Coloma and Palacio Valdés. Benito Pérez Galdós and the 'Generation of 98' were less well represented, and Pío Baroja's *Zalacaín el aventurero*, brought to the screen by Juan de Orduña (1954), passed without notice. Juan Bardem began the ambitious project of adapting the iconoclastic *Sonatas* of Ramón del Valle-Inclán in 1959, but the end product was a flop. It was not until 1964 that Miguel Picazo launched his successful adaptation of Unamuno's *La tía Tula*, which availed itself of the comparatively tolerant mood of the time such a provocative text to translate to the screen.

A significant number of novels by writers of the Falange were filmed: José María Sánchez Silva's *Marcelino, pan y vino* (Ladislao Vajda, 1954); *La paz empieza nunca* by Emilio Romero (Leon Klimovski, 1960), and *Cuerda de*

---

years later, the need for evasiveness continued to ensure the popularity of Álvarez Quintero's *sainetes*; among those filmed were *Terremoto* (Benito Perojo, 1939), *Malvaloca* (Luis Marquina, 1942, directed again later by Ramón Torrado in 1954), and *Cinco lobitos* (Ladislao Vajda 1945). The humor in such pieces serves to destabilize any possible criticism they may contain, as the texts alternate between conformism and dissidence. Benavente's comedies still enjoyed huge success, even though during the war he had been on the Republican side. *La malquerida* (José López Rubio, 1940) and *Rosas de otoño* (Juan de Orduña, 1943) were made into highly successful films, as was the Machado brothers' *La Lola se va a los puertos* (Juan de Orduña, 1947), where a frieze of regional stereotypes and the glorification of the Spanish nation did much to ensure its popularity. Woods (2004) explores the transgressive element present in Francoist cinema, in particular in Luis Marquina's *Torbellino* (1941). Andalusian 'casticismo' that did so much to fix for many years an image of Spain in the public eye was reinforced by the success of two remakes centered around folkloric stereotypes: *Malvaloca* (Ramón Torrado, 1954), the third adaptation of Álvarez Quintero's play (the first being by Benito Perojo in 1926, and the second by Luis Marquina in 1942), and the same author's *Morena Clara*, twice adapted for the screen: by Luis Lucía (1954) and Florián Rey (1936).

presos by Tomás Salvador, founder of the National Police Force, or Cuerpo General de Policía (Pedro Lazaga, 1955). The novels and stories of exiled writers (Aub, Sender, Chacel, Ayala) remained off-limits until much later, as did works by writers who had defended the Republican cause, such as García Lorca or Benjamín Jarnés.

The exile of intellectuals and artists with links to the cinema (such as Aub, Sender, and Ayala) was a great loss to Spanish cinema. Many more film professionals who could have contributed to the development of the national industry went into exile, among them directors Luis Buñuel, Luis Alcoriza, and Jaime Salvador; scriptwriters Julio Alexander and Eduardo Ugarte; and composer Gustavo Pitaluga, who went to work on soundtracks for Mexican cinema. The adaptations of Galdós's works that Buñuel directed in Mexico and Spain deserve separate mention. Even though Buñuel acquired a thorough understanding of Mexican culture, and enjoyed universal appeal, his essential Spanishness is plain to see in *Nazarín* (1957), *Tristana* (1969), and *Viridiana* (1961).[5] These are films that clearly capture the iconoclastic and anticlerical spirit of Galdós.

The most successful authors of the post-war period, Cela and Delibes, played no part in the Spanish cinema of their day. The films *La familia de Pascual Duarte* and *La colmena* would not be released until 1975 and 1982 (directed by Ricardo Franco and Mario Camus, respectively), and the only adaptation of Delibes's work to be released during the Franco era was *El camino* (1962). What little social criticism there was came in the form of high-quality comedies, influenced by Italian neorealism of the kind developed by Marco Ferreri; films of this kind depicted, often without overt comment, the squalid social realities of the time. Examples are *El pisito* (1958) and *El cochecito* (1960), based on two stories by Rafael Azcona, *El pisito* and *El paralítico*.

The rebirth of Spanish cinema began with José María García Escudero. As Director-General of Cinematography between 1962 and 1967, he was charged with making Spanish films exportable to the rest of Europe. A Catholic but one open to different points of view, García Escudero was the ideal candidate for the job. What he did was to reject the literary tradition in favor of a more critical exploration of contemporary reality, and yet one that still acceptable politically. The adaptation of *Lazarillo de Tormes* from this period stands out for its picturesque views of Spanish rural and urban landscapes interwoven with allusions to Spain's efforts to promote itself as a tourist destination. As Vilarós has noted (2002: 202), this film was 'a detailed catalogue of places of tourist interest in Castile'. Another successful comedy redolent of the period

---

[5]   *Viridiana*'s success at the Cannes Film Festival, where it won the coveted Palme d'Or, provoked a huge outcry in Spain and the film was promptly 'disappeared'.

is *Bienvenido Mr. Marshall* (Andrés Berlanga 1962), a film that cloaks its criticism of the status quo with a *castizo* (pure-blooded) and comic slant. Directors who favored the New Spanish Cinema, most of them opposed to Francoism, distrusted this new promotion of the film industry and feared exploitation by politicians.

In spite of a reduction in the number of literary adaptations, there was a significant dialogue between film and the written word, and several writers considered proponents of social realism and defenders of objectivism displayed a clear affinity for the films of their day, as we can see from their aesthetic, ideological and technical approaches to writing. The influence exerted by film on the generation of the mid-1950s is obvious in the neorealist narratives of Ignacio Aldecoa, Rafael Sánchez Ferlosio, Martín Gaite, García Hortelano, and Jesús Fernández Santos. *Young Sánchez* (1963) and *Con el viento solano* (1965), both by Aldecoa, were adapted by Mario Camus. The influence of Sánchez-Ferlosio's **El Jarama* is acknowledged in a key film of the New Spanish Cinema, *Los golfos*, directed by Carlos Saura (1959). Two other films of the time, based on Miguel de Unamuno's **La tía Tula* (Miguel Picazo, 1964) and Pío Baroja's **La busca* (Angelino Fons, 1966), show a style of adaptation which is quite detached from the text that inspired it, especially when it comes to character, and which is existentialist in its approach and use of metaphor. Zunzunegui (2002: 106) emphasizes this aim of the New Spanish Cinema's to articulate a 'cinematographic realism' unrelated to the novel, departing from the old 'the literary and literaturizing perspective [that] tries to turn the cinema into one more link in a long, unbroken chain stretching from the picaresque novel to the present'.

The final years of the Franco dictatorship were marked by what has been called '*dictablanda*' ('light dictatorship') and by a weakening of censorship. Franco's death, the restoration of democracy, and the victory of the social-ists gave way to one of the most complex and convulsive periods in Spanish culture. Three key factors affected the process of change. The disappear-ance of censorship (softened after 1966, but officially in place until 1978) sparked a desire to reconstruct the past from a new perspective and to rede-fine Spain's image internally and abroad. When the time came to rewrite history and to profile the new democracy, film and novels, along with the mass media, would prove useful: driven by the desire to normalize every-thing that the censors had prohibited, cinema would join forces with fiction to offer a liberal worldview opposed to Francoism. So, we have the vibrant adaptations of Valera's **Pepita Jiménez* (Rafael Moreno Alba, 1975), and of the bawdy fourteenth-century classic *El libro de buen amor* (Jaime Bayarri, 1975), both of which keep faith with the written original as a way of justi-fying the film's sexual content. The adaptations of Max Aub's *Las buenas intenciones* (*Soldados*: Alfonso Hungría, 1978) and Eduardo Mendoza's **La verdad sobre el caso Savolta* (Antonio Drove, 1979) also show interest in opening up the screen to new perspectives and political subjects. Ricardo Franco's *Pascual Duarte* (1975) adds a political dimension also, and, as Marvin d'Lugo points out (1997: 23), the director 'modified [Cela's] contemporary masterpiece to coincide with a critique of the political forces shaping social behavior in Spain'. The way in which content and form are brought together make this a film with a 'minimalist aesthetic' Santoro (1996: 88), but one which nevertheless embraces the unmotivated nature of the crimes committed by the protagonist.

With the restoration of democracy, it became government policy to use film once more both for its own sake and as a means of diffusing cultural values, and to that end there was a series of government subsidies, including the so-called '1300 Million Decree'.[6] The controversial Miró law, enacted in 1982, was a milestone in cinema-literature relations because it established an accredited institutional model designed to encourage collaboration, without any of the more complex, riskier, and less commercial aesthetic or ideological approaches that had characterized such joint ventures in the past. The goal was to create a cinema equal in stature to what was on offer elsewhere in Europe, adding cultural prestige to film by linking it to fiction, and taking advantage of the ensuing collaboration to project an image of a Spain that was culturally at ease with its own traditions and history. Some of the most celebrated 'literary' films of the Spanish cinema come from this socialist stable: Miguel Delibes's *Los santos inocentes* (Mario Camus, 1984), Luis Martín Santos's *Tiempo de silencio* (Vicente Aranda, 1986), Cela's *La colmena* (Mario Camus, 1981); Adelaida García Morales's *El sur* (Víctor Erice, 1983), Fernando Fernán Gómez's *Las bicicletas son para el verano* (Jaime Chavarri, 1984), Ramón Sender's *Réquiem por un campesino español* (Betriú, 1985), Eduardo Mendoza's *La verdad sobre el caso Savolta* (Antonio Drove, 1979); and Mercè Rodoreda's *La plaza del diamante* (Francesc Betriú, 1981).[7]

---

6 This public competition, promoted in 1979 by the UCD (Democratic Center Party) to promote the Spanish film industry, is just one example of government subsidy. On offer as a prize was the chance to direct a TV series. The rules of the contest stipulated that the series should be based on a literary work, and this was seen as a way of encouraging collaboration between literature, film, and television. As it turned out, the same guidelines that were developed for television came to apply also to film. Among the reasons for that was that many TV series were conceived with the idea that they would later be turned into feature-length films. The decree laid down ground rules for adaptations, which would later be endorsed by the PSOE (Spanish Socialist Party) when it came to power.

7 In *La plaza del diamante*, there is a clear re-politicization of the film text. Stanley (2004: 64) puts it in these terms: 'The written work counters patriarchy and by extension Francoist fascism; the screen adaptation explicitly politicizes Natàlia's tale, evincing not only anti-Francoism ideology but also boasting both Republican and Catalanist sentiments'.

Some 194 films based on published texts were made between 1975 and 1989, and the success of Delibes in the cinema is clearly exceptional. His ability to create character and the documentary-style nature of his work led to adaptations of twelve of his novels between 1962, when Ana Marshal filmed *El camino*, and 1998, the year in which Francisco Betriú brought *Diario de un jubilado* to the screen under the title *Una pareja perfecta. Los santos inocentes* and the three films directed by Antonio Jiménez Rico – *Retrato de familia* (1976)*, El disputado voto del señor Cayo* (1986) and **Las ratas* (1997) – stand out as especially felicitous choices (see Arbona Abascal 2002). Here we have titles that were equally successful on page and on screen and which share the same critical sociodemocratic subtext as both.

These films may have been box-office successes, but they have been criticized for a certain uniformity, part of which may be due to norms imposed by the socialist government. They are often didactic, and perhaps too much so, and many do not try to translate to the screen version the complexities and subtleties of the original. Their aim is patently to achieve a straightforward, 'realistic' film, accessible to the general public and with a convincing and commercially successful message. Isolina Ballesteros's view is that they also do something more:

> In the post-Franco era, the masses progressively become *voyeurs*, spectators of their historical and literary past, leaving it to the cultural apparatus of the state to choose what they would see, by turning into spectacles those literary texts that best represent their hidden, Francoist past, and do so through a socialist ideological filter. (1994: 171)

Socialist policy on cinema did manage, on the other hand, to replace the old folkloric, populist, and often comic adaptations with something new and closer to the audience's own experiences. The result was a homegrown product so markedly Spanish that, in spite of its quality, it did not prove easy to export. Although cinema played a key role in the consolidation of Spain's new image at a national level, its international impact was limited. Antoine Jaime takes a positive view of this lengthy dialogue between film and literature at this period and suggests the two did enrich each other:

> The desire carefully to recreate on screen great moments in literature was born of a conviction that the future of the country was at stake and that there was a need to disseminate serious works and ideas so that the social debate about improved and enhanced democracy would be better informed. It has meant that comparisons have been made between the literary originals and their screen adaptations. The choice of themes and subjects, the inner emotional journeys of characters, their deep feelings, nuances of meaning that encourage reflection on the fundamental problems of society,

all of these have forced film-makers to develop techniques as delicate and as convincing as those of the wonderful texts that inspired them.

(2000: 321)

At present, the tendency to revise the past and reinvent national identity has gone and what we have in its place are films and novels detached from political issues and centered on contemporary reality – and on the commodification of art. The ideological burden and the restrictions typical of first the Franco regime and then the socialist government have gone. The criteria for making films have become more and more commercial, and the themes they treat are accordingly to do with the problems of the new generation, their transgressions, their nihilism. The most highly praised writers and film directors are keen to document the current, unstable global reality and to captivate spectators/readers between the ages of 15 and 30, with whom they themselves identify. The protagonists of such films and stories are disoriented and gravitate toward hedonism, alcohol, drugs, and marginality, rambling through urban spaces to the spasmodic beat of the big city.

The impact of visual culture on young writers, especially those of the so-called 'Generation X' (see above, Chapter 14), and the handling of references and techniques that come from several audiovisual fields (rock, comedy, video clips) is evident in everything, from the fragmented structuring of novels as film scripts, to the dominance of dialogue and constant allusions to cinema. Typical of these trends are José Ángel Mañas, author of *Historias del Kronen* (Montxo Armendáriz, 1995) and *Mensaka* (Salvador García, 1998); Ray Loriga, author and director of *La pistola de mi hermano*, and Lucía Etxebarria, involved in the adaptation of her own novel, *Amor, curiosidad, prozac y dudas* (Miguel Santesmanes, 2001).[8] Isolina Ballesteros summarizes this recent phenomenon in the following terms:

> It is a fact that the simulated universe of the image (film, television, video) is reality for Generation X and determines its cultural experience. It is not surprising then, that the new generation of narrators and film directors should construct texts that constantly allude to that world, nor that film directors should take some of those texts and bounce them back in the form of screen adaptations. (1994: 244)

Alongside 'Generation X' are other well known writers whose upbringing was more literary than visual but who are interested in integrating film into

---

[8]   There are wide differences between Armendáriz's version of *Historias del Kronen*, which attenuates the amoral and nihilistic posture of the characters, and Salvador García's take on *Mensaka* which concentrates on the protagonists' vacuity and makes no effort to humanize them. See Fouz-Hernández (2000).

their creative process. Among these we have Antonio Muñoz Molina, three of whose works have been transferred to the silver screen: *Beltenebros (Pilar Miró, 1991), *El invierno en Lisboa (José Antonio Zorrilla, 1991) and Plenilunio (Imanol Uribe, 2000), while Rosa Montero's La hija del caníbal (Lucía, Lucía: Antonio Serrano, 2003), Belén Gopegui's Las razones de mis amigos (Gerardo Herrero, 2000), and *Todas las almas (El último viaje de Robert Rylands: Gracia Querejeta, 1996) by Javier Marías, have all made it into the cinema.[9] Similarly artistic films have been made out of two nouvelles – Manuel Rivas's *La lengua de las mariposas (José Luis Cuerda, 1999) and Manuel Vázquez Montalbán's *El pianista (Mario Gas, 1999) – and one Bildungsroman: Almudena Grandes's Malena es un nombre de tango (Gerardo Herrero, 1996). Arturo Pérez Reverte's *El maestro de esgrima (Pedro Olea, 1992) and La novena puerta (Roman Polanski, 1999) have enjoyed international success, and Juan Marsé's *El embrujo de Shanghai, which was to have been adapted by Víctor Erice, ended up being directed in 2002 by Fernando Trueba.

Erotic novels have also been a happy hunting ground for the film-maker. There was real commercial appeal in the case of Almudena Grandes's *Las edades de Lulú (Bigas Luna, 1990), Antonio Gala's La pasión turca (Vicente Aranda, 1994), and Manuel Vicent's Son de mar (Bigas Luna, 2001). Commercial success was also the driving force that led to the adaptation of several prize-winning novels, including Juan José Millás's *La soledad era esto (Sergio Renán, 2002), Andrés Sopeña's El florido pensil (Juan José Porto, 2002), Lorenzo Silva's El alquimista impaciente (Patricia Ferreira, 2002), Vázquez Montalbán's El misterio Galíndez (Gerardo Herrero, 2003), Manuel Rivas's *El lápiz del carpintero (Antón Reixa, 2003), Eduardo Mendoza's *El año del diluvio (Jaime Chavarri, 2004), Bernardo Atxaga's *Obaba(koak) (Montxo Armendáriz, 2005), and Javier Cercas's *Soldados de Salamina (David Trueba, 2002).

Adaptations continue to be important in current Spanish cinema (more than a hundred of them were filmed between 1990 and 2006) and this conjunction has clearly been advantageous from the commercial point of view, so that producers, taking advantage of the supposed benefits of adapting a best-selling novel, have not hesitated to make lucrative offers to writers in exchange for the film rights to their works.[10]

---

[9] This 'free' adaptation of *Todas las almas gave rise to a lawsuit brought by Marías against the producer. The Court found in favor of the writer and awarded him damages.

[10] In Pedro Almodóvar's films, although they are not based on fictional adaptations, literature is always present. The question of authorship runs throughout his work, as Marvin d'Lugo has shown (2002). Writers figure as characters in several films: Pablo Quintero in La ley del deseo (1987), Amanda Gris in La flor de mi secreto (1995), and Esteban in Todo sobre mi madre (1999).

As for social cinema, there have been several recent adaptations based on issues of the day. Imanol Uribe's *Días contados* (1994) is based on a novel by Juan Madrid about violence by ETA, the Basque separatist group; Uribe's film *Bwana* (1996) is based on a play by Ignacio de Moral, and *Said* (Llorenç Soler, 1998), is an adaptation of Joseph Lorman's novel, *L'aventure de Said* (Said's Adventure), These last two deal with immigration issues, while *Bajarse al moro* (Fernando Colomo, 1989) is based on José Luis Alonso Santos's play about crime and drugs.

Adaptations of classics continue to be brought to the big screen, nowadays with outstanding visual effects; among the best of these are Lope de Vega's splendid *El perro del hortelano* (Pilar Miró, 1996), Lorca's *Yerma* (Pilar Tavora, 1998), and Galdós's 1904 play *El abuelo* (José Luis Garcí, 1998). *Don Quijote* has several times been filmed, most recently by Manuel Gutiérrez Aragón (2002); there have been four adaptations of *Celestina,* by Cesar Ardavín (1969), Miguel Sabido (1976), Juan Guerrero Zamora (1982), and Gerardo Vera (1996); and three of *El Lazarillo de Tormes*: César Ardavín (1925), Florián Rey (1959), and Fernando Fernán Gómez (2000).

It is perhaps possible to identify four constants in the long dialogue between film and the novel in Spain. First, it has been strongly marked by ideology and political circumstance, as well as a penchant for propaganda and didacticism. Second, the importance of the market and of commercial success has dictated the choice of texts to be adapted. Third, government subsidies have played a big role in shaping the bonds between cinema and literature, as the texts adapted had to please the government financing the project. And, fourth, success in the cinema has helped to boost sales of the novels involved.

Further reading

Barbáchano (2000), Cabello-Castellet *et al.* (1992, 1995, 1997, and 2000), Chatman (1978 and 1990), Desmond & Hawkes (2005), Eisenstein (1949a), Font (2002), Fuentes (2003), Gimferrer (1985), Gómez Mesa (1978), Martínez-Carazo (2005), McFarlane (1996), Méndez Leite (1997), Merino (1997), Naremore (2000), Ríos Carratalá (1997 and 2002), Stam (2005), Turner (1990), Valis (1990), Vanoye (1995).

VI

PLURILINGUAL SPAIN

16

The Catalan Novel

JOSEP MIQUEL SOBRER

One of the driving forces of Catalan literature in the twentieth century has been the determination to modernize, the feeling that it was imperative to look to Europe and not to gaze back fondly over the glories of Spain's erstwhile empire. But to identify oneself culturally with things Catalan was to accept not only a language but a tradition and a sense of nationhood that could be restored by looking back at history. Modern Catalan culture is characterized by this push and pull between tradition and innovation. Catalan writers have had to compensate for the fact that, in living memory, their country was relegated to a peripheral and often subordinate role in a version of Spanish history and culture determined by Madrid. They have done so by committing themselves to the modern as much as the traditional. In 1906 Eugeni d'Ors coined the term *noucentisme* to differentiate emerging Catalan modes and styles from turn-of-the-century *modernisme*. Both terms bear witness to the Catalan determination to engage with all things modern.[1]

Caterina Albert i Paradís, a writer who sheltered from the public gaze behind the pseudonym 'Víctor Català', published in 1905 what was to become a trail-blazing novel, *Solitud*. It tells the story of a young woman, Mila, whose marriage falls apart when she realizes her husband can offer her neither material comfort nor sexual satisfaction. As it turns out, he cannot even offer her protection: when she is raped by the villain of the piece, known only by his Jungian-sounding nickname 'l'Ànima', he turns a blind eye to what has happened, and there is even a hint that he may have been complicit in it. The basic plot is as black-and-white as it could be: an earnest young woman, a wise old man (assassinated by the villain), a frustrated love interest, a spineless husband, and a thoroughly evil villain. Yet even today the novel has an extraordinary impact on the reader: the narrative is vivid, and the descriptions evocative. The novel begins with a physical ascent and ends with the protagonist's return to the plain below. That physical progres-

---

[1]   The fullest account of Catalan literature is Molas (1986–88). For a dictionary of authors and titles see Bou (2000). Terry (2003) offers a short but insightful overview in English.

sion contrasts with the moral temper of the story which turns the climb into a descent into a spiritual hell and the final descent into the moment when the protagonist comes of age. *Solitud reads like a critique of patriarchal social mores and, as such, has generated much enthusiasm among feminist critics, some of whom insist on using the author's actual name rather that the nom de plume she herself affected.

Quite unlike *Solitud, Prudenci Bertrana's Josafat (1906) is a work that seems perfectly at ease with patriarchal and even perverted modes of sexuality. It reads like a degenerate version of Hugo's Notre-Dame de Paris, though one set against the humbler cathedral backdrop of Girona (where one of the bell-ringers is involved in sadistic relationships with young prostitutes that lead into necrophilia). Bertrana's characters are more tormented than evil and the novel's accusations are leveled not at them but at the clerical establishment. The author's interest was clearly more psychological than mythical, as we see from his 1925 novel Jo! (Memòries d'un metge filòsof), a pseudo-autobiography based on the life of a friend of the author (a friend, that is, until he read the published book).

Bertrana's work marks a departure from the traditional Catalan literary contrast between the desolation of the mountains and rural areas and the urbanized plains and coast. Another work to do much the same is Raimon Casellas's Els sots feréstecs (1901). For Casellas, as for Català/Albert, the hills are alive with the stench of evil. The mythical battle in Els sots pits a well-meaning rural priest against a flamboyant whore who, just in case the reader has missed the earlier symbolism, goes on to celebrate a Black Mass. Casellas's novel is modern also in the way it inverts the romantic cliché of the purity of mountains and countryside, even though the tension between priest and prostitute takes us all the way back way to the Eve legend.

The noucentistes appeared on the literary scene armed with a bourgeois sense of revulsion for such Miltonian conflicts. They wanted to 'civilize' (a favorite word with Eugeni d'Ors) the novel, making it urban and middle-class and peopling it with characters who brushed their teeth twice a day. Yet theirs was a generation that wrote very few novels (Yates 1975). Eugeni d'Ors wrote a couple of narratives that might be considered novels, albeit with a pronounced essayistic bent. The more famous of these is La ben plantada (1911) in which the main character, Teresa, is glorified as an embodiment of everything that is good and Catalan. It tends to be read as an allegory, even though recent research (Mas 2006) suggests that the 'handsome woman' of the title was based on the flesh-and-bones figure of a real lady by the name of Teresa Mestre de Baladia.[2]

---

[2]   The term 'ben plantada' is hard to translate since it is calqued upon 'ben plantat,' a term of praise for masculine good looks. But it does also carry a suggestion of 'well planted'.

More typical of what *noucentisme* was trying to do with the novel are the three works with a woman's name as their title written by Carles Soldevila, a man whose mission as a writer it was to bring modern cosmopolitanism into Catalan culture. His *Fanny* (1929), the story of a young middle-class woman who makes a living as a cabaret artiste when her family falls on hard times, was followed by *Eva* (1931) and *Valentina* (1933). In these novels Soldevila portrays upper middle-class characters who drink tea and go on pleasure cruises but who are nevertheless prey to strong passions, some of which may strike a modern reader as a little over-Freudian. He made a good living as a writer, and was keen to bring an elegant social polish and cultural refine-ment to his work; unsurprisingly, he loathed the fiction of *modernistes* like Caterina Albert and Raimon Casellas.

Soldevila's contemporary, Josep Maria de Sagarra, parts company from mainstream *noucentisme*. Best known as a poet and dramatist, he wrote jour-nalism, essays, travelogues, narratives, and memoirs, as well as three full-length novels. Of these, *All i salobre* (1928), a story of Costa Brava fishermen of the kind we find in stage successes such as his *costumbrista El cafè de la Marina* (1933), was followed by *Vida privada* (1932), a gossipy story set in Barcelona amid the upper bourgeoisie and petty nobility and involving two brothers from a distinguished but down-at-heel family, their affairs, and their betrayals. Written with verve, this second novel shows Sagarra at his best: his mastery of the language, his powers of observation, his splendid sense of the comic. Yet, although influenced to some extent by Marcel Proust, it cannot shake itself free of a didacticism that tends to make its characters into ciphers rather than real people.

A cluster of writers, known as the Grup de Sabadell because they were born in that industrial town near Barcelona, emerged in the years immediately prior to the great catastrophe that was 1936–39. The best known member of the group was Francesc Trabal. His most successful novel, *Vals* (1935), gives a clear indication of what these writers were attempting to do: unadorned prose, an interest in experimentation and the exploration of the absurd, and a disdain for characterization and verisimilitude. Trabals's novels are more like Soldevila's work than they are like Sagarra's, and take an ironic, detached view. The Sabadell group was interested in experimentation and understood literature as playfulness. As we shall soon see, they were to have an impact on later writers such as Pere Calders and Quim Monzó.

The Civil War and its long aftermath dealt a severe blow to aspirations for Catalan self-rule and to writers' ambitions for Europeanization and modernity. The country was forcibly returned to the old ways: Catholicism, Castilian monolingualism, and conservative social and political structures. Catalan culture was once again marginalized and the cultural scaffolding assembled by the *noucentistes* and their successors was ruthlessly disman-tled. Many of the generation of writers who had begun to publish during

the brief Republican interlude before the war (1931–36), found themselves
forced into exile as the conflict developed. It was the experience of exile
itself that inspired Lluís Ferran de Pol's *Érem quatre* (1960), a narrative set
in Mexico and dealing with the sense of defeat and failure that the war had
provoked in someone who, just like Ferran, had fought on the losing side.
Arguably the most successful of these exiled writers, also a man who had seen
service under the Republic, was Pere Calders. His novel of exile, *L'ombra de
l'atzavara* (1964) is very different from *Érem quatre* as it does not involve
a heroic or adventurous plot and also shuns the mythical dimension so dear
to Ferran. *L'ombra de l'atzavara* is the story of an indecisive Catalan, Joan
Deltell, who, exiled in Mexico City, tries to put his life together and run a
small business, only to find himself baffled by the ways of the locals. He
views the people he is dealing with, including the woman he marries and her
immediate family, as indolent and untrustworthy. Many readers have projected
those prejudices onto the author himself and accused him of Eurocentrism,
but one must bear in mind that Calders's talent runs to the satirical, sometimes to the bitterly satirical, and his *L'ombra* is certainly a sardonic view
of the country which, during the presidency of Lázaro Cárdenas, welcomed
numerous Spanish Republican exiles. Calders is best known for his short,
at times extremely short, stories: whimsical pieces that blur the distinction
between the mundane and the absurd. In his other novel, *Ronda naval sota la
boira* (1966), a number of characters whom the reader can easily identify as
familiar types find themselves aboard a ship caught in such thick fog that it
can only go round in circles. The reactions of the characters remain absurdly
in the realm of the familiar, despite the catastrophe threatening them. *Ronda*
is a comic masterpiece and perhaps its author's most experimental and daring
work.

The Spanish war itself has been treated sparingly in novels in Catalan. The
reason surely has to do with the post-war cultural repression by the Franco
regime which made it unthinkable to publish a novel in Spain dealing with the
war from a Republican or Catalanist perspective. A possible exception to this
rule is *Incerta glòria* (1956; definitive edition 1971) by Joan Sales, a writer
whose firm Catholic convictions may have made the regime regard him as
less of a threat. *Incerta glòria* is an ambitious work whose characters have
been compared to those of Dostoyevsky, standing as they do midway between
the prophetic and the everyday.

Even if only indirectly, the war did inspire one of the best novels written
in Catalan in the twentieth century, Mercè Rodoreda's *La plaça del Diamant*
(1962). Related in the first person, it tells the story of Natàlia, a working-
class woman. The narrative begins at the moment when she meets her first
husband at a dance in the square of the Barcelona neighborhood of Gràcia
that gives the title to the novel, and it closes with her as a contented middle-
aged woman dancing at her daughter's wedding. Her life story straddles the

war, in which Quimet, her first husband, fights and is killed. The stream-of-consciousness narrative deals with Natàlia's experiences in a war-devastated Barcelona beset by hunger; the ruin of all her hopes has led her to plumb the depths of despair. There is also a strong allegorical element here: Quimet, who always calls his wife Colometa ('little pigeon'), starts a second business breeding carrier pigeons, and these, far from symbolizing freedom or peace, intrude upon Natàlia's life and add to her material discomfort and spiritual alienation. Natàlia's liberation starts when she begins to destroy the birds.

*La plaça del Diamant, written from exile in Geneva, was published by Joan Sales in Barcelona. In the early 1960s the Catalan cultural establishment used the literary prizes it had in its gift to hedge its bets. One such was the Premi Sant Jordi, awarded for an unpublished novel. Rodoreda submitted her manuscript under the title Colometa; Sales, it seems, later convinced Rodoreda to change it. The Sant Jordi prize of 1961, however, went to Enric Massó's Viure no és fàcil, a novel that has since faded from public view. Critics have since wondered why a jury consisting of some of the most distinguished names in Catalan letters failed to see the superiority of Rodoreda's submission. Years later, one of those jury members, Joan Fuster, gave his version of the affair. A fellow jury member, the influential and popular essayist Josep Pla, who had not bothered, or so Fuster says, to read the manuscript, convinced his colleagues that the award, at this moment of national reconstruction, should not go to a novel 'that has a sardana for a title' (Ferré 2000: 127–28), the sardana being the Catalan folk dance par excellence. Yet, surely, Pla and his acquiescent fellow jury members should have seen the winning submission for what it was: folksy, backward looking, and lightweight.

Despite the jury's verdict, *La Plaça del Diamant went on to become a critical success and cemented its author's reputation. Rodoreda's style subsequently evolved from the stark realism of *La Plaça to a more mysterious experimentalism. Her *Mirall trencat (1974) shows her beginning to move in that direction. A novel of reflection and fragmentation, as Christine Arkinstall points out, it consists of fifty-two short chapters, arranged into three parts and tracing three generations of a single Barcelona family. Each chapter takes a slightly different narrative point of view. It is interesting to compare this novel with Sagarra's Vida privada: each focuses on the dissolution of a single family, but Rodoreda's more restrained prose avoids the judgmental pitfalls into which the earlier writer stumbles as she presents her characters with the detached empathy that makes her novel such a triumphant success. Understandably, she herself has had a tremendous influence on younger writers, particularly women. She has also attracted a great deal of scholarly attention, mainly from American critics, a rare achievement for someone writing in Catalan (Martí-Olivella 1987; McNerney & Vosburg 1994).

As Catalan culture slowly recovered after the war a new generation of writers began to emerge. Among them was the prolific Manuel de Pedrolo.

His *Una selva com la teva* (1960) is a good example of his work from the middle period of the Franco dictatorship. It tells the story of two young people who meet by chance, have an affair, and eventually drift apart. Their story is told in a number ways, among them excerpts from the young man's journals and a police report on the young woman. Heavily influenced by existentialist thinking, the characters act out the Sartrian concepts of *ensoi* and *poursoi*: life in oneself and for oneself.

Pedrolo played a major part in the renaissance of Catalan literature in the 1960s. He is part of that quest for modernity we mentioned earlier, although, of course, what is modern changes all the time. He became fascinated by the hard-boiled American detective novel, taught himself English so that he could translate foreign authors, and was instrumental in the development of a series of highly popular mystery novels in Catalan called *La cua de palla*.[3] Later in his career, ever keen on the new, he turned to science fiction, writing *Mecanoscrit del segon origen* (1979), the story of a dystopian future with a human population on the verge of extinction. As a writer, Pedrolo clearly had a cause: to bring Catalan literature to as wide an audience as possible and to make it as international as he could. This he sought to do by producing, and translating into Catalan, the kinds of writing that had made household names out of Dashiell Hammett, Georges Simenon, and Isaac Asimov.

The detective genre has continued to be popular and has been cultivated by a good number of writers (see above, Chapter 8). One such is Ferran Torrent, whose detective, one Toni Butxana, is the hero (or anti-hero) of several novels. Butxana appears, for example, in *Cambres d'acer inoxidable* (2000), snooping around the seedy underbelly of urban Valencia.

Another writer of that same generation, Joan Perucho, brought out his *Les històries naturals* in the same year (1960) and with the same publishing-house as *Una selva com la teva,* yet no two stories could be more different and no writer could be less Sartrian than Perucho. *Les històries naturals* is a romance that blends fictional characters with historical ones, most notably the Carlist general Ramón Cabrera. The novel's 1840s ambiance is charming, but the main characters are flat. The most appealing of them is probably Onofre de Dip who holds the distinction of being the only Catalan character specifically conceived as a vampire. This Onofre is a melancholy and world-weary vampire, very eager to call it, at long last, a day.

Quite a different kind of writer, and one unique in Catalan letters in that he was no enemy of the Franco regime, was the Mallorcan Llorenç Villalonga. *Mort de dama* (1931) had not enjoyed much success outside Mallorca before the author sent it to Joan Sales, the novelist who had created the publishing

---

[3] The phrase means 'the tail of straw' and it is an idiom close in meaning to the English 'chip on the shoulder.'

venture 'El club dels novel.listes' which had brought out the first edition of Rodoreda's *La Plaça del Diamant*. Sales reissued the novel in 1954 and at once Villalonga had found his publisher and his readership. It is a satirical examination of the Mallorcan aristocratic class in the modern age of business, the death of the title referring not only to the main character but also to her social class. One reason for its success may have been that Catalan readers were at long last being offered a novel not about Paris or New York or the concerns of contemporary Barcelona, but about the stuffy, insular, class-ridden, Catalan-speaking world of Mallorca.

After *Mort de Dama*, Villalonga went on to produce his greatest work, one I would unhesitatingly place among the two or three best novels of the century: *Bearn o la sala de les nines* (1961; revised 1966). Villalonga's irony is wonderful. The Marquès Don Toni de Bearn's story is told by his family's young confessor, and the author hints to the reader that this narrator, although he does not suspect it, is in fact the marquis's natural son. Don Toni is a fascinating Enlightenment figure (the novel is set in the early nineteenth century) who nevertheless feels quite at ease in Catholic Mallorca. He adores his pious wife and accompanies her to Rome for an audience with the Pope, after convincing her, and the priest-narrator, that the way from Palma to Rome goes by way of Paris. Love for his wife aside, Don Toni pursues romantic interests elsewhere and also delves into the occult. The fascination of *Bearn*, perhaps even more so than plot, rests on Don Toni's reflections and observations about life ('all paradises are lost paradises' is one of his maxims), most of which are apparently delphic as far as the narrator is concerned. The narrative itself, then, has this extra layer of dialogism to it.

Baltasar Porcel is another to set much of his fiction in his native Mallorca. His early works are broad, almost mythical in scope as they seek inspiration in the convoluted lives of the sea-faring families of the port town of Andratx. His most successful novels, which include *Cavalls cap a la fosca* (1975) and *Les primeveres i les tardors* (1986), show that Catalan fiction is perfectly capable of dealing with universal subject matter. In these works we can see a change from those pre-war writers who tried to escape their sense of provincialism by embracing the new and the cosmopolitan; Porcel turns inwards to the most specific of provincial locations, and yet also manages to convey a sense of the wider world, as his pirates and merchants sail the seas to such destinations as North Africa and the Americas.

Those making their debuts in the 1970s were born after World War II. The most flamboyant of this 'Generation of the '70s' has to be Terenci Moix (see also above, pp. 180–81). His first success, *El dia que va morir Marilyn* (1969), is a morality tale that is the first novel in Catalan to have central characters who are homosexual. It is a critique of the Catalan middle class, viewed through a highly sarcastic lens. More innovative is his fantasy *Món mascle* (1971) about a complacent and rabidly patriarchal society. Moix's interest in the queer is matched only by his interest in kitsch; the universe he creates is full of references to pop idols, glamorous figures, and the techniques of the comic strip. Ramón Buckley has hailed *Món mascle* as a book that 'represents the most complete expression of radical thought in Spain' (1996: 101) in its creation of a universe that entraps its characters as much as it does the author and his readers. Catalan gay fiction, which has a decided penchant for the dubious middle ground between modernity and tradition, poses fascinating questions for the critic, as Josep-Anton Fernàndez's excellent study of 'the tension between the nation and the body' makes clear (2000: 1).

A few years older than Moix, Robert Saladrigas explores a different kind of modernity. His *Memorial de Claudi M. Broch* (1986) illustrates some of the new trends of form and content we find in the Catalan novel. There are multiple narrators and stories are included simply because they are thematically related to at least part of the novel. The narrative moves in a historical sweep covering the main events of the twentieth century: war and revolution, in Europe and elsewhere.

A near contemporary of Moix, Montserrat Roig has transformed modern Catalan fiction in a number of ways. She was among the first, if not the first Catalan novelist to draw characters from the immigrant population of Barcelona. A good example is *El temps de les cireres* (1977). This novel, whose title comes from a French popular song, recounts the experiences of a modern young woman who has spent a long time in England after having terminated an unwanted pregnancy. Such an eventuality was not, of course, unheard of in Catalonia, but writers from previous generations either found such subjects too risqué or feared that they would be excised by the censor. It fell to Roig to put it down like it was, and, by the time she was writing, sex and its consequences were being more openly discussed.

Although more accomplished as a short-story writer, Quim Monzó has published a couple of novels, taking to witty extremes the absurdist line typical of the Grup de Sabadell. Novels like *Benzina* (1983) and *La magnitud de la tragèdia* (1989) turn their back on verisimilitude. Monzó subordinates characterization to plot, drawing attention to the fact by giving his characters unbelievably coincidental names (in *Benzina* they all have names beginning with H-; in *La magnitud* they all have hyphenated first names). The basic plot situations also tend to be arbitrary. In *La magnitud* we have a man with a permanent erection; nothing he does triggers detumescence. Such hyperbolic playfulness works better in a short story than it does in the longer, novel format: for the reader, if not the protagonist, the joke pretty quickly falls flat.

Where do you go once you have stripped the bones of fiction bare? The favourite ploys of postmodernity cannot endure for long, and after modernity is, in Zigmunt Bauman's word for it, 'liquified', its inevitably vanishes. Thus, one unexpected consequence of modernity is a loss of faith in progress.

Increased competition for the attention of the public (from film, television, and the internet) only adds to the malaise, and the globalization of cultural products complicates the matter. Art must find other avenues to explore, even if this means turning to the past once more, as happened in Catalonia as the twentieth century wore on. The whole century had been packaged as aspiring to modernity as a remedy for cultural subordination. But modernity is an insatiable beast, always devouring those who sire it; there is no such thing as being modern enough, and sooner or later this realization sinks in. In the late 1980s and '90s interest once again grew in the historical novel. Jaume Cabré's highly acclaimed *Senyoria* (1991) is an excellent example, as well as an engaging read. It is a morality tale featuring the man who was the civil governor of Barcelona at the beginning of the nineteenth century. Cabré plays with as many registers as he can, from the satirical to the tragic, from the comical to the pathetic, from social portraiture to sexual innuendo. The narrative flows seamlessly, with its multiple characters and their personal idiosyncracies. One might argue that this is an overpolished performance, as though the novelist had erected for himself a series of hurdles which he has then skilfully overcome. But, in Catalan literature one is grateful for a beautifully polished performance, whether or not there is much substance to it.

Carme Riera did something similar. *Dins el darrer blau* (1994) is a well-researched tale set in a period ignored by previous authors: the Castilian-dominated seventeenth century. It is a tour de force of period setting, characterization, and language. At its center beats a heart that makes this novel the most ambitious from her pen to date. It tells the story of a group of Mallorcan Jews who attempt to escape their world of repression and persecution. Their flight is discovered, the group is detained, and they are eventually brought to trial and paraded in an auto-da-fé. The novel works, despite its many lengthy disquisitions: on collusion between the Holy Office and the secular authorities, from the humblest jailer to representatives of the Crown, and on the criminal indifference of the Catholic population. Riera here tackles a subject, the Inquisition, that is large and difficult, and she does so without sermonizing or sentimentality, and without in any way sacrificing the grand sweep of the narrative. The horrors of the events she recounts are attenuated only by her skill as a narrator. She later went on to write the story of a descendant of one of that same group of Jews some two centuries later in *Cap al cel obert* (2000), a less heroic and more intimate novel but one almost as satisfying.

The protagonist of *Cap al cel obert* attempts to rebuild her life in Cuba, still a Spanish colony at the time the story is set. The island also figures prominently in *L'herència de Cuba* (1997), Margarida Aritzeta's novel chronicling the plight of the rural poor of Catalonia in a changing economic landscape, and the emigration of entire agricultural communities either to greener pastures (as Cuba was supposed to be) or to the industrial areas of Barcelona itself. The vision she offers of the country differs both from the repulsion of the *modernistes* and the disregard of the *noucentistes* at the beginning of the century. Her novel calls attention to the losers in contemporary history. Another to embrace that same theme, Maria Barbal, then explores it in several novels, beginning with *Pedra de tartera* (1985), a bittersweet story quite elegant in its simplicity. Through the eyes of Barbal's characters, we see Barcelona as a huge graveyard, gasping for air, deprived of the smell of new-mown hay, indifferent to the seasons, and cut off from the sources of sustenance, perhaps even from life itself.

Jesús Moncada brings together both these themes, the historical and the rural, in his highly acclaimed *Camí de sirga* (1988), a tale of the last days of the town of Mequinença, the old section of which was submerged forever under a man-built reservoir. This is a story about a past that is lost forever, drowned beneath a tide of modernity. It sounds the depths of such oblivion. Recent interest among Catalan novelists in themes such as these may tell us something about a culture in transition and an eleventh-hour interest in a past almost beyond recall. *Camí de sirga* shows empathy with the ebbing ancestral culture of the Catalan countryside, and its success may be an indication that Moncada's readers feel that empathy, too.

The historical and the rural have come to dominate the Catalan novel at the turn of the twenty-first century and perhaps they suggest a way of resolving the tension between tradition and modernity which clearly dogged Catalan culture for most of the twentieth-century. The mixture of resignation and nostalgia (in its proper sense of 'homesickness') in the fictions of the last quarter of the century may indicate where Catalan culture may be going next. The quest for modernity is ebbing, and may have gone for good. But then Catalans are not the only ones to sense that faith in the future has become increasingly problematic.

Further reading

Arkinstall (2004), Arnau (1987), Bauman (1992), Bordons & Subirana (1999), Bou (2000), Bover (1993), Bru (1999), Buckley (1996), Charlon (1964), Febrés (1985), Fernàndez (2000), Ferraté (1992), Ferré (2000), Keating (1996), Massot (1979), McNerney (1999), McNerney & Vosburg (1994), Molas (1978 and 1983), Orja (1989), Payne (2004), Resina (1996), Resina & Sobrer (2000), Terry (2003), Triadú (1978), Vicens (1954), Yates (1975).

17

The Galician Novel

KATHLEEN N. MARCH

To understand the current Galician novel, it is necessary to understand the history and status of the geographical region and its language over the centuries. There is occasionally some confusion as to what constitutes a Galician novel, because of the complex circumstances that led to the creation of the autonomous region today. It is easy to identify a Galician novelist by his or her place of birth, which would be one of the four provinces in the northwestern corner of the Iberian Peninsula: A Coruña, Lugo, Ourense, and Pontevedra. A fair number of novelists from previous centuries would fit this description and many are extremely well known: Emilia Pardo Bazán, Ramón del Valle-Inclán, Wenceslao Fernández Flórez, Elena Quiroga, and even Camilo José Cela. For our purposes, however, Galician novels are those that are written in the Galician language, even though this narrower criterion excludes some if not all of the work of other famous figures, such as Rosalía de Castro in the nineteenth century and Rafael Dieste in the twentieth.

The Kingdom of Galicia, which originally included part of what is today northern Portugal, was established in 1065, and it has always had ties of one sort or another to its Portuguese-speaking neighbor to the south. The relationship between the two languages and their mutual antipathy to Castilian is important even today. Yet there is still no unanimity about which form of Galician is the 'correct' one (an experience which replicates arguments several decades ago about the 'modalities' of Catalan), and deliberations about that issue may have implications for the sense of autonomy and independence that a particular writer may feel since, when Galician readers look at a text, they simultaneously tend to enquire about the author's political and cultural intentions. In the thirteenth century, King Alfonso X, 'the Wise', King of Leon and Castile, wrote important poetic works in Galician-Portuguese and for a time this became the language of literary culture in Iberia. Despite that early prestige, the language fell into disuse in cultured circles for about four centuries. Kept alive in oral traditions and especially in the rural areas (and until very recently Galicia remained predominantly rural), the language finally began to re-emerge in the nineteenth century.

In 1856, intellectuals, students, and workers joined in the *Banquete de Conxo*, a public gathering (punctuated with poetic toasts) organized to draft a liberal democratic declaration of solidarity with Galician ideals and support for the Galician language. The other date of significance is 17 May 1863, when Rosalía de Castro's *Cantares gallegos* (Galician Songs) became the first book to appear in modern times in the Galician language. While the author published five books of verse in all, her five novels in Spanish remained virtually unread for years and were afterwards often ignored by scholars because they were not written in the vernacular. For the same reason, the novels by her husband Manuel Murguía, one of the major players in the *Rexurdimento* or Renaissance spearheaded by his wife's book, tend not be thought of as Galician, either.

During the nineteenth century, many Galicians emigrated to Latin America because of famine and unemployment at home. It would be groups of emigrants living in cities like Havana, Montevideo, and Buenos Aires who provided support over the years for writers publishing back home. In 1880, the journal *La Ilustración Gallega y Asturiana* published, in instalments, the first novel in Galician. Marcial Valladares's *Maxina, ou a filla espúrea* is the story of a rape, told in a romantic style full of local color. Written ten years before it first appeared, it vanished from sight for almost a century until Ricardo Carvalho Calero published it as a separate title. *¡A besta!*, by Xan de Masma (the pseudonym of Patricio Delgado Luaces), also appeared in instalments in Havana between 1899 and 1901. It, too, would have to wait a long time – until 1993 – to be published in a single volume. Centering on a *cacique* or local boss, it is a social commentary written in a style that borrows from both naturalism and sentimentalism.

The closing years of the nineteenth century and the first few of the twentieth saw the appearance of three historical novels by Antonio López Ferreiro: *A tecedeira de Bonaval* (1894), *O castelo de Pambre* (1895), and *O niño de pombas* (1905). These works mix fact with romance, the past with the present. Concern for renewal and modernization, coupled with a clearer sense of Galician nationalism, the legacy of Conxo and the *Rexurdimenti*, began to appear at the beginning of last century alongside more traditional narrative pieces. A major factor in the development of a distinct identity and the confidence to use the vernacular in fiction was the creation at A Coruña in 1916 of the *Irmandades da Fala*, organizations committed to the promotion of the Galician language and of all other aspects of *galeguidade*. The *Irmandades*, which flourished until the outbreak of war in 1936, associated the Galician language with the idea of separate nationhood and it was their members who went on to found the Galician-language publishing house A Nosa Terra. Their goals included official recognition of the equal status of Galician and Castilian, political autonomy, a federalist relationship with Portugal, and equal rights for women. Many of those associated with this ideology would subsequently either be killed or forced into exile during the Civil War. But before that, many narrative texts were published, often in the supplement of a local newspaper, *El Noroeste*, or the journal *Alborada*. In 1922 the Céltiga collection was founded, and in 1924 an important sequence of short novels was published by Carré Alvarellos and Anxel Casal in the series *Lar*. These novelettes were consciously promoted as an important way of getting writing in Galician to tackle modern subjects. This is not to say that the styles and themes chosen did not include the usual rural sentimentalism, but there were new narrative forms and a measure of social realism of the kind we find in Xosé Lesta Meis's *Manecho o da rúa* (1926) and *Estebo* (1927).

Not all the intellectuals of this period were of the same mind, however. Despite splits in the national cultural movement (one example being the appearance of the group *Nós* in Ourense), even the more conservative or cautious writers treated some of these issues in their works. Common themes included Celtism and the importance of the Atlantic world (*Atlantismo*), both seen as counters to the centralizing tendencies of the Madrid government and its ideology of Castilianism.

In 1920 there appeared the first novel in Galician to be published by a woman. Francisca Herrera Garrido's *Néveda*, whose title shares its name with the female protagonist, may be a post-romantic tale set in the countrysides but its author is clearly trying to create a new kind of narrative. She would subsequently publish two novels in Spanish and three more in Galician: *A ialma de Mingos* (1922), *Martes de Antroido* (1925), and *A neta de Naipera* (1925). It would be some years, however, before there was what we might call a tradition of women novelists in Galician. Herrera Garrido was the first woman to be elected to the Galician Language Academy, although it appears that her admission was deferred long enough to ensure that she died before she could take up her seat.

While conditions have improved to some extent for women writers in Galicia, an intellectual like Francisca Herrera Garrido could not compete with the men who came to be known as the *Xeración Nós*, of which the main figures were Vicente Risco, Daniel Rodríguez Castelao, and Ramón Otero Pedrayo. The group's name derives from the journal *Nós*, founded in 1920 in Ourense by intellectuals who held a more conservative political outlook than that of the *Irmandades*, but who were equally innovative in literary terms. The group focused on defining Galician identity by placing it squarely within a European context, and for them prose was the most appropriate medium for this. Novels with urban settings represent, at this time, a conscious effort to combat the widespread assumption that the Galician language was best suited to bucolic verse and descriptions of peasant life. Carré Alvarellos, the editor of *Lar*, was always on the lookout for novels that would sell, and he sponsored a new series that began with Wenceslao Fernández Flórez' nouvelle, *A miña muller* (1924), and included his own *Naiciña* (1925), which, although of more dubious literary quality, gave a new impetus to writing and reading in Galician.

One of the most complex of Galician intellectuals, both in terms of his ideological shifts (he would at one point promote a right-wing party and support Franco) and for his exploration of a diverse range of themes and literary techniques, some quite elitist, is Vicente Risco. Despite his esoteric literary proclivities, here is a writer who questions social conditions. His *O porco de pé* (1928) is a parody of the typical local figure who becomes leader of his town, has little talent as a politician, and even less honesty. The sense of satire and fun in this work is not uncommon in Galician fiction. The fun derives from allusions to the *Entroido* (or *Antroido*), a specifically Galician mode of pre-Lenten celebration which, under Franco, would be ruthlessly suppressed. As with Carnival and its associated motif of the world-upside-down, the *Entroido* allows for social criticism, even perhaps for a glimpse of a world where justice might prevail, and as such is an ideal vehicle for covert reference to the abandonment of Galicia by the central government in Madrid and the injustices perpetrated by the latter.

Alfonso Daniel Rodríguez Castelao, another multifaceted intellectual (politician, doctor, artist, and author of prose fiction and essays), is a major figure of this period and still remains so today. His nouvelle, *Un ollo de vidro: Memorias dun esquelete* (1922), contains profound political criticism under the guise of a grotesquely humorous essay. His only novel, *Os dous de sempre* (1934), shows him attempting fresh narrative structures. The unity of the work comes from the parallel stories of the two protagonists, while the narrator enters into a dialogue with the reader, distancing both author and reader from the events of the novel. This complicity between narrator and reader was a new departure for the Galician novel. After 1939, Castelao served as a minister in the Republican government in exile and was President of the Consello de Galiza, which operated out of Buenos Aires. Although these two novels appeared before the Civil War, the political voice is still there in his *Sempre en Galiza* (1944), required reading for an understanding of Galician nationalism from the 1930s right down to the present day.

Ramón Otero Pedrayo, who laid the cornerstone for the novel in Galicia and was one of the most prolific members of *Nós*, published a trilogy, *Os camiños da vida*, in 1928 and a single, seminal novel, *Arredor de sí*, two years later. The latter has become a point of reference for students of contemporary Galician literature, as it is reminiscent of the 'Generation of 98' (Unamuno, Machado, Baroja, and the others who tried to redefine Spain after the loss of its remaining colonies). Its protagonist, Adrián Solovio, is shown traveling through Spain and Europe in search of his identity, before finally returning to his beloved Galicia where, and despite the apparent mismatch between his own sophistication and the unlettered life of the rural area, he finds himself most at home. Otero Pedrayo would later experiment more technically in

Devalar (1935), a work which, in its innovative techniques and impressionist style, points to the author's hope for progress in his country. His other novels in Galician include *A romeiría de Xelmírez* and *Fra Vernero*, both of which appeared in 1934. *Xelmírez* is a historical novel dealing with the life of the famous Archbishop who was a main figure in the construction and promotion of the cathedral in Santiago de Compostela, later a major pilgrimage site. The central character embodies a triumphant, Catholic, traditional Galicia, a nation deserving of recognition in Europe. With the Spanish Civil War, Otero Pedrayo would have to curtail his literary production in the vernacular and his only novel in Galician after the war was over was *O señorito da Reboraina* (1960).

The goal of awakening and strengthening a sense of national identity in readers shaped the techniques that writers employed, among which were the creation of the implicit, active reader and the use of non-linear narrative structures. Nevertheless, the traditional reiteration of the importance of the land and the *Nós* Generation's attachment to it is still very much there. This rural influence is not limited to narrators (and poets) born in the countryside, because, as both motif and motive, it made a clear distinction between the climate and geography of Galicia and the arid plains of Castile, and thus the rest of Spain. Another common denominator among many writers was the use of what has long been considered a Galician brand of humor. That humor is sometimes quite boisterous, but more often than not it is *xorne* – a subtle, tongue-in-cheek, irony that plays to readers alert to its double entendres and its indirect allusions to social problems. Humor can help to create group identity, especially when that group feels exploited by outside forces, and it can serve to express veiled criticism of social and economic conditions. Galician humor often works in this way. The self-deprecating *xome*, also called *retranca*, was highly critical of the grotesque poverty suffered by Galicians even while they were supposedly citizens of a united Spain. It would be easy to link this latter use of humor with the *esperpentos* of Valle-Inclán, but that might be to overlook the intentions of writers who were consciously denouncing the constant famine and the Civil War, both decisive factors in triggering the Galician diaspora.

The pre-war activities of the *Nós* group included a multifaceted approach to the discovery and forging of local identity through the study of history, anthropology, and archaeology. The *Seminario de Estudos Galegos*, founded with this purpose in mind, brought together a number of young intellectuals. Active from 1923 until the outbreak of war, it had close links with the University of Santiago. Some members of the group would continue to write, translate, and research for a long time; a few would produce novels, some of which did not see the light of day until many years later. In 1944, the group reformed under the aegis of the *Instituto de Estudos Galegos Padre Sarmiento*, though many of its original members had by then disappeared.

The post-war period in Galicia was, as elsewhere in Spain, one of fear and silence. Few dared to use the language in ways that might attract attention. In 1949, the periodical *La Noche* began issuing a highbrow Saturday supplement that brought together intellectuals, young and old. The following year saw the creation of what would be known as the Galaxia Group, named after the publishing house they ran. Galaxia, in turn, came to produce the journal *Grial,* still important today as a way of disseminating literary and other cultural scholarship. Galaxia would promote an *enxebrista,* or nativist narrative, realist in focus, infused with rural nationalism, and peopled by characters representing the soul or essence of Galicia. This was homegrown literature, and yet it was not a return to the picture-postcard world of the nineteenth century. Those involved were political moderates keen to promote a detached, scientific vision of what it meant to be Galician.

In 1951, Ricardo Carvalho Calero published the first post-war novel in Galician, *Xente da Barreira.* More important, however, were his contemporaries Álvaro Cunqueiro and the anthropologist Anxel Fole (the latter's documentary fieldwork on popular folk tales was much admired). Despite his fascist leanings and the fact that he frequently wrote in Castilian, Cunqueiro rapidly earned a reputation as a major Galician novelist. His use of the fantastic set him apart from the kind of rural realism encouraged by Galaxia, but his technical innovations blended well with the widespread desire among the Galician literarchy to forge a local literature. The fact that his irony derives from popular culture persuaded readers to accept the more sophisticated and ambitious facets of his output. His most important novels in Galician are *Merlín e familia* (1955), *As crónicas do sochantre* (1956) and *Si o vello Sinbad volvese ás illas* (1961). Some readers claim to see in his stories, with their complex plots and polyphonic voices, the legacy of Galician traditional narrative.

During these years, some of those Galicians living in exile as a result of the Civil War wrote novels. A number of them had pre-war experiences in Latin America: some had even been born there. Some were based in one particular country, and others moved about. During the nineteenth century, Havana had been the major center of Galician culture, but it was Buenos Aires that became the magnet for the post-war diaspora of writers and artists committed to the Galician cause.

Xosé Neira Vilas is the most widely read emigrant author of the post-war generation. His works depict childhood memories of the village he had to leave in order to make a living. The settings of his novels are best seen as an amalgam of Galician village life, fondly remembered, and the world of the immigrant exile. The author of many short story collections as well, he has published the novels *Memorias dun neno labrego* (1961), *Camiño bretemoso* (1967), *Remuiño de sombras* (1973), and *Querido Tomás* (1980).

Eduardo Blanco Amor's *A esmorga* (1959), with its the theme of genetic determinism and its apocalyptic portrayal of mayhem and drunkenness, fell foul of the censor who disapproved of its unflattering portrayal of poverty-stricken Galician youth but, technically and thematically, it is a classic still worth reading today. His other Galician language novel, *Xente ao lonxe* (1972), appeared after he had returned to his native Ourense (thinly disguised as Auria). Once again Blanco Amor had produced an innovative work, dealing this time with the political repression of peasants.

Silvio Santiago, exiled during the Civil War, went to Cuba and then to Venezuela, where he founded the Centro Galego and directed *Casa Galicia, Lar Gallego,* and several journals. He eventually returned to his native Vilardevós, and, in the novel *Vilardevós* (1961), provides an autobiographical portrait of his childhood in the village. *O silencio redimido,* his story of the Civil War, flight and exile, includes scenes set in a jail. For years it was banned by the Franco regime, but was finally published in 1976.

Ramón de Valenzuela's novels, again chronicles of personal experiences during and after the war, were published years apart from one another: *Non agardei por ninguén* (1957) and *Era tempo de apandar* (1980). The writer had been conscripted into the fascist forces, but deserted, and contacted Castelao. He became a supporter of Galician nationalism, was imprisoned under Franco, and escaped to Buenos Aires, where he worked with the exile community until he was able to return to Europe.

Xosé Luis Méndez Ferrín, one of the major living Galician writers and editor-in-chief of the Galician journal of critical thought, *A Trabe de Ouro,* has published in a variety of genres and is one of the best when it comes to dealing with modern subjects and techniques without compromising the quality of the language used. He was a member of the nationalist literary group *Brais Pinto,* founded in 1958 by a group of young intellectuals who managed to publish in Galician in a Madrid which showed little if any sympathy for the peripheral languages. Ever on the cutting edge of Galician issues, Ferrín was also the first to use the term New Galician Narrative, in the relatively sympathetic pages of the Barcelona journal *Destino.*

One of the best known New Narrative authors was Gonzalo Mourullo. He published *Nasce un árbore* (1954) and the innovative *Memorias de Tains* (1956), the latter a novel whose protagonist travels to the imaginary, lost village of Tains whence he writes a series of letters to his family and friends. After these two novels, Mourullo did not pursue a career as a writer, save for one short story 'Lembranza dunha morte regramentaria', published in a collection of short fiction entitled *Relatos de Medusa* (1984).

In the context of post-war Spain, 'new' meant the hope of freedom from fascism and rebellion both political and cultural. 'New', anti-realist aesthetic tendencies would emerge, not only in literary circles but also in music and the other creative arts. The French model of the *nouveau roman* provided further impetus. But 'newness' was tempered in Galicia by the desire to define a popular, still rural culture emerging from several decades of imposed silence. Unlike the original poetic avant-garde of Manoel-Antonio and his contemporaries in the 1920s and '30s, this second post-war avant-garde, was more in evidence in prose writing than in poetry. Fresh narrative voices emerged and nonlinear structures of the kind that were on display in the work of European and peninsular cutting-edge writers, though even one of its most ardent supporters, Xosé Luis Méndez Ferrín, admits that some of the experiments proved unsuccessful. Aside from his oft-cited and read collections of poetry and short stories, Ferrín's novels include *Arrabaldo do norte* (1964), the novelette *Retorno a Tagen Ata* (1971), *Antón e os inocentes* (1976), *Bretaña, Esmeraldina* (1987) and *No ventre do silencio* (1999). *Arrabaldo* shows the influence of French writers and Kafka in its dehumanized protagonist's wandering search for meaning. Tagen Ata is a thinly disguised Galicia in which there develops a conflict between conservative and radical nationalist groups. *Antón* portrays post-war Galicia and utilizes memory as well as monologue to create a sense of timelessness. *Bretaña*'s blind protagonist struggles for the independence of Tagen Ata, while *Silencio* depicts the horrors of the 1950s in post-war Galicia. In general, Ferrín's imagination and inventiveness suggest comparisons with Cunqueiro, but he uses experimental techniques and the world of fantasy to express nationalistic sentiments and to make a case for the prosecution (not for nothing was he imprisoned by the Franco regime). His insistence on medieval, Arthurian, and Celtic motifs goes beyond mere whim: it takes on political color. Ferrín furnishes truly literary accounts of the years of repression, which is a change from the usual pamphlets denouncing political leaders and advocating change.

María Xosé Queizán is perhaps the most prolific woman writer in Galicia today and she has written fiction, essay, drama, and poetry. Her novel *A orella no buraco* (1965) is a *nouveau roman* influenced by French writers and was the first published by a woman since *Néveda* in 1920. Markedly feminist, she addresses the theme of homosexuality and the destructive effect of social norms. Subsequent novels include *Amantia* (1984), a historical view on feminism, literary women, and what became known as 'Priscilianism' in the fourth-century Roman province of Gallaecia; *O segredo da Pedra Figueira* (1986), where the young female protagonist is a model for childhood feminism; the drama of sex-change in *A semellanza* (1988); *Amor de tango* (1992); and *O solpor da cupletista* (1995) which recalls the figure of La Bella Otero, the young woman who left her small town to make her way in French society, and *Ten o seu punto a fresca rosa* (2000). Queizán is a major literary and cultural figure in Galicia, not only for her impressive, often avant-garde, literary output but also for her work in encouraging women of all ages to participate in helping to make Galicia a progressive and inclusive nation. Her editorship of the journal *Festa da palabra silenciada* and her leadership in the feminist party FIGA are further evidence of her legacy to Galicia.

Adiós, María (1971), a novel by Xohana Torres, who is perhaps better

known for her poetry and plays, earned her membership in the Nova Narrativa Galega. Awarded the Premio Galicia of Buenos Aires, its focus is the
world of women in the 1960s. The novel looks at emigration, the growth of
capitalism, reconversion, and the impact of the media on daily life. All are
viewed critically and negatively.

Not all Galician novelists have received the recognition they deserve.
Ferrín observes that while writers such as Manuel Rivas and Carlos Casares
are familiar to everyone, the work of another Nova Narrativa Galega member,
Camilo González Suárez-Llanos, is not nearly so well known. Under the
name Camilo Gonsar, he has written several novels, including *Como calquera
outro día* (1962), *Cara a Times Square* (1980), *A desfeita* (1983), and *A noite
da aurora* (2003). *Aurora* links Galicia with other countries (in this case,
Iceland). It brings into play dialogues between friends, ethical decision-
making, and the lasting effects of being uprooted when young.

María Pilar (Marilar) Jiménez Aleixandre was born in Madrid, but since
arriving in Vigo she has adopted Galician as her literary medium. Her
novels include *Tránsito dos gramáticos* (1993); *A compañía clandestina de
contrapublicidade* (1998), which won the Álvaro Cunqueiro award for best
novel; *A banda sen futuro* (1999); *Unha presa de terra* (2001); and *Teoría do
caos* (2001), winner of the Premio Xerais. By her own observation, two of the
main themes in her work are the ways we betray ourselves and the difficulties
of family relationships.

Most recent prose fiction has been in the shorter genres. The long, historical novel does not seem to have developed as successfully as has the short
story, the journal article, and the novelette. This may be a contemporary
literary trend elsewhere, too, but in a Galician context it cannot be entirely
divorced from the strength of the oral tradition, with its polyphonic narrative structures typical of rural communities where people frequently get
together to tell stories. At one stage there was even debate about whether the
language could cope with subjects such as eroticism, but that debate missed
the point: it is not the language but the writers who lack the necessary experience to treat topics not considered inaccessible in other peninsular languages.
Debates about Galicians' creative capacity still do take place from time to
time, showing that the language is still seen as being inextricably linked to
rural experience and occasionally tentative about tackling urban subjects.
There is, of course, still a collective awareness of the dangers of Castilian
influence in the media and other public fora and of whether writers should
publish in the 'language of Madrid' even if it might be seen as a betrayal of
Galician interests.

The programme to standardize and promote (*normativizar* and *normal-
izar*) Galician, official policy since the passage of the Constitution in 1976,
is fraught with tension. Official bodies such as the Real Academia Galega,
the Xunta, (autonomous government), and the Instituto da Lingua Galega, as

well as local literary and cultural groups such as A Mesa, the PEN Clube, the Asociación de Escritores en Lingua Galega, and publishing houses have conflicting ideas about correctness in matters orthographic and lexical and also when it comes to the subjects treated in fiction. The role played by literary prizes in dictating the length, genre, and themes of literary works is also clearly an influential one. Sometimes that influence affects only the length of a novel, as it does in the case of the Premio Blanco Amor, initiated in 1981, which started out by stipulating that all works submitted had to be at least 300 pages long, a figure since reduced to 200 and, recently, to 150. Early novels were accordingly longer and their themes naturally reflected wider national questions or had a historical focus. Among such early works were Daniel Cortezón's *A vila sulagada* (1981), Víctor Freixanes's *O trián-gulo inscrito na circunferencia* (1982), and *Beiramar* (1983) by Xosé Manuel Martínez Oca. Another important award is the Premio Xerais, founded in 1984. Its first recipient was Carlos Reigosa, who won it for a detective story, *Crime en Compostela*. The fact that such a prize could be awarded to crime fiction in Galician was at least as important as any literary virtues that partic-ular work might have. As with his two multi-author volumes of erotic short stories, Reigosa's attempts to introduce new modalities into the literature of the vernacular, modernizing and demonstrating the capacity of Galician to keep up with the times, appealed to a broad reading public. Aníbal Malvar has followed in Reigosa's path with several detective novels of his own.

Among those now proving themselves in the newer and popular genres are Xosé Fernández Ferreiro, author of a western, *A morte de Frank González* (1975), a science-fiction tale, *Reportaxe cósmico* (1982), and the novels *Morrer en Castrelo de Miño* (1978), *Corrupción e morte de Brigitte Bardot* (1981), *O minotauro* (1989) and *Agosto do 36* (1991). Antón Risco, the son of Vicente and an accomplished literary critic who lived in Canada, came to creative fiction somewhat late, and his decision to publish in Galician as well as Castilian was controversial. His works include a novelette, *Margarida de Ouridac* (1992); *O caso* (1989); *As metamorfoses de Proteo* (1989), a portrait of a local boss whose personality dominates all those around him; *O Embrión* (2002), a novel of exploration and return; the science-fiction piece *Hipó-grifo* (1994); and *Mascarada* (1995), a somewhat surprising psychodrama about interpersonal relationships. Risco's predilection is for fantasy, and this figures in his novels; he also wrote (Risco 1993) about the role fantasy plays in the works of others, including Rosalía de Castro's *El caba-llero de las botas azules* (1867).

Two of the best-known modern Galician novelists are Carlos Casares and Manuel Rivas. Casares, who has a reputation as a writer of children's stories, had already published some of his Galician novels in Castilian. *Ilustrísima* (1980) depicts a small town affected by film and its modernizing agenda and by the subsequent reaction of the Church, which sees this as undermining traditional social structures. The atmosphere becomes highly charged and intolerance based on dogmatism leads to violence. His first novel, *Cambio en tres* (1969), was reissued in 2004, after his death. Ferrín comments on the experimental nature of the text, and it has recently been seen as pioneering a fresh approach to the traditional subject of emigration through the use of interior monologue. *Xoguetes pra un tempo prohibido* (1975), awarded the Premio Galaxia, shows the same experimental tendency in its depiction of the post-war period under Franco and its effects on children and adolescents. Eventually, Casares returned to a more traditional style: *Os mortos daquel verán* (1987) is a familiar treatment of violence and the Civil War, but close in mood to the *roman noir*, while *O sol de verán* (2004), Casares's last work, centers on a love and death conflict. His other titles include *Os escuros soños de Clio* (1979) and *Deus sentado nun sillón azul* (1996). A sometime director of the Consello da Cultura Galega, Casares also had an established reputation as an essayist, journalist, and literary critic, as well as editor of *Galaxia* and *Grial*.

Manuel Rivas raised a few eyebrows among Galician critics with his early publications in Spanish. However, titles like *Galicia, un millón de vacas* (1989) were not superficial portraits of his native land. Rivas was a founding member of Greenpeace in Spain and nobly used his skills as a writer to raise consciousness of the dire situation created by the oil spill of the tanker Prestige in late 2002. He is a prolific writer and two of his narratives, **O lapis do carpinteiro* and the short story **A lingua das bolboretas*, have been made into films. His other works include *Os comedores de patacas* (1991), *En salvaxe compaña* (1993), and the short-prose collections *Ela, maldita alma* (1999), *Galicia, Galicia* (1999), *As chamadas perdidas* (2002), and *Os libros arden mal* (2006). In his newspaper columns Rivas consistently asks difficult, no-holds-barred, ethical questions about contemporary Galicia, its history, post-war cultural repression, the rural economy (and its present crisis), and the local effects of globalization. Readers get the impression that literary innovations are important in Rivas's work, but that they do not take precedence over the validity of his ideas and the need for contemporary social awareness.

In general, the efforts to express contemporary and pop culture in the Galician language have produced mixed results. Most readers may welcome the new writing, but others may feel that both the quality of the language and the techniques employed leave something wanting and are nakedly commercial. Yet there is a form of Galician nationalism in some of these more modern literary experiments, which could even be said to parody pop culture. Novels such as these often use a complex narrative to present situations which can be viewed from several different perspectives.

One final factor to be noted regarding the contemporary scene is the practice of reprinting older novels and putting them on the secondary school curriculum. The relatively recent birth of Galician literature and especially the Galician novel means that an official form of cultural affirmation is important. Many of the novels reissued in this fashion come complete with a critical study, corrections, and annotations, many of them emphasizing the political issues in play. The linguistic questions that face Galicians on a daily basis – not just in regard to using Spanish but also in regard to which kind of Galician they should be using – are also as present in these novels as they are in the debates conducted by academics. More subtly, political identity also influences choice when it comes to literary subject-matter and style. This makes reading and studying novels like these all the more challenging, as it demands a thorough understanding of the development of narrative in Galician, a language considered by many to be endangered even though it remains the cornerstone of national identity.

Further reading

Álvaro Cunqueiro (1993), Bermúdez *et al.* (2002), Blanco (1991), Blanco Torres (1930a), Bobillo (1981), Bommel (1993), Carvallo (1981), Casares (2004), Casas (1990 and 1994), Castro (1992), Fernández del Riego (1973 and 1978), Figueroa (2001), Freixeiro (1995), García Negro (1999), Gómez & Queixas (2000), González-Millán (1991, 1994, 1996, and 2002), Hermida (1995), Irizarri (1979), King (2003), McNerney & Enríquez (1994), March (1987), Molina (1989), Montero (1995), Patterson (2006), Pena (2002), Queixas (1999), Rodríguez Sánchez (1991), Tarrío (1988 and 1994), Torre (1988), Vilavedra (1999), Zubatsky (1992 and 1995).

18

Basque Fiction*

MARI JOSE OLAZIREGI

Most introductions to Basque literature begin with a survey of the language and of present-day Basque society. This is because Basque literature is virtually unknown outside the country and few Basque authors have managed to cross frontiers. But it is also the case that the socio-historical context itself, and particularly the language, have played a large part in shaping the written word.

We are not dealing here with Basque authors of international standing who wrote in Spanish, such as Pío Baroja, Miguel de Unamuno, Gabriel Celaya, Blas de Otero, Ignacio Aldecoa, or Luis Martín-Santos, but of Basque authors who used *euskara*, the Basque language. Indeed, as Lasagabaster suggests (2002: 24), it would be more appropriate to speak of Basque *literatures* than of Basque literature, since Basque writers have written and continue to write not only in Basque but also in Spanish and French. It would be fair to say that, in a sense, Basque writers are classified less according to their nationality or place of birth than by the language they choose to write in. As Claudio Guillén says (1995), it is language that serves to differentiate the various literatures and the literary systems that support them. Although the fact of writing in Basque, a pre-Indo-European language (and the most ancient language in Western Europe) currently spoken by some 700,000 people, does not in and of itself present an insurmountable barrier, it is true that the development of literature in Basque has been closely linked to the socio-historical fortunes of the spoken language. In a well-known poem, used as an epigraph to his *Obabakoak* (1992), Bernardo Atxaga compares Basque literature to a hedgehog that woke up in the twentieth century after a lengthy period of hibernation.

The most important period of Basque literary history is accordingly the last hundred years; before that, most literature in Basque was religious or written with some other extra-literary purpose in mind.[1] The first signs of

---

* This essay was translated from Spanish by Kristin Addis.
[1] Between 1545, when the first book written in Basque was printed (Etxepare's collection of poems *Linguae Vasconum Primitiae*), and 1879, 101 books were published in Basque, of which only four were literary works.

a new dawn – one that would effect a root-and-branch change in Basque letters – came in the last decade of the nineteenth century. Works of religious teaching began to take a back seat and new narrative genres, particularly the novel, burst onto the scene. The disappearance, after the second Carlist war (1873–76), of traditional local legal traditions going back to the early Middle Ages (the so-called Fueros), coincided with the onset of this Basque literary renaissance. It was at this time, and particularly in the works of Sabino Arana, that Basque nationalism took root, and this was to influence all Basque literature during the first third of the twentieth century. The dominance of nationalist ideology meant that literary production during this period was once again dictated by extra-literary objectives, and that Basque missed out on the European modernist movement, which attempted to adapt traditional structures and language in ways that might make them better suited to contemporary concerns.

By the close of the nineteenth century, the socio-cultural conditions that facilitated the appearance of the Basque novel were becoming stable. The number of readers increased, thanks to industrialization, improvements in education, and the founding of a number of literary journals, some 140 of the latter appearing for the first time between 1876 and 1936. Although schools were still relatively few, local councils began in 1920 to open their own and the number of those conducting their teaching in Basque (the *ikastolas*) grew steadily through the 1920s and '30s.

Regional literary competitions or *juegos florales* encouraged the writing of turn-of-the-century historical fiction. Writers such as Navarro Villoslada and Juan Venancio Araquistain produced Spanish historical romances modelled on those of Sir Walter Scott. The first novel written in Basque, Txomin Agirre's *Auñemendiko lorea* ('The Flower of Auñemendi', 1898) was in the same romantic vein, as was Francisco Navarro Villoslada's highly popular *Amaya o los vascos en el siglo VIII*. Agirre's influence would be crucial in the evolution of Basque fiction, especially for the descriptions of local customs and the countryside that we find in his later novels, *Kresala* ('Saltwater', 1906) and *Garoa* ('The Fern', 1912). He depicted an idealized, traditionalist version of the Basque Country infused with the kind of nationalist ideology that inspired Basque narratives until the middle of the twentieth century. As with the paintings of the Zubiaurre and the Arrue brothers, in which nationalism created its own iconography, the Basque novel reflected an undisturbed and fundamentalist world in sharp contrast with the reality of the industrial cities that were springing up at the time. Novels like these, narrated by an omniscient narrator, were based on descriptions of customs and folklore rather than on action or plot, and turned on three primary axes: faith, patriotism and 'Basqueness'. Agirre's works may be considered idyllic, to use the term Montesinos employs of Pereda's novels (Montesinos 1969), in that they evoke the lives and tribulations of nineteenth-century Basque fishermen and shepherds. Other authors who published novels in the early twentieth century, such as José Manuel Etxeita, Resurrección M. Azkue, Jean Barbier and Pierre Lhande, followed the same route as Agirre. Interestingly, short stories describing local customs were even more popular with Basque readers during this era than were full-length novels; they include Jean Etxepare's *Buruxkak* ('Ears of Wheat', 1910) and *Berebilez* ('By Car', 1934), as well as two important collections by Evaristo Bustintza (known as 'Kirikiño'): *Abarrak* ('Branches', 1918) and *Bigarren abarrak* ('More Branches', 1930).[2]

The Second Republic (1931–39) saw a literary renaissance in the southern Basque Country: *Euzko Pizkundea*, or Basque cultural renaissance. Nationalism and cultural activism went hand in hand and it was poets rather than novelists who were the driving force, poetry and theater being much more firmly rooted in Basque traditions than fiction. Lizardi (José M. Agirre) and Lauaxeta (Esteban Urquiaga) cultivated a post-symbolist poetry, which explored and stretched the expressive possibilities of the Basque language; both actively participated in this cultural renaissance. Agustin Anabitarte's novels, *Usauri* (1929) and *Donostia* (1929), and Tomas Agirre's *Uztaro* ('Harvest Time', 1937) also came out of this movement. Although these are works that clearly subscribe to a traditional Basque poetic aesthetic, they do show signs of innovation at a narrative level. *Usauri*, for example, tells about the customs and ways of a coastal town and, although it still has the usual omniscient narrator, it includes many passages that are more objective than any we find in Anabitarte's earlier works. *Donostia* (1931), also an award winner, is a historical novel describing turn-of-the-century San Sebastian, but the descriptions given do nothing to explain how the society depicted has come to be as it is. Some years later, Anabitarte published two more novels: *Poli* (1958), about the life of a mischievous orphan, and *Aprika-ko basam- ortuan* ('In the Desert of Africa', 1961), a description of the author's trip across the Sahara in 1954. Agirre was a man of great culture who translated Walter Scott, S. Pellico and Giovanni Papini into Basque. His novel *Uztaro* is traditional in form (an omniscient narrator, a clear distinction between

---

2   The more open political atmosphere led to the formation of cultural associations such as *Euskaltzaleak,* which organized Basque Poetry Days starting in 1930 and which, together with the journal *Antzerti*, was the driving force behind Basque Theater Day (1934–36). Theater was in fact the genre that dominated Basque literary production from 1876 to 1935, comprising 51 per cent of all published literary texts. Audiences, who were largely illiterate, could in this way get to know works by José M. Soroa, Toribio Altzaga and Avelino Barriola. *Garbiñe* (1916), a play by Katarine Eleizegi, is an excellent example of the contribution women made to the literary life of the time. She, along with other female authors such as Rosario Artola, Sorne Unzueta, Tene Muxika, Julia Gabilondo, María Pilar Lekuona, and Julene Azpeitia, were regular contributors to literary journals and other publications. Nuñez Betelu (2001) shows how they responded positively to the role that Basque nationalism ascribed to women and mothers at the time as the prime conduits for the Catholic faith and the Basque language.

good characters and bad, rabid chauvinism, and so on) but it carries a heavier thematic charge than do the works of Anabitarte.

The Spanish Civil War had a devastating effect on Basque literature, with many writers dying or going into exile, and brutal reprisals by the victors. The Franco regime imposed its will on every aspect of daily life: Basque names were prohibited, as were inscriptions in Basque on tombstones; street names and government buildings were all in Castilian, and the world of the arts was subject to stringent censorship. The post-war generation was nevertheless one of the most important in the history of Basque literature because it enjoyed something not often vouchsafed previous generations: continuity. The most popular genre of the time was poetry, partly because it was easier to publish a few short poems than a longer work, and partly because, from 1940 to 1950 at least, any normal publishing activity was to all intents and purposes out of the question. In the case of the Basque novel, nine years passed between the publication of the last pre-war work, *Uztaro* (1937) and the appearance, in 1946, of *Joanixio* by Juan Antonio Irazusta, published in Buenos Aires by Ekin.

The first novel published in Basque after the Spanish Civil War did not appear until 1950. It was also a historical piece, *Alos-Torrea* ('The Tower of Alos'), and was the work of Jon Etxaide, a prolific writer also responsible for the translation of Baroja's novels into Basque. In his later novels *Joanak joan* ('Past Times', 1955) and *Gorrotoa lege* ('Law of Hatred', 1964), Etxaide attacked the discredited idylls of his earlier work. In 1955, Juan Antonio Loidi published the first Basque crime novel, *Amabost egun Urgain'en* ('Two Weeks in Urgain'). Although its dialogue is weak and it is riddled with meta-narrative comments that destroy the suspense and impede the flow of the story, it continues to be popular with younger readers.

In the middle of last century, we see the emergence of a new generation of writers who set about bringing Basque literature up to date. The group included Federico Krutwig, Gabriel Aresti, Juan San Martín, José Luis Alvarez Enparantza (known as 'Txillardegi'), and Jon Mirande; most were non-native Basque speakers, agnostics, and had a wide range of political credos, ranging from Communism (Aresti) to the extreme right (Mirande). Above all, they distanced themselves from traditional nationalism, having themselves grown up during the emergence of the armed separatist group Euskadi Ta Askatasuna (ETA), founded in 1959, and started writing in the atmosphere of political radicalization that has divided Basque cultural life ever since.

In the 1950s, Basque literature aligned itself to a growing degree with European literary currents at the time. There was also great interest in Basque translations, of Homer and Shakespeare among others, which lent a legitimacy to Basque as a literary language; the practice has continued and there are now Basque versions of Hemingway, Tagore, Ionesco, Cela,

Brecht, Camus, Kafka, Stevenson and Twain (as well as Baroja and Juan Ramón Jiménez). The creation by the publishing house Editorial Itxaropena of the series 'Kulixka Sorta' in 1952 gave fresh impetus to this modernizing tendency and acted as a catalyst for a new crop of journals such as *Jakin* (1956), *Karmel* (1950) and *Anaitasuna* (1953), which have become important shop windows for Basque culture.

Post-war Basque fiction evolved from the description of local customs to existentialist concerns of the kind best exemplified by Txillardegi's innovative *Leturiaren egunkari ezkutua* ('The Secret Diary of Leturia', 1957). Like Roquentin in Sartre's *Nausea*, its central figure, Leturia, is a problematic hero. He senses the lack of meaning to human existence and experiences solitude, failure, pain, and the anguish of choice. Txillardegi's *Peru Leartzako* (1960) and *Elsa Scheelen* (1969) also tell existentialist tales that have little to do directly with the peculiarities of life in the Basque Country.

With tales like these, the Basque novel had abruptly entered the modern age, leaping in a single bound from idyllic descriptions of local customs to French existentialism without passing through the intermediary typologies of realism. Lasagabaster considers the change too drastic and reflects on what Basque narrative missed by not following the example of Baroja, whose impressionist techniques, inclusion of philosophical debate, travelogues, satire, and existential angst were traits the Basque novel would not incorporate until much later. According to Lasagabaster, 'the Basque novel must make more of an effort to follow in Baroja's footsteps if writing in Basque, whatever the genre involved, is to be a broad church in which Basque readers can become fully involved' (2002: 137–38).[3]

Jon Mirande, a poet of distinction from the post-war years and whose lyrical works transcend the religiosity of so much Basque poetry, also wrote an important psychological novel, *Haur besoetakoa* ('The Goddaughter', published 1970). Written in 1959, the novel's transgressive content – the relationship between a mature man and his very young goddaughter, reminiscent of Nabokov's *Lolita* – did not pass unnoticed by Basque critics. Gabriel Aresti, also a poet, energetically tried to get this controversial novel published. In addition to his collected poems, *Harri eta herri* ('Stone and Country', 1964), one of the most significant landmarks in the whole of Basque literature, Aresti was also a novelist, short-story writer, playwright, and a key figure in the movement to modernize the Basque language. A man of intellect and charisma, he translated T.S. Eliot, Boccaccio, and the modern Turkish poet

---

3   Pío Baroja's artful descriptions of Basque society and countryside include observations on his compatriots and a stream of unforgettable characters such as Mari Belcha, Tellagorri and Zalacaín. They have stood the test of time and remain credible and appealing today. In contrast, Baroja's contemporaries portrayed an idealized and Manichaean world in which Basque readers did not recognize themselves.

Nâzim Hikmet into Basque, and played a large part in the country's cultural life during the 1960s and '70s.

The number of novels published in Basque increased significantly during the 1960s, doubling in relation to the preceding decade and, perhaps for the first time, the novel began to live up to the expectations of its readers, who were also increasing in number. In the 1960s and '70s, political activism against the Franco regime went hand in hand with a cultural activism that supported literacy campaigns, the consolidation of the *ikastolas*, the unification of the Basque language, the founding of new Basque publishing houses (the first Basque Book Fair was held in Durango in 1965), and the diffusion of modern Basque music through groups like *Ez dok amairu*. The poet Aresti, the philologist Luis Mitxelena, and the sculptor Jorge Oteiza were the principal figures in this movement for cultural renewal.

In 1969, the publication of *Egunero hasten delako* ('Because It Begins Every Day') by Ramón Saizarbitoria signaled the decline of existentialism and social realism in the novel in favor of experimental fiction similar to the French *nouveau roman*. The publication of social novels (by Xabier Amuriza, Txomin Peillen, and Xabier Gereño, for example) and of allegories (by Anjel Lertxundi and Mikel Zarate) designed to circumvent Francoist censorship, was followed by more self-reflective and literary works mirroring the changes that were taking place in the novel in the 1970s. *Egunero hasten delako* features two independent and alternating narratives. One is the story of a young student seeking an abortion, narrated in a dispassionate, objectivist style; the other takes the form of a conversation in a railway station between a stranger and a number of anonymous interlocutors, and is presented as the transcription of just the one side of that dialogue (a technique already used in 1956 in Camus' *La chute*). Saizarbitoria's second novel, *Ehun metro* ('A Hundred Meters', 1976), has been translated into Spanish, French, English and Italian, and was filmed in 1985 by the director Alfonso Ungría. The main story, the last hundred meters run by an ETA activist before he is shot by the police, significantly influenced the political interpretation of the novel; although Saizarbitoria's best known work, it is also, according to Jon Juaristi (1987: 88), one of the most misread novels in the whole of Basque literature. Not only did the authorities suppress the first edition, but readers chose to see it as a nationalist manifesto, quite failing to give due credence to the writer's deliberately objective account of events. Techniques such as the use of the second person, striking anachronisms, the inclusion of extracts from the press and from tourist flyers, and the use of six levels of narrative attest to the technical modernity of the novel. The use of Spanish in certain sections of the work, such as police interrogations and press clippings, intensified the debate about the novel's linguistic realism and whether or not it credibly reflected the diglossic situation of *euskara*.

The publication of Saizarbitoria's metanovel *Ene Jesus* ('Oh, Jesus!',

1976) marked the end of his experimental phase. As in Beckett's *Malone dies* (1951), the protagonist tries to kill the time he has left him by telling stories, which are nevertheless interrupted over and over again, emphasizing the sheer impossibility of ever achieving a coherent narrative.

Although the advent of democracy in 1975 did not bring about any drastic change in Basque writing, it nevertheless created the conditions under which the Basque literary establishment was able to consolidate. The passing of the statute establishing autonomous states (1979) and the law permitting the use of Basque language (1982) permitted, among other things, bilingual education and assistance for publishing in Basque. With these changes, new publishing houses were established and the number of books published in Basque increased significantly. Between 1876 and 1975, an average of 31.5 books was published annually in Basque, while when we get to the period 1976 to 1994 that annual average has increased to 660. At present, some 1500 books are published each year, 59 per cent of which are narratives of one kind or another (Olaziregi 2005: 25–38). This is a huge increase, as narrative accounted for only 18.7 per cent of the titles published between 1876 and 1935; the figure rose steadily from 23.8 per cent for the period 1936–1975 to 48.5 per cent for 1976–96. The Basque literary world now boasts more than 100 publishing houses and some 300 writers (15 per cent of whom are women). In addition, the 1980s saw the establishment of a university degree in Basque philology as well as the foundation of organizations like EIE, the Basque writers' association (www.idazleak.org), and EIZIE, the Association of translators, revisers and interpreters of the Basque language (www.eizie.org). The quality of translations into Basque (of Faulkner, Hölderling, Maupassant, and so on) is not matched, however, by any concomitant push for the translation of Basque works into other languages (a list of Basque works that have been translated can be found at www.basqueliterature.com).

As has happened in contemporary Spanish fiction, the novel has become the genre with the greatest impact and literary prestige in Basque; it is also, of course, the one that promises the greatest returns for the publishing houses. We could say that the Basque novel of the last three decades has adopted the postmodern premiss that everything has already been told, but that we must now remember it. After the experimental period of the 1970s, the contemporary novel seems to have rediscovered the pleasures of storytelling. Contemporary Basque novelists are extremely eclectic in their influences and play with multiple literary intertexts. Although they have adopted many of the techniques of European modernism, they enjoy creating parodic and ironic combinations of genres and offer a considerable diversity of typologies. It could be said that most Basque novels of the last thirty years look inwards (they are concerned with the subjective point of view, the narrative 'I'), and that when they do look outwards, rather than a realism understood as a mimesis or representation of reality, they reflect a subjective realism that affirms that anything and everything is a linguistic construct. Other types of novels to become popular include genre novels (crime novels, comic novels, and travelogues), historical novels (including historiographic metafiction), and hybrids that mix fiction and essay: further evidence of that same eclecticism.

Special mention should be made here of the highly lyrical novels that are rooted in subjectivity and which often reflect a feminine/feminist point of view. These began to appear in number in the late 1970s and include, among others, *Zergatik Panpox* ('Why Panpox', 1979) and *Koaderno Gorria* ('The Red Notebook', 1998) by Arantxa Urretabizkaia; **Eta emakumeari sugeak esan zion* (2000; *And the Serpent Said to the Woman*, 2005) by Miren Lourdes Oñederra; *Sísifo maite minez* ('Sisyphus in Love', 2001) by Laura Mintegi; *Agur, Euzkadi* ('Goodbye, Basque Country', 2001) by Juan Luis Zabala; *SPrako tranbia* by Unai Elorriaga ('Streetcar to SP'), which won the Spanish National Prize for Narrative in 2002; *Larrepetit* (2002) by Pello Lizarralde, and *Negutegia* ('Winter Quarters', 2006) by Ixiar Rozas. Women writers (Urretabizkaia, Oñederra, Mintegi, Rozas) are particularly conspicuous and tend to employ innovative narrative strategies to give a voice to the kinds of people who were previously silent in Basque writing.

Another genre which has recently become popular in Basque fiction is the crime novel (compare Chapter 8, above). The influence of the American detective novel is particularly evident in the Chandleresque *Rock 'n' Roll* (2000) by Aingeru Epaltza, *Euliak ez dira argazkietan ateratzen* ('No Flies in Photos', 2000) by Joxemari Iturralde, or the intriguing *Beluna Jazz* ('Dark Jazz', 1996) and *Pasaia Blues* (1999) by Harkaitz Cano. These are writers who seduce the reader with suspense stories and often do so by subverting the parameters of crime fiction. Other recent novels employ different types of realist strategy. Although today's realist novels deal with conditions as they are now, they most often provide a subjective take on them. To do this, they import into the literary language a number of different images, be they memories, dreams, fantasies, or even naturalist representations of contemporary society. There are also examples of magic realism in recent Basque novels: Juan Mari Irigoien's *Poliedroaren hostoak* ('The Leaves of the Polyhedron', 1982) and *Babilonia* (1989), Bernardo Atxaga's **Bi anai* (1985, *Two Brothers*), and Anjel Lertxundi's *Hamaseigarrenean, aidanez* ('On the Sixteenth, They Say', 1983). Examples of gritty urban realism include Edorta Jimenez's *Speed gauak* ('Speed Nights', 1991) and Ur Apalategi's *Gauak eta hiriak* ('Nights and Cities', 1997).

Contemporary Basque novels offer writers a privileged vehicle for analysis and reflection upon historical events such as the Spanish Civil War or the development of ETA terrorist violence. In novels like these we can see the urge to analyze conflicts past and present, as well as a conviction that fiction can be truer than fact – as well, of course, as the almost cathartic need to reflect on the political violence that has marked Basque life for much of the past hundred years. We could say that these writers revisit recent Basque history in order to explore an historical discourse that is alien to its citizens. The novels written by Saizarbitoria and Atxaga in the 1990s do this. Saizarbitoria's *Hamaika pauso* ('Innumerable Steps', 1995), a chronicle of the 1970s generation that participated in ETA, and *Bihotz bi: Gerrako kronikak* ('Love and War', 1999) present scenes of the Spanish Civil War that serve as a counterpoint to the domestic war that we witness going on between the two main characters. Saizarbitoria's five stories collected in *Gorde nazazu lurpean* ('Let Me Rest', 2000), reflect two major threads of his recent work: the problems of communication between men and women, and the disastrous experiences of Basque soldiers in the Spanish Civil War (two of these stories could be considered historiographic metafictions). Whether recounting the roller-coaster existence of Basque soldiers in 1936 or retelling the burden that nationalism imposed on his generation, Saizarbitoria conjures many of the ghosts that haunt and divide contemporary Basque society.

Atxaga's novels, *Gizona bere bakardadean* (1993, *The Lone Man*), *Zeru horiek* (1995, *The Lone Woman*) and *Soinujolearen semea* (2003, *The Accordionist's Son*) deal with ETA violence and the personal and social fragmentation the terrorist struggle has left in its wake. Atxaga employs subjective realism in order to give voice to characters and situations that rarely figure in the never-ending media bombardment about the 'Basque troubles'. The loss of revolutionary ideals in *Gizona bere bakardadean*, the political re-insertion of ETA prisoners in *Zeru horiek*, and the betrayal of the armed group by one of its members in *Soinujolearen semea* are examples of a decision to destabilize the authorial monologue (nationalist or non-nationalist) and to create an *oeuvre* that reflects the author's rejection of violence and his love of life (Olaziregi 2005: 214).

Anjel Lertxundi is another whose work is not only extensive but also offers continuous aesthetic innovation, with magical realist novels (*Hamaseigarren aidanez*, 1982), fantasy literature (*Azkenaz beste*, 'Endings', 1996) and even suggestive metanovels (*Argizariaren egunak*, 'Days of Wax', 1998). His latest work, *Zorion perfektua* (2003, *Perfect happiness*), is a realist novel with lyrical overtones. It explores the effect that witnessing a terrorist assassination has on the life of a sixteen-year-old girl. The novel is moral but not moralistic, because by confronting such horror, the author takes a clear stand against a hedonism based on the failure to listen to one's conscience.

The short story is a relatively recent genre in Basque, for it was not until the 1950s and 1960s that writers like Aresti and Mirande first published stories in the modern manner of Poe, Gogol, and Maupassant (Olaziregi 2004: 11–27). Basque critics consider Lertxundi's *Hunik arrats artean* ('Until Nightfall', 1970) the first book of modern stories in Basque, with its echoes of a magical realism (García Márquez, Rulfo, and so on) influenced by the literature of the absurd (of Kafka, Artaud, and others). Other collections of stories published in that same decade were more traditional, or incorporated the experimentalism that was so much in vogue in the novel at the time. The 1980s mark a definitive turning point in the evolution of the modern Basque story. As in the case of Spanish literature, the greater numbers of literary journals, prizes, and anthologies encouraged a renaissance of the genre. Basque 'short' genres (short stories and poetry) were also revolutionized by the work of the Pott group (1978–80) which included writers such as Bernardo Atxaga, Joseba Sarrionandia, Joxemari Iturralde and Ruper Ordorika, who were greatly influenced by the Anglo-Saxon tradition (crime novels, cinema, adventure stories, and so on).[4]

The Basque short story could be said to have come of age in its most translated work, and the one that has received the most prizes: *Obabakoak (1988) by Bernardo Atxaga. With the success of this collection, Atxaga demonstrates that, although Basque writing may be described as 'peripheral' or as belonging to a minority literature, this does necessarily imply that it does not travel: it is possible to be international without forfeiting one's genuine Basque identity. The emotional and mythical landscape of the imaginary town of Obaba is described as a virtual infinity in which the memory of the narrator weaves a suggestive framework of stories that combine metanarrative reflection with the strategies of fantasy literature. For this purpose, the narrator departs on an intertextual voyage beginning with the *Thousand and One Nights* and ending with allusions to the great storytellers of recent times (Poe, Chekov, Maupassant, Villiers de l'Isle Adam, Waugh, Borges, Cortázar, Calvino). That voyage allows Atxaga to reflect on the relationship between literature and life and on the battle between nature and civilization.

The vitality of contemporary Basque fiction and its eclecticism suggest that the future is a promising one, and that it will include more translations both from and into Basque, thus ensuring the continuing enrichment of Basque literature by an expanding national and international readership interested in the cultural survival of one of Europe's most fascinating minorities.

---

[4]   As in the case of the novel, Basque short stories display a richness and diversity of both form and content. Basque fiction tends toward realism, whether of the psychological-cum-fantasy variety (as in the stories of Elorriaga), or of a more objective and detached kind such as we encounter in American 'dirty realist' authors such as Raymond Carver or Tobias Wolff (Xabier Montoia, Arantxa Iturbe, Pello Lizarralde). There are also metafictional stories (Juan Garzia, Iban Zaldua), absurdist tales (Karlos Linazasoro, Harkaitz Cano) and microstories (Joseba Sarrionandia). The experimentalism of the 1970s has given way to the simple pleasure of storytelling. The new modes of narration, rhythms, and linguistic registers also show the influence of oral culture and of cinema, television, music and advertising.

Further reading

Abellán *et al.* (2000), Amado & Pablo (2000), Aretxaga *et al.* (2005), Badiola & López (1981), Douglass *et al.* (1999), Douglass & Zulaika (2007), Etxeberria (2002), Gabilondo (1999 and 2000), Juaristi (1999), Kurlansky (2001), Kortazar (1998, 1999, and 2003), Lanz (1993), Lasagabaster (1990), McNerney & Enríquez (1994), Martín (2000), Olaziregi (2000a, 2000b, and 2008), Sarasola (1976), Toledo (1989), Urquizu *et al.* (2000), Villasante (1961).

CHRONOLOGY

1898 Spanish-American War. Vicente Blasco Ibáñez, *La barraca*, a book that will eventually sell more than one million copies in English translation.

1902 Valle-Inclán, *Sonata de Otoño*. Unamuno, *Amor y pedagogía*. Baroja, *Camino de perfección*. Blasco Ibáñez, *Cañas y barro*, written after Blasco met Zola in Paris.

1909 *Setmana tràgica* in Barcelona. Trial and execution of Ferrer Guardia after anarchist revolts triggered by conscription for war in Morocco.

1914 Blasco Ibáñez, *Los cuatro jinetes del apocalipsis*, the first anti-war bestseller, confirms Blasco as an international celebrity.

1917 General Strike in Catalonia. CNT (Anarchist Workers' Party) has 750,000 members; Catalonia becomes 'anarchist capital of Europe'.

1918 Antonio Maura elected prime minister.

1921 (July) Defeat at Battle of Annual (Morocco) leaves 20,000 dead.

1923 (September) Miguel Primo de Rivera launches military coup. His dictatorship lasts until January 1930. José Ortega y Gasset founds *La Revista de Occidente*.

1924 Unamuno exiled to Fuerteventura by a Royal Decree. In July he travels to France, choosing to ignore an amnesty. He remains there until fall of Primo de Rivera (1930).

1925 Ortega y Gasset, *La deshumanización del arte*.

1929 International Exhibition, Barcelona.

1931 Alfonso XIII abdicates. Proclamation of Second Republic (April); Niceto Alcalá Zamora President. *Generalitat* (autonomous government of Catalonia) formed.

1932 Agrarian reform laws (September).

1933 (January) Attacks on Manuel Azaña's government after repression of peasant uprising in Casas Viejas (Cádiz). José Antonio Primo de Rivera founds fascist *Falange Española* (October). Alejandro Lerroux elected Prime Minister after November election.

1934 Fusion of *Falange* with J.O.N.S. (*Juntas de Ofensiva Nacional Sindicalista*). Miners' revolt, Asturias (October).

1935 Assassination of General Castillo (July) by right-wing activists followed by assassination of minister Joaquín Calvo Sotelo.

1936 Popular Front wins election (February); Manuel Azaña President, Casares Quiroga Prime Minister (May). Civil War beings (July). José Antonio Primo de Rivera executed.

1937 Picasso paints *Guernica* to commemorate the air-raid on Basque town by German squadrons. Magazine *Destino* founded in Burgos by writer and journalist Ignacio Agustí with Catalan *Falange* colleagues.

1938 Orwell, *Homage to Catalonia* (Spanish version 1944).

1939 (April) Civil War ends. Spain declares neutrality (September) in World War II. More than 20,000 Republican dissidents executed 1940–51.

1940 (October) Hitler meets Franco in Hendaya.

1942 Internal struggle between monarchists and falangists. Cela, *La familia de Pascual Duarte* (banned until 1946 after only two editions).

1943 Centenary of Galdós's birth.

1944 Laforet, *Nada*, wins Nadal prize. Ignacio Agustí, *Mariona Rebull* (first part of saga *La ceniza fue árbol*. Dámaso Alonso, *Hijos de la ira*, heralds social/existential emphasis of post-war poetry.

1945 Fascist salute abolished. The regime emphasizes Catholic ideology over Fascism.

1947 Franco bestows Cross of Isabel La Católica on Evita Perón.

1950 United Nations revokes 1946 condemnation of Franco.

1951 Tram strike, Barcelona. Cela, *La colmena*. Rafael Sánchez-Ferlosio, *Alfanhuí*.

1952 Ninth Eucharistic Congress, Barcelona (May). Food rationing ends. Cardenal Spellman visits Spain and praises its anti-communism.

1953 Treaty between Franco and Eisenhower assures financial and military aid. Spain agrees to host the US Navy VI Fleet. Agreement between Franco and Vatican to more Church control in Spain. Spain joins UNESCO. SEAT car factory opens in Barcelona with production of 100 cars per month. Gironella,*Los cipreses creen en Dios*, the first novel to attempt a non-partisan account of the Civil War.

1955 Spain admitted to membership of the United Nations (December).

1956 Student revolt in Madrid against monopoly Falange Student Union. Franco grants independence to Spanish Morocco. Sánchez Ferlosio, *El Jarama*. Fernández Santos, *Los bravos*. Pío Baroja dies.

1957 Franco appoints Opus Dei members to government. Cela elected to Royal Spanish Academy.

1958 Severe recession (until 1961) creates a massive rural migration to Spanish towns and cities and overseas. Franco creates government-assisted migration programs reversing rural policies of immediate post-war period in order to slow the influx of peasants to the cities.

1959 Liberalization of the economy stimulates foreign investment and Spain fully embraces capitalism. ETA founded in Basque country. Protests against director of Barcelona newspaper *La Vanguardia* for insulting

Catalan language. Martín Gaite, *La búsqueda del interlocutor y otras búsquedas*.

1960 Civil disobedience by Jordi Pujol, singing the Catalan anthem at the Barcelona Palau de la Música. Matute, *Primera memoria*.

1962 Spain initiates negotiations to enter European Community (February). Student revolts. Success of Mario Vargas Llosa's *La ciudad y los perros* opens door for other Latin American novelists to publish in Europe, leading to the 'Boom' of 1974–75.

1963 *I Plan de desarrollo* initiates era of rapid economic growth.

1964 Minister of Culture and Tourism Manuel Fraga Iribarne organizes the campaign *25 años de paz,* celebrating Franco regime.

1965 Mercè Rodoreda, *La Plaça del Diamant,* instant bestseller throughout Spain.

1966 Press Law issued by Fraga opens new cultural era by loosening censorship of films and fiction. Exiled writers begin publishing in Spain. Juan Goytisolo's *Señas de identidad*. Juan Marsé's neopicaresque *Últimas tardes con Teresa*.

1967 Admiral Luis Carrero Blanco appointed Deputy Head of State (September).

1968 Paris student riots have repercussions in Madrid and Barcelona. Government disbands *Comisiones Obreras*, allowing only official government-approved trade unions. Communists in charge of all working class organizations.

1969 Curfew imposed (January–March). Opus Dei militants in Franco cabinet. Franco asks Parliament to approve Prince Juan Carlos as his successor (July). Matesa scandal brings about government changes (October). Sender, *Requiem por un campesino español*. Vázquez Montalbán, *Una educación sentimental*.

1970 ETA trial Burgos (December). Immigrants from south to Barcelona total 712,000. *Asamblea de Catalunya* is formed as unified opposition group seeking Catalan autonomy.

1972 One million tourists visit Spain. Torrente Ballester*, La saga-fuga de J B*, bestseller of the year.

1973 Luis Carrero Blanco officially appointed Prime Minister (June). Assassinated by ETA 20 December. Arias Navarro appointed as his successor. Luis Goytisolo begins quartet *Recuento*. Cela, *Oficio de tinieblas 5*.

1974 Franco seriously ill (July). Juan Carlos temporary Head of State. Opposition forms *Junta Democrática* (July). Ultra-right terrorist movements FRAP and GRAPO founded. Felipe González elected Secretary-General of the Socialist Party.

1975 Execution of five members of ETA and FRAP (September) under new anti-terrorist legislation that prescribes mandatory death sentences for terrorism. Death of Franco (November). King Juan Carlos I sworn in as Head of State by the President of the Cortes (November). Carlos Arias Navarro Prime Minister of provisional government. Economic recession. Eduardo Mendoza's *La verdad sobre el caso Savolta* in its 18th edition.

1976 Arias Navarro resigns (July). King appoints Adolfo Suárez as Prime Minister. Lourdes Ortiz, *Luz de la memoria*. Film documentary *El desencanto* (Jaime Chavarri) reflects disconcerting nature of transition to democracy.

1977 First free elections since 1936 (June). Lidia Falcón founds Spanish Feminist Party. Esther Tusquets, *El mismo mar de todos los veranos*. Juan José Millás, *Visión del ahogado*.

1978 New Spanish Constitution adopted. *Estatut* giving autonomy to Catalan region approved. Martín Gaite's *El cuarto de atrás* wins National Literary Prize. Recession intensifies. Delibes parodies the first democratic electoral process in *El disputado voto del Señor Cayo*.

1979 Rosa Montero, *Crónica del desamor*.

1980 Amendment to Divorce Law (revoked by Franco in 1938). Benet, *Saúl ante Samuel*.

1981 King condemns abortive military coup staged in Spanish Parliament (February) and appeals to citizens to remain calm. Adolfo Suárez resigns. Guelbenzu, *El río de la luna*.

1982 Victory of Socialist Party. Felipe González Prime Minister (until 1995). Spain enters NATO.

1983 Elena Quiroga elected to Royal Spanish Academy. Film director Luis Buñuel dies.

1984 Pombo, *El héroe de las mansardas de Mansard*.

1986 Eduardo Mendoza, *La ciudad de los prodigios*. Galician letters recognized by award of National Literary Prize to Alfredo Conde's *Xa vai o griffón no vento*.

1987 Rosa Chacel awarded National Literary Prize for lifetime achievement.

1988 Javier Marías, *Todas las almas*. Francisco Ayala awarded National Literary Prize for lifetime achievement.

1989 Cela wins Nobel Prize. Atxaga receives the National Literary Prize for *Obabakoak*. Almudena Grandes, *Las edades de Lulú*.

1990 Rosa Chacel dies.

1991 Vázquez Montalbán wins the National Literary Prize for historical novel *Gálindez*. Miguel Delibes receives the National Literary Prize.

1992 Madrid named European Capital of Culture. Olympic Games held in Barcelona. Seville hosts EXPO 92.

1994 Carmen Martín Gaite awarded National Literary Prize.

1995 Ana María Matute elected to Royal Spanish Academy. Manuel Vázquez Montalbán awarded National Literary Prize.

1996 Assassination by ETA of Professor Francisco Tomás y Valiente, a member of the Constitutional Tribunal. Centre-rightist Partido Popular wins elections. José María Aznar becomes Prime Minister. Antonio Muñoz Molina elected to Royal Spanish Academy.

1997 Mass protests throughout Spain after ETA assassinates a young congressman of the People's Party. Francisco Umbral awarded National Literary Prize.

2000 Partido Popular obtains absolute majority. Javier Cercas, *Soldados de Salamina*. Carmen Martín Gaite dies.

NOVELS IN ENGLISH TRANSLATION

Note. Only translations into English of Spanish novels discussed in this *Companion* are listed. Some have been translated in English more than once; the list does not necessarily contain every version.

Alas, Leopoldo
La Regenta. 1984. Tr. John Rutherford. Harmondsworth: Penguin.
Atxaga, Bernardo
Obabakoak. 1992. Tr. Margaret Jull Costa. London: Hutchinson.
The Lone Man (Gizona bere bakardadean). 1997. Tr. Margaret Jull Costa. London: Harvill.
The Lone Woman (Zeru horiek). 1999. Tr. Margaret Jull Costa. London: Harvill.
Two Brothers (Bi anai). 2000. Tr. Margaret Jull Costa. London: Harvill.
Aub, Max
Field of Honour (Campo cerrado). 1988. Tr. Gerald Martin. London & New York: Verso.
Ayala, Francisco
The Lamb's Head: A Translation and Critical Study of La cabeza del cordero *by Francisco de Ayala*. 1971. Tr. Cecile Craig Fitzgibbons Wiseman. Dissertation: University of Texas at Austin.
Usurpers (Los usurpadores). 1996. Tr. Carolyn Richmond. New York: Penguin.
Azorín (José Martínez Ruiz)
Journeys in Time and Space (Las confesiones de un pequeño filósofo and *La ruta de don Quijote)*. 2002. Tr. Walter Borenstein. Rock Hill SC: Spanish Literature Publications.
Azúa, Félix de
Diary of a Humiliated Man (Diario de un hombre humillado). 1996. Tr. Julie Jones. Cambridge MA: Lumen.
Barea, Arturo
The Forging of a Rebel. 1984. Tr. Isla Barea [1943–46]. Fontana.
Baroja, Pío
Caesar, or Nothing (César o nada). 1919. Tr. Louis How. New York: Knopf. Repr. New York: H. Fertig, 1976.
The City of the Discreet (La ciudad de la niebla). 1917. Tr Jacob S. Fassett. New York: Knopf.

The House of Aizgorri (La casa de Azgorri). 1921. Tr. Laura Lorine Donnelly. Dissertation: University of Califonia at Berkeley.

Paradox, King: A Novel (Paradox, rey). 1931. Tr. Neville Barbour. London: Wishart. Repr. 1983.

The Quest (La busca). 1922. Tr. Isaac Goldberg. La Lucha por la Vida 1. New York: Knopf.

Red Dawn (Aurora roja). 1924. Tr. Isaac Goldberg. La Lucha por la Vida 3. New York: Knopf.

The Restlessness of Shanti Andía. and Other Stories (Las inquietudes de Shanti Andía). 1962. Tr. Anthony & Elaine Kerrigan. New York: New American Library of World Literature.

The Road to Perfection (Camino de perfección). 2007. Ed. & Tr. Walter Borenstein. Hispanic Classics. Warminster: Aris & Phillips.

The Tree of Knowledge (El árbol de la ciencia). 1922. Tr. Aubrey F.G. Bell. New York: Knopf.

Weeds (Mala hierba). 1923. Tr. Isaac Goldberg. La Lucha por la Vida 2. New York: Knopf.

Zalacaín the Adventurer : The History of the Good Fortune and Wanderings of Martín Zalacaín of Urbia (Zalacaín el aventurero: Historia de las buenas andanzas y fortunas de Martín Zalacaín de Urbia). 1997. Tr. James P. Diendl. Fort Bragg CA: Lost Coast.

Benet, Juan

Return to Region (Volverás a Región). 1985. Tr. Gregory Rabassa. New York: Columbia University Press.

Blasco Ibáñez, Vicente

Blood and Sand (Sangre y arena). 1913. Tr. Mrs W. A. Gillespie. London: [s.n.].

The Cabin (La barraca). 1919. Tr. Francis Hafkine Snow & Beatrice M. Mekota. New York: Knopf.

The Four Horsemen of the Apocalypse (Los cuatro jinetes del Apocalípsis. 1918. Tr. Charlotte Brewster Jordan. New York: Dutton.

Our Sea (Mare nostrum). 1919. Tr. Charlotte Brewster Jordan. New York: Burt.

The Torrent (Entre naranjos). 1921, Tr. Isaac Goldberg & Arthur Livingston. New York: Dutton.

Catalá , Víctor (Caterina Albert i Paradís)

Solitude (Solitud). 1992. Tr. David H. Rosenthal. Columbia LA: Readers International.

Cela, Camilo José

Boxwood (Madera de Boj). 2002. Tr. Patricia Haugaars. New York: New Directions.

The Hive (La colmena). 1954. Tr. J.M. Cohen, with Arturo Barea. New York: New American Library.

The Family of Pascual Duarte (La familia de Pascual Duarte). 1964. Tr. Anthony Kerrigan. Boston MA: Little, Brown & Co. Repr. 1990.

Mazurka for Two Dead Men (Mazurca para dos muertos). 1992. Tr. Patricia Haugaars. New York: New Directions.

San Camilo, 1936: The Eve, Feast, and Octave of St Camillus of the Year 1936 in Madrid (Vísperas, festividad y octava de San Camilo del año 1936 en Madrid). 1991. Tr. John H. R. Polt. Durham NC: Duke University Press.

Cercas, Javier

Soldiers of Salamis (Soldados de Salamina). 2004. Tr. Anne McLean. London: Bloomsbury.

Chacel, Rosa

Memoirs of Leticia Valle (Memorias de Leticia Valle). 1994. Tr. Carol Maier. Lincoln NE: University of Nebraska Press.

Chacón, Dulce

The Sleeping Voice (La voz dormida). 2006. Tr. Nick Caistor. London: Harvill Secker.

Coloma, Luis

Currita, Countess of Albornoz: A Novel of Madrid Society (Pequeñeces). 1900. Tr. Estelle Huyck Attwell. Boston MA: Little, Brown & Co.

Delibes, Miguel

Five Hours with Mario (Cinco horas con Mario). 1988. Tr. Frances Lopez-Morillas. New York: Columbia University Press.

The Hedge (Palabra de náufrago). 1983. Tr. Frances Lopez-Morillas. New York: Columbia University Press.

The Path (El camino). 1961. Tr. John & Brita Haycraft. New York: John Day & London: Hamish Hamilton.

The Prince Dethroned (El príncipe destronado). 1986. Tr. Thomas Molloy. Madrid: Iberia.

Smoke on the Ground (Las ratas). 1972. Tr. Alfred Johnson. Garden City NY: Doubleday.

Falcón, Lidia

No Turning Back (Camino sin retorno). 1999. Tr. Jessica K. Knauss. Dissertation: University of Iowa.

Fernán Gómez, Fernando

Bicycles are for Summer (Las bicicletas son para el verano). 1992. Tr. Dale Hartkemeyer. In: *Plays of the New Democratic Spain (1975–1990)*, ed. Patricia W. O'Connor. Lanham MD: University Press of America: 193–311.

Fernàndez, Lluís

The Naked Anarchist (El anarquista desnudo). 1990. Tr. Dominic Lutyens. London: Gay Men's Press.

Fernández Santos, Jesús

Extramuros. 1984. Tr. Helen R. Lane. New York: Columbia University Press.

Fuguet, Albert

Bad Vibes (Mala onda). 1997. Tr. Kristina Cordero. New York: St Martin's.

García Pavón, Francisco

The Crimson Twins (Las hermanas coloradas). 1999. Tr. Susan Neve. A & B Crime. London: Allison & Busby.

García Morales, Adelaida

The South, and Bene (El sur, seguido de Bene). 1999. Tr. Thomas G. Deveny. Lincoln NE: University of Nebraska Press.

The Silence of the Sirens (El silencio de las sirenas). 1989. Tr. Concilia Hayter. London: Flamingo.

Gironella, José María

The Cypresses Believe in God (Los cipreses creen en Dios). 1955. Tr. Harriet de Onís. 2 vols. New York: Knopf.

One Million Dead (Un millón de muertos). 1963. Tr. Joan MacLean. Garden City NY: Doubleday.

Peace after War (Ha estallado la paz). 1969. Tr. Joan MacLean. New York: Knopf.

Goytisolo, Juan

Children of Chaos (Duelo en el Paraíso). 1958. Tr. Christine Brooke-Rose. London: Macgibbon.

Count Julian (Reivindicación del conde don Julián). 1974. Tr. Helen R. Lane. New York: Viking. Reissued Champaign IL : Dalkey Archive Press, 2007.

Fiestas. 1960. Tr. Herbert Weinstock. London: MacGibbon & Kee.

Forbidden Territory: The Memoirs of Juan Goytisolo, 1931–1956 (Coto vedado). 1988. Tr. Peter Bush. London: Quartet.

Juan the Landless (Juan sin tierra). 1977. Tr. Helen R. Lane. New York: Viking.

Landscapes after the Battle (Paisajes después de la batalla). 1987. Tr. Helen R. Lane. New York: Seaver.

Makbara. 1981. Tr. Helen R. Lane. New York: Seaver. Reissued Champaign IL: Dalkey Archive, 2008.

Marks of Identity (Señas de identidad). 1969. Tr. Gregory Rabassa. London: Serpent's Tail. Repr. 2003.

The Young Assassins (Juegos de manos). 1959. Tr. John Rust. New York: Knopf.

The Virtues of the Solitary Bird (Las virtudes del pájaro solitario). 1991. Tr. Helen R. Lane. London: Serpent's Tail.

Grandes, Almudena

The Ages of Lulu (Las edades de Lulu), 1994. Tr. Sonia Soto. New York: Grove.

Laforet, Carmen

Nada: A Novel (Nada). 1958. Tr. Inez Muñoz. London: Weidenfeld & Nicolson.

Nada: A Novel (Nada). 2007. Tr. Edith Grossman. Introd. Mario Vargas Llosa. London: Harvill Secker.

Lerxtundi, Anjel

Perfect Happiness (Zorion perfektua). 2006. Tr. Amaia Gabantxo. Basque Literature Series 4. Reno NV: University of Nevada.

Loriga, Ray

My Brother's Gun (Caídos del cielo). 1997. Tr. Kristina Cordero. New York: St Martin's.

Marías, Javier

All Souls (Todas las almas). 1992. Tr. Margaret Jull Costa. London: Harvill.

Marsé, Juan de

The Fallen (Si te dicen que caí). 1979. Tr. Helen R. Lane. Boston MA. Little, Brown.

Shanghai Nights (El embrujo de Shangai). 2006. Tr. Nick Caistor. London: Harvill Secker.

Martín Gaite, Carmen

The Back Room (El cuarto de atrás). 1983. Tr. Helen R. Lane. New York: Columbia University Press. Reissued San Francisco CA: City Lights, 2007.

Behind the Curtains (Entre visillos). 1990. Tr. Frances Lopez-Morillas. New York: Columbia University Press.

Courtship Customs in Postwar Spain (Usos amorosos de la postguera española). 2004. Tr. Margaret E.W. Jones. Lewisburg PA: Bucknell University Press.

Martín-Santos, Luis

Time of Silence (Tiempo de silencio). 1965. Tr. George Leeson. London: Calder.

Matute, Ana María

Celebration in the North-West (Fiesta al noroeste). 1997. Tr. Phoebe Ann Porter. Lincoln NE: University of Nebraska Press.

The Lost Children (Los hijos muertos). 1965. Tr. Joan Maclean. New York: Macmillan.

School of the Sun (Primera memoria). 1969. Tr. Elaine Kerrigan. Los Mercaderes 1. New York: Columbia University Press.

Soldiers Cry by Night (Los soldados lloran de noche). 1994. Tr. Robert Nugent & María José de la Cámara. Los Mercaderes 2. Pittsburg PA: Latin American Literary Review.

The Trap (La trampa). 1996. Tr. Robert Nugent & María José de la Cámara. Los Mercaderes 3. Pittsburg PA: Latin American Literary Review.

Medio, Dolores

We, the Riberos (Nosotros los Rivero). 1978. Tr. Kathleen A. Leder. Dissertation: Eckerd College, St Petersburg FL.

Mendicutti, Eduardo

Seven against Georgia; Erotic Fiction (Siete contra Georgia). 2003. Tr. Kristina Cordero. New York: Grove.

Mendoza, Eduardo

The City of Marvels (La ciudad de los prodigios). 1986. Tr. Bernard Molloy. San Diego CA: Harcourt Brace Jovanovich.

The Truth about the Savolta Case (La verdad sobre el caso Savolta). 1992. Tr. Alfred MacAdam. New York: Pantheon.

No Word from Gurb (Sin noticias de Gurb). 2007. Tr. Nick Caistor. London: Telegram.

The Year of the Flood (El año del diluvio). 1995. Tr. Nick Caistor. London: Harvill.

Millás García, Juan José

That was Loneliness (La soledad era esto). 2000. Tr. Allison Beeby. London: Allison & Busby.

Moix, Ana María

Julia. 2004. Tr. Sandra Kingery. Lincoln NE: University of Nebraska Press.

Montero, Rosa
Absent Love (Crónica del desamor). 1991. Tr. Cristina de la Torre & Diana Glad. Lincoln NE: University of Nebraska Press.
The Delta Function (La función delta). 1991. Tr. Kari Easton & Yolanda Molina Gavilán. Lincoln NE: University of Nebraska Press.

Monzó, Quim
The Enormity of the Tragedy (La magnitud de la tragèdia). 2007. Tr. Peter Bush. London & Chester Springs PA; Peter Owen.

Muñoz Molina, Antonio
Prince of Shadows (Beltenebros). 1993. Tr. Peter R. Bush. London: Quartet.
Sepharad (Sefarad). 2003. Tr. Margaret Sayers Peden. Orlando FL: Harcourt.
Winter in Lisbon (El invierno en Lisboa). 1999. Tr. Sonia Soto. London: Granta.

Navarro, Julia
The Brotherhood of the Holy Shroud (La hermandad de la sábana santa). 2007. Tr. Andrew Hurley. New York: Dell.

Oñederra, Miren Lourdes
And the Serpent Said to the Woman (Eta emakumeari sugeak esan zion). 2005. Tr. Kristin Addis. Basque Literature Series 2. Reno NV: Center for Basque Studies, University of Nevada.

Ortega y Gasset, José
The Dehumanization of Art and *Notes on the Novel (La deshumanización del arte y Ideas sobre la novela).* 1948. Tr. Helena Weyl. Princeton NJ: Princeton University Press.
Man and Crisis (En torno a Galileo). 1962. Tr. Mildred Adams. New York: Norton.
The Modern Theme (El tema de nuestro tiempo). 1933. Tr. James Cleugh. New York: Norton.
The Revolt of the Masses (La rebelión de las masas). 1932. Anonymous. London: Allen & Unwin.

Palacio Valdés, Armando
Sister Saint Sulpice (La hermana san Sulpicio). 1890. Tr. Nathaniel Haskell Dole. New York: Crowell.

Pérez de Ayala, Ramón
Tiger Juan (Tigre Juan). Tr. Walter Starkie. 1933. New York: Macmillan & London: Cape.

Pérez Galdós, Benito
Fortunata y Jacinta. 1973. Tr. Lester Clark. Harmondsworth: Penguin.

Pérez Reverte, Arturo
Captain Alatriste (El Capitán Alatriste). 2005. Tr. Margaret Sayers Peden. The Adventures of Captain Alatriste 1. New York: G.P. Putnam's Sons.
The Fencing Master (El maestro de esgrima). 1999. Tr. Margaret Jull Costa. London: Harvill.
The King's Gold (El oro del rey). 2008. Tr. Margaret Sayers Peden. The Adventures of Captain Alatriste 4. New York: G.P. Putnam's Sons.

The Ninth Gate (El Club Dumas). 1999. Tr. Margaret Jull Costa. London: Harvill.

Purity of Blood (Limpieza de sangre). 2006. Tr. Margaret Sayers Peden. The Adventures of Captain Alatriste 2. New York: Penguin.

Sun over Breda (El sol de Breda), 2007. Tr. Margaret Sayers Peden. The Adventures of Captain Alatriste 3. New York: G.P. Putnam's Sons.

Perucho, Joan

Natural History (Les històries naturals). 1988. Tr. David H. Rosenthal. New York: Knopf.

Pombo, Álvaro

The Hero of the Big House (El héroe de las mansardas de Mansard). 1988. Tr. Margaret Jull Costa. London: Chatto & Windus.

Porcel, Baltasar

Horses into the Night (Cavalls cap a la fosca). 1995. Tr. John L. Getman. Fayeteville AR: University of Arkansas Press.

Springs and Autumns (Les primeveres i les tardors). 2000. Tr. John L. Getman. Fayeteville AR: University of Arkansas Press.

Queizán, María Xosé

The Likeness (Semellanza). 1999. Tr. Ama M. Spitzmesser. New York: Peter Lang.

Riera, Carme

In the Last Blue (Dins el darrer blau). 2007. Tr. Jonathan Dunne. Woodstock NY: Overlook.

Rivas, Manuel

The Butterfly's Tongue (A lingua das bolboretas). 2006. Tr. Jennifer Leigh Pittman. Montgomery AL: Huntington College.

The Butterfly's Tongue: Three stories translated from the Galician (A lingua das bolboretas). 2000. Tr. Margaret Jull Costa. London: Harvill.

The Carpenter's Pencil (O lapis do carpinteiro). 2001. Tr. Jonathan Dunne. Woodstock NY: Overlook.

In the Wilderness (En salvaxe compañía). 2003. Tr. Jonathan Dunne. London: Harvill.

Rodoreda, Mercé

A Broken Mirror (Mirall trencat). 2006. Tr. Josep Miquel Sobrer. European Women Writers. Lincoln NE: University of Nebraska Press.

Camelia Street (El Carrer de les Camèlies). 2006. Tr. David H. Rosenthal. St Paul MN: Graywolf.

The Pigeon Girl: A Novel (La Plaça del Diamant). 1967. Tr. Eda O'Shiel. London: Deutsch.

The Time of the Doves (La Plaça del Diamant). 1980. Tr. David H. Rosenthal. New York: Taplinger.

Ruiz Zafón, Carlos

The Shadow of the Wind (La sombra del viento). 2004. Tr. Lucia Graves. New York: Penguin.

Sales, Joan
Uncertain Glory (Incerta glòria). 2002. Tr. David H. Rosenthal. Houston TX: American Institute for Catalan Studies.
Saizarbitoria, Ramón
A Hundred Meters (Ehun metro). 1985. Tr. Gloria Castresana Waid. Basque Translations 1. Reno NV: Basque American Foundation.
Sánchez Ferlosio, Rafael
The Adventures of the Ingenious Alfanhuí (Alfanhuí). 2000. Tr. Margaret Jull Costa. Sawtry: Dedalus.
The River (El Jarama). 2004. Tr. Margaret Jull Costa. Sawtry: Dedalus.
Sánchez Silva, José María
The Miracle of Marcelino (Marcelino, pan y vino). 1963. Tr. John Paul Debicki. Chicago IL: Scepter.
Sender, Ramón
Dark Wedding (Epitalamio del Prieto Trinidad). 1943. Tr. Eleanor Clark. Garden City NY: Doubleday.
Mr Witt among the Rebels (Mr. Witt en el Cantón). 1938. Tr. Peter Chalmers Mitchell. Boston MA: Houghton Mifflin.
Requiem for a Spanish Peasant (Réquiem por un campesino español). 1960. Tr. Elinor Randall. Preface Maír José Benardete. New York: Las Américas.
Seven Red Sundays (Siete domingos rojos). 1936. Tr. Peter Chalmers Mitchell. New York: Liveright.
The War in Spain: A Personal Narrative (Contraataque). 1937. Tr. Peter Chalmers Mitchell. London: Faber & Faber.
Torrente Ballester, Gonzalo
Don Juan. 1986. Tr. Bernard Molloy. Madrid: Iberia.
Tusquets, Esther
Love is a Solitary Game (El amor es un juego solitario). 1985. Tr. Bruce Penman. London: Calder & New York: Riverrun.
Never to Return (Para no volver). 1999. Tr. Barbara F. Ichiishi. Lincoln NE: University of Nebraska Press.
The Same Sea as Every Summer (El mismo mar de todos los veranos). 1990. Tr. Margaret E.W. Jones. Lincoln NE: University of Nebraska Press.
Stranded (Varada tras el ultimo naufragio). 1991. Tr. Susan E. Clark. Elmwood Park IL: Dalkey Archive Press.
Unamuno, Miguel de
Ábel Sanchez and Other Stories (Abel Sánchez). 1956. Tr. Anthony Kerrigan. Chicago: Gateway.
Aunt Tula (La tía Tula). 1921. Ed. & tr. Stanley Appelbaum. Mineola NY: Dover.
Love and Pedagogy (Amor y pedagogía). 1996. Tr. Michael Vande Berg. New York: Peter Lang.
Mist (Niebla). 1928. Tr. Warner Fite. New York: Knopf.
Peace in War (Paz en la Guerra). 1983. Ed. & tr. Allen Lacy & Martin Nozick. Bollingen Series 85/i. Princeton NJ: Princeton University Press.

St Manuel Bueno, Martyr (San Manuel bueno, mártir). 2007. Ed. & tr. Pals Burns & Salvador Ortiz-Carboneres. Hispanic Classics. Oxford: Oxbow.

Three Exemplary Novels (Tres novelas ejemplares y un prólogo). 1930. Tr. Ángel Flores. Introd. Ángel del Río. Repr. 1997.

Valera, Juan

Pepita Jiménez. *1908*. Tr. G. L. Lincoln. Boston MA: Heath.

Valle-Inclán, Ramón del

Divine Words: A Village Tragicomedy (Divinas palabras). 1977. Tr. Trader Faulkner. London: Heinemann, in association with the National Theatre.

The Pleasant Memoirs of the Marquis of Bradomin: Four Sonatas (Sonatas: Memorias del marqués de Bradomín). 1924. Tr. May Heywood Braun & Thomas Walsh. New York: Harcourt Brace. Repr. New York: H. Fertig, 1984.

The Tyrant: A Novel of Warm Lands (Tirano Banderas). 1929. Tr. Margarita Pavitt. New York: Holt.

Vázquez Montalbán, Manuel

The Angst-ridden Executive (La soledad del manager). 1990. Tr. Ed Emery. London: Serpent's Tail.

Barcelonas. 1992. Tr. Andy Robinson. London & New York: Verso.

The Buenos Aires Quintet (Quinteto de Buenos Aires). 1997. Tr. Nick Caistor. London: Serpent's Tail.

Galíndez. 1992. Tr. Carol & Thomas Christensen. New York: Atheneum & Toronto: Macmillan Canada.

Murder in the Central Committee (Asesinato en el Comité Central). 1981. Tr. Patrick Camiller. Chicago IL: Academy.

Off Side (El delantero centro fue asesinado al atardecer). 1996. Tr. Ed Emery. London & New York: Serpent's Tail.

An Olympic Death (Laberinto griego). 1992. Tr. Ed Emery. London: Serpent's Tail.

The Pianist (El pianista). 1989. Tr. Elisabeth Plaister. London & New York: Quartet.

Southern Seas (Los mares del Sur). 1986. Tr. Patrick Camiller. London: Pluto.

Vila Matas, Enrique

Bartleby & Co. (Bartleby y Compañía). 2000. Tr. Jonathan Dunne. New York: New Directions.

Montano's Malady (El mal de Montano). 2007. Tr. Jonathan Dunne. New York: New Directions.

Villalonga, Llorenç

Bearn, or the Doll's Room (Bearn, o la sala de les nines). 1986. Tr. Deborah Bonner. Madrid: Iberia.

BIBLIOGRAPHY

Abel, Elizabeth, Marianne Hirsch, and Elizabeth Langland. 1983. *The Voyage: Fictions of Female Development*. Hanover & London: University Press of New England.

Abella, Rafael. 1992. *Finales de enero, 1939: Barcelona cambia de piel.* Espejo de España 154. Barcelona: Planeta.

Abellán, José L. (ed.). 1977. *El exilio español de 1939*. 4 vols. Madrid: Taurus.

—— et al. 2000. *Memoria del exilio vasco: Cultura, pensamiento y literatura de los escritores transterrados en 1939*. Ed. Emilio Palacios Fernández. Introd. José Paulino Ayuso. Ensayos. Madrid: Biblioteca Nueva.

Abellán, Manuel L. 1980. *Censura y creación literaria en España (1939–1976)*. Temas de Historia y Política Contemporáneas 9. Barcelona: Península.

Acland, Charles R. 2004. 'Fresh Contacts: Global Culture and the Concept of Generation', in Campbell 2004: 31–52.

Agawu-Kakraba, Yaw. 2002. 'José Ángel Mañas's Literature of Insurgency: *Historias del Kronen*', *Revista Hispánica Moderna* 55: 188–203.

Aguilar Fernández, Paloma. 2002. *Memory and Amnesia: The Role of the Spanish Civil War in the Transition to Democracy*. Tr. Mark Gordon Oakley. New York and Oxford: Berghahn.

Agustí, Ignacio. 1962. *Mariona Rebull* [1944]. La Ceniza Fue Árbol 1. Barcelona: Argos.

——. 1974. *Ganas de hablar.* Espejo de España 3. Barcelona: Planeta.

Alarcón, Pedro Antonio de. 1999. *El escándalo* [1875]. Ed. Juan Bautista Montes Bordajandi. Letras Hispánicas 253. Madrid: Cátedra.

——. 2001. *La pródiga* [1882]. Ed. Filomena Liberatori. Clásicos Castalia 261. Madrid: Castalia

Alas, Leopoldo (Clarín). 1995. *La Regenta* [1884]. Oviedo: Biblioteca Artes y Letras.

Alas Mínguez, Leopoldo. 1994. *De la acera de enfrente: Todo lo que se debe saber de los gays y nadie se ha atrevido a contar*. El Papagayo 83. Madrid: Temas de Hoy.

Albaladejo Mayordomo, Tomás, F. Javier Blasco, and Ricardo de la Fuente (eds). 1992. *Las vanguardias.* Renovación de los Lenguajes Poéticos 2. Ensayos Júcar 6. Madrid: Júcar.

Alberich, José. 1966. *Los ingleses, y otros temas de Pío Baroja*. Hombres. Hechos e Ideas 9. Madrid: Alfaguara.

——. 1970. 'Mariona Rebull, o la burguesía inútil', *Revista de Occidente* 2ª época 28/lxxxii: 23–38.

Albert i Paradís, Catalina (Victor Català). 1905. *Solitud.* Barcelona: Publicació Joventut.

Alborg, Concha. 1993. *Cinco figuras en torno a la novela de posguerra: Galvarriato, Soriano, Formica, Boixadós y Aldecoa.* Avefénix Textos: Ensayos 51. Madrid: Libertarias.

Alborg, Juan L. 1958–62. *Hora actual de la novela española.* 2 vols. Madrid: Taurus.

Aldecoa, Ignacio. 1954a. *Con el viento solano.* Autores Españoles e Hispanoamericanos. Barcelona: Planeta. 3rd edn 1970.

——. 1954b. *El fulgor y la sangre.* Autores Españoles e Hispanoamericanos. Barcelona: Planeta. 3rd edn 1970.

——. 1955a. *Espera de tercera clase: Narraciones.* Madrid: Puerta del Sol.

——. 1955b. *Vísperas del silencio.* Con el Tiempo 2. Madrid: Taurus.

——. 1957. *Gran Sol.* Galería Literaria. Barcelona: Noguer. 3rd edn 1969.

——. 1967. *Parte de una historia.* Galería Literaria. Barcelona: Noguer.

Aldecoa, Josefina. 1990. *Historia de una maestra.* Narrativas Hispánicas 97. Barcelona: Anagrama.

——. 1994. *Mujeres de negro.* Narrativas Hispánicas 160. Barcelona: Anagrama.

——. 1997. *La fuerza del destino.* Narrativas Hispánicas 230. Barcelona: Anagrama.

Aldekoa, Iñaki. 2004. *Historia de la literatura vasca.* Donostia/San Sebastián: Erein.

Aldridge, John W. (ed.). 1952. *Critiques and Essays on Modern Fiction, 1920–1951: Representing the Achievement of Modern American and British Critics.* Intro. Mark Shorer. New York: The Ronald Press.

Aliaga, Juan V. and José M. G. Cortés. 1997. *Identidad y diferencia: Sobre la cultura gay en España: Ensayo.* Barcelona: Gay y Lesbiana (Egales).

Aliaga, Juan V. *et al.* (eds). 2001. *Miradas sobre la sexualidad en el arte y la literatura del siglo XX en Francia y España.* Valencia: Universitat de València.

Alonso, Santos. 1983. *La novela en la transición (1976–1981).* Libros Dante. Madrid: Puerta del Sol.

——. 1988. *La verdad sobre el caso Savolta: Eduardo Mendoza.* Guías de Lectura. Barcelona: Alhambra.

——. 2003. *La novela española en el fin de siglo, 1975–2001.* Estudios y Ensayos 3. Madrid: Mare Nostrum.

——. 2005. La novela entre la autonomía literaria y la industria', in *Novelistas en el siglo XXI. Creación, Mercado y Lectores. Actas del XVII Congreso de Literatura española contemporánea (Noviembre 2003).* Ed. Salvador Montesa. Ediciones del Congreso de la Universidad de Málaga: 53–69.

Alonso Santos, José Luis. 1988. *Bajarse al moro.* Ed. Fermín Tamayo and Eugenia Popeanga. Letras Hispánicas 289. Madrid: Cátedra.

Alonso Zaldívar, Carlos and Manuel Castells. 1992a. 'La revolución silenciosa: Las nuevas españolas', in Alonso & Castells 1992b: 53–56.

—— and ——. 1992b. *España fin de siglo.* Madrid: Alianza.

Altisent, Marta E. 1992. *Los artículois de Gabriel Miró en la prensa barcelonesa, 1911–1920*. Pliegos de Ensayo 78. Madrid: Pliegos.

——. 2002. 'Barcelona: Del homenaje a la invectiva', in Bermúdez *et al.* 2002: 117–43.

—— and Cristina Martínez-Carazo (eds). 2005. *Twentieth-century Spanish Fiction Writers*. Dictionary of Literary Bibliography 322. Detroit MI: Gale Thomson.

Álvarez, Blanca. 1992. *La soledad del monstruo*. Letras Hispánicas 5. Madrid: Grupo 88.

Álvarez-Ude, Carlos (ed.). 1990. 'Novela española 1989–1990', *Ínsula* 525: 9–24.

Álvaro Cunqueiro. 1993. *Álvaro Cunqueiro: Actas do Congreso celebrado en Mondoñedo entre os días 9 a 13 de setembro de 1991*. Santiago de Compostela: Xunta de Galicia.

Amado Castro, Víctor M. and Santiago de Pablo. 2001. *Los vascos y Europa*. Besaide Bilduma 9. Vitoria-Gasteiz: Fundación Sancho El Sabio.

Amat, Nuria. 1997. *La intimidad*. Barcelona: Alfaguara.

——. 1999. *El país del alma*. Biblioteca Breve. Barcelona: Seix Barral.

Amell, Samuel. 1986. 'La novela negra y los narradores españoles actuales', *Revista de Estudios Hispánicos* 20/i: 91–102.

—— (ed.). 1992. *España frente al siglo XXI: Cultura y literatura*. Encuentros Cátedra. Madrid: Cátedra & Ministerio de Cultura.

—— (ed.). 1996. *The Contemporary Spanish Novel: An Annotated, Critical Bibliography, 1936–1994*. Bibliographies and Indexes in World Literature 50. Westport CT: Greenwood.

Anderson, Reed. 1978. 'Luis Martín-Santos and Juan Goytisolo: Irony and Satire in the Contemporary Spanish Novel,' *Orbis Litterarum* 33: 359–74.

Anderson Imbert, Enrique. 1976. *El realismo mágico y otros ensayos*. Caracas: Monte Avila.

Annesley, James. 1998. *Blank Fictions: Consumerism, Culture and the Contemporary American Novel*. New York: St. Martin's.

Arbona Abascal, Guadalupe. 2002. 'Delibes y el cine: Una aproximación sin polémicas', *Espéculo: Revista de Estudios Literarios* = <http://www.ucm.es/info/especulo/delibes/cine.html>.

Arconada, César M. 1930. *La turbina*. Madrid and Buenos Aires: Iberoamericana.

——. 1933. *Los pobres contra los ricos*. Literatura. Madrid: Publicaciones Izquierda.

——. 1934. *Reparto de tierras*. Paris and Seville: Publicaciones Izquierda.

Arderíus, Joaquín. 1931. *Campesinos*. Madrid: Zeus.

——. 1934. *Crimen: Suceso*. Madrid: Castro.

Aretxaga, Begoña *et al.* (eds). 2005. *Empire and Terror: Nationalism/ Postnationalism in the New Millennium*. Center for Basque Studies Conference Papers 1. Reno NV: University of Nevada, Reno.

Arguloll, Rafael *et al.* 1989. *Cuentos barceloneses*. Barcelona: Icaria.

Arias Careaga, Raquel. 2005. *Escritoras españolas (1939–1975): Poesía, novela y teatro.* Arcadia de Las Letras 29. Madrid: Laberinto.

Aritzeta i Abad, Margarida. 1997. *L'herència de Cuba.* Col.lecció Clàssica 229. Barcelona: Columna.

Arkinstall, Christine R. 2002. 'Towards a Female Symbolic: Re-presenting Mothers and Daughters in Contemporary Spanish Narrative by Women', in Giorgio 2002: 47–84.

——. 2004. *Gender, Class, and Nation: Mercè Rodoreda and the Subjects of Modernism.* Lewisburg PA: Bucknell University Press.

Arnau, Carme. 1987. *Marginats i integrats a la novel.la catalana (1925–1938): Introducció a la novel.lística de Llor, Arbó, Soldevila i Trabal.* Llibres de l'Abast. Barcelona: Edicions 62.

——. 1991 'Barcelona in the Contemporary Catalan Novel', *Catalan Writing* 7: 11–15.

Arniches y Barrera, Carlos. 1995. *La señorita de Trevélez* [1916]. Ed. Andrés Amorós. Letras Hispánicas 405. Madrid: Cátedra.

Asís Garrote, María D. de. 1992. *Última hora de la novela en España.* Biblioteca Eudema. Madrid: Pirámide.

Atxaga, Bernardo. 1992. *Obaba(koak).* Erein Literatura 48. Donosta/San Sebastián: Erein.

Aub, Max. 1943. *Campo cerrado: Novela.* El Laberinto Mágico 1. Mexico City: Tezontle.

——. 1954. *Las buenas intenciones.* Mexico City: Tezontle.

——. 1988. *Diarios, 1939–1972.* Ed. Manuel Aznar Soler. Barcelona: Alba.

——. 2002. *Obras completas, III-B: El laberinto mágico, II. Campo de los almendros.* Ed. Francisco Caudet and Luis Llorens Marzo. Valencia: Biblioteca Valenciana.

Axeitos, Xosé L. (ed.). 1995. *Rafael Dieste: Actas del congreso celebrado na Coruña os días 25, 26 e 27 de maio de 1995.* Santiago: Xunta de Galicia.

Ayala, Francisco. 1949a. *Los usurpadores.* Introd. F. de Paula A. G. Duarte. Buenos Aires: Sudamericana.

——. 1949b. *La cabeza del cordero.* Buenos Aires: Losada.

——. 1983. *La cabeza del cordero.* Libro de Bolsillo 982. Madrid: Alianza.

——. 1988a. *Cazador en el alba* [1929]. Introd. Rosa Navarro Durán. Alianza Tres 225. Madrid: Alianza.

——. 1988b. *El escritor y el cine.* Ensayos 43. Madrid: Aguilar.

Azaña, Manuel. 1977. *Defensa de la autonomía de Cataluña.* Colección Textos 2. Barcelona: Undarius.

Azcoaga, Enrique. 1949. *El empleado.* Madrid: Revista de Occidente.

Azcona, Rafael. 1960. *Pobre, paralítico y muerto.* Madrid: Arión.

——. 2005. *El pisito: Novela de amor e inquilinato* [1957]. Ed. Juan A. Ríos Carralatá. Letras Hispánicas 581, Madrid: Cátedra.

Azevedo, Milton. 1993. 'Code-switching in Catalan Literature'. *Antipodas: Journal of Hispanic Studies of the University of Auckland* 5 [special number on Catalan literature, ed. Robert Archer]: 223–32.

Azorín (José Martinez Ruiz). 1943a. 'Superrealismo', in Azorín 1943b.

——. 1943b. *Obras selectas*. Madrid: Biblioteca Nueva.

——. 1953. *El cine y el momento*. Madrid: Biblioteca Nueva.

——. 1955. *El efímero cine*. Más Allá 12. Madrid: Afrodisio Aguado.

——. 1973. *Doña Inés: Historia de amor*. Ed. Elena Catena. Clásicos Castalia 53. Madrid: Castalia.

Azúa de, Félix. 1987. *Diario de un hombre humillado*. Narrativas Hispánicas 56. Barcelona: Anagrama.

——. 1994. *Demasiadas preguntas*. Narrativas Hispánicas. Barcelona: Anagrama.

——. 1996. *Salidas de tono: Cincuenta observaciones de un ciudadano*. Barcelona: Anagrama.

——. 1997. *Historia de un idiota contada por él mismo*. Compactos 71. Barcelona: Anagrama.

——. 1998. *Lecturas compulsivas: Una invitación*. Introd. Ana Dexeus. Argumentos 215. Barcelona: Anagrama.

——. 1999. *La invención de Caín*. Textos de Escritor. Madrid: Alfaguara.

Badiola Rentería, María P. and Josefina López Sainz. 1981. *La literatura en lengua vasca*. Cuardernos de Estudio: Literatura 32. Madrid: Cincel.

Baker, Edward. 1991. *Materiales para escribir Madrid: Literatura y espacio urbano de Moratín a Galdós*. Lingüística y Teoría Literaria. Madrid: Siglo XXI.

—— (ed.). 1999. 'Madrid Writing/Reading Madrid', *Arizona Journal of Hispanic Cultural Studies* 3 (special number): 71–219.

Bakhtin, Mikhail M. 1981. *The Dialogic Imagination: Four Essays*. Ed. Michael Holquist. Tr. Caryl Emerson and Michael Holquist. Slavic Series 1. Austin TX: University of Texas Press.

——. 1990. *Art and Answerability: Early Philosophical Essays*. Ed. Michael Holquist and Vadim Liapunov. Tr. Vadim Liapunov. Slavic Series 9. Austin TX: University of Austin Press.

Bal, Mieke. 1997. *Narratology: An Introduction to the Theory of Narrative*. Tr. Christine van Boheemen. 2nd edn. Toronto: University of Toronto Press.

Balibrea, Mari P. 1999. *En la tierra baldía: Manuel Vázquez Montalbán y la izquierda española en la postmodernidad*. Barcelona: El Viejo Topo.

Ballester, Josep. 1992. *Temps de quarantena: Cultura i societat a la postguerra (1939–1959)*. Valencia: Eliseu Clement.

Ballesteros, Isolina. 1994. *Escritura femenina y discurso autobiográfico en la nueva novela española*. American University Studies II. 207. New York: Peter Lang.

——. 2001. *Cine (ins)urgente: Textos fílmicos y contextos culturales de la España posfranquista*. Arte 126. Madrid: Fundamentos.

Baquero Goyanes, Mariano. 1970. *Estructuras de la novela actual*. Ensayos Planeta. Barcelona: Planeta. 2nd edn 1975.

Barbachano, Carlos J. 2000. *Entre cine y literatura*. Ensayo 4. Zaragoza: Prames.

Barbal, Maria. 1985. *Pedra de tartera*. Barcelona: Laia.

——. 1999. *Carrer Bolívia*. Balancí 349. Barcelona: Columna.

Barea, Arturo. 1984a. *La forja de un rebelde* [1958]. 3 vols. Colección Turner 73–75. Madrid: Ediciones Turner.

——. 1984b. *The forging of a rebel*. Tr. Isla Barea [1943–46]. Fontana.

Barella Vigal, Julia, Francisco Gutiérrez Carbajo and Francisco Solano (eds). 1995. *Madrid en la novela*. Vol. V, 'Prólogo' and 'Introducción'. Madrid: Comunidad de Madrid. Conserjería de Educación y Cultura: 9–31.

Barella Vigal, Julia and Francisco Gutiérrez Carbajo (eds). 1997. *Madrid en la novela*. Vol. VI, 'Prólogo'. Madrid: Comunidad de Madrid. Conserjería de Educación y Cultura: 9–26.

Baroja, Pío. 1946. *La busca* [1903–04] in Baroja 1946–: I. 259–380.

——. 1946–. *Obras completas*. 8 vols. Madrid: Biblioteca Nueva.

——. 1999. *Las inquietudes de Shanti Andía* [1882]. Letras Hispánicas 73. Madrid: Castalia.

——. 2004. *Zalacaín el aventurero: Historia de las buenas andanzas y fortunas de Martín Zalacaín de Urbia*. [1909]. Libro de Bolsillo. Madrid: Alianza.

Barral, Carlos. 1975. *Años de penitencia: Memorias I*. Alianza Tres 13. Madrid: Alianza.

——. 1979. *Usuras y figuraciones*. Poesía 32. Barcelona: Lumen.

——. 1982. *Los años sin excusa: Memorias II*. Madrid: Alianza.

Barreiro Barreiro, Xosé L. (ed.). 1990. *O pensamento galego na historia*. Santiago de Compostela: Universidade de Santiago. 2nd edn 1992.

Barth, John. 1995. *Further Fridays: Essays, Lectures, and other Nonfiction, 1984–94*. Boston: Little, Brown & Co.

Barthes, Roland. 1953. *Le degré zero de l'écriture*. Paris: Éditions du Seuil.

——. 1970. *S/Z*. Paris: Éditions du Seuil.

——. 1972. *Mythologies*. Ed. and tr. Annette Lavers. New York: Hill and Wang. Repr. 1978.

——. 1978. *A Lover's Discourse: Fragments*. Tr. Richard Howard. New York: Farrar, Straus & Giroux.

Basanta, Ángel. 1979. *Cuarenta años de novela española*. 2 vols. Grandes Obras de la Literatura Universal 400–401. Madrid: Cincel-Kapelusz.

——. 1990. *La novela española de nuestra época*. Biblioteca Básica. Madrid: Anaya.

Basdekis, Demetrios. 1974. *Unamuno and the Novel*. Estudios de Hispanófila 31. Madrid: Castalia & Chapel Hill NC: Hispanófila.

Batchelor, Ronald E. 1972. *Unamuno Novelist: A European Perspective*. Oxford: Dolphin.

Baudelaire, Charles. 1980. *Oeuvres complètes*. Ed. Michel Jamet. Prologue Claude Roy. Paris: Laffont.

Bauman, Zygmunt. 1992. *Intimations of Postmodernity*. London and New York: Routledge.

Beilín, Katarzyna Olga. 2004. *Conversaciones literarias con novelistas contemporáneos*. Támesis A 203. Woodbridge: Tamesis.

Belic, Oldrich. 1968. *La estructura narrativa de 'Tirano Banderas'*. Cuadernos Ateneo 43. Madrid: Editora Nacional.

Benet, Juan. 1967. *Volverás a Región*. Ancora y Delfín 295. Barcelona: Destino.

——. *¿Qué fue la guerra civil?* 1976. Biblioteca de Divulgación Política. Barcelona: Gaya Ciencia.

——. 1983–86. *Herrumbrosas lanzas*. 3 vols. Literatura Alfaguara 122, 158, 213. Madrid: Alfaguara.

Benjamin, Walter. 1968a. *Illuminations: Essays and Reflections*. Ed. Hannah Arendt. Tr. Harry Zohn. New York: Schocken.

——. 1968b. 'The Flaneur', in Benjamin 1968a: 253–64.

Bergmann, Emilie L. and Richard Herr (eds). 2007. *Mirrors and Echoes: Women's Writing in Twentieth-century Spain*. Berkeley CA and London: University of California Press.

Bergmann, Emilie L. and Paul J. Smith (eds). 1995. *¿Entiendes?: Queer Readings, Hispanic Writings*. Series Q. Durham NC: Duke University Press.

Berman, Marshall. 1988. *All that is Solid Melts into Air: The Experience of Modernity*. 2nd edn. New York: Penguin.

Bermúdez, Silvia, Antonio Cortijo Ocaña and Timothy McGovern (eds). 2002. *From Stateless Nations to Postnational Spain/De naciones sin estado a la España postnacional*. Boulder, CO: Society of Spanish and Spanish-American Studies.

Bernstein, Jerome S. 1972. *Benjamín Jarnés*. TWAS 128. New York: Twayne.

Bértolo Cadenas, Constantino. 1984. 'Apéndice', in Lacruz 1984: 203–30.

——. 1989. 'Introducción a la narrativa española actual', *Revista de Occidente* 98/99: 29–60.

Bertrana, Prudenci. 1978. *Jo! (Memòries d'un metge filòsof)* [1925]. Les Millors Obres de la Literatura Catalana 4. Barcelona: Edicions 62.

——. 1985. *Josafat* [1906]. Història de la Literatura Catalana 60. Barcelona: Edicions 62.

Bertrand de Muñoz, Maryse. 1982–87. *La guerra civil española en la novela: Bibliografía comentada*. 3 vols. Ensayos. Madrid: José Porrúa Turanzas.

——. 1996. 'Novela histórica, autobiografía y mito', in Romera Castillo *et al.* 1996: 19–38.

Bieder, Maryellen. 1981. 'De *Señas de identidad* a *Makbara*: Estrategia narrativa en las novelas de Juan Goytisolo', tr. Philip Metzidakis, *Revista Iberoamericana* 116/117: 89–96.

Blanchot, Maurice. 1969. *El espacio de la literatura*. Letras Mayúsculas 10. Buenos Aires: Paidós.

Blanco, Carmen. 1991. *Literatura galega da muller*. Vigo: Edicións Xerais de Galicia.

Blanco Aguinaga, Carlos. 1975a. 'Sobre la "Reivindicación del Conde don Julián": La ficción y la historia', in Blanco Aguinaga 1975b: 51–100.

——. 1975b. *De mitólogos y novelistas*. Ediciones 19. Madrid: Turner.

——, Julio Rodríguez Puértolas and Iris M. Zavala. 1978–79. *Historia social de la literatura española (en lengua castellana)*. 3 vols. Madrid: Castalia.

Blanco Amor, Eduardo. 2003. *Xente ao lonxe* [1972]. 13th edn. Biblioteca Blanco Amor 2. Vigo: Galaxia.

——. 2004. *A esmorga* [1959]. Biblioteca Blanco Amor 4. Vigo: Galaxia.

Blanco Torres, Roberto. 1930a. 'La nueva generación literaria gallega', in Blanco Torres 1930b.

——. 1930b. *De esto y de lo otro*. Coruña: Nós.

Blasco Ibáñez, Vicente. 1997. *Entre naranjos* [1900]. Ed. José Mas and María Teresa Mateu. Letras Hispénicas 435. Madrid: Cátedra.

——. 1998a. *Sangre y arena* [1908]. Libro de Bolsillo. Madrid: Alianza.

——. 1998b. *Mare nostrum* [1918]. Ed. María José Navarro. Letras Hispánicas 470. Madrid: Castalia.

——. 2004. *La barraca* [1917]. Ed. José Mas and María Teresa Mateu. 5th edn. Letras Hispánicas 440. Madrid: Cátedra

Bobillo, Francisco Javier. 1981. *Nacionalismo gallego: La ideología de Vicente Risco*. Akal Universitaria: Sociología 36. Madrid: Akal.

Bohigas, Oriol, Peter Buchanan, and Vittorio Magnago Lampugnani. 1990. *Barcelona: Arquitectura y ciudad, 1980–1992*. Barcelona: Gustavo Gili.

Bommel, Antón van. 1993. 'El realismo mágico en la obra de Álvaro Cunqueiro: *Merlín e familia*', in *Álvaro Cunqueiro* 1993: 175–96.

Booth, Wayne. 1961. *The Rhetoric of Fiction*. Chicago IL and London: University of Chicago Press.

Bordons, Glòria and Jaume Subirana (eds). 1999. *Literatura catalana contemporània*. Barcelona: Universitat Oberta de Catalunya and Edicions Proa.

Bou, Enric (ed.). 2000. *Nou diccionari 62 de la literatura catalana*. Barcelona: Edicions 62.

Bourneuf, Roland and Réal Ouellet. 1975. *La novela*. Tr. Enric Sullà. Letras e Ideas: Instrumenta 9. Barcelona: Ariel.

Bover i Font, August. 1993. *Manual de catalanística*. Prologue Josep Massot i Muntaner. Biblioteca Serra d'Or 124. Barcelona: Abadia de Montserrat and Tarragona: Diputació de Tarragona.

Boves Naves, María del Carmen. 1996. 'Novela histórica femenina', in Romera Castillo *et al.* 1996: 39–54.

Boyd, Carolyn P. 1997. *Historia patria: Politics, History, and National Identity in Spain, 1875–1975*. Princeton NJ: Princeton University Press.

Brabazon, Tara. 2005. *From Revolution to Revelation: Generation X, Popular Memory and Cultural Studies*. Aldershot: Ashgate.

Bretz, Mary L. 1979. *La evolución novelística de Pío Baroja*. Studia Humanitatis. Madrid: Jose Porrúa Turanzas.

Brihuega, Jaime. 1982. *La vanguardia y la república*. Cuadernos Arte 14. Madrid: Cátedra.

Briones García, Ana I. 1999. 'Novela policiaca española y postmodernismo historicista en los años ochenta', *Anales de la Literatura Española Contemporánea* 24: 65–83.

Bristow, Joseph. 1997. *Sexuality*. New Critical Idiom. London: Routledge.

Brooks, Peter. 1984. *Reading for the Plot: Design and Intention in Narrative*. New York: Random House.

——. 1994. *Psychoanalysis and Storytelling*. Bucknell Lectures in Literary Theory 10. Oxford and Cambridge MA: Blackwell.

Brown, Gerald G., 1972. *The Twentieth Century*. History of Spanish Literature. New York: Barnes & Noble.

Brown, Joan L. (ed.). 1991. *Women Writers of Contemporary Spain: Exiles in the Homeland*. Newark NJ: University of Delaware Press and London: AUP.

Bru de Sala, Xavier. 1999. *El descrèdit de la literatura*. Assaig: Minor 15. Barcelona: Quaderns Crema.

—— and Javier Tusell (eds). 1990. *Ideas '92'*. Miami: University of Miami: Iberian Studies Institute/North South Center.

—— and —— (eds). 1997. *Barcelona–Madrid, 1898–1998: Sintonies i distàncies*. Barcelona: Centre de Cultura Contemporània de Barcelona.

—— and —— (eds). 1998. *España, Catalunya: Un diálogo con futuro*. Introd. Josep A. Duran i Lleida. Documento. Barcelona: Planeta.

Buckley Planas, Ramón. 1996. *La doble transición: Política y literatura en la España de los años setenta*. Madrid: Siglo XXI.

—— and John Crispin. 1973. *Los vanguardistas españoles, 1925–1935*. Madrid: Alianza.

Buñuel, Luis. 1929. *Un chien andalou*. Screenplay Salvador Dalí and Luís Buñuel. France: Ursulines Film Studio.

Buschman, Albrecht (ed.). 2002. 'Dossier: La novela negra española', *Iberoamericana* ns 7: 93–149.

Bussière-Perrin, Annie (ed.), 1998. *Le roman espagnol actuel: Tendances et perspectives, 1975–2000*, I. Éditions du Cerf : Études Critiques. Montpellier: Université de Montpellier.

Bustelo, Gabriela. 1996. *Veo veo*. Contraseñas 155. Barcelona: Anagrama.

——. 2001. *Planeta hembra*. Barcelona: RBA.

Butler, Judith, 1990. *Gender Trouble: Feminism and the Subversion of Identity*. Thinking Gender. New York and London: Routledge.

Butt, John. 1978. *Writers and Politics in Modern Spain*. London: Hodder & Stoughton.

——. 1981. *Miguel de Unamuno: San Manuel Bueno, mártir*. Critical Guides to Spanish Texts 31. London: Grant & Cutler/Tamesis.

Buxán, Xosé M (ed.). 1997. *Conciencia de un singular deseo: Estudios lesbianos y gays en el estado español*. Rey de Bastos 27. Barcelona: Laertes.

Caballé, Anna *et al.* 2006. 'Madrid y Barcelona: Memorias de dos ciudades', *Revista de Occidente* 292: 5–96.

Caballero Bonald, José Manuel. 1962. *Dos días de setiembre*. Biblioteca Breve. Barcelona: Seix Barral.

Cabello-Castellet, George *et al.* (eds). 1992. *Cine-Lit: Essays on Peninsular Film and Fiction*. Corvallis OR: Portland State University and Oregon State University.

—— *et al.* (eds). 1995. *Cine-Lit II: Essays on Hispanic Film and Fiction*. Corvallis OR: Portland State University and Oregon State University.

—— *et al.* (eds). 1997. *Cine Lit III: Essays on Hispanic Film and Fiction*. Corvallis OR: Oregon State University.

—— *et al.* (eds). 2000. *Cine-Lit 2000: Essays on Hispanic Film and Fiction*. Corvallis OR: Oregon State University.

—— *et al.* (eds). 2004. *Cine-Lit V: Essays on Hispanic Film and Fiction.* Corvallis OR: Oregon State University.

Cabré, Jaume. 1991. *Senyoria.* Biblioteca A Tot Vent 294. Barcelona: Proa.

Cagigao, José L., John Crispin, and Enrique Pupo-Walker (eds). 1982. *España 1975–1980: Conflictos y logros de la democracia.* Ensayos. Madrid: José Porrúa Turanzas.

Cahoone, Lawrence E. (ed.). 1996. *From Modernism to Postmodernism: An Anthology.* Oxford and Cambridge MA: Blackwell.

Calders, Pere. 1964. *L'ombra de l'atzavara.* Barcelona: Selecta.

——. 1966. *Ronda naval sota la boira.* Biblioteca Selecta 384. Barcelona: Selecta.

Callinicos, Alex. 1990. *Against Postmodernism: A Marxist Critique.* New York: Saint Martin's.

Calvo Serer, Rafael. 1949. 'España, sin problema', *Arbor*, 14/xlv–xlvi: 160–73.

——. 1962. *La literatura universal sobre la guerra de España.* O Crece o Muere 167–68. Madrid: Ateneo.

Campbell, Neil (ed.). 2004. *American Youth Cultures.* New York: Routledge.

Candel Crespo, Francesc. 1964. *Els altres Catalans.* Col.lecció a l'Abast 13. Barcelona: Edicions 62.

Capmany, Maria Aurèlia. 1972. *El jaqué de la democràcia.* Col·lecció J.M. 6. Barcelona: Nova Terra.

——. 1980. *Vés-te'n ianqui! o, si voleu, traduït de l'americà* [1959]. 2nd edn. Les Eines 61. Barcelona: Laia.

Carbonell, Antoni *et al.* 1979. *Literatura catalana dels inicis als nostres dies.* El Punt 6. Barcelona: Edhasa.

Cardín, Alberto (ed.). 1991. *SIDA: Enfoques alternos.* Colección Rey de Bastos. Barcelona: Laertes.

Cardona, Rodolfo. 1957. *Ramón: A Study of Gómez de la Serna and his Works.* New York: E. Torres.

—— (ed.). 1976. *Novelistas españoles de posguerra.* Escritor y la Crítica: Persiles 96. Madrid: Taurus.

Carr, David. 1986. *Time, Narrative, and History.* Studies in Phenomenology and Existential Philosophy. Bloomington IA: Indiana University Press.

Carr, Raymond. 2001. *Modern Spain, 1875–1980* [1980]. Oxford: Oxford University Press.

—— and Juan Pablo Fusi Aizpurúa. 1991. *Spain: Dictatorship to Democracy.* London and New York: Routledge.

Carrasquer, Francisco. 1970. *'Imán' y la novela histórica de Sender.* Támesis A 17. London: Tamesis Books Ltd.

Carré Alvarellos, Leandro. 1925. *Naiciña.* Lar 4. A Coruña: Imp. Moret.

Carvallo Calero, Ricardo. 1981. *Historia da literatura galega contemporánea, 1808–1936.* 3rd edn. Vigo: Galaxia.

——. 2002. *Xente da Berreira* [1951]. Biblioteca Galega 120: 27. A Coruña: Voz de Galicia.

Casares, Carlos. 1996. *Deus sentado nun sillón azul.* Literaria 138. Vigo: Galaxia.

——. 2000. *Ilustrísima* [1980]. Literaria: Ensino 2. Vigo: Galaxia.

——. 2004a. *Conciencia de Galicia: Risco, Otero, Curros: Tres biografías*. Biblioteca Carlos Casares 4. Vigo: Galaxia.

——. 2004b. *Cambio en tres* [1969]. 2nd edn. Biblioteca Carlos Casares 1. Vigo: Galaxia.

——. 2004c. *Os mortos daquel verán* [1987]. Biblioteca Carlos Casares 2. Vigo: Galaxia.

——. 2004d. *O sol de verán*. Biblioteca Carlos Casares 3. Vigo: Galaxia.

——. 2006. *Os escuros soños de Clio* [1979]. Biblioteca Carlos Casares 14. Vigo: Galaxia.

Casas, Arturo. 1990. 'Las artes del trasgo: Primeras ficciones de Rafael Dieste', *Ínsula* 525: 29–30.

——. 1994. *Rafael Dieste e a súa obra literaria en galego*. Agra Aberta 19. Vigo: Galaxia.

Casellas, Raimon. 1980. *El sots feréstecs* [1901]. Prologue Jordi Castellanos. Los Eines de Butxaca 9. Barcelona: Laia.

Castellet, José M. 1957. *La hora del lector: Notas para la iniciación a la literatura narrativa de nuestros días*. Biblioteca Breve 111. Barcelona: Seix Barral.

—— (ed.). 1970. *Nueve novísimos poetas españoles*. Libros de Enlace 4. Barcelona: Barral.

Castells, Manuel. 1983. *The City and the Grassroots: A Cross-cultural Theory of Urban Social Movements*. California Series in Urban Development. Berkeley CA: University of California Press.

Castle, Gregory. 2006. *Reading the Modernist Bildungsroman*. Gainesville FL: University Press of Florida.

Castro, Américo. 1971. *The Spaniards: An Introduction to their History*. Tr. Willard F. King and Selma Margaretten. Berkeley CA: University of California Press.

Castro, Rosalía de. 2005. *Cantares gallegos* [1863]. Ed. Ricardo Carvalho Calero. Letras Hispánicas 26. 12th edn. Madrid: Cátedra.

——. 1995. *El caballero de las botas azules* [1867]. Ed. Ana Rodríguez-Fischer. Letras Hispánicas 399. Madrid: Cátedra.

Castro, X. Antón. 1992. *Arte y nacionalismo: La vanguardia histórica gallega (1925–1936)*. Sada and A Coruña: Castro, 1992.

Cebrián, Juan L. 1982. 'La experiencia del periodo constituyente', in Cagigao *et al.* 1982: 13–24.

Cela, Camilo J. 1942. *La familia de Pascual Duarte*. Madrid: Aldecoa.

——. 1944. *Nuevas andanzas y desventuras del Lazarillo de Tormes*. Madrid: La Nave.

——. 1951. *La colmena*. Buenos Aires: Emecé.

——. 1969. *Vísperas, festividad y octava de San Camilo del año 1936 en Madrid*. Alfaguara Literaria 24. Madrid: Alfaguara.

——. 1987. *La colmena*. Ed. Raquel Asún. Clásicos Castalia 24. Madrid: Castalia. Repr. 1990, etc.

——. 1993. *Memorias, entendimientos y voluntades*. Cambio 16. Barcelona: Plaza y Janés.

Cercas, Javier. 2001. *Soldados de Salamina*. Andanzas 433. Barcelona: Tusquets.

Cerezo Galán, Pedro. 1992. 'El pensamiento filosófico: De la generación trágica a la generación clásica: Las generaciones del 98 y del 14', in Laín Entralgo 1992: I. 133–315.

Certeau, Michel de. 1993. 'Walking in the City', in *During 1993*: 151–60.

Chacel, Rosa. 1945. *Memorias de Leticia Valle*. Colección Hórreo. Buenos Aires: Emecé.

Chacón, Dulce. 2002. *La voz dormida*. Madrid: Alfaguara.

Charlon, Anne. 1964. *La condició de la dona en la narrativa femenina catalana (1900–1983)*. Tr. Pilar Canal. Llibres a l'Abast 256. Barcelona: Edicions 62.

Chatman, Seymour. 1978. *Story and Discourse: Narrative Structure in Fiction and Film*. Ithaca and London: Cornell University Press.

——. 1990. *Coming to Terms: The Rhetoric of Narrative in Fiction and Film*. Ithaca and London: Cornell University Press.

Christian, Edward (ed.). 2001. *The Post-colonial Detective*. Crime Films. Basingstoke: Palgrave and St. Martin's Press.

Christie, Ruth, Judith Drinkwater, and John Macklin. 1995. *The Scripted Self: Textual Identities in Contemporary Spanish Narrative*. Re-reading Spanish Literature. Warminster: Aris and Phillips.

Cillero Goiriastuena, Javi. 2000. 'The Moving Target: A History of Basque Detective and Crime Fiction'. Unpublished doctoral dissertation. University of Nevada, Reno.

Ciplijauskaité, Biruté. 1972. *Baroja: Un estilo*. Madrid: Ínsula.

——. 1988. *La novela femenina contemporánea. 1970–1985: Hacia una tipología de la narración en primera persona*. Autores, Textos y Temas: Literatura 3. Barcelona: Anthropos.

Clarke, Anthony H. (ed.). 1999. *A Further Range: Studies in Modern Spanish Literature from Galdós to Unamuno: In memoriam Maurice Hemingway*. Exeter: University of Exeter Press.

Cleckley, Hervey. 1988. *The Mask of Sanity: An Attempt to Clarify some Issues about the So-called Psychopathic Personality*. New York: Hartford.

Collins, Marsha Suzan. 1986. *Pío Baroja's 'Memorias de un hombre de acción' and the Ironic Mode: The Search for Order and Meaning*. Támesis A 124. London: Tamesis.

Colloquium. 1978. *First Colloquium of Catalan Studies in North America*. Urbana IL: University of Illinois.

Colmeiro, José F. 1989. 'Stretching the Limits: Pedrolo's Detective Fiction', *Catalan Review* 3/ii: 59–70.

——. 1994a. *La novela policiaca española: Teoría e historia crítica*. Biblioteca A 9. Barcelona: Anthropos.

——. 1994b. 'The Spanish Connection: Detective Fiction after Franco', *Journal of Popular Culture* 28/i: 151–61.

——. 1996. *Crónica del desencanto: La narrativa de Manuel Vázquez Montalbán*. Letras de Oro. Coral Gables FL: North-South Center, University of Miami.

——. 2001. 'The Spanish Detective as Cultural Other', in Christian 2001: 176–92.

——. 2002. 'Detective Fiction by Spanish Women Writers', in Pérez 2002b: I. 166–71.

——. 2005. *Memoria histórica e identidad cultural: De la postguerra a la postmodernidad.* Memoria Rota: Exilios y Heterodoxos 40. Barcelona: Anthropos.

—— (ed.). 2007. *Manuel Vázquez Montalbán: El compromiso con la memoria.* Támesis A 250. Woodbridge: Tamesis.

Coloma, Luis. 1999. *Pequeñeces* [1890]. Ed. Rubén Benítez. Letras Hispánicas 28. 6th edn. Madrid: Castalia.

Conde Guerri, Maria José, and Manuel Longares (eds). 1993. *Madrid en la novela.* Vol. IV, 'Prólogo' and 'Introducción'. Madrid: Comunidad de Madrid. Conserjería de Educación y Cultura: 9–24.

Conte, Rafael. 1978. 'La maldición del Planeta'. *El País*, 10 November: 2.

——. 1985a. 'En busca de la novela perdida', in Conte *et al.* 1985: 1, 24.

—— *et al.* 1985b. [Special number on the novel], *Ínsula* 464/465 (July–Aug.): 1–26.

Corrales Egea, Jesús. 1971. *La novela española actual: Ensayo de ordenación.* Libros de Bolsillo. Madrid: Cuadernos para el Diálogo.

Cortezón Álvarez, Daniel. 1981. *A vila sulagada.* Narrativa. A Coruña: Castro.

Coupland, Douglas. 1991. *Generation X: Tales for an Accelerated Culture.* New York: St Martin's.

Cox, Randolph C. Jr. 1973. *Aspects of Alienation in the Novels of Juan Goytisolo.* Doctoral dissertation, University of Wisconsin, 1972. Ann Arbor MI: University Microfilms.

Criado Miguel, Isabel. 1986. *Las novelas de Miguel de Unamuno: Estudio formal y crítico.* Acta Salmanticensia: Filosofía y Letras 186. Salamanca: Universidad de Salamanca.

Culler, Jonathan. 1975. *Structuralist Poetics: Structuralism, Linguistics, and the Study of Literature.* London: Routledge and Kegan Paul.

Cunningham, Valentine (ed.). 1986. *Spanish Front: Writers on the Civil War.* Oxford and New York: Oxford University Press.

Cunqueiro, Álvaro. 1999. *Si o vello Sinbad volvese ás illas* [1961]. Literaria 10. 9th edn. Vigo: Galaxia.

——. 2001. *Merlín e familia* [1955]. Literaria 2. Vigo: Galaxia.

——. 2002. *As crónicas do sochantre* [1956]. Biblioteca Galega 32. A Coruña: Voz de Galicia.

Curutchet Garaffo, Juan C. 1973. *Introducción a la novela española de la postguerra: Cuatro ensayos sobre la novela española.* Mundo Actual. Montevideo: Alfa.

Davies, Catherine (ed.). 1993. *Women Writers in Twentieth-century Spain and Spanish America.* Lewiston NY and Lampeter: Edwin Mellen.

——. 1998. *Spanish Women's Writing 1849–1996.* Women in Context. London and Atlantic Highlands NJ: Athlone.

De Juan Bolufer, Amparo. 2000. *La técnica narrativa en Valle-Inclán.* Lalia: Maior 13. Santiago: Universidade de Santiago de Compostela.

Delibes, Miguel. 1959. *La hoja roja*. Ancora y Delfín 168. Barcelona: Destino.
——. 1962. *Las ratas*. Ancora y Delfín 218. Barcelona: Destino.
——. 1966. *Cinco horas con Mario*. Ancora y Delfín 281. Barcelona: Destino.
——. 1969. *Parábola del náufrago*. Ancora y Delfín 329. Barcelona: Destino.
——. 1973. *El príncipe destronado*. Ancora y Delfín 436. Barcelona: Destino.
——. 1975. *Las guerras de nuestros antepasados*. Ancora y Delfín 457. Barcelona: Destino.
——. 1978. *El disputado voto del señor Cayo*. Ancora y Delfín 553. Barcelona: Destino.
——. 1981. *Los santos inocentes*. Narrativa 48. Barcelona: Planeta.
——. 1995. *Diario de un jubilado*. Ancora y Delfín 738. Barcelona: Destino.
——. 1997. *El camino* [1950]. Ed. Marisa Sotelo Vázquez. Clásicos Contemporáneos 3. 2nd edn. Barcelona: Destino.
De Man, Paul. 1984. *The Rhetoric of Romanticism*. New York: Columbia University Press.
Desmond, John M. and Peter Hawkes. 2005. *Adaptation: Studying Film and Literature*. Boston MA: McGraw-Hill.
Deveny, Thomas G. 1999. *Contemporary Spanish Film from Fiction: Literary Texts on Screen*. Lanham MD and Folkestone: Scarecrow.
Díaz de Castro, Francisco J. and Alberto Quintana Peñuela. 1984. *Juan Marsé: Ciudad y novela, Últimas tardes con Teresa: Organización del espacio y producción de imagen*. Palma de Mallorca: Universidad de Palma de Mallorca.
Díaz-Diocaretz, Myriam and Iris M. Zavala (eds). 1993–2000. *Breve historia feminista de la literatura española (en lengua castellana)*. 6 vols. Pensamiento Crítico 80, 90, 92, 98, 101, 112. Barcelona: Anthropos and Madrid: Dirección General de la Mujer.
Díaz Fernández, José. 1985. *El nuevo romanticismo: Polémica de arte, política y literatura*. Ed. José M. López de Abiada. Madrid: José Esteban.
Díaz Migoyo, Gonzalo. 1985. *Guía de 'Tirano Banderas'*. Ensayo 84. Madrid: Fundamentos.
Díez Hochleitner, Ricardo. 1976. *El desarrollo estético de la novela de Unamuno*. Colección Nova Scholar. Madrid: Playor.
Díez de Revenga, Francisco J. 2005. *Poetas y narradores: La narrativa breve en las revistas de vanguardia en España (1918–1936)*. Devenir: Ensayo 4. Madrid: J. Pastor.
D'Lugo, Marvin. 1997. *Guide to the Cinema of Spain*. Reference Guides to the World's Cinema. Westport CT and London: Greenwood.
——. 2002. 'Pedro Almodóvar y la autoría literaria', in Mínguez Arranz 2002: 79–96.
Docherty, Thomas. 1996. *Alterities: Criticism, History, Representation*. Oxford and New York: Clarendon.
Dolgin, Stacey L. 1991. *La novela desmitificadora española, 1961–1982*. Ámbitos Literarios: Ensayo 38. Barcelona: Anthropos.
Dollimore, Jonathan. 1991. *Sexual Dissidence: Augustine to Wilde, Freud to Foucault*. Oxford and New York: Oxford University Press.

Domingo, José. 1973. *La novela española del siglo XX*. 2 vols. Nueva Colección Labor 147, 149. ii: *De la postguerra a nuestros días*. Barcelona: Labor.

Domínguez Olano, Antonio. 1974. *Carta abierta a un muchacho 'diferente'*. Madrid: Ediciones 99.

Dorca, Toni. 1997. 'Joven narrativa en la España de los noventa: La generación X', *Revista de Estudios Hispánicos* 31: 309–24.

D'Ors, Eugenio. 2004. *La ben plantada* [1911]. Barcelona: Quaderns Crema.

Dougherty, Dru. 1999. *Guía para caminantes en Santa Fe de Tierra Firme; Estudio sistémico de 'Tirano Banderas'*. Pre-Textos 415. Valencia: Pre-Textos.

Douglass, William A. *et al*. (eds). 1999. *Basque Cultural Studies*. Basque Studies Program Occasional Papers 5. Reno NV: University of Nevada.

—— and Joseba Zulaika. 2007. *Basque Culture: Anthropological Perspectives*. Basque Textbooks. Reno NV: University of Nevada Press.

Durán, Manuel. 1986. 'Fiction and Metafiction in Contemporary Spanish Letters', *World Literature Today* 60/iii: 398–402.

During, Simon (ed.). 1993. *The Cultural Studies Reader*. London and New York: Routledge.

Dynes, Wayne R. *et al*. (eds). 1990. *Encyclopedia of Homosexuality*. 2 vols. New York: Garland.

Ealham, Chris and Michael Richards. 2005a. 'History, Memory and the Spanish Civil War: Recent Perspectives', in Ealham and Richards 2005b: 1–22.

—— and ——. 2005b. *The Splintering of Spain: Cultural History and the Spanish Civil War, 1936–1939*. Cambridge and New York: Cambridge University Press.

Eisenberg, Daniel. 1990. 'Spain', in Dynes *et al*. 1990: ii. 1236–43.

Eisenstein, Sergei. 1949a. *Film Form: Essays in Film Theory* Ed. and tr. Jay Leyda. New York: Harcourt Brace.

——. 1949b. 'Dickens, Griffith, and the Film Today', in Eisenstein 1949a: 195–255.

Elliott, John H. 1963. *Imperial Spain, 1469–1716*. New York: New American Library.

Ellis, Bret Easton. 1985. *Less than Zero*. New York: Simon & Schuster.

Encinar, Ángeles. 1991. *La novela española actual: La desaparición del héroe*. Pliegos de Ensayo 52. Madrid: Pliegos.

—— and Kathleen M. Glenn (eds). 2005. *La pluralidad narrativa: Escritores españoles contemporáneos (1984–2004)*. Estudios Críticos de Literatura 20. Madrid: Biblioteca Nueva.

——, Eva Lofquist *et al*. (eds). 2006. *Género y géneros: Escritura y escritoras iberoamericanas*. 2 vols. Estudios 117. Madrid: Universidad Autónoma de Madrid.

Eoff, Sherman H. 1961. *The Modern Spanish Novel: Comparative Essays Examining the Philosophical Impact of Science on Fiction*. New York: New York University Press.

Epps, Bradley S. 1966. *Significant Violence: Oppression and Resistance in the Narratives of Juan Goytisolo, 1970–1990*. Oxford Hispanic Series. Oxford: Oxford University Press.

—— (ed.). 2002. 'Barcelona and the projection of Catalonia', *Hispanic Cultural Studies* 6 (special section): 193–269.

—— and Luis Fernández Cifuentes. 2005. *Spain beyond Spain: Modernity, Literary History, and National Identity.* Lewisburg PA: Bucknell University Press.

Esslin, Martin. 1961. *Brecht: The Man and his Work.* Anchor Books A 245. Garden City NY: Anchor Books.

Estruch Tobella, Joan. 1994. 'El català en la narrativa castellana escrita a Catalunya: Els casos de Mendoza, Marsé i Vázquez-Montalbán', *Catalan Review* 8/i–ii: 153–60.

Etxeberria, Hasier. 2002. *Cinco escritores vascos: Entrevistas de Hasier Etxeberria.* Irún: Alberdania.

Etxebarria, Lucía. 1997. *Amor, curiosidad, prozac y dudas.* Ave Fénix: Mayor 64. Barcelona: Plaza y Janés.

——. 1998. *Beatriz y los cuerpos celestes.* Ancora y Delfín 810. Barcelona: Destino.

Falcón, Lidia. 1992. *Camino sin retorno.* Ámbitos Literarios: Narrative 38. Barcelona: Anthropos.

Faulkner, Sally. 2004. *Literary Adaptations in Spanish Cinema.* Támesis A 202. London: Tamesis.

Febrés, Xavier (ed). 1985. *Isabel-Clara Simó, Montserrat Roig.* Diàlegs a Barcelona 5. Barcelona: Laia.

Fernán Caballero (Cecilia Böhl de Faber). 1997. *La familia de Alvareda* [1849]. Madrid: Alba.

Fernán Gomez, Fernando. 1984. *Las bicicletas son para el verano.* Austral 124. Madrid: Espasa-Calpe.

Fernàndez, Josep-Anton. 2000. *Another Country: Sexuality and National Identity in Catalan Gay Fiction.* MHRA Texts and Dissertations 50. Leeds: Maney for The Modern Humanities Research Association.

Fernández, Luis M. 1992. *El neorrealismo en la narración española de los años cincuenta.* Monografías da Universidade. Santiago de Compostela: Universidade de Santiago de Compostela.

Fernàndez, Lluís. 1979a. *L'anarquista nu.* El Balanci 13. Barcelona: Edicions 62.

——. 1979b. *El anarquista desnudo.* Contraseñas 19. Barcelona: Anagrama.

Fernández Cifuentes, Luis. 1982. *Teoría y mercado de la novela en España: Del 98 a la República.* Biblioteca Románica Hispánica: Estudios y Ensayos 321. Madrid: Gredos.

——. 1993. 'Fenomenología de la vanguardia: El caso de la novela', *Anales de Literatura Española* 9: 45–59.

Fernández Cubas, Cristina. 1988a. 'La ventana del jardín', in Fernández Cubas 1988b: 33–52.

——. 1988b. *Mi hermana Elba, y Los altillos de Brumal.* Andanzas. Barcelona: Tusquets.

——. 1990. *El ángulo del horror.* Andanzas 119. Barcelona: Tusquets.

——. 1994. *El año de Gracia.* Fábula 13. Barcelona: Tusquets.

Fernández Ferreiro, Xosé. 1981. *Corrupción e morte de Brigitte Bardot.* Montes e Fontes 21. Vigo: Xerais de Galicia.

——. 1982. *Reportaxe cósmico.* Sada: Castro.

——. 1989. *O minotauro.* Medusa: Narrativa. Barcelona: Sotelo Blanco.

——. 1991a. *A morte de Frank González.* [1975]. 2nd edn. Sada: Castro.

——. 1991b. *Agosto do 36.* Narrativa: Xerais de Galicia.

——. 1995. *Morrer en Castrelo de Miño* [1978]. 2nd edn. Vigo: Xerais de Galicia.

Fernández Florez, Wenceslao. 1924. *A miña mulher.* Lar 1. A Coruña: Tip. Moret.

Fernández del Riego, Francisco de. 1973. *Un país e unha cultura: A idea de Galicia nos nosos escritores.* Vigo: Artes Gráficas Galicia for Real Academia Gallega.

——. 1978. *Manual de historia da literatura galega* [1951]. Repr. Vigo: Galaxia, 1995.

Fernández Santos, Jesús. 1954. *Los bravos.* Ancora y Delfín 174. Barcelona: Destino.

——. 1957. *En la hoguera.* Espejo y Flor. Madrid: Anoli.

——. 1958. *Cabeza rapada.* Biblioteca Breve 136. Barcelona: Seix Barral.

——. 1964. *Laberintos.* Biblioteca Formentor. Barcelona: Seix Barral.

——. 1969. *El hombre de los santos.* Ancora y Delfín 320. Barcelona: Destino.

——. 1978. *Extramuros.* Barcelona: Argos Vergara.

Ferran de Pol, Lluís. 1960. *Érem quatre: Novel.la.* Biblioteca Catalana de Novel.la 15. Barcelona : Club.

Ferraté, Joan. 1992. 'Deu anys de producció literaria', *El País*, 22 October.

Ferré Pavia, Carme. 2000. *Intel.lectualitat i cultura resistents: 'Serra d'Or', 1959–1977.* Cabrera de Mar: Galerada.

Ferreras, Juan I. 1970. *Tendencias de la novela española actual, 1931–1969: Seguidas de un catálogo de urgencia de novelas y novelistas de la posguerra española.* Paris: Ediciones Hispanoamericanas.

——. 1988. *La novela en el siglo XX (hasta 1939).* 2 vols. Historia Crítica de la Literatura Española 22–23. Madrid: Taurus.

Ferrés, Antonio. 1959. *La piqueta.* Ancora y Delfín 172. Barcelona: Destino.

—— and Armando López Salinas. 1960. *Caminando por las Hurdes.* Biblioteca Breve. Barcelona: Seix Barral.

Figueroa, Antón. 2001. *Nación, literatura, identidade: Comunicación literaria e campos sociais en Galicia.* Universitaria. Vigo: Edicións Xerais de Galicia.

Flint, Weston and Noma Flint. 1983. *Pío Baroja: Camino de perfección.* Critical Guides to Spanish Texts 37. London: Grant & Cutler/Tamesis.

Fole, Anxel *et al.* 1984. *Relatos de Medusa.* Barcelona: Sotelo Blanco.

Folkart, Jessica. 2002. *Angles on Otherness in Post-Franco Spain: The Fiction of Cristina Fernández Cubas.* Lewisburg PA: Bucknell University Press.

Font, Doménech. 2002. 'Dos no son siempre pareja', in Heredero 2002: 323–38.

Forrest, Gene S. 1977. 'El mundo antagónico de Terenci Moix'. *Hispania* (Worcester MA) 60: 927–35.

Fortes, José A. (ed.). 1984. *La novela joven de España*. Granada: Aula de Narrativa, Universidad de Granada.

——. 1996. 'Del 'realismo sucio' y otras imposturas en la novela española última'. *Ínsula* 589/590: 21, 27.

Foster, David. 1999. *Spanish Writers on Gay and Lesbian Themes: A Bio-critical Sourcebook*. Westport CT: Greenwood.

Foster, Hal. 1996. *The Return of the Real: The Avant-garde at the End of the Century*. Cambridge MA: MIT.

Foucault, Michel. 1976–84. *The History of Sexuality*. 3 vols. Tr. Robert Hurley. New York: Vintage.

——. 1988. 'What is an author?', in Lodge 1988: 197–210.

Fouz-Hernández, Santiago. 2000. '¿Generación X?: Spanish Urban Youth Culture at the End of the Century in Mañas's Armendáriz's *Historias del Kronen*', *Romance Studies* 18: 83–98.

Fox, E. Inman. 1992. *Azorín: Guía de la obra completa*. Literatura y Sociedad 52. Madrid: Castalia.

Foxá, Agustín. 1938. *Madrid de Corte a checa*. San Sebastián: Librería Internacional.

Frank, Joseph. 1952. 'Spatial Form in the Modern Novel', in Aldridge 1952: 43–66.

Freixanes, Víctor. 1982. *O triángulo inscrito na circunferencia*. Vigo: Galaxia.

Freixas, Laura (ed.). 1996. *Madres e hijas*. Narrativas Hispánicas 195. Barcelona: Anagrama.

Freixeiro Mato, Xosé R. 1995. 'A lingua en Rafael Dieste', in Axeitos 1995: 137–88.

Friedman, Norman. 1955. 'Point of View in Fiction: The Development of a Critical Concept', *PMLA* 70 (1955): 1160–84.

Frye, Northrop. 1973. *Anatomy of Criticism: Four Essays* [1957]. Princeton NJ: Princeton University Press.

Fuentes, Víctor. 2003. *Clarín y Buñuel* = <http://cvc.cervantes.es/actcult/clarin/catalogo/articulos/fuentes01.htm.>

Fuguet, Albert. 1991. *Mala onda*. Biblioteca del Sur. Buenos Aires: Planeta.

Fuster, Jaume. 1972. *De mica en mica s'omple la pica*. El Balancí 76. Barcelona: Edicions 62.

Gabilondo, Joseba. 1999. 'Before Babel: Global Media, Ethnic Hybridity, and Enjoyment in Basque Culture', *Revista Internacional de Estudios Vascos* 44/i: 7–49.

——. 2000. 'Bernardo Atxaga's Seduction: On the Symbolic Economy of Postcolonial and Postnational Literatures in the Global Market', in Douglass *et al.* 1999: 106–33.

——. 2007. 'Olvidar a Galíndez: Violencia, otredad y memoria histórica en la globalización hispano-atlántica', in Colmeiro 2007: 159–83.

Gala, Antonio. 1993. *La pasión turca*. 3rd edn. Autores Españoles e Hispanoamericanos. Barcelona: Planeta.

Galerstein, Carolyn L. and Kathleen McNerney (eds). 1986. *Women Writers of*

Spain: An Annotated Bio-bibliographical Guide. Bibliographies and Indexes in Women's Studies 2. New York and Westport CT: Greenwood.

García de Cortázar, Fernando. 2003. *Los mitos de la historia de España*. Historia y Sociedad. Barcelona: Planeta.

García Fernández, Carlos J. 2002. *Contrasentidos: Acercamiento a la novela española contemporánea*. Trópica: Anexos de Tropelías 10. Zaragoza: Tropelías.

García Galiano, Ángel and Andrés Sánchez Magro. 2001. 'Narrativa española de los noventa', *Reseña* 277: 2–6.

García Morales, Adelaida. 1985. *El Sur, seguido de Bene*. Narrativas Hispánicas 21. Barcelona: Anagrama.

——. 1985. *El silencio de las sirenas*. Narrativas Hispánicas 28. Barcelona: Anagrama.

——. 1990. *La lógica del vampiro*. Narrativas Hispánicas 95. Barcelona: Anagrama.

García Negro, Pilar. 1999. *Sempre en galego* [1993]. 2nd edn. Ensaio 25. Santiago de Compostela: Laiovento.

García de Nora, Eugenio. 1963–70. *La novela española contemporánea (1898–1927)*. 2nd edn. 2 vols. Madrid: Gredos.

García Pavón, Francisco. 1999. *Las hermanas coloradas*. Ed. José F. Colmeiro. Clásicos Contemporáneos Comentados 30. Barcelona: Destino.

Garino Abel, Laurence. 1998. 'Eduardo Mendoza', in Bussière-Perrin 1998: I. 223–246.

Garrido, Vicente. 2000. *El psicópata: Un camaleón en la sociedad actual*. Sin Fronteras 4. Alzira: Algar.

Genette, Gerard. 1972. *Nouveau discours du récit*. Paris: Éditions du Seuil.

Gies, David T. (ed.). 1999. *The Cambridge Companion to Modern Spanish Culture*. Cambridge and New York: Cambridge University Press.

—— (ed.). 2004. *The Cambridge History of Spanish Literature*. Cambridge and New York: Cambridge University Press.

Gil-Albert, Juan. 1974. *Valentín: Homenaje a William Shakespeare*. Serie del Volador. Mexico City: J. Mortiz.

——. 1975. *Heraclés: Sobre una manera de ser* [1955]. Ensayo Humanístico 17. Madrid: J. Betancor.

——. 1979. *Razonamiento inagotable, con una cartafinal*. Héroe 2. Madrid: Caballo Griego.

——. 1981. *Los arcángeles: Parábola*. Laia 23. Barcelona: Laia.

——. 1984. *Fuentes de la constancia* [1972]. Ed. José C. Rovira. Letras Hispánicas 205. Madrid: Cátedra.

——. 1989. *Tobeyo, o Del amor*. Pre-Textos 114. Valencia: Pre-Textos.

Gil Casado, Pablo. 1973. *La novela social española, 1920–1971* [1968]. 2nd edn. Barcelona: Seix Barral.

——. 1977. *El paralelepípedo*. Nueva Narrativa Hispánica. Mexico: Joaquín Mortiz.

——. 1981. '*Makbara* es un cementerio', *Cuadernos Americanos* 239 (Nov.–Dec.): 217–26.

——. 1990. *La novela deshumanizada española (1958–1988)*. Barcelona: Anthropos.

Gilligan, Carol. 1982. *In a Different Voice: Psychological Theory and Women's Development*. Cambridge MA: Harvard University Press.

Gimferrer, Pere. 1985. *Cine y literatura*. Ensayo 32. Barcelona: Planeta.

Giorgio, Adalgisa (ed.). 2002. *Writing Mothers and Daughters: Renegotiating the Mother in Western European Narratives by Women*. New York: Berghahn.

Gironella, José M. 1962. *Un millón de muertos* [1961]. Barcelona: Planeta.

——. 2003. *Los cipreses creen en Dios* [1953]. Barcelona: Planeta.

Glenn, Kathleen M. 1973. *The Novelistic Technique of Azorín (José Martínez Ruiz)*. Plaza Mayor Scholar 22. Madrid: Playor.

——. 1981. *Azorín (José Martínez Ruiz)*. TWAS 604. Boston: Twayne.

Godsland, Shelley (ed.). 2002. 'La novela criminal femenina', *Letras Femeninas* 28/i (special number): 11–173.

—— and Stewart King. 2006. 'Crimes Present, Motives Past: A Function of National History in the Contemporary Spanish Detective Novel', *Clues* 24/iii: 30–40.

—— and Nickianne Moody (eds). 2004. *Reading the Popular in Contemporary Spanish Texts*. Monash Romance Studies. Newark DE: University of Delaware.

Gómez Mesa, José L. 1978. *La literatura española en el cine nacional, 1907–1877: Documentación y crítica*. Madrid: Filmoteca Nacional de España.

Gómez Sánchez, Anxo and Mercedes Queixas Zas. 2000. *Historia xeral da literatura galega*. Vigo: A Nosa Terra.

Gómez de la Serna, Ramón. 1916. *La viuda blanca y negra*. Madrid: Biblioteca Nueva.

——. 1920. *Toda la historia de la Puerta del Sol*. Madrid.

——. 1923a. *El chalet de las rosas*. Valencia: Sempere.

——. 1923b. *Cinelandia*. Valencia: Sempere.

——. 1925. *La casa triangular*. Madrid: Revista de Occidente.

——. 1945. *Greguerías, 1940–1945*. Austral 143. Buenos Aires: Espasa-Calpe.

——. 1948. *Automoribundia, 1888–1948*. Buenos Aires: Sudamericana.

——. 1975. *Ismos*. Punto Omega: Literatura Moderna 197. Madrid: Guadarrama.

——. 1981. *Descubrimiento de Madrid*. Ed. Tomás Borrás. 3rd edn. Madrid: Cátedra.

——. 2003. *Dalí*. Madrid: Espasa-Calpe.

Gonsar, Camilo (pseudonym of Camilo González Suárez-Llanos). 1984. *Como calquera outro día* [1962]. Montes e Fontes 49. Vigo: Xerais de Galicia.

——. 1987. *A desfeita (semirreportaxe)* [1983]. 2nd edn. Prologue Xavier Rodríguez Baixeras. Vigo: Xerais de Galicia.

——. 2003. *A noite da aurora*. Vigo: Galaxia.

——. 2007. *Cara a Times Square* [1980]. Vigo: Xerais de Galicia.

González-Millán, Xoan. 1991. *Silencio, parodia e subversión: Cinco ensaios sobre narrativa galega contemporánea*. Universitaria. Vigo: Xerais de Galicia.

——. 1994. *Literatura e sociedade en Galicia, 1975–1990*. Universitaria. Vigo: Xerais de Galicia.

——. 1996. *A narrativa galega actual (1975–84): Unha historia social.* Universitaria. Vigo: Xerais de Galicia.

——. 2002. 'El exilio gallego y el discurso de la restauración nacional', *Arizona Journal of Hispanic Cultural Studies* 6: 7–25.

Goytisolo, Juan. 1954. *Juegos de manos.* Ancora y Delfín 104. Barcelona: Destino.

——. 1955. *Duelo en el Paraíso.* Ancora y Delfín 183. Barcelona: Destino.

——. 1959. *Problemas de la novela.* Biblioteca Breve 141. Barcelona: Seix Barral

——. 1970. *Reivindicación del Conde don Julián.* Barcelona: Seix Barral.

——. 1975. *Juan sin tierra.* Biblioteca Breve 378. Barcelona: Seix Barral.

——. 1976. *Señas de identidad.* Biblioteca Breve; Mayor 32. Barcelona: Seix Barral. Repr. 1976, 1977.

——. 1978. *Libertad, libertad, libertad.* Ibérica 8. Barcelona: Anagrama.

——. 1980. *Makbara.* Biblioteca Breve 453. Barcelona: Seix Barral.

——. 1982. *Paisajes después de la batalla.* Visió Tundali: Contemporáneos 18. Barcelona: Montesinos.

——. 1985 *Coto vedado.* Biblioteca Breve 665. Barcelona: Seix Barral.

——. 1988. *Las virtudes del pájaro solitario.* Biblioteca Breve. Barcelona: Seix Barral.

Goytisolo, Luis. 1973. *Recuento,* Biblioteca Breve 358. Barcelona: Seix Barral.

——. 1988. *Fábulas* [1981]. Literatura 250. Madrid: Alfaguara.

Gracia García, Jordi. 2000. *Los nuevos nombres, 1975–2000: Primer suplemento.* Historia y Crítica de la Literatura Española 9/i, supplement. Barcelona: Crítica.

——. 2001. *Hijos de la razón: Contraluces de la libertad en las letras españolas de la democracia.* El Puente. Barcelona: Edhasa.

Graham, Helen and Jo Labanyi (eds). 1995. *Spanish Cultural Studies, an Introduction: The Struggle for Modernity.* Oxford and New York: Oxford University Press.

—— and Antonio Sánchez. 1995. 'The politics of 1992', in Graham and Labanyi 1995: 406–18.

Grandes, Almudena. 1989. *Las edades de Lulú.* La Sonrisa Vertical 61. Barcelona: Tusquets.

——. 1994. *Malena es un nombre de tango.* Andanzas 211. Barcelona: Tusquets.

Grossberg, Lawrence. 1984. 'I'd Rather Feel Bad than not Feel Anything at All', *Enclitic* 8: 94–111.

Grosso, Alfonso. 1961a. *La zanja.* Ancora y Delfín 199. Barcelona: Destino.

——. 1961b. *Un cielo difícilmente azul.* Biblioteca Formentor. Barcelona: Seix Barral.

——. 1963. *Testa de copo.* Biblioteca Formentor. Barcelona: Seix Barral.

——. 1966. *El capirote.* Serie del Volador. Mexico City: Joaquín Mortiz.

Guasch, Oscar. 1991. *La sociedad rosa.* Argumentos 122. Barcelona: Anagrama.

Gubern, Román. 1981. *La censura: Función política y ordenamiento jurídico bajo el franquismo (1836–1975)*. Historia, Ciencia y Sociedad 166. Barcelona: Península.

——. 1997. *Viaje de ida*. Biblioteca de la Memoria 14. Barcelona: Anagrama.

——. 1999. *Proyector de luna: La generación del 27 y el cine*. Argumentos 231. Barcelona: Anagrama.

——. 2002. 'Mirando hacia otro lado: Literatura y cine en los años cuarenta', in Heredero 2002: 57–76.

Guillamón, Julià. 2001. *La ciutat interrompuda: de la contracultura a la Barcelona posolímpica*. Barcelona: La Magrana.

Guillén, Claudio. 1995. 'Lo uno con lo diverso: Literatura y complejidad', *1616: Anuario de la Sociedad Española de Literatura General y Comparada 9:* 51–66.

——. 1998. *Múltiples moradas. Ensayo de literatura comparada*. Barcelona: Tusquets

Guirao, Olga. 1992. *Mi querido Sebastián*. Narrativas Hispánicas 135. Barcelona: Anagrama.

Gullón, Agnes and Germán Gullón (eds). 1974. *Teoría de la novela (aproximaciones hispánicas)*. Persiles 75. Madrid: Taurus.

Gullón, Germán. 1992. *La novela moderna en España (1995–1902): Los albores de la modernidad*. Persiles 204. Madrid: Taurus.

——. 1996. 'Cómo se lee una novela de la última generación (apartado X)', *Ínsula* 589/590: 31–33.

——. 2004. *Los mercaderes en el templo de la literatura*. Barcelona: Caballo de Troya.

——. 2006. *La modernidad silenciada: La cultura española en torno a 1900* . Biblioteca Otras Eutopías 26. Madrid: Biblioteca Nueva.

Gullón, Ricardo. 1964. *Autobiografías de Unamuno*. Biblioteca Románica Hispánica: Estudios y Ensayos 76. Madrid: Gredos.

——. 1969. *La invención del 98 y otros ensayos*. Biblioteca Románica Hispánica: Campo Abierto 23. Madrid: Gredos.

——. 1979. *Psicologías del autor y lógicas del personaje*. Persiles 109. Madrid: Taurus.

——. 1980. *Espacio y novela*. Ensayo 8. Barcelona: A. Bosch.

——. 1983a. *El cosmos de Antagonía: Incursiones en la obra de Luis Goytisolo*. Prologue Salvador Clotas. Barcelona: Anagrama.

——. 1983b. 'Un texto de aire y de fuego', in Gullón 1983a: 49–73.

——. 1984. *La novela lírica*. Crítica y Estudios Literarios. Madrid: Cátedra.

——. 1994. *La novela española contemporánea: Ensayos críticos*. Alianza Universidad 796. Madrid: Alianza.

—— et al. 1979. [Special number on the novel], *Ínsula* 396/397 (Nov.–Dec.): 1–22.

—— et al. 1989. [Special number on the novel], *Ínsula* 512/513.

Hall, Peter G. 1998. *Cities in Civilization*. New York: Pantheon.

Hardin. James N. (ed.). 1991. *Reflection and Action: Essays on the Bildungsroman*. Columbia SC: University of South Carolina Press.

Hare, Robert D. 1999. *Without Conscience*. New York: Guildford.

Harrison, Joseph and Alan Hoyle (eds). 2000. *Spain's 1898 Crisis: Regeneration, Modernism, Post-colonialism*. Manchester and New York: Manchester University Press.

Hart, Patricia. 1987. *The Spanish Sleuth: The Detective in Spanish Fiction*. Rutherford: Fairleigh Dickinson University Press.

Hart, Stephen M. (ed.). 1988. *No pasarán: Art, Literature, and the Spanish Civil War*. Támesis A 86. London: Tamesis.

——. 1993. *White ink: Essays on Twentieth-century Feminine Fiction in Spain and Latin America*. Támesis A 156. London: Tamesis.

Haubrich, Walter. 1986. 'Angst für neuen Wunden. Spanien erinnert sich seines Bürgerkrieges', *Frankfurter Allgemeine Zeitung*. 4 August.

Havard, Robert (ed.). 2004. *Companion to Spanish Surrealism*. Támesis A 206. Woodbridge: Tamesis.

Henseler, Christine. 2003. *Contemporary Spanish Women's Narrative and the Publishing Industry*. Hispanisms. Urbana IL: University of Illinois Press.

—— and Randolph D. Pope (eds). 2007. *Generation X Rocks: Contemporary Fiction, Film, and Rock Culture*. Hispanic Issues 33. Nashville TN: Vanderbilt University Press.

Heredero, Carlos (ed.). 2002. *La imprenta dinámica: Literatura española en el cine español*, Cuadernos de la Academia 11/12. Madrid: Academia de las Artes y las Ciencias Cinematográficas de España.

Hermida García, Modesto. 1995. *Narrativa galega: Tempo do rexurdimento*. Xerais Universitaria. Vigo: Xerais de Galicia.

Hernández Les, Juan A. 2005. *Cine y literatura: Una metáfora visual*. Imágenes. Madrid: Ediciones JC.

Heron, Liz (ed.). 1993. *City Women: Stories of the World's Great Cities*. Boston MA: Beacon.

Herrera y Garrido, Francisca. 1925. *Martes de Antroido*. Lar 6. A Coruña: [s.n.].

——. 1981. *Néveda* [1920]. Montes e Fontes 19. Vigo: Xerais de Galicia.

Herzberger, David K. 1995. *Narrating the past: Fiction and Historiography in Postwar Spain*. Durham NC: Duke University Press.

Hiriart, Rosario. 1972. *Los recursos técnicos en la obra de Francisco Ayala*. Madrid: Ínsula.

Holloway, Vance. 1999. *El posmodernismo y otras tendencias de la novela española (1967–1995)*. Espiral Hispanoamericana 36. Madrid: Fundamentos.

Hooper, John. 1995. *The New Spaniards*. London: Penguin Books.

Hopewell, John. 1986. *Out of the Past: Spanish Cinema after Franco*. London: British Film Institute.

Hughes, Robert. 1992. *Barcelona*. New York: Alfred A. Knopf.

Humphrey, Robert. 1968. *Stream of Consciousness and the Modern Novel* [1954]. Berkeley CA: University of California Press.

Hutcheon, Linda. 1988. *A Poetics of Postmodernism: History, Theory, Fiction*. New York and London: Routledge.

Ilie, Paul. 1968. *The Surrealist Mode in Spanish Literature: An Interpretation of Basic Trends from Post-romanticism to the Spanish Vanguard.* Ann Arbor: University of Michigan Press.

——. 1980. *Literature and Inner Exile: Authoritarian Spain, 1939–1975.* Baltimore MA: Johns Hopkins University Press.

Inglehart, Ronald *et al.* 1990–97. *World Values Surveys and European Values Surveys, 1981–1984, 1990–1993, and 1995–1997.* CSM: UC Berkeley <http://nds.umdl.umich.edu/w/wevs/wevs.htm>.

—— *et al.* 2004. *Human Beliefs and Values: A Cross-cultural Sourcebook Based on the 1999–2002 Values Surveys.* Mexico City: Siglo XXI.

Irisarri, Ángeles de and Magdalena Lasala. 2002. *Moras y cristianas* [1998]. 9th edn. Barcelona: Salamandra.

Irizarry, Estelle. 1971. *Teoría y creación en Francisco Ayala.* Biblioteca Románica Hispánica: Estudios y Ensayos 151. Madrid: Gredos.

——. 1979. *Rafael Dieste.* TWAS 554. Boston: Twayne.

Iser, Wolfgang. 1974. *The Implied Reader: Patterns of Communication in Prose Fiction from Bunyan to Beckett.* Baltimore MA: Johns Hopkins University Press.

Iturralde, Juan. 2000. *Días de llamas* [1979]. Madrid: Debate.

Izquierdo, José M. 2001. 'Narradores españoles novísimos de los años noventa', *Revista de Estudios Hispánicos* 35: 293–308.

Jaime, Antoine. 2000. *Literatura y cine en España, 1975–1995.* Tr. María Pérez Harguindey and Manuel Talens. Signo e Imagen. Madrid: Cátedra.

Jakobson, Roman. 1973. *Questions de poétique.* Poétique. Paris: Éditions du Seuil.

James, Henry. 2003. *Otra vuelta de tuerca.* Tr. José Bianco. Escolar de Literatura. Madrid: Siruela.

Jameson, Fredric. 1981. *Postmodernism, or The Cultural Logic of Late Capitalism.* Durham NC: Duke University Press,.

Japtok, Martin. 2005. *Growing Up Ethnic: Nationalism and the Bildungsroman in African American and Jewish American Fiction.* Iowa City IA: University of Iowa Press.

Jarnés, Benjamín. 1926. *El profesor inútil.* Madrid: Revista de Occidente.

——. 1928. *El convidado de piedra: Novela* [1924]. Madrid: Historia Nueva.

——. 1929a. *Paula y Paulita: Novela.* Madrid: Revista de Occidente.

——. 1929b. *Locura y muerte de nadie: Novela.* Madrid: Oriente.

——. 1930. *Teoría del zumbel: Novela.* Madrid: Espasa-Calpe.

Jauss, Hans R. 1976. *La literatura como provocación.* Ediciones de Bolsillo 483. Barcelona: Península.

Jeffers, Thomas L. 2005. *Apprenticeships: The Bildungsroman from Goethe to Santayana.* New York and Basingstoke: Palgrave MacMillan.

Jiménez Aleixandre, Marilar. 1993. *Tránsito dos gramáticos.* Narrativa. Vigo: Xerais de Galicia.

——. 1998. *A compañía clandestina de contrapublicidade.* Literatura 151. Vigo: Galaxia.

——. 2001a. *Unha presa de terra.* Vigo: Indo Imp.

——. 2001b. *Teoría do caos.* Narrativa 169. Vigo: Xerais de Galicia.

——. 2003. *A banda sen futuro* [1999]. Fora de Xogo 40. Vigo: Xerais de Galicia.

Johnson, Roberta. 1993. *Crossfire: Philosophy and the Novel in Spain, 1900–1934*. Studies in Romance Languages 35. Lexington KY: University Press of Kentucky.

——. 1999. 'Narrative in culture, 1868–1936', in Gies 1999: 123–33.

——. 2003. *Gender and Nation in the Spanish Modernist Novel*. Nashville TN: Vanderbilt University Press.

Jordan, Barry. 1990. *Writing and Politics in Franco's Spain*. London and New York: Routledge.

——. 1995. 'The Emergence of a Dissident Intelligentsia', in Graham and Labanyi 1995: 245–55.

—— and Rikki Morgan-Tamosunas (eds). 2000. *Contemporary Spanish Cultural Studies*. London: Arnold and New York: Oxford University Press.

Juaristi, Jon. 1987. *Literatura vasca*. Historia Crítica de la Literatura Hispánica 29. Madrid: Taurus.

——. 1999. *El chimbo expiatorio: La invención de la tradición bilbaina, 1876–1939*. Fórum: Ensayo y Pensamiento. Madrid: Espasa-Calpe.

Jurkevich, Gayana. 1991. *The Elusive Self: Archetypal Approaches to the Novels of Miguel de Unamuno*. Columbia MO: University of Missouri Press.

——. 1999. *In Pursuit of the Natural Sign: Azorín and the Poetics of Ekphrasis*. Lewisburg PA: Bucknell University Press.

Kafka, Franz. 1971a. 'The Care of the Family Man', in Kafka 1971b: 427–29.

——. 1971b. *The Complete Stories*. Ed. Nahum N. Glatzer. New York: Schocken.

Keating, Michael. 1996. *Nations against the State: The New Politics of Nationalism in Quebec, Catalonia, and Scotland*. New York: St. Martin's Press.

Kelly, Dorothy, 2000. 'Selling Spanish "Otherness" since the 1960s', in Jordan and Morgan-Tamosunas 2000: 29–37.

King, Stewart. 2003. 'Condenada a la modernidad: Memoria e identidad cultural en la novela criminal gallega', in Sibbald *et al.* 2003: 183–93.

——. 2005. ' "Un personaje genuinamente español": National Discourses in Jorge Martínez Reverte's *Gálvez en Euskadi*', *Hispanic Research Journal* 6/i: 29–38.

Kirkpatrick, Susan. 2003. *Mujer, modernismo y vanguardia en España, 1898–1931*. Tr. Jacqueline Cruz. Feminismos 73. Madrid: Cátedra.

Kortazar, Jon. 1998. *Literatura vasca: Siglo XX*. Donostia/San Sebastián: Etor.

——. 1999. *La pluma y la tierra: Poesía vasca contemporánea, 1978–1995*. Las Tres Sorores 3. Zaragoza: Prames.

——. 2003. *Literatura vasca desde la transición: Bernardo Atxaga*. Biblioteca Crítica de las Literaturas Hispánicas 5. Madrid: Ediciones del Orto and Minneapolis MN: University of Minnesota.

Krauel, Ricardo. 2001. *Voces desde el silencio: Heterologías genérico-sexuales en la narrativa española moderna, 1875–1975*. Universidad 26. Madrid: Libertarias.

Krause, Anna. 1955. *Azorín, el pequeño filósofo: Indagaciones en el origen de una personalidad literaria.* Tr. Luis Rico Navarro. Prologue Amancio Martínez Ruiz. Madrid: Espasa-Calpe.

Kristeva, Julia. 1972. *Semeiotike/Semiótica.* Tr. José Martín Arancibia. 2nd edn. 2 vols. Espiral 25–26. Madrid: Fundamentos.

Kurlansky, Mark. 2001. *The Basque History of the World* [1999]. New York: Penguin.

Kushigian, Julia A. 2003. *Reconstructing Childhood: Strategies of Reading for Culture and Gender in the Spanish American Bildungsroman.* Bucknell Studies in Latin American Literature and Theory. Lewisburg PA: Bucknell University Press.

Labanyi, Jo. 1985. *Ironía e historia en 'Tiempo de silencio'.* Persiles 162. Madrid: Taurus.

——. 1989. *Myth and History in the Contemporary Spanish Novel.* Cambridge and New York: Cambridge University Press.

——. 1999. 'Narrative in Culture, 1975–1996', in Gies 1999: 147–162.

—— (ed.). 2002. *Constructing Identity in Contemporary Spain: Theoretical Debates and Cultural Practice.* Oxford: Oxford University Press.

Lacarta, Manuel. 1986. *Madrid y sus literaturas.* Madrid: Avapiés.

Lacruz, Mario. 1984. *El inocente.* Tus Libros Policiacos 46. Madrid: Anaya.

Laforet, Carmen. 1945. *Nada,* Barcelona: Destino.

——. *La insolación.* 1963. 3rd edn. Tres Pasos Fuera del Tempo 1. Barcelona: Planeta.

Lain Entralgo, Pedro (ed.). 1992. *La Edad de Plata de la cultura española (1898–1936).* 2 vols. Historia de España, ed. Ramón Menéndez Pidal, XXXIX. Madrid: Espasa-Calpe,

Landeira, Richard and Luis T. González del Valle (eds). 1987. *Nuevos y novísimos: Algunas perspectivas críticas sobre la narrativa española desde la década de los sesenta.* Boulder CO: Society of Spanish and Spanish American Studies.

Lanz, Juan J. 1993. *La luz inextinguible: Ensayos sobre literatura vasca actual.* Lingüística y Teoría Literaria. Madrid: Siglo XXI.

Larra, Mariano José de. 1998a. 'El Día de difuntos de 1836', in Larra 1988b: 469–78.

——. 1998b. *Artículos de costumbres.* Ed. Luis F. Díaz Larrios. 10th edn. Austral 99. Madrid: Espasa-Calpe.

Larson, Susan and Eva M. Woods (eds). 2005. *Visualizing Spanish Modernity.* Oxford and New York: Berg.

La Rubia Prado, Francisco. 1996. *Alegorías de la voluntad: Pensamiento orgánico, retórica y deconstrucción en la obra de Miguel de Unamuno.* Universidad 18. Madrid: Libertarias/Prodhufi.

——. 1999. *Unamuno y la vida como ficción.* Biblioteca Románica Hispánica: Estudios y Ensayos 412. Madrid: Gredos.

Lasagabaster Madinabeitia, Jesús M. (ed.). 1990. *Contemporary Basque fiction: An anthology.* The Basque Series. Reno NV: University of Nevada Press.

——. 2002. *Las literaturas de los vascos.* Ed. Ana Toledo Lezeta. Donostia/San Sebastián: Universidad de Deusto.

Lecuona Lerchundi, Lourdes. 1993. *Presencia de lo inglés en Pío Baroja*. Monografías 36. San Sebastián: Instituto Dr Camino.

Lehan, Richard D. 1998. *The City in Literature: An Intellectual and Cultural History*. Berkeley CA: University of California Press.

Lera, Ángel M. de. 1957. *Los olvidados: Novela*. Madrid: Aguilar.

——. 1958. *Los clarines del miedo*. Ancora y Delfín 143. Barcelona: Destino.

——. 1960. *Bochorno*. Novela Nueva. Madrid: Aguilar.

——. 1963. *Hemos perdido el sol*. Novela Nueva. Madrid: Aguilar.

——. 1964. *Tierra para morir, y las cien casas cerradas no se abrirán ya nunca*. Novela Nueva. Madrid: Aguilar.

Lesta Meis, Xosé. 1981. *Estebo* [1927]. Ed. Benito Varela Jácome. Montes e Fontes 18. Vigo: Xerais de Galicia.

——. *Manecho o da rúa* [1926]. Froita do Tempo 7. Vigo: A Nosa Terra.

Levinas, Emmanuel. 1995a. 'La proximité d'autre', in Levinas 1995b: 10–19.

——. 1995b. *Alterité et transcendance*. Preface Pierre Hyayat. Saint-Clément-la-Rivière: Fata Morgana.

——. *Alterity and Transcendence*. 1999. Tr. Michael Smith. New York: Columbia University Press.

Levine, Linda G. 1976. *Juan Goytisolo: La destrucción creadora*. Confrontaciones. Mexico: Joaquín Mortiz.

—— and Ellen E. Marson (eds). 1997. *Proyecciones sobre la novela: Actas del XIV congreso de literatura latinoamericana, Montclair State University*. Montclair NJ and Hanover NH; Ediciones del Norte.

——, ——, and Gloria Waldman (eds). 1993. *Spanish Women Writers: A Bio-bibliographical Source Book*. Westport CT: Greenwood.

Lewis. Tom. 1994. 'Aesthetics and Politics: Afterword', in López *et al*. 1994.

Livingstone, Leon. 1970. *Tema y forma en las novelas de Azorín*. Biblioteca Románica Hispánica: Estudios y Ensayos 141. Madrid: Gredos.

Lizarraga, Xavier *et al*. 1978. *El homosexual ante la sociedad enferma*. Ed. José Ramón Enríquez. Acracia 25. Barcelona: Tusquets.

Llamas, Ricardo. 1998. *Teoría torcida: Prejuicios y discursos en torno a 'la homosexualidad'*. Teoría. Madrid: Siglo XXI.

—— and Francisco Javier Vidarte. 1999. *Homografías*. Madrid: Espasa-Calpe.

Llarena Rosales, Alicia. 1996. 'Claves para una discusión: El "realismo mágico" y "lo real maravilloso americano"', *Inti* 43/44: 21–44.

Lodge, David (ed.). 1988. *Modern Criticism and Theory: A Reader*. London and New York: Longman.

——. 1990. *After Bakhtin: Essays on Fiction and Criticism*. London and New York: Routledge.

——. 1994. *The Art of Fiction: Illustrated from Classic and Modern Texts* [1992]. London: Penguin.

——. 2002. *Consciousness and the Novel: Connected Essays* London: Secker & Warburg.

Longhurst, Carlos A. 1974. *Las novelas históricas de Pío Baroja*. Punto Omega 171. Madrid: Guadarrama.

——. 1977. *Pío Baroja: El mundo es ansí*. Critical Guides to Spanish Texts 20. London: Grant & Cutler/Tamesis.

López, Silvia L., Jenaro Talens, and Darío Villanueva (eds). 1994. *Critical Practices in Post-Franco Spain*. Hispanic Issues 11. Minneapolis MN: University of Minnesota Press, 1994.

López-Cabrales, María del Mar. 2000. *Palabras de mujeres: Escritoras españolas contemporáneas*. Colección Mujeres. Madrid: Narcea.

López-Criado, Fidel. 1998. *El erotismo en la novela ramoniana*. Espiral Hispanoamericana 9. Madrid: Fundamentos.

López Ferreiro, Antonio. 1978. *O niño de pombas* [1905]. Santiago de Compostela: Universidade de Santiago, Departmento de Filoloxía Galega.

——. 1996. *O castelo de Pambre* [1895]. A Nosa Literatura 16. Vigo: Asociación Socio-Pedagóxica Galega.

——. 2001. *A tecedeira de Bonaval* [1894]. Biblioteca Galega 120: 9. A Coruña: Voz de Galicia.

López-Morillas, Juan. 1972. *Hacia el 98: Literatura, sociedad, ideología*. Letras e Ideas: Minor 2. Barcelona: Ariel.

López-Pacheco, Jesús. 1958. *Central eléctrica*. Ancora y Delfín 149. Barcelona: Destino.

——. 1961a. *Canciones del amor prohibido*. Colección Colliure. Barcelona: Literaturasa.

——. 1961b. *Mi corazón se llama Cudillero*. Mieres: El Ventanal.

——. 1973. *La hoja de parra*. Nueva Narrativa Hispánica. Mexico: Joaquín Mortiz.

López Salinas, Armando. 1960a. *Año tras año*. Paris: Ruedo Ibérico.

——. 1960b. *La mina*. Ancora y Delfin 180. Barcelona: Destino.

Loriga, Ray. 1992. *Lo peor de todo*. Literatura 102. Madrid: Debate.

——. 1995. *Caídos del cielo*. Ave Fénix: Mayor 27. Barcelona: Plaza & Janés.

——. 2003. *Héroes* [1993]. Barcelona: Random House Mondadori.

Lott, Robert E. 1981. 'Sobre el método narrativo y el estilo en las novelas de Azorín', in Villanueva 1983: 64–91.

Lough, Francis (ed.). 2000. *Hacia la novela nueva: Essays on the Spanish Avantgarde Novel*. Oxford and New York: Peter Lang.

Lukács, György. 1976. *La novela histórica*. Tr. Manuel Sacristán. Obras Completas de György Lukács 9. Barcelona: Grijalbo.

Lyon, John E. 1979. 'Don Pedro's Complicity: An Existential Dimension of *Tiempo de silencio*', *Modern Language Review* 74: 69–78.

Lyotard, Jean-François. 1988. *The Differend: Phrases in Dispute*. Tr. Georges van den Abbeele. Theory and History of Litterature 46. Minneapolis MN: University of Minnesota Press.

——. 1992. 'Answering the Question: What is Postmodernism?', in Waugh 1992a: 117–24.

McFarlane, Brian. 1996. *Novel to Film: An Introduction to the Theory of Adaptation*. Oxford and New York: Clarendon.

McNerney, Kathleen (ed.). 1999. *Voices and Visions: The Words and Works of Mercè Rodoreda*. Selinsgrove PA: Susquehanna University Press.

—— and Cristina Enríquez de Salamanca (eds). 1994. *Double Minorities of Spain: A Bio-bibliographic Guide to Women Writers of the Catalan, Galician, and Basque Countries.* New York: Modern Language Association of America.

—— and Nancy Vosburg (eds). 1994. *The Garden across the Border: Mercè Rodoreda's Fiction.* Selinsgrove PA: Susquehanna University Press.

Madrid, Juan. 1993. *Días contados.* Hispánica 99. Madrid: Alfaguara.

Maestre, Pedro. 1996. *Matando dinosaurios con tirachinas.* Ancora y Delfín 757. Barcelona; Destino.

Mainer, José-Carlos. 1980. *Modernismo y 98.* Historia y Crítica de la Literatura Española 6. Barcelona: Crítica, 1980.

——. 1981. *La Edad de Plata (1902–1939): Ensayo de interpretación de un proceso cultural.* Madrid: Cátedra.

——. 1994. *De postguerra, 1951–1990.* Filología. Barcelona: Crítica.

——. 2005. *Tramas, libros, nombres: Para entender la literatura española, 1944–2000.* Argumentos 333. Barcelona: Anagrama.

Mandrell, James. 2007. ' "Como un hombre invisible": El imposible objeto del deseo', in Colmeiro 2007: 143–55.

Manteiga, Robert C., Carolyn L. Galerstein, and Kathleen McNerney (eds). 1988. *Feminine Concerns in Contemporary Spanish Fiction by Women.* Scripta Humanistica 44. Potomac MD: Scripta Humanistica.

Mañas, José A. 1995. *Mensaka.* Ancora y Delfín 753. Barcelona: Destino.

——. 1999. *Historias del Kronen* [1994]. Ed. Germán Gullón. Barcelona: Destino.

Maragall, Pasqual. 1986. *Refent Barcelona.* Col.lecció Ramon Llull: Assaig 3. Barcelona: Planeta.

—— and Jaume Guillamet. 1991. *Barcelona: La ciutat retrobada.* Llibres a l'Abast 263. Barcelona: Edicions 62.

Maravall, Antonio. 1986. *La cultura del Barroco: Análisis de una estructura histórica* . Letras e Ideas: Studia. 4th edn. Barcelona: Ariel.

March, Kathleen N. (ed.). 1987. *First Galician Studies Conference: October 10–11, 1985, University of Maine, Orono, Maine.* Orono ME: University of Maine Press.

Marco, Joaquín, 1972. *La nueva literatura en España y América.* Palabra Seis 10. Barcelona: Lumen.

Marí, Jorge. 2003. *Lecturas espectaculares: El cine en la novela española desde 1970.* Universidad 29. Madrid: Libertarias.

Marías, Javier. 1994. *Todas las almas.* Narrativas Hispánicas 78. Barcelona: Anagrama.

Marías, Julián. 1994. *Consideración de Cataluña* [1966]. Barcelona: Acervo.

Marqués López, Antonio J. 2000. *Francisco García Pavón y su detective Plinio.* Tomelloso: Souvriet.

Marra-López, José R. 1963. *Narrativa española fuera de España, 1939–1961.* Crítica y Ensayo 39. Madrid: Guadarrama.

Marsé, Juan. 1966. *Últimas tardes con Teresa.* Biblioteca Breve. Barcelona: Seix Barral.

——. 1973. *Si te dicen que caí*. Mexico City: Novaro.

——. 1984. *Ronda del Guinardó*. Biblioteca Breve. Barcelona: Seix Barral.

——. 1987. *Teniente bravo*. Biblioteca Breve. Barcelona: Seix Barral.

——. 1991. *El amante bilingüe*. Autores Españoles e Hispanoamericanos. Barcelona: Planeta.

——. 1993. *El embrujo de Shangai*. Ave Fénix: Mayor 1. Barcelona: Plaza y Janés.

Marsh, Steven and Parvati Nair (eds). 2004. *Gender and Spanish Cinema*. Oxford and New York: Berg.

Martín, Andreu. 1980. *Prótesis*. Círculo del Crímen 21. Madrid: Sedmay.

——. 1983. *Si es no es*. Fábula 116. Barcelona: Planeta.

——. 1987. *Barcelona Connection*. Barcelona: Cosecha Roja.

Martín, Annabel. 2000. 'Modulations of the Basque Voice: An Interview with Bernardo Atxaga', *Journal of Spanish Cultural Studies* 1: 193–204.

Martín, Gregorio C. (ed). 1984. *Selected Proceedings: 32nd Mountain Interstate Foreign Language Conference*. Winston-Salem NC: Wake Forest University.

Martín Gaite, Carmen. 1957. *Entre visillos*. Ancora y Delfín 147. Barcelona: Destino.

——. 1960. *Las ataduras: Relatos*. Ancora y Delfín 185. Barcelona: Destino.

——. 1978. *El cuarto de atrás*. Ancora y Delfín 530. Barcelona: Destino.

——. 1987. *Usos amorosos de la postguerra española*. Argumentos 85. Barcelona: Anagrama.

——. 1994. *Esperando el porvenir: Homenaje a Ignacio Aldecoa*. Libros del Tiempo 73. Madrid: Siruela.

Martín Santos, Luis. 1962. *Tiempo de silencio*. Biblioteca Formentor. Barcelona: Seix Barral.

Martínez Cachero, José M. 1960. *Las novelas de Azorín*. Ínsula 37. Madrid: Ínsula.

——. 1979. *Historia de la novela española entre 1961 y 1975*. Literatura y Sociedad 20. Madrid: Castalia.

——. 1985. *La novela española entre 1936 y 1980: Historia de una aventura*. Literatura y Sociedad 37. Madrid: Castalia.

Martínez-Carazo, Cristina. 2006. *De la visualidad literaria a la visualidad fílmica: 'La Regenta' de Leopoldo Alas 'Clarín'*. Signos 2. Gijón: Llibros del Pexe.

Martínez-Expósito, Alfredo. 1998. *Los escribas furiosos: Configuraciones homoeróticas en la narrativa española actual*. Iberian Studies 27. New Orleans LA: University Press of the South.

——. 2004. *Escrituras torcidas: Ensayos de crítica 'queer'*. Rey de Bastos 44. Barcelona: Laertes.

Martínez Latre, María P. 1979. *La novela intelectual de Benjamín Jarnés*. Tesis Doctorales 34. Zaragoza: Institución 'Fernando el Católico'.

Martínez Oca, Xosé Manuel. 1983. *Beiramar*. Vigo: Xerais de Galicia.

Martínez Reverte, Jorge. 1979. *Demasiado para Gálvez: El caso 'Sérfico'*. Literatura. Madrid: Debate.

——. 1983. *Gálvez en Euskadi*. Contraseñas 50. Barcelona: Anagrama.

——. 1995. *Gálvez y el cambio del cambio.* Contraseñas 154. Barcelona: Anagrama.

——. 2001. *Gálvez en la frontera.* Barcelona: Anagrama.

——. 2005. *Gudari Gálvez.* Madrid: Espasa.

Martí-Olivella, Jaume (ed.). 1987. *Catalan Review* 2/ii [Special number dedicated to Mercè Rodoreda]: 1–278.

Marx, Karl. 1984a. 'Alienated Labor' in Marx 1984b: 130–44.

——. 1984b. *The Portable Karl Marx.* Ed. and tr. Eugene Kamenka. Harmondsworth: Penguin.

Mas, Ricard. 2006. 'De *La ben plantada* ...', *Avui*, 6 August.

Masma, Xan de (pseudonym of Patricio Delgado Luaces). 1993. *¡A besta!* [1899]. Narrativa de Onte 1. Vigo: Galaxia.

Massó, Enric. 1961. *Viure no és fàcil.* Barcelona: Selecta.

Massot i Montaner, Joan. 1979. 'La represa del llibre català a la postguerra', *Els Marges* 17: 82–102.

Mata Moncho Aguirre, Juan de. 1986. *Cine y literatura: La adaptación literaria en el cine español.* Valencia: Generalitat Valenciana.

Matute, Ana M. 1959. *Primera memoria* [*Los mercaderes*, 1]. Ancora y Delfín 179. Barcelona: Destino.

——. 1963. *Los soldados lloran de noche* [*Los mercaderes*, 2]. Ancora y Delfín 250. Barcelona: Destino.

——. 1969. *La trampa* [*Los mercaderes*, 3]. Ancora y Delfín 324. Barcelona: Destino.

——. 1971. *La torre vigía.* Palabra Seis 1. Barcelona: Lumen.

——. 1983. *Fiesta al noroeste* [1952]. Ancora y Delfín 246. Barcelona: Destino.

Mayans Natal, María-Jesús. 1984. 'El lenguaje del feminismo en la narrativa española contemporánea', in Martín 1984: 217–24.

Mayock, Ellen C. 2004. *The 'Strange Girl' in Twentieth-century Spanish Novels Written by Women.* New Orleans LA: University Press of the South.

Mechthild, Albert (ed.). 2005. *Vanguardia española e intermedialidad: Artes escénicas, cine y radio.* La Casa de la Riqueza 7. Madrid: Iberoamericana and Frankfurt am Main: Vervuert.

Medina Domínguez, Alberto. 2001. *Exorcismos de la memoria: Políticas y poéticas de la melancolía en la España de la transición.* Estudios Literarios: Universidad 27. Madrid: Ediciones Libertarias.

Medio, Dolores. 1953. *Nosotros los Rivero.* Ancora y Delfín 82. Barcelona: Destino.

——. 1956. *Funcionario público.* Ancora y Delfín 128. Barcelona: Destino.

Méndez Ferrín, Xosé Luis. 1976. *Antón e os inocentes.* Biblioteca de Autores Galegos 49–50. Vigo: Diario 16.

——. 1987. *Retorno a Tagen Ata* (1971). 2nd edn. Vigo: Xerais.

——. 1999a. *Arrabaldo do norte* (1964). Peto Literaria 15. Vigo: Xerais de Galicia.

——. 1999b. *No ventre do silencio.* Narrativa 150. Vigo: Xerais.

——. 2007. *Bretaña, Esmeraldina* (1987). Ed. Anxo Angueira Viturro. Clásicos 7. Vigo: Xerais.

Méndez Leite, Fernando. 1997. 'Adaptación cinematográfica de *La Regenta*'. *República de las Letras: Cine y literatura* 54: 147–56.

Mendicutti, Eduardo. 1974. *Cenizas*.

——. 1985. *El salto del angel*. Alcalá Narrativa 8. Madrid: Fundación Colegio del Rey.

——. 1987. *Siete contra Georgia*. Sonrisa vertical. Barcelona: Tusquets.

——. 1988a. *Una caricia para Rebeca Soler*. Cuento 8. San Sebastián: Caja de Guipúzcoa.

——. 1988b. *Una mala noche la tiene cualquiera*. Flauta Mágica 14. Barcelona: Tusquets.

——. 1989. *Tiempos mejores*. Flauta Mágica 18. Barcelona: Tusquets.

——. 1991a. *El palomo cojo*. Andanzas 145. Barcelona: Tusquets.

——. 1991b. *Última conversación*. Flauta Mágica 27. Barcelona: Tusquets.

——. 1993. *Los novios búlgaros*. Andanzas 203. Barcelona: Tusquets.

——. 1997. *Yo no tengo la culpa de haber nacido tan sexy*. Andanzas 313. Barcelona: Tusquets.

——. 2000. *El beso del cosaco*. Andanzas 401. Barcelona: Tusquets.

——. 2002. *El ángel decuidado*. Andanzas 484. Barcelona: Tusquets.

——. 2003a. *Duelo en Marilyn City*. Madrid: La Esfera de los Libros.

——. 2003b. *La Susi en el vestuario blanco*. Madrid: La Esfera de los Libros.

Mendilow, Adam A. 1972. *Time and the Novel* [1952]. Introd. J. Isaacs. New York: Humanities Press.

Mendoza, Eduardo. 1975. *La verdad sobre el caso Savolta*. Nueva Narrativa Hispánica. Barcelona: Seix Barral .

——. 1979. *El misterio de la cripta embrujada*. Nueva Narrativa Española. Barcelona: Seix Barral.

——. 1982. *El laberinto de las aceitunas*. Barcelona: Seix Barral.

——. 1986. *La ciudad de los prodigios*. Biblioteca Breve. Barcelona: Seix Barral.

——. 1991. *Sin noticias de Gurb*. Biblioteca Breve. Barcelona: Seix Barral.

——. 1992. *El año del diluvio*. Biblioteca Breve. Barcelona: Seix Barral.

——. 2001. *La aventura del tocador de señoras*. Biblioteca Breve. Barcelona: Seix Barral.

Merino, José M. 1990a. 'La imposibilidad de la memoria', in Merino 1990b: 57–74.

——. 1990b. *El viajero perdido*. Alfaguara Hispánica 69. Madrid: Alfaguara.

——. 1997. 'Texto verdadero y versión cinematográfica', *República de las Letras: Cine y Literatura* 54: 125–28.

——. 2000. *Los invisibles*. Espasa Narrativa. Madrid: Espasa.

Mermall, Thomas. 1989. *Las alegorías del poder en Francisco Ayala*. 2nd edn. Madrid: Guadarrama.

Michelena, Luis. 1960. *Historia de la literatura vasca*. Biblioteca Vasca 7. Madrid: Minotauro.

Michener, James A. 1968. *Iberia: Spanish Travels and Reflections*. New York: Random House.

Middleton, Peter and Tim Woods (eds). 2000. *Literatures of Memory: History,*

Time, and Space in Postwar Writing. Manchester and New York: Manchester University Press.

Millás, Juan J. 1994. *La soledad era esto* [1990]. 9th edn. Ancora y Delfín 649. Barcelona: Destino.

——. 2002. *Dos mujeres en Praga*. Espasa Narrativa. Madrid: Espasa.

Mínguez-Arranz, Norberto (ed.). 2002. *Literatura española y cine*. Compás de Letras. Madrid: Complutense.

Mira Nouselles, Alberto. 2004. *De Sodoma a Chueca: Una historia cultural de la homosexualidad en España en el siglo XX*. Colección G. Madrid: Egales.

Moix, Ana M. 1970. *Julia*. Nueva Narrativa Hispánica. Barcelona: Seix Barral.

——. 1973. *Walter, ¿por qué te fuiste?* Hispánica Nova 55. Barcelona: Seix Barral.

——. 1994. *Vals negro*. Femenino Singular 15. Barcelona: Lumen.

—— and Terenci Moix. 1988. *Els Barcelonins*. Photography Colita, Oriol Maspons and Xavier Miserachs. Barcelona: Edicions 62.

Moix, Terenci. 1968. *La torre dels vicis capitals*. Narracions 61. Barcelona: Selecta.

——. 1969. *El dia que va morir Marilyn*. El Balancí 60. Barcelona: Edicions 62.

——. 1970. *Món mascle*. Barcelona: Aymá.

——. 1974a. 'Lilí Barcelona', in Moix 1974b: 91–110.

——. 1974b. *La torre de los vicios capitales*. Tr. Joan Emric Lahosa. Barcelona: Seix Barral.

——. 1990. *El peso de la paja*. 3 vols. Barcelona: Plaza y Janés.

——. 1992. *Lleonard, o El sexo de los ángeles*. Tr. Terenci and Ana María Moix. Autores Españoles e Hispanoamericanos. Barcelona: Planeta.

——. 1998. *Extraño en el paraíso* [*El peso de la paja*, 3]. Autores Españoles e Iberoamericanos: Memorias. Barcelona: Planeta.

Molas, Joaquim. 1978. 'Panorama de la literatura catalana de postguerra', *El País* (suplemento literario), 5 February: 3–4.

——. 1983. *La literatura catalana d'avantguarda, 1916–1938*. Barcelona: Antoni Bosch.

——. 1986–88. *Història de la literatura catalana*. Vols. 8–11: *Part moderna, II*. Barcelona: Ariel.

——. 1996a. 'La literatura catalana sota el franquisme (1939–1959)', *L'Avenç* 6: 39–43.

——. 1996b. *La literatura catalana de posguerra*. Barcelona: Rafael Dalmau.

Molina, César A. 1989. *Prensa literaria en Galicia (1920–1960)*. Universitaria. Vigo: Xerais de Galicia.

Molinaro, Nina. 2005. 'Facing towards Alterity and Spain's "Other" New Novelists'. *Anales de la Literatura Española Contemporánea* 30/i–ii: 301–24.

Moncada, Alberto. 1995. *España americanizada*. España Hoy 42. Madrid: Temas de Hoy.

Moncada, Jesús. 1988. *Camí de Sirga*. Ales Esteses 39. Barcelona: La Magrana.

Monleón, José B. (ed). 1995. *Del franquismo a la posmodernidad: Cultura española 1975–1990*. Akal Universitaria 176. Madrid: Akal.

Monteath, Peter. 1994. *The Spanish Civil War in Literature, Film, and Art: An International Bibliography of Secondary Literature*. Bibliographies and Indexes in World Literature 43. Westport CT: Greenwood.

Montero, Rosa. 1981. *La función Delta*. Colección Literatura. Madrid: Debate.

——. 1997. *La hija del caníbal*. Espasa Narrativa. Madrid: Espasa.

Montero, Xesús A. 1995. 'A palabra e o silencio na obra de Rafael Dieste', in Axeitos 1995.

Monzó, Quim. 1983. *Benzina*. Biblioteca Mínima 8. Barcelona: Quaderns Crema.

——. 1989. *La magnitud de la tragèdia*. Biblioteca Mínima 20. Barcelona: Quaderns Crema.

—— and Biel Mesquida. 1977. *Self-service*. Ucronia. Barcelona: Iniciativas.

—— and ——. 1978. *-Uf, va dir ell*. Quaderns Crema: Narrativa 2. Barcelona: Antoni Bosch.

Moreiras Menor, Cristina. 2002. *Cultura herida: Literatura y cine en la España democrática*. Universidad 28. Madrid: Libertarias.

Moretti, Franco. 2000. *The Way of the World: The Bildungsroman in European Culture*. Tr. Alberto J. Sbragia. London and New York: Verso.

Morris, Barbara and Lou Charnon-Deutsch. 1993–94. 'Whose masochism? Whose submission? Regarding the Pornographic Subject in *Las edades de Lulú*', *Letras Peninsulares* 6/ii–iii: 301–19.

Morris, C. Brian. 1972. *Surrealism and Spain, 1920–1936*. Cambridge: Cambridge University Press.

Mourullo, Gonzalo R. 2001. *Nasce un árbore* [1954]; *Memorias de Tains* [1956]. Ed. María Teresa Bermúdez Montes. Biblioteca das Letras Galegas 50. Vigo: Xerais de Galicia.

Mumford, Lewis. 1961. *The City in History: Its Origins, its Transformations, and its Prospects*. New York: Harcourt Brace.

Muñoz Molina, Antonio. 1987. *El invierno en Lisboa*. Barcelona: Siex Barral.

——. 1989. *Beltenebros*. Biblioteca Breve. Barcelona: Seix Barral.

——. 1991. *El jinete polaco*. Autores Españoles e Hispanoamericanos. Barcelona: Planeta.

——. 1993. *Nada del otro mundo*. Austral. Madrid: Espasa-Calpe.

——. 1997. *Plenilunio*. Madrid: Alfaguara.

——. 1999. *Carlota Fainberg*. Madrid: Alfaguara.

——. 2001. *Sefarad: Una novela de novelas*. Madrid: Alfaguara.

Murphy, Katharine. 2004. *Re-reading Pío Baroja and English Literature*. European Connections 17. Oxford and New York: Peter Lang.

Naremore, James (ed.). 2000. *Film Adaptation*. Depth of Field. New Brunswick NJ: Rutgers University Press.

Navajas, Gonzalo. 1979. *La novela de Juan Goytisolo*. Temas 15. Madrid: Sociedad General Española de Librería.

——. 1987. *Teoría y práctica de la novela española posmoderna*. Ibérica 45. Barcelona: Ediciones del Mall.

——. 1996a. 'Narrativa y género: La ficción actual desde la mujer', *Ínsula*, 589/590: 37–39.

——. 1996b. *Más allá de la posmodernidad: Estética de la nueva novela y cine españoles.* Humanidades 10. Barcelona: EUB.

——. 2002. *La narrativa española en la era global: Imagen, comunicación, ficción.* Humanidades 19. Barcelona: EUB.

——. 2004. *La modernidad como crisis. Los clásicos modernos ante el siglo XXI.* Otras Eutopías 10. Madrid: Biblioteca Nueva.

Neira Vilas, Xosé. 1988. *Querido Tomás* [1980]. 4th edn. Coruña: Castro.

——. 1991a. *Remuíño de sombras* [1973]. Narrativa 89. Vigo: Galaxia.

——. 1991b. *Camiño bretemoso* [1967]. Narrativa 96. Vigo: Galaxia.

——. 2002. *Memorias dun neno labrego* [1961]. Biblioteca Galega 120: 39. A Coruña: Voz de Galicia.

Nicholas, Robert L. 1987. *Unamuno, narrador.* Literatura y Sociedad 42. Madrid: Castalia.

Nichols, Geraldine C. 1989. *Escribir, espacio propio: Laforet, Matute, Moix, Tusquets, Riera y Roig por sí mismas.* Literature and Human Rights 7. Minneapolis MN: Institute for the Study of Ideologies and Literature.

——. 1992. *Des/cifrar la diferencia: Narrativa femenina de la España contemporánea.* Lingüística y Teoría Literaria. Mexico City: Siglo XXI de España.

——. 2005. 'Blank spaces: Literary History, Spain, and the Third Millennium', in Epps and Fernández 2005: 253–69.

Nieto, Ramón. 1957. *La tierra.* Madrid: Agora.

——. 1958. *Los desterrados.* Leopoldo Alas 5. Barcelona: Rocas.

——. 1959. *La fiebre.* Altor 24. Madrid: Cid.

——. 1961. *El sol amargo.* Altor 30. Madrid: Cid.

——. 1962. *La patria y el pan.* Biblioteca Formentor. Barcelona: Seix Barral.

——. 1963. *La cala.* Volvo. Madrid: Aula.

——. 1964. *Vía muerta.* Biblioteca de Literatura Actual 5. Madrid: Horizonte.

Nieva de la Paz, Pilar. 2004. *Narradoras españolas en la transición política (textos y contextos).* Espiral 53. Madrid: Fundamentos.

Nora, Eugenio de. 1958. *La novela española contemporánea.* 2nd edn. 3 vols. Biblioteca Románica Hispánica: Estudios y Ensayos 41. Madrid: Gredos.

Olaziregi, Mari J. 1998. 'Bernardo Atxaga: El escritor deseado', *Ínsula* 623: 7–11.

——. 2000a. 'La literatura vasca en Europa', in Amado Castro & de Pablo 2000: 125–55.

——. 2000b. 'Un siglo de novela en euskera', in Urquizu 2000: 504–88.

——. 2004. *An Anthology of Basque Short Stories.* Reno NV: Center for Basque Studies, University of Nevada.

——. 2005. *Waking the Hedgehog: The Literary Universe of Bernardo Atxaga.* Basque Textbooks 11. Reno NV: Center for Basque Studies, University of Nevada.

——. 2008. *History of Basque Literature.* Reno NV: Center for Basque Studies, University of Nevada.

——, Linda White, and Kristin Addis (eds). 2004. *An Anthology of Basque Short*

Stories. Basque Literature Series 1. Reno: Center for Basque Studies, University of Nevada.

Olson, Paul R. 1984. *Unamuno: Niebla*. Critical Guides to Spanish Texts 40. London: Grant & Cutler/Tamesis.

———. 2002. *The Great Chiasmus: Word and Flesh in the Novels of Unamuno*. Purdue Studies in Romance Literatures 26. West Lafayette IN: Purdue University Press.

Ordóñez, Elizabeth J. 1987. 'Inscribing difference: "L'écriture féminine" and new narrative by women', *Anales de la Literatura Española Contemporánea* 12/i–ii: 45–58.

———. 1991. *Voices of Their Own: Contemporary Spanish Narrative by Women*. Lewisburg PA: Bucknell University Press.

Orja, Joan. 1989. *Fahrenheit 212: Una aproximació a la literatura catalana recent*. Cotlliure 12. Barcelona: La Magrana.

Ortega, José. 1969. 'Realismo dialéctico de Martín-Santos en *Tiempo de silencio*', *Revista de Estudios Hispánicos* 3: 33–42.

———. 1972. *Juan Goytisolo: Alienación y agresión en 'Señas de identidad' y 'Reivindicación del conde don Julián'*. Torres Library of Literary Studies 12. New York: Eliseo Torres & Sons.

Ortega y Gasset, José. 1925. *La deshumanización del arte: Ideas sobre la novela*. Madrid: Revista de Occidente.

———. 1929. *La rebelión de las masas*. Madrid: Revista de Occidente.

Ortiz, Lourdes. 1991. *Urraca*. Literatura 88. Madrid: Debate.

Orwell, George. 1967. *Homage to Catalonia* [1938]. Introd. Lionel Trilling. Boston: Beacon.

Otaola, Javier. 2003. *La brocheta de carne*. Nueva Narrativa. San Sebastián: Hiria.

Otero Pedrayo, Ramón (ed.). 1934. *A romeiría de Xelmírez*. Nós 72. Santiago de Compostela: Nós.

———. 1935. *Devalar*. Nós 72. Santiago de Compostela: Nós.

——— (ed.). 1974. *Gran Enciclopedia Gallega*. Santiago de Compostela: Silverio Cañada & Novos Vieros.

———. 1988 *Fra Vernero* [1934]. Colección Literaria: Narrativa 64. 2nd edn. Vigo: Galaxia.

———. 1996. *O señorito da Reboraina* [1960]. Ed. Xosé Manuel Salgado. Obras de Otero Pedrayo 10. Vigo: Galaxia.

———. 2002a. *Os camiños da vida* [1928]. Ed. Ramón Mariño Paz. 13th edn. Obras de Otero Pedrayo 3. Vigo: Galaxia.

———. 2002b. *Arredor de si* [1930]. Biblioteca Galega 120: 20. A Coruña: Voz de Galicia.

Øveraas, Anne M. 1993. *Nivola contra novella*. Biblioteca Unamuno 15. Salamanca: Universidad de Salamanca.

Palacio Valdés, Armando. *La hermana san Sulpicio*. [1889]. Austral 76. 16th edn. Madrid: Espasa-Calpe.

Palol, Miquel de. 1989. *El jardí dels set sepulcres*. 3 vols. Biblioteca a Tot Vent 273–75. Barcelona: Proa.

Pàmies, Sergi. 1998. *La gran novela sobre Barcelona.* Tr. Javier Cercas. Narrativas Hispánicas 253. Barcelona: Edicions 62.

Parsons, Deborah L. 2003. *A Cultural History of Madrid: Modernism and the Urban Spectacle.* Oxford and New York: Berg.

Patterson, Craig. 2006. *Galician Cultural Identity in the Works of Ramón Otero Pedrayo.* Lewiston NY: Mellen.

Payne, John. 2004. *Catalonia: History and Culture.* Nottingham: Five Leaves.

Pedraza Giménez, Felipe B. and Milagros Rodríguez Cáceres. 1980–2005. *Manual de literatura española.* 4th edn. 16 vols. Pamplona: Cénit. See vol. XIII: *Posguerra: Narradores.*

Pedrolo, Manuel de. 1960. *Una selva com la teva.* El Dofi. Barcelona: Destino.

——. 1965. *Joc Brut.* La Cua de Palla 32. Barcelona: Edicions 62.

——. 1968. *Mossegar-se la cua* [1967]. La Cua de Palla 58. Barcelona: Edicions 62.

——. 1974. *Mecanoscrit del segon origen.* El Trapezi 24. Barcelona: Edicions 62.

——. 1991. *L'inspector fa tard* [1954]. La Negra 20. Barcelona: Magrana.

Pena, Xosé Ramón. 2002. 'Nacionalismo y vanguardia en la literatura gallega', in Bermúdez *et al.* 2002: 81–90.

Peña-Ardid, Carmen. 1996. *Literatura y cine: Una aproximación comparativa.* 2nd edn. Signo e Imagen 28. Madrid: Cátedra.

Pereiro, Peregrina. 2002. *La novela española de los noventa: Alternativas éticas a la postmodernidad.* Pliegos de Ensayo 163. Madrid: Pliegos.

Pérez, Genaro J. 1987. 'Construcción y destrucción en *Paisajes después de la batalla*', *Ínsula* 42 (March): 7.

——. 2002a. *Ortodoxia y heterodoxia de la novela policíaca hispana: Variaciones sobre el género negro.* Hispanic Monographs. Newark DE: Juan de la Cuesta.

Pérez, Janet D. (ed.). 1983. *Novelistas femeninas de la posguerra española.* Studia Humanitatis. Madrid: José Porrúa Turanzas.

——. 1988. *Contemporary Women Writers of Spain.* TWAS 798. Boston MA: Twayne.

——. 1990. 'Teaching Allegory and Concealment: Covert Dissent from Within the Franco Camp', in Valis 1990: 172–83.

—— (ed.). 2000b. *Feminist Encyclopedia of Spanish Literature.* 2 vols. Westport CT: Greenwood.

—— and Genaro J. Pérez (eds). 1987. 'Hispanic Science-Fiction/Fantasy and the Thriller', *Monographic Review/Revista Monográfica*, 3/i–ii.

Pérez Bazo, Javier (ed.). 1998. *La Vanguardia en España: Arte y literatura.* Toulouse: CRIC and Paris: Ophrys.

Pérez Bowie, José A. 2004. *Cine, literatura y poder: La adaptación cinematográfica durante el primer franquismo (1939–1950).* Salamanca: Cervantes.

Pérez-Díaz, Víctor M. 1993. *The Return of Civil Society: The Emergence of Democratic Spain.* London and Cambridge MA: Harvard University Press.

Pérez Embid, Florentino. 1949. 'Ante la nueva actualidad del "Problema de España"', *Arbor* 14/xlv–xlvi: 149–60.

Pérez Firmat, Gustavo. 1981. 'Repetition and Excess in *Tiempo de silencio*', *Publications of the Modern Language Association of America* 96: 194–209.
——. 1982. *Idle Fictions: The Hispanic Vanguard Novel, 1926–1934*. Durham NC: Duke University Press.
Pérez Galdós, Benito. 1904. *El abuelo: Drama en cinco actos*. Madrid: Obras de Pérez Galdós.
——. 2003. *Fortunata y Jacinta: Dos historias de casadas*. Ed. Santiago Fortuño Llorens. 2 vols. Castalia Didáctica 59. Madrid: Castalia.
Pérez López, Manuel M. 1974. *Azorín y la literatura española*. Acta Salmanticensia: Filosofía y Letras 83. Salamanca: Universidad de Salamanca.
Pérez Minik, Domingo. 1957. *Novelistas españoles de los siglos XIX y XX*. Crítica y Ensayo 3. Madrid: Guadarrama.
Pérez Reverte, Arturo. 1988. *El maestro de esgrima*. Madrid: Mondadori.
——. 1999. *El Club Dumas: La novena puerta*. Madrid: Alfaguara.
Perriam, Christopher. 2000. *A New History of Spanish Writing, 1939 to the 1990s*. Oxford and New York: Oxford University Press.
Perucho, Joan, 1960. *Les històries naturals*. Barcelona: Destino.
Pino, José M. del. 1995. *Montajes y fragmentos: Una aproximación a la narrativa española de vanguardia*. Teoría Literaria: Textos y Teoría 15. Amsterdam-Atlanta: Rodopi.
Pla, Josep. 1951. *Un senyor de Barcelona*. Biblioteca Selecta 90. Barcelona: Selecta.
Pombo, Álvaro. 1977. *Relatos sobre la falta de substancia*. Barcelona: La Gaya Ciencia.
——. 1983. *El héroe de las mansardas de Mansard*. Narrativas Hispánicas 1. Barcelona: Anagrama.
——. 1986a. *Los delitos insignificantes*. Narrativas Hispánicas 3. Barcelona: Anagrama.
——. 1986b. *El hijo adoptivo*. Narrativas Hispánicas 4. Barcelona: Anagrama.
——. 1990. *El metro de platino iridiado*. Narrativas Hispánicas 100. Barcelona: Anagrama.
——. 1996. *Donde las mujeres*. Narrativas Hispánicas 200. Barcelona: Anagrama.
——. 1997. *Cuentos reciclados*. Narrativas Hispánicas 232. Barcelona: Anagrama.
——. 2001. *El cielo raso*. Narrativas Hispánicas 298. Barcelona: Anagrama.
——. 2005. *Contra natura*. Narrativas Hispánicas 388. Barcelona: Anagrama.
Ponce de León, José L. 1971. *La novela española de la guerra civil (1936–1939)*. Madrid: Ínsula.
Pons, María C. 1996. *Memorias del olvido: Del Paso, García Márquez, Saer y la novela histórica de fines del siglo XX*. Mexico City: Siglo XXI.
Pope, Randolph D. 1984. *Novela de emergencia: España 1939–1954*. Temas 22. Madrid: Sociedad General Española de Librería.
——. 1995. *Understanding Juan Goytisolo*. Columbia SC: University of South Carolina Press.
——. 1999. 'Narrative in Culture, 1936–1975', in Gies 1999: 134–46.

Porcel, Baltasar. 1975. *Cavalls cap a la fosca*. El Balancí 96. Barcelona: Edicions 62.

——. 1986. *Les primavers i les tardors*. A Tot Vent 255. Barcelona: Proa.

Pozuelo Yvancos, José M. 1993. *Poética de la ficción*. Teoría de la Literatura y Literatura Comparada. Madrid: Síntesis.

Preston, Paul. 1986. *The Spanish Civil War, 1936–1939*. Chicago IL: Dorsey.

——. 1986. *The Triumph of Democracy in Spain*. London and New York: Methuen.

——. 1993a. 'War of Words: The Spanish Civil War and the Historians', in Preston 1993b: 1–13.

—— (ed.). 1993b. *Revolution and War in Spain, 1931–1939* [1984]. London and New York: Routledge.

Prince, Gerald. 1982. *Narratology. The Form and Functioning of Narrative*. Janua Linguarum: Maior 108. Berlin and New York: Mouton.

Puértolas, Soledad. 1992. *Días del Arenal*. Colección Autores Españoles e Hispanoamericanos. Barcelona: Planeta.

Pulgarín, Amalia. 1995. *Metaficción historiográfica: La novela histórica en la narrativa hispánica posmodernista*. Espiral 23. Madrid: Fundamentos.

Queixan, María Xosé. 1984a. *A orella no buraco* [1965]. 2nd edn. Narrativa 49. Vigo: Galaxia.

——. 1984b. *Amantia*. Vigo: Xerais de Galicia.

——. 1995a. *A semellanza* [1977]. 3rd edn. Barcelona: Sotelo Blanco.

——. 1995b. *O solpor da cupletista*. Relatos Dunha Hora 12. Vigo: Nigra.

——. 2003. *O segredo da Pedra Figueira* [1986]. Fora de Xogo 69. Vigo: Xerais de Galicia.

——. 2007. *Amor de tango* [1992]. 5th edn. Narrativa 73. Vigo: Xerais.

Queixas Zas, Mercedes. 1999. *Breve historia da literatura galega*. Vigo: A Nosa Terra: Promocións Culturais Galegas.

Quiroga, Elena. 1960. *Tristura*. Galería Literaria 23. Barcelona. Noguer.

——. 1965. *Escribo tu nombre*. Galería Literaria. Barcelona. Noguer.

Ramsden, Herbert. 1974. *The 1898 Movement in Spain: Towards a Reinterpretation, with Special Reference to 'El torno al casticimso' and 'Idearium español'*. Manchester: Manchester University Press and Totowa NJ: Rowman & Littlefield.

——. 1982. *Pío Baroja: La busca*. Critical Guides to Spanish Texts 32. London: Grant & Cutler/Tamesis.

Redondo Goicoechea, Alicia (ed.). 2003. *Mujeres novelistas: Jóvenes narradoras de los noventa*. Mujeres. Madrid: Narcea.

Regás, Rosa (ed.). 1989. *Cuentos barceloneses*. Barcelona: Icaria.

—— (ed.). 1998. *Barcelona, un día: Un llibre de contes de la ciutat*. Extra Alfaguara. Madrid: Santillana.

Reigosa, Carlos. 2001. *Crime en Compostela* [1984]. Biblioteca Galega 120: 65. A Coruña: Voz de Galicia.

Resina, Joan R. 1993. 'Desencanto y fórmula literaria en las novelas policiacas de Manuel Vázquez Montalbán', *Modern Language Notes* 108: 254–82.

—— (ed.). 1994. *Disremembering the Dictatorship: The Politics of Memory in*

the Spanish Transition to Democracy. Portada Hispánica 8. Amsterdam and
Atlanta GA: Rodopi.

——. 1996. 'Hispanism and its Discontents', *Siglo XX/20th Century* 14/i–ii:
85–135.

——. 1997. *El cadáver en la cocina: La novela criminal en la cultura del desencanto.* Contemporáneos 48. Barcelona: Anthropos.

Rey, Alfonso. 1977. *Construcción y sentido de 'Tiempo de silencio'.* Ensayos.
Madrid: José Porrúa Turanzas.

Ribbans, Geoffrey. 1971. *Niebla y soledad: Aspectos de Unamuno y Machado.*
Biblioteca Románica Hispánica: Estudios y Ensayos 162. Madrid: Gredos.

Ricoeur, Paul. 1983–85. *Temps et récit.* 3 vols. L'Ordre Philosophique. Paris:
Éditions du Seuil.

Riera, Carme. 1975. *Te deix, amor, la mar com a penyora.* Les Eines 12. Barcelona: Laia.

——. 1994. *Dins el darrer blau.* Ancora 65. Barcelona: Destino.

——. 2000. *Cap el cel obert.* Ancora 134. Barcelona: Destino.

Ríos Carratalá, Juan A. 2002. 'La semilla y sus frutos: Lo sainetesco en el cine
español', in Heredero 2002: 247–61.

—— and John D. Sanderson (eds). 1997. *Relaciones entre el cine y la literatura:
El guión.* Alicante: Universidad de Alicante.

Ríos-Font, Wadda C. 2005. 'National Literature in the Protean Nation: The Question of Nineteenth-century Spanish Literary History', in Epps and Fernández
2005: 127–47.

Risco, Antón. 1989a. *O caso.* Medusa: Narrativa. Barcelona: Sotelo Blanco.

——. 1989b. *As metamorfoses de Proteo* (1989). Narrativa 77. Vigo: Galaxia.

——. 1992. *Margarida de Ouridac.* Narrativa. A Coruña: Castro.

—— (ed.). 1993. *Antoloxía da literatura fantástica en lingua galega.* 3rd edn.
Colección Literaria 94. Vigo: Galaxia.

——. 1994. *Hipógrifo.* Narrativa. Xerais de Galicia.

——. 1995. *Mascarada.* Literaria 188. Vigo: Galaxia

——. 2002. *O Embrión.* Literaria 188. Vigo: Galaxia.

Risco, Antonio. 1980. *Azorín y la ruptura con la novela tradicional.* Estudios 8.
Madrid: Alhambra.

——. 1987. *Literatura fantástica en lengua española: Teoría y aplicaciones.*
Persiles 179. Madrid: Taurus.

Risco, Vicente. 2002. *O porco de pé* [1928]. Biblioteca Galega 120: 18. A
Coruña: Voz de Galicia.

Rivas, Manuel. 1991. *Os comedores de patacas.* Narrativa. Vigo: Xerais de
Galicia.

——. 1993. *En salvaxe compaña.* Narrativa. Vigo: Xerais de Galicia.

——. 1998a. *O lapis do carpinteiro.* Narrativa 145. Vigo: Xerais de Galicia.

——. 1998b. *El lápiz del carpintero.* Tr. Dolores Vilavedra. Madrid, Alfaguara.

——. 1999a. *Ela, maldita alma.* Literatura. Vigo: Galaxia.

——. 1999b. *Galicia, Galicia.* Ed. Xosé A. Mato Domínguez. Vigo: Xerais de
Galicia.

——. 2002. *As chamadas perdidas.* Narrativa 185. Vigo: Xerais de Galicia.

——. 2005. *A lingua das bolboretas*. Vigo: Galaxia.

——. 2006. *Os libros arden mal*. Narrativa 228. Vigo: Xerais de Galicia.

——. 2007. *Un millón de vacas* [1989]. 11th edn. Narrativa 42. Vigo: Xerais de Galicia.

Rivas Hernández, Ascensión. 1998. *Pío Baroja: Aspectos de la técnica narrativa*. Cáceres: Universidad de Extremadura.

Rivera, Haydée. 1972. *Pío Baroja y las novelas del mar*. New York: Anaya.

Rivière, Margarita. 1995. *La década de la decencia: Intolerancias 'prêt-à-porter', moralina mediática y otras indecencias de los años noventa*. Prologue Manuel Vázquez Montalbán. Argumentos 161. Barcelona: Anagrama.

——. 2000. *El problema: Madrid Barcelona*. 2nd edn. Barcelona: Plaza y Janés.

Rix, Rob (ed.). 1992. *Leeds Papers on Thrillers in the Transition: 'Novela negra' and Political Change in Spain*. Leeds Iberian Papers. Leeds: Trinity and All Saints College.

Robbe-Grillet, Alain. 1957. *La jalousie*. Paris: Éditions de Minuit.

——. 1959. *Jealousy*. Tr. Richard Howard. Evergreen 193. New York : Grove.

Ródenas de Moya, Domingo. 1998. *Los espejos del novelista: Modernismo y autorreferencia en la novela vanguardista española*. Historia, Ciencia y Sociedad 274. Barcelona: Península.

Rodoreda, Mercè. 1962. *La Plaça del diamant: Novel.la*. Biblioteca Catalana de la Novel.la 22. Barcelona: Club.

——. 1966. *El Carrer de les Camèlies*. Biblioteca Catalana de la Novel.la 37. Barcelona: Club.

——. 1974. *Mirall trencat: Novel.la*. Biblioteca Catalana de la Novel.la 81–82. Barcelona: Club.

Rodríguez, María P. 2000. *Vidas im/propias: Transformaciones del sujeto femenino en la narrativa española contemporánea*. Purdue Studies in Romance Literatures 19. West Lafayette IN: Purdue University Press.

Rodríguez Castelao, Daniel. 1980. *Un ollo de vidrio: Memoria dun esquelete* [1922]. Céltiga 7. A Coruña: Rueiro.

——. 2001. *Os dous de sempre* [1934]. Ed. Henrique Monteagudo. Vigo. Galaxia.

——. 2004. *Sempre en Galiza* [1944]. Biblioteca Castelao 1. Vigo: Galaxia.

Rodríguez-Fisher, Ana. 1998. *Batir de alas*. Club 20. Madrid: Acento.

Rodríguez Sánchez, Francisco. 1991. *Conflito lingüístico e ideoloxía na Galiza*. 3rd edn. Laiovento 7. Santiago de Compostela: Laiovento.

Roig, Montserrat. 1977. *El temps de les cireres*. El Balancí 105. Barcelona: Edicions 62.

——. 1987. *Barcelona a vol d'ocell*. Vida i Costums dels Catalans. Photography Xavier Miserachs. Barcelona: Edicions 62.

Roig Roselló, Antonio. 1977. *Todos los parques no son un paraíso: Memorias de un sacerdote*. Fábula 14. Barcelona: Planeta.

——. 1979. *Vidente en rebeldía: Un proceso en la Iglesia*. Fábula 45. Barcelona: Planeta.

Romera Castillo, José, Francisco Gutiérrez Carbajo, and Mario García-Page (eds).

1996. *La novela histórica a finales del siglo XX: Actas del V seminario inter-nacional del Instituto de Semiótica Literaria y Teatral del la UNED, Cuenca, UIMP, 3–6 de julio, 1995*. Biblioteca Filología Hispana 26. Madrid: Visor.

Romero, Emilio. 1957. *La paz empieza nunca*. Autores Españoles Contemporá-neos. Barcelona: Planeta.

Romero, Luis. 1951. *La noria: Premio Eugenio Nadal 1951*. Ancora y Delfín 65. Barcelona: Destino.

Rosa Camacho, Isaac. 2007. *¡Otra maldita novela sobre la Guerra Civil!: Lectura crítica de 'La malamemoria'*. Biblioteca Breve. Barcelona: Seix Barral.

Round, Nicholas G. 1974. *Unamuno: Abel Sánchez*. Critical Guides to Spanish Texts 12. London: Grant & Cutler/Tamesis.

Ruiz Zafón, Carlos. 2001. *La sombra del viento*. Autores Españoles e Ibero-americanos. Barcelona: Planeta.

Rus, Miguel Ángel de. 2000. *Dinero, mentiras y realismo sucio*. Colección de Narrativa 4. Madrid: Ediciones Irreverentes.

Rusiñol, Santiago. 1973. *L'Auca del senyor Esteve* [1907]. 10th edn. Biblioteca Selecta 80: Novel.la 21. Barcelona: Selecta.

Ruz Velasco, David. 1999. '*La soledad era esto* y la posmodernidad: El sujeto escriptivo, el sueño mimético y la antípoda'. *Espéculo: Revista de Estudios Literarios* 11 = <http://www.ucm.es/info/especulo/numero11/millas.html>.

Sabas, Martín (ed.). 1997. *Páginas amarillas: Antología*. Nueva Biblioteca 17. Madrid: Lengua de Trapo.

Sagarra, Josep M. de. 1928. *All i salobre*. Barcelona: Llibreria Catalònia.

——. 1932. *Vida privada: Novel.la*. 2 vols. Barcelona: Llibreria Catalònia.

Salabert, Juana. 1996. *Arde lo que será*. Ancora y Delfín 758. Barcelona: Destino.

Saladrigas, Robert. 1986. *Memorial de Claudi M. Broch*. Lletres Catalanes: Novel.la. Barcelona: Plaza y Janés.

Sales, Joan. 1971. *Incerta glòria* [1956]. 4th edn. Biblioteca Catalana de Novel.la 54–56. Barcelona: Club.

Salgués Cargill, Maruxa. 1973. *'Tirano Banderas': Estudio crítico-analítico*. Jaén: Gráficas Nova.

Salisachs, Mercedes. 1983. *El volúmen de tu ausencia: Novela*. Autores Espa-ñoles e Hispanoamericanos. Barcelona: Planeta.

Saludes, Esperanza G. 1981. *La narrativa de Luis Martín-Santos a la luz de la psicología*. Colección de Estudios Hispánicos. Miami FL: Universal.

Salvador, Tomás. 1953. *Cuerda de presos*. Barcelona: Luis de Caralt.

Sammons, Jeffrey L. 1991. 'The Bildungsroman for Non-specialists: An Attempt at Clarification', in Hardin 1991: 26–45.

Sánchez, Antonio. 2002. 'Barcelona's Magic Mirror: Narcissim or the Redisco-very of Public Space and Collective Identity?', in Labanyi 2002: 294–310.

Sánchez-Ferlosio, Rafael. 1951. *Industrias y andanzas de Alfanhuí*. Madrid: Talleres Gráficos.

——. 1956. *El Jarama*. Ancora y Delfín 121. Barcelona: Destino.

Sánchez Noriega, José L. 2000. *De la literatura al cine: Teoría y análisis de la adaptación*. Comunicación 118. Barcelona: Paidos.

Sánchez Silva, José María. 1999. *Marcelino, pan y vino* [1952]. 8th edn. Barcelona: Andrés Bello.

Sánchez Vázquez, Adolfo. 1980. *Estética y marxismo: Presentación y selección de los textos*. 4th Spanish edn. 2 vols. El Hombre y su Tiempo. Mexico City: Era.

Sanrune, Carlos. 1992. *El gladiador de Chueca: De chaperos y clients*. Barcelona: Laertes.

Santana, Mario. 2000. *Foreigners in the Homeland: The Spanish American New Novel in Spain, 1962–1974*. Bucknell Studies in Latin American Literature and Theory. Lewisburg PA: Bucknell University Press.

Santiago, Silvio. 1982. *Vilardevós* [1961]. Literatura 40. Vigo: Galaxia.

——. 1989. *O silencio redimido: Historia dun home que pode ser outro* [1976]. Literaria 33. Vigo: Galaxia.

Santiáñez-Tió, Nil. 2002. *Investigaciones literarias: Modernidad, historia de la literatura y modernismos*. Letras de Humanidad. Barcelona: Crítica.

Santoro, Patricia J. 1996. *Novel into Film: The Case of 'La familia de Pascual Duarte' and 'Los santos inocentes'*. Newark DE: University of Delaware Press.

Santos, Juliá. 2004. *Historias de las dos Españas*. Historia. Madrid: Taurus.

Sanz Villanueva, Santos. 1972. *Tendencias de la novela española actual (1950–1970)*. Bolsillo 175. Madrid: Cuadernos para el Diálogo.

——. 1980. *Historia de la novela social española (1942–1975)*. 2 vols. Estudios 6. Madrid: Alambra.

——. 1984. *Literatura actual*. Historia de la Literatura Española 6/ii. Barcelona: Ariel.

——. 1992. 'La novela', in Villanueva 1992a: 249–84.

Sarasola, Ibon. 1976. *Historia social de la literatura vasca*. Akal 74: 59. Madrid: Akal.

Scarlett, Elizabeth A. 1994. *Under Construction: The Body in Spanish Novels*. Charlottesville VA: University Press of Virginia.

Schaefer-Rodríguez, Claudia. 1984. *Juan Goytisolo: Del realismo crítico a la utopía*. Ensayos. Madrid: José Porrúa Turanzas.

——. 1990. 'On the Waterfront: Realism meets the Postmodern in Post-Franco Spain's *novela negra*', *Hispanic Journal* 11/i: 133–46.

Schiavo, Leda. 1980. *Historia y novela en Valle-Inclán: Para leer 'El ruedo ibérico'*. Literatura y Sociedad 25. Madrid: Castalia.

Schumm, Sandra J. 1999. *Reflection in Sequence: Novels by Spanish Women, 1944–1988*. Lewisburg PA: Bucknell University Press.

Sempronio. 1980. *Barcelona era una festa*. Biblioteca Selecta 503: Historia 46. Barcelona: Selecta.

Senabre, Ricardo. 1995. 'La novela española hacia el año 2000', *Letras de Deusto* 25/lxvi: 23–38.

Sender, Ramón J. 1932. *Siete domingos rojos (novela)*. Barcelona: Balagué.

——. 1934. *Viaje a la aldea del crimen (documental de Casas Viejas)*. Madrid: Impr. de Juan Pueyo

——. 1936. *Mr. Witt en el Cantón*. Madrid: Espasa-Calpe.

——. 1937. *The War in Spain: A Personal Narrative*. Tr. Peter Chalmers Mitchell. London: Faber & Faber. [First Spanish edn 1938, entitled *Contraataque*.]

——. 1953. *Mosén Millán: Novela*. Mexico City: Aquelarre.

——. 1957. *Los cinco libros de Ariadna*. New York: Ibérica. (See also Sender 2004.)

——. 1965–66. *Crónica del alba* [1963]. Biblioteca Literaria Aymá 2 4–5. Barcelona: Delos-Aymá.

——. 1974. *Réquiem por un campesino español* [1960]. Ancora y Delfín 460. Barcelona: Destino.

——. 1978. *Contraataque* [1938]. Patio de Escuelas. Salamanca: Almar.

——. 2004. *Los cinco libros de Ariadna* [1957]. Ed. Patricia McDermott. Larumbe 35. Zaragoza: Prensas Universitarias de Zaragoza.

Senov Kanev, Venko. 1996. 'Lo real maravilloso: un método definidor en las letras hispanoamericanas', *Alba de América* 75.

Serrahima, Maurici. 1967. *Realidad de Catalunya: respuesta a Julián Marías*. Barcelona: Aymá.

Serrano Ajenjo, José E. 1992. *Ramón y el arte de matar: El crimen en las novelas de Gómez de la Serna*. Biblioteca de Ensayo 8. Granada: Caja General de Ahorros de Granada.

Servodidio, Mirella (ed.). 1987. 'Reading for difference: Feminist Perspectives on Women Novelists of Contemporary Spain', *Anales de la literatura española contemporánea* 12 (special issue).

Shaw, Donald. 1975. *The Generation of 1898 in Spain*. New York: Barnes and Noble & London: Benn.

Sibbald, Kay, Jesús Pérez Magallón, & Ricardo de la Fuente Ballesteros (eds). 2003. *Memorias y olvidos: Autos y biografías (reales, ficticias) en la cultura hispánica*. Cultura Iberoamericana 16. Valladolid: Universitas Castellae.

Silva, Lorenzo. *El alquimista impaciente*. Ancora y Delfín 890. Barcelona: Destino.

Sinclair, Alison. 1977. *Valle-Inclán's 'Ruedo Ibérico': A Popular View of Revolution*. Támesis A 43. London: Tamesis.

——. 2001. *Uncovering the Mind: Unamuno, the Unknown, and the Vicissitudes of Self*. Manchester & New York: Manchester University Press.

Smith, Edmund J. 1991. *Postmodernism and Contemporary Fiction*. London:

Smith, Paul J. 1992. *Laws of desire: Questions of Homosexuality in Spanish Writing and Film, 1960–1990*. Oxford: Clarendon & New York: Oxford University Press.

——. 1998. 'Modern Times: Francisco Umbral's Chronicle of Distinction', *Modern Language Notes* 113: 324–38.

——. 2000a. 'Cross-cut: City' in Smith 2000b: 108–32.

——. 2000b. *The Moderns: Time, Space, and Subjectivity in Contemporary Spanish Culture*. Oxford & New York: Oxford University Press.

Smith, Verity. 1971. *Valle-Inclán: Tirano Banderas*. Critical Guides to Spanish Texts 3. London: Grant & Cutler/Tamesis.

Sobejano, Gonzalo. 1967. *Forma literaria y sensibilidad social (Mateo Alemán,*

Galdós, Clarín, el 98 y Valle-Inclán). Biblioteca Románica Hispánica: Campo Abierto 19. Madrid: Gredos.

——. 1970. *Novela española de nuestro tiempo (en busca del pueblo perdido)*. 2nd edn, rev. El Soto 10. Madrid: Prensa Española.

——. 1985. 'La novela poemática y sus alrededores', in Conte *et al.* 1985: 1, 26.

——. 1987. *Juan Millás, fabulador de la extrañeza*. Buenos Aires: Alfaguara.

——. 1988. 'La novela ensimismada (1980–1985)', *España contemporánea* 1/i 1–26.

——. 1989. 'Novela y metanovela en España', in Gullón *et al.* 1989: 4–6.

——. 1996. 'Novelistas de 1950 al final del siglo', *Ínsula* 589/590: 43–44.

Sobrer, Josep M. 1978. 'Literature, Disglossia, Dictatorship: The Case of Catalonia', in *Colloquium* 1978: 51–65.

——. 1992. *Catalonia: A Self-portrait*. Bloomington IA: Indiana University Press.

—— and Joan R. Resina. 2000. 'Catalan Literature as National Literature: Origins, Development, and Future', *Catalan Review* 14/i–ii (special number): 1–190.

Soldevila, Carles. 1929. *Fanny: Novel.la*. Barcelona: Llibreria Catalònia.

——. 1931. *Eva: Novel.la*. Barcelona: Llibreria Catalònia.

——. 1933. *Valentina*. Barcelona: Llibreria Catalònia.

Soldevila-Durante, Ignacio. 1977. 'Para una hermenéutica de la prosa vanguardista española (A propósito de Francisco Ayala)', *Cuadernos Hispanoamericanos* 110/cccxxix–cccxxx: 356–65.

——. 1980. *La novela desde 1936*. Historia de la Literatura Española Actual: Estudios. Madrid: Alhambra.

——. 1989. 'Esfuerzo titánico de la novela histórica', in Gullón *et al.* 1989: 8.

——. 2001. *Historia de la novela española (1936–2000)*. Crítica y Estudios Literarios. Madrid: Cátedra.

Sopeña Monsalve, Andrés. 1994. *El florido pensil: Memoria de la escuela nacionalcatólica*. Crítica. Barcelona: Grijalbo Mondadori.

Soria Olmedo, Andrés. 1930. *Vanguardismo y crítica literaria en España (1910–1930)*. Bella Bellatrix. Madrid: Istmo.

Sotelo Vázquez, Adolfo. 2005. *Viajeros en Barcelona*. Divulgación: Historia. Barcelona: Planeta.

Soto Puente, Juan. 1993. *Un hombre llamado Katy*. Ediciones La Palma 25. Madrid: La Palma.

Southworth, Herbert R. 1963. *El mito de la cruzada de Franco*. Crítica 1. Paris: Ruedo Ibérico.

Speratti-Piñero, Emma S. 1957. *La elaboración artística en 'Tirano Banderas'*. Publicaciones de la Nueva Revista de Filología Hispánica 4. Mexico City: El Colegio de México. Repr. in Speratti-Piñero 1968.

——. 1968. *De 'Sonata de otoño' al esperpento: Aspectos del arte de Valle-Inclán*. Támesis A 11. London: Tamesis.

——. 1974. *El ocultismo en Valle-Inclán*. Támesis A 34. London: Tamesis.

Spires, Robert C. 1978. *La novela española de postguerra: Creación artística y experiencia personal*. Planeta Universidad 20. Madrid: Cupsa.

——. 1984. *Beyond the Metafictional Mode: Directions in the Modern Spanish Novel*. Studies in Romance Languages 30. Lexington KY: University Press of Kentucky.

——. 1988. *Transparent Simulacra: Spanish Fiction, 1902–1926*. Columbia MO: Missouri University Press.

——. 1996. *Post-totalitarian Spanish Fiction*. Columbia MO: University of Missouri Press.

Stam, Robert. 2005. *Literature through Film: Realism, Magic, and the Art of Adaptation*. Oxford & Malden MA: Blackwell.

Stanley, Maureen T. 2004. 'Rodoreda's Feminist Vindication of Maternal Symbolic Order Contrasted with Betriú's Apotheosis of the Republican Cause', in Cabello-Castellet *et al.* 2004: 64–72.

Stoker, Bram. 2001. *Drácula*. Barcelona: Óptima.

Suárez Cortina, Manuel. 2006. *La sombra del pasado: Novela e historia en Galdós, Unamuno y Valle-Inclán*. Historia Biblioteca Nueva. Madrid: Biblioteca Nueva.

Subirats, Eduardo. 1995. *España: Miradas fin de siglo*. La Tronera 8. Madrid: Akal.

Sueiro, Daniel. 1961. *La criba*. Biblioteca Formentor. Barcelona: Seix Barral.

Suñén, Luis. 1978. 'El juego (cruel) de la memoria', *Ínsula* 378: 5.

Tarrío Varela, Anxo. 1988. *Literatura gallega*. Historia Crítica de la Literatura Hispánica 28. Madrid: Taurus.

——. 1994. *Literatura galega: Aportacións a unha historia crítica*. Universitaria. Vigo: Xerais de Galicia.

Terry, Arthur. 2003. *A Companion to Catalan Literature*. Támesis A 193. London: Tamesis.

Thomas, Gareth. 1990. *The Novel of the Spanish Civil War*. Cambridge & New York: Cambridge University Press.

Thompson-Casado, Kathleen. 2004. 'On the Case of the Spanish Female Sleuth', in Godsland & Moody 2004: 136–49.

Todó, Lluis M. 1994. *El joc del mentider*. Columna 129. Barcelona: Columna.

Todorov, Tzvetan. 1973. *The Fantastic: A Structural Approach to a Literary Genre*. Tr. Richard Howard. Cleveland OH: Case Western Reserve University.

——. 1987. *Introducción a la literatura fantástica*. 3rd edn. Mexico City: Premià.

Toledo Lezeta, Ana M. 1989. *Domingo Agirre: Euskal eleberriaren sorrera*. Bilbao: Bizkaiko Foru Aldundia.

Tomachevskii, Boris V. 1972. *Teoría de la literatura*. Tr. Marcial Suárez. Introd. Fernando Lázaro Carreter. Akal Universitaria 15. Madrid: Akal.

Tomeo, Javier. 1989. *La ciudad de las palomas*. Narrativas Hispánicas 73. Barcelona: Anagrama.

Torre, Cristina de la. 1988. *La narrativa de Álvaro Cunqueiro*. Pliegos de Ensayo 30. Madrid: Pliegos.

Torrecilla, Jesús. 2004. *España exótica: La formación de la imagen española moderna*. Boulder CO: Society of Spanish and Spanish-American Studies.
——. 2006. *La actualidad de la generación del 98: Algunas reflexiones sobre el concepto de lo moderno*. Ensayos Literarios 15. Mérida: Editora Regional de Extremadura.
Torrent, Ferran. 2000. *Cambres d'acer inoxidable*. 3rd edn. Col.lecció Clàssica 408. Barcelona: Columna.
Torres, Maruja. 1998. *Un calor tan cercano*. Bolsillo 114. Madrid: Alfaguara.
Torres, Xohana. 1971. *Adiós María*. Buenos Aires: Galicia.
Trabal Benessat, Francesc. 1936. *Vals*. Barcelona: Proa.
Triadú, Joan. 1978. *Una cultura sensa llibertat*. Col.lecció La Mirada. Barcelona: Proa.
Tucker, Peggy L. 1980. *Time and History in Valle-Inclán's Historical Novels and 'Tirano Banderas'*. Albatros Hispanófila 7. Valencia: Albatros.
Tuñón de Lara, Manuel. 1973. *Medio siglo de cultura española (1885–1936)*. 3rd edn. Madrid: Tecnos.
Turner, David G. 1974. *Unamuno's Webs of Fatality*. Támesis A 45. London: Tamesis.
Turner, Harriet S. 1990. 'From the Verbal to the Visual in *La Regenta*', in Valis 1990: 67–86.
—— and Adelaida López de Martínez (eds). 2003. *The Cambridge Companion to the Spanish Novel from 1600 to the Present*. Cambridge Companions to Literature. Cambridge & New York: Cambridge University Press.
Tusquets, Esther. 1978. *El mismo mar de todos los veranos*. Palabra Menor 50. Barcelona: Lumen.
——. 1979. *El amor es un juego solitario*. Palabra Menor 53. Barcelona: Lumen.
——. 1980. *Varada tras el último naufragio*. Palabra Menor 56. Barcelona: Lumen.
——. 1981. *Siete miradas en un mismo paisaje*. Palabra Menor 60. Barcelona: Lumen.
——. 1985. *Para no volver*. Palabra en el Tiempo 161. Barcelona: Lumen.
——. 1997. *Con la miel en los labios*. Narrativas Hispánicas 235. Barcelona: Anagrama.
Tussell, Javier. 1991. *La transición española a la democracia*. Biblioteca Historia 16: 31. Madrid: Historia 16.
Ugarte, Miguel. 1981. '*Tiempo de silencio* and the Language of Displacement,' *Modern Language Notes* 96: 340–57.
——. 1982. *Trilogy of Treason: An Intertextual Study of Juan Goytisolo*. Columbia MO: University of Missouri Press.
——. 1996. *Madrid 1900: The Capital as Cradle of Literature and Culture*. Penn State Studies in Romance Literatures. University Park PA: Pennsylvania State University Press.
Umbral, Francisco. 1970. *El Giocondo: Novela*. Autores Españoles e Hispano-americanos. Barcelona: Planeta.
——. 1977. *Tratado de perversiones*. Barcelona: Argos.

——. 1978. *Ramón y las vanguardias*. Selecciones Austral 50. Madrid: Espasa-Calpe.

——. 1988. *Un carnívoro cuchillo*. Narrativa 102. Barcelona: Planeta.

——. 1993. *La década roja*. Documento 332. Barcelona: Planeta.

Unamuno, Miguel de. 1974. *Niebla (nivola)*. 5th edn. Temas de España 28. Madrid: Taurus.

——. 1981. *Amor y pedagogía*. Austral 141. 12th edn. Madrid: Espasa-Calpe.

——. 1995. *Abel Sánchez: Una historia de pasión* [1917]. Ed. Carlos A. Longhurst. Letras Hispánicas 398. Madrid: Castalia.

Urioste, Carmen. 1997–98. 'La narrativa española de los noventa: ¿Existe una "generación X"?', *Letras Peninsulares* 10/ii–iii: 455–47.

Urquizu Sarasua, Patricio *et al.* (eds). 2000. *Historia de la literatura vasca*. Aula Abierta 36140. Madrid: Universidad Nacional de Educación a Distancia.

Urrutia, Jorge. 1984. *Imago litterae: Cine, literatura*. Semiótica y Crítica 1. Seville: Alfar.

Utrera, Rafael. 1985. *Escritores y cinema en España: Un acercamiento histórico*. Imágenes 6. Madrid: Ediciones JC.

——. 2002. 'Entre el rechazo y la fascinación: Los escritores del 98 ante el cinematógrafo', in Heredero 2002: 221–45.

Valenzuela, Ramón de. 1989. *Non agardei por ninguén* [1967]. Ed. Modesto Hermida García. Biblioteca das Letras Galegas 10. Vigo: Xerais de Galicia.

——. 1997. *Era tempo de apandar* [1980]. O Fardel da Memoria 4. Vigo: A Nosa Terra.

Valera, Juan. 2001. *Pepita Jiménez*. [1874]. Ed. Leonardo Romero. Letras Hispánicas 290. 11th edn. Madrid: Cátedra.

Valis, Noël M. (ed.). 1990. '*Malevolent Insemination' and Other Essays on Clarín*. Romance Studies 10. Ann Arbor MI: Department of Romance Languages, University of Michigan.

—— (ed.). 2007. *Teaching Representations of the Spanish Civil War*. New York: Modern Language Association.

Valladares, Marcial. 1991. *Maxina, ou a filla espúrea* [1880]. Ed Anxo Tarrío *et al.* Vigo: Xerais de Galicia.

Valles Calatrava, José R. 1991. *La novela criminal española*. Crítica Literaria 113. Granada: Universidad de Granada.

Valls, Fernando. 1989. 'La literatura femenina en España, 1975–1989', in Gullón *et al.* 1989: 13.

——. 2003. *La realidad inventada: Análisis crítico de la novela española actual*. Letras de Humanidad. Barcelona: Crítica.

Van Guardia, Lola. 1997. *Con pedigree: Culebrón lésbico por entregas*. Salir del Armario 6. Barcelona: Gay y Lesbiana.

——. 1999. *Plumas de doble filo*. Salir del Armario 23. Barcelona: Egales.

——. 2002. *La mansión de las tríbadas*. Salir del Armario 40. Barcelona: Egales.

Vanoye, Francis. 1995. *Récit écrit, récit filmique*. Cinéma et Récit 1. Paris: Nathan.

Vauthier, Bénédicte. 2004. *Arte de escribir e ironía en la obra narrativa de*

Miguel de Unamuno. Biblioteca Unamuno 27. Salamanca: Universidad de Salamanca.

Vázquez Cuesta, Pilar (ed.). 2002. *Nós: A literatura galega.* Lisbon: Horizonte.

Vázquez Medel, Manuel A. (ed.). 1998. *Francisco Ayala y las vanguardias.* Universidad 35. Sevilla: Alfar.

Vázquez Montalbán, Manuel. 1979. *Los mares del sur.* Autores Españoles e Hispanoamericanos. Barcelona: Planeta.

——. 1984. *La rosa de Alejandría.* Autores Españoles e Hispanoamericanos. Barcelona: Planeta.

——. 1985. *El pianista.* Biblioteca Breve 672. Barcelona: Seix Barral.

——. 1988. *El delantero centro fue asesinado al atardecer.* Carvalho 14. Barcelona: Planeta.

——. 1989. 'Contra la novela policiaca', in Gullón *et al.* 1989: 9.

——. 1990a. *Galíndez.* Barcelona: Seix Barral.

——. 1990b. "El amante trilingüe; La nueva novela de Juan Marsé, entre la sociolingüística y la depresión'. *El País,* 30 September: 1, 3.

——. 1992. *Autobiografía del General Franco.* Autores Españoles e Hispanoamericanos. Barcelona: Planeta.

——. 2003. 'Milenio', *El País,* 3 August.

——. 2004. *Milenio Carvalho.* 2 vols. Autores Hispánicos e Hispanoamericanos. Barcelona: Planeta.

—— & Eduard Moreno. 1991. *Barcelona, cap a on vas? Diàlegs per a una altra Barcelona.* Descoberta 8. Barcelona: Llibres de l'Index.

Vicens Vives, Jaume. 1954. *Notícia de Catalunya.* Ancora y Delfín 100. Barcelona: Destino.

Vicent, Manuel. 2001. *Son de mar.* Mexico City: Alfaguara.

Vidal-Folch, Xavier (ed.) 1994. *Los catalanes y el poder.* Nuevo Siglo. Madrid: El País & Aguilar.

Vila-Matas, Enrique. 1985. *Historia abreviada de la literatura portátil.* Narrativas Hispánicas 23. Barcelona: Anagrama.

——. 1991. *Suicidios ejemplares.* Narrativas Hispánicas 107. Barcelona: Anagrama.

——. 1993. *Hijos sin hijos.* Narrativas Hispánicas 138. Barcelona: Anagrama.

——. 1997. *Extraña forma de vida.* Narrativas Hispánicas 218. Barcelona: Anagrama.

——. 1999. *El viaje vertical.* Narrativas Hispánicas 260. Barcelona: Anagrama.

——. 2000. *Bartleby y compañía.* Narrativas Hispánicas 279. Barcelona: Anagrama.

——. 2002. *El mal de Montano.* Narrativas Hispánicas 334. Barcelona: Anagrama.

Vilarós, Teresa M. 1998. *El mono del desencanto: Una crítica cultural de la transición española, 1973–1993.* Sociología y Política. Mexico City: Siglo XXI.

——. 2002. 'Cine y literatura en la España de los sesenta: Testimonio de un primer proceso de desideologización', in Mínguez Arranz 2002: 193–206.

Vilas, Santiago. 1968. *El humor y la novela española contemporánea.* Punto Omega 47. Madrid: Guadarrama.

Vilavedra Fernández, Dolores. 1999. *Historia da literatura galega*. Manuais 2. Vigo: Galaxia.

Villalonga, Llorenç. 1931. *Mort de dama*. Palma de Mallorca.

——. 1966. *Bearn o la sala de les nines*. 3rd edn. Barcelona: Club.

Villanueva, Darío. 1977. *Estructura y tiempo reducido en la novela española contemporánea*. Biblioteca Filológica: Manuales 4. Valencia: Bello.

—— (ed.). 1983. *La novela lírica*. 2 vols. Persiles 141–42. Madrid: Taurus.

—— (ed.). 1992a. *Los nuevos nombres, 1975–1990*. Historia y Crítica de la Literatura Española 9. Barcelona: Crítica.

——. 1992b. *Teorías del realismo literario*. Madrid: Instituto de España and Espasa-Calpe.

——. 1997. *Theories of Literary Realism*. Tr. Mihai I. Spariosu & Santiago García Castañón. The Margins of Literature. Albany NY: State University of New York Press.

Villasante, Luis. 1961. *Historia de la literatura vasca*. Colección Larrún. Bilbao: Sendo.

Villegas, Juan. 1973. *La estructura mítica del héroe en la novela del siglo XX*. Ensayos Planeta de Lingüística y Crítica Literaria 26. Barcelona: Planeta.

Villena, Luis A. de. 1980. *Para los dioses turcos*. Barcelona: Laertes.

——. 1982. *Ante el espejo: Memorias de una adolescencia*. En Cuarto Mayor 125. Madrid: Argos Vergara.

——. 1983. *Amor pasión*. Literatura Contemporánea en Castellano 37. Barcelona: Laertes.

——. 1989. *Chicos*. Narrativa Mondadori. Madrid: Mondadori.

——. 1994. *Divino*. Autores Españoles y Hispanoamericanos. Barcelona: Planeta.

——. 1999. *El mal mundo*. Sonrisa Vertical 109. Barcelona: Tusquets.

——. 2004a. *Huesos de Sodoma*. Hetereo 2. Madrid: La Odisea and Siglo XXI.

——. 2004b. *Patria y sexo*. Los Tres Mundos. Barcelona: Seix Barral.

Vollendorf, Lisa (ed.). 2001. *Recovering Spain's Feminist Tradition*. New York: Modern Language Association of America.

Waugh, Patricia. 1984. *Metafiction: The Theory and Practice of Self-conscious Fiction*. New Accents. London and New York: Methuen.

—— (ed.). 1992a. *Postmodernism: A Reader*. London and New York: Edward Arnold.

——. 1992b. *Practising Postmodernism, Reading Modernism*. Interrogating Texts. London and New York: Edward Arnold.

Weeks, Jeffrey. 1985. *Sexuality and its Discontents: Meanings, Myths, and Modern Sexualities*. London and Boston MA: Routledge and Kegan Paul.

——. 1995. *Invented Moralities: Sexual Values in an Age of Uncertainty*. London: Polity and New York: Columbia University Press.

Wellek, René and Austin Warren. 1953. *Teoría literaria*. Tr. José M. Gimeno Capella. Introd. Dámaso Alonso. Biblioteca Románica Hispánica: Trados y Monografías 2. Madrid: Gredos.

Wentzlaff-Eggebert, Harald. 1991. *Las literaturas hispánicas de vanguardia:*

Orientación bibliográfica. Bibliotheca Iberoamericana 38. Frankfurt am Main: Vervuert.

——. 1999. *Las vanguardias literarias en España: Bibliografía y antología crítica*. Madrid: Iberoamericana and Frankfurt am Main: Vervuert.

White, Hayden. 1987. *The Content of the Form: Narrative Discourse and Historical Representation*. Baltimore: Johns Hopkins University Press.

Williams, Mark. 1992. *The Story of Spain*. Málaga: Santana.

Woods, Eva. 2004. 'Radio Free *Folklóricas*: Cultural, Gender, and Spatial Hierarchies in *Torbellino* (1941)', in Marsh and Nair 2004: 201–18.

Wyers, Frances. 1976. *Miguel de Unamuno: The contrary self.* Támesis A 61. London: Tamesis.

Yates, Alan. 1975. *Una generació sense novel.la?: La novella catalana entre 1920–1925*. Llibres a l'Abast 122. Barcelona: Edicions 62.

Ynduráin, Domingo (ed.). 1981. *Época contemporánea (1939–1980)*. Historia y Crítica de la Literatura Española 8. Barcelona: Crítica.

Zamora Vicente, Alonso. 1983. *Las sonatas de Valle-Inclán* [1951]. 2nd edn. Biblioteca Románica Hispánica: Estudios y Ensayos 40. Madrid: Gredos.

Žižek, Slavoj. 2000. *The Fragile Absolute, or Why is the Christian Legacy Worth Fighting for?*. London and New York: Verso.

Zubatsky, David S. 1992. *Spanish, Catalan, and Galician Literary Authors of the Twentieth Century: An Annotated Guide to Bibliographies*. Metuchen NJ: Scarecrow.

——. 1995. *Spanish, Catalan, and Galician Literary Authors of the Eighteenth and Nineteenth Centuries: An Annotated Guide to Bibliographies*. Metuchen NJ: Scarecrow.

Zuffi, María G. 1996. 'Identidad/otredad: Algunas estrategias conceptuales', *Osamayor: Graduate Student Review* 6/ix: 45–58.

Zuleta, Emilia de. 1977. *Arte y vida en la obra de Benjamín Jarnés*. Biblioteca Románica Hispánica: Estudios y Ensayos 267. Madrid: Gredos.

Zulueta, Carmen de. 1977. 'El monólogo interior de Pedro en *Tiempo de silencio*,' *Hispanic Review* 45: 297–309.

Zunzunegui, Santos. 2002. 'De cuerpo presente: En torno a las raíces del nuevo cine español', in Heredero 2002: 103–16.

INDEX

An asterisk * against a title indicates that it has been translated into English